Learning From Resilient People

*This book is dedicated to the resilient children who endure traumas
to the body and to the spirit, yet survive and live astonishing lives. It is also dedicated to the
victims and survivors of genocide and state-sponsored terror that my parents endured in the
killing fields of Eastern Europe. Growing up with stories of atrocities makes me wish, fervently, that
we never again need to use the word "survivor" knowing that it means surviving the banality of evil.*

Learning From Resilient People

Lessons We Can Apply to Counseling and Psychotherapy

Morley D. Glicken

Institute for Personal Growth: A Research, Treatment, and Training Cooperative, Los Angeles, California

SAGE Publications
Thousand Oaks ▪ London ▪ New Delhi

KH

For information:

Sage Publications, Inc.
2455 Teller Road
Thousand Oaks, California 91320
E-mail: order@sagepub.com

SAGE Publications Ltd
1 Oliver's Yard
55 City Road
London EC1Y 1SP
United Kingdom

Sage Publications India Pvt. Ltd.
B-42, Panchsheel Enclave
Post Box 4109
New Delhi 110 017 India

Printed in the United States of America

Library of Congress Cataloging-in-Publication Data

Glicken, Morley D.
Learning from resilient people : lessons we can apply to counseling and psychotherapy / Morley D. Glicken.
    p. cm.
Includes bibliographical references and index.
ISBN 1-4129-0484-6 (cloth)
   1. Resilience (Personality trait) I. Title.
BF698.35.R47G55 2006
155.2′4—dc22

                       2005035897

This book is printed on acid-free paper.

06 07 08 09 10 9 8 7 6 5 4 3 2 1

Acquisitions Editor:	Kassie Graves
Editorial Assistant:	Veronica Novak
Typesetter:	C&M Digitals (P) Ltd.

9/19/07

Contents

Preface

This book is about the ways resilient people navigate the troubled waters of life's traumas and how human service professionals can apply that information to our work. While a number of researchers believe that understanding resilience is the key to knowing how people successfully cope with traumatic life events and why they often come out of a crisis stronger and more certain of their goals and directions in life, the concept of resilience is still fairly new in the research literature. Although we think we know what it means to be resilient, we know far less about why some people are resilient, or how their resilience functions across the life cycle and through multiple life events. All of these issues will be discussed at length in this book.

This book continues the development of ideas found in two other books I've written: *Using the Strengths Perspective in Social Work Practice* (2004a) and *Improving the Effectiveness of the Helping Professions: An Evidence-Based Approach to Practice* (2005b). In both books I've argued for a knowledge-guided approach to practice that focuses on client strengths. Much of what I've found in researching each book leads me to believe there is demonstrable evidence that many people are resilient and that we can learn about how they cope with traumas and apply those successful approaches to our clinical work. Knowing how resilient people cope could lead to breakthroughs in the way we provide treatment.

Instead of writing a purely research-oriented book, I've combined discussions of the current research with stories resilient people have shared with me about the traumas they've successfully resolved. I've then compared their coping strategies with the existing research. To gather stories about resilience for this book, I asked people at professional and social functions, friends, colleagues, and people I met randomly who had stories of resilience, to send them to me. The stories were to contain the traumas experienced by the storyteller, when they were experienced, what they did to cope with the traumas, and why their coping approaches seemed to work. I tried to only use those stories that met all of these prior expectations. Some of the stories were told to me, and I wrote them with the storyteller's permission. Several of the stories and cases in the book are based upon multiple composites of people and situations and were written by me because I felt the stories were necessary to tell. In a few instances I wrote stories about my own life experiences. It felt right to me to do this since my family suggests many examples of resilience. When I had all the stories for the book, I compared each story to the existing research on resilience to determine whether it confirmed or departed from current beliefs about resilience. The coping strategies that were clearly identified in the stories and seemed consistent throughout the book were then summarized in a series of suggestions for clinical practice.

This approach combines the objective with the more subjective. Although the stories included are single events and generalizing to other populations of people experiencing similar traumas may be difficult, still, there is much to be learned from a more subjective approach. Proving or disproving theories of resilience becomes more of a possibility when we observe how the bulk of the over 50 stories included in this book agree or disagree with the existing research. This approach also answers fundamental questions about resilience throughout the life span and the ability of resilient people to cope with multiple traumas. Since I have included interviews with some of the people whose stories appear in the book, the reader has an opportunity to obtain additional information about resilience not necessarily included in the stories.

Like many people who grew up in families that were overwhelmed with life problems, I learned about resilience from my working class, immigrant parents. They dealt with illness, lack of finances, and social isolation, as well as prejudice against immigrant Jews, in ways that modeled resilience. But being resilient and surviving serious life problems, while still achieving at a high level, isn't done without a price, and this is why throughout this book *resilience* is defined as successful social functioning that may or may not include happiness and self-fulfillment.

Not everyone is resilient, of course, and to remember the many among us who suffer because of the harm done to them by others, this book is written for the abused and neglected, the homeless and the hungry, the victims of terror, the immigrants who suffer indignities to the body and to the spirit, the children who grow up with violence, and for our fellow citizens who live with unimaginable social and emotional pain. Their anguish should motivate all helping professionals to open our hearts and minds to new ideas and new treatment approaches and, in Bertrand Russell's words, to have "unbearable sympathy for the suffering of others."

—Morley D. Glicken, DSW

Acknowledgments

I want to thank the many wonderful people who contributed stories to this book. Their willingness to share difficult and often painful life experiences made this book possible. I'm very touched that so many people were willing to share such traumatic and personal stories. Courage like theirs is one of the reasons so many of us feel blessed to be in the helping professions.

I also want to thank my amazing editor at Sage Publications, Dr. Arthur Pomponio, for supporting and encouraging the writing of this book, my second book for Sage. Any writer who finds an editor and a publisher who believe in his or her work finds a home. Veronica Novak, Dr. Pomponio's assistant, has been wonderful to work with. Special thanks also to Patricia Fox for helping me with so many aspects of the book and for providing me with an emotional and creative safe haven.

You draw inspiration for books from your own life experiences. My inspiration comes from the resilience of my parents, Rose and Sam Glicken, and my daughter, Amy Glicken. These special people give me hope each day and make me believe that when life is approached with love, humor, spirituality, and deep conviction, anything is possible. My daughter, Amy, sums up this belief when she writes, "Many of us are overwhelmed with our daily lives. But each of us has a gift that we can use to make our lives much better than they are. The task is simply to discern what our gifts are and to utilize them. Because, in the end, we are each our own Tooth Fairies, taking what has been lost and giving gold in return." I am grateful for the gifts of these special people.

PART I

What We Can Learn From Resilient People

CHAPTER 1

Understanding Resilience

This book on resilience takes stories of and from resilient people and evaluates key elements of the stories that appear to explain why some people cope so well with highly traumatic and disturbing life experiences while others don't. The stories of resilience are presented as I received them, with a minimum of editing or changes, although some changes were necessary to protect confidentiality and to keep stories anonymous. In several cases, the stories were told to me and I wrote them, but then I shared stories with the individuals to check for accuracy. You will be alerted to it when others' stories were written by me. Although I asked for narrative stories, some people sent back poems and short stories. You may wonder if stories done in formats that suggest a fictionalized account are accurate and true. In each case, I received assurances that all of the stories were absolutely accurate and that more creative forms of conveying the story to the reader were used because it felt more impactful to write a short story or a poem. I tend to agree, and I urge you to approach stories with an open mind even when they don't appear to suggest resilience or when they are written in dramatic forms. The writers are successful people trying to cope with serious life issues. If a story doesn't appear to convey resilience, the section following the story, entitled "Lessons to Be Learned From This Story," will, I hope, fully serve to clarify the story and suggest reasons why the person in the story is resilient and why the story should matter to us.

The primary purpose of this book is to analyze stories of resilience so that we might apply what is learned from resilient people to our own practice. A second purpose of the book is to help practitioners who want to use a wellness or strengths model to develop practice philosophies that use what we know about people who cope well with traumas and apply that knowledge to those who cope less well. Two of my prior books (Glicken, 2004a, 2005b) have discussed ways of helping therapists work more effectively by using the strengths perspective and evidence-based practice (EBP). Much of the research found for those two books points to the existence of resilience in explaining why some people cope well with traumas while others don't. Because resilience plays such a crucial role in well-being, and since the research on resilience is limited, I believe that a book of stories from resilient people will help us understand why they've done so well. In addition to the stories, I've included current and seminal research on resilience to lend support to or offer disagreement with the stories' perspectives. I've also included a critical evaluation of each story to determine why the subjects have dealt so well with traumas. In each case, I've asked the story-teller why he or she was able to cope so well with such a serious trauma. This information is reported in direct written statements by the storyteller, in conversations between the storyteller and myself, and in my analysis of the story.

In writing this book, I'm mindful that a bias sometimes exists among some practitioners favoring the use of a pathology model. The information in my book on evidence-based practice (Glicken, 2005b) convinces me that many long-held beliefs in the helping professions lead to ineffective practice. Practitioners often make serious errors in diagnosis, often stemming from racial, ethnic, and gender biases. Helping approaches are chosen that support the practitioner's bias rather than the existing evidence confirming that an approach will work with a specific client. Helping approaches are often chosen in support of existing mythologies rather than best evidence. Few therapists do even the most elementary form of evaluation to determine whether clients have been helped and, if so, why.

Because our work isn't always effective, increasing numbers of people reject professional help, opting instead for self-help groups using wellness approaches that often lead to clients feeling more optimistic about the future. Natural healing in addictions and in traumatic events suggests that resilience exists in many people, permitting them to cope with serious problems on their own and without professional assistance. Seeing this information unfold has convinced many third-party payers and policy analysts that therapy isn't especially helpful, which has resulted in limited numbers of paid therapy sessions or, in some cases, a complete elimination of payments for therapy. In its place, there is an increasingly unsupported and sometimes dangerous use of psychotropic medications.

If we are to develop the new models of helping that might improve our level of effectiveness, then we should study healthy people who overcome terrible life tragedies with the same intensity that we've studied people who develop pathologies and who require the best help possible. The knowledge gained from studying successful ways of coping with traumas might then be applied to troubled people in treatment. If we can utilize what we know about resilient people and apply it successfully to people who are not doing well, then perhaps we will have begun to overcome the lack of success that seems to be so evident with a variety of client problems, and we can then move therapy to a new level of efficacy.

Definitions of Resilience

Walsh (2003) defines resilience as "the ability to withstand and rebound from disruptive life challenges. Resilience involves key processes over time that foster the ability to 'struggle well,' surmount obstacles, and go on to live and love fully" (p. 1). Gordon (1996) defines resilience as "the ability to thrive, mature, and increase competence in the face of adverse circumstances" (p. 1). Glick (1994) writes, "'Resilience' is the ability to 'bounce back' from adversity, to overcome the negative influences that often block achievement. Resilience research focuses on the traits and coping skills and supports that help kids survive, or even thrive, in a challenging environment" (p. 1). Henry (1999) suggests that the notion of resilience was created to help explain why some children do well under very troubled circumstances. Resilience describes children who grow up in highly unfavorable conditions without showing negative consequences. Henry (1999) defines resilience as "the capacity for successful adaptation, positive functioning, or competence despite high risk, chronic stress, or prolonged or severe trauma" (p. 521). In a further definition of resilience, Abrams (2001) indicates that resilience may be seen as the ability to readily recover from illness, depression, and adversity. Walsh (2003) says that "the concept of family resilience extends our understanding of healthy family functioning to situations of adversity. Although some families are shattered by crisis or chronic stresses, what is remarkable is that many others emerge strengthened and more resourceful" (p. 1). Anderson (1997) reports that resilient people have been described as being

> socially, behaviorally, and academically competent despite living in adverse circumstances and environments as a result of poverty (Werner & Smith, 1982), parental mental illness (Beardslee & Podorefsky, 1988), interparental conflict (Neighbors, Forehand, & McVicar, 1993), inner-city living (Luthar, 1993), and child abuse and neglect (Farber & Egeland, 1987). Resilient children who are functioning well despite enduring hardships often do not receive treatment services because they find ways to be successful despite their troubled environments. (p. 594)

Mandleco and Peery (2000) are concerned about the inconsistent meaning of the term *resilience* and wonder if it has begun to mean whatever the person writing about it wishes it to. For example, resilience has been described as a personality characteristic not related to stress; a characteristic of some children from at-risk environments; the absence of psychopathology in a child whose parents have serious emotional problems; success in meeting societal expectations or developmental tasks; characteristics which help children to succeed who were expected to fail; the ability to restore equilibrium and adapt to life situations. The authors note that Polk (1997) tried to synthesize a model of resilience suggesting that "resilience is a midrange theory with a four-dimensional construct, where dispositional, relational, situational, and philosophical patterns intermingle with the environment to form resilience" (Mandleco & Peery, 2000, p. 100). The result of these various definitions of resilience is that while a "commonsense universal definition is assumed, when one attempts to identify specifics affecting resilience, these definitions are inadequate and confusing" (Mandleco & Peery, 2000, p. 100).

Attributes of Resilient People

A consistent finding over the last 20 years of resilience research is that most children from highly dysfunctional families or very poor communities do well as adults. This finding applies to almost all populations of children found to be at risk for later life problems, including children who experience divorce, children who live with stepparents, children who have lost a sibling, children who have attention deficit disorder or suffer from developmental delays, and children who become delinquent or run away. More of these children make it than don't. Furstenberg (1998) and Wilkes (2002a) reviewed the research and found that almost 75% of children at risk do well in later life, including children born to teenage mothers, children who were sexually abused (Wilkes, 2002b), children who grew up in substance-abusing or mentally ill families (Werner & Smith, 2001), and children who grew up in poverty (Vaillant, 1993). Even when children had experienced multiple risks, Rutter (2003) found that half of them overcame adversity and achieved good emotional and social development.

Masten (2001) believes that resilience is part of the genetic makeup of humans and that it is the norm rather than the exception:

> What began as a quest to understand the extraordinary has revealed the power of the ordinary. Resilience does not come from rare and special qualities, but from the everyday magic of ordinary, normative human resources in the minds, brains, and bodies of children, in their families and relationships, and in their communities. (p. 9)

We tend to think that traumas will generally lead to malfunctioning behavior in children and adults, but often this isn't the case. A good example of how well people actually cope with trauma may be seen in the response to the World Trade Center bombings. Gist and Devilly (2002) report that the estimates of posttraumatic stress disorder (PTSD) after the 9-11 attacks dropped by almost two thirds within 4 months of the tragedy. The authors concluded that "these findings underscore the counterproductive nature of offering a [treatment] with no demonstrable effect, but demonstrated potential to complicate natural resolution, in a population in which limited case-conversion can be anticipated, strong natural supports exist, and spontaneous resolution is prevalent" (p. 742). In other words, resilience to severe traumas exists when people heal on their own and when they have strong social and emotional supports. Introducing treatment too early in the process may actually interfere with resilience.

Mandleco and Peery (2000) describe one effort to understand resilience by focusing on the self-righting tendencies that propel children toward normal development under adverse circumstances. This work identifies common dispositions and situations that describe resilient behavior in children and seem crucial in their ability to respond to stress and adversity while still maintaining control and competence in their lives—even when challenged by physical handicaps, a pathological family environment, or the adverse effects of poverty, war, or dislocation. Mandleco and Peery (2000) note that "these commonalities generally have been organized into three categories: personal predispositions of the child, characteristics of the family environment, and the presence of extra familial support sources" (p. 101).

Werner and Smith (1982, 1992, 2001) identify protective factors that tend to counteract the risk of stress. Protective factors include genetic factors (e.g., an easygoing disposition), strong self-esteem and sense of identity, intelligence, physical attractiveness, and supportive caregivers. Garmezy, Masten, and Tellegen (1964) note that there are three protective factors in resilient children: dispositional attributes of the child, family cohesion and warmth, and availability and use of external support systems by parents and children. Seligman (1992) believes that resilience exists when people are optimistic; have a sense of adventure, courage, and self-understanding; use humor in their lives; have a capacity for hard work; and possess the ability to cope with and find outlets for emotions. Findings by Luthar and Zigler (1991) indicate that resilient children are active, humorous, confident, competent, prepared to take risks, flexible, and, as a result of repeated successful coping experiences, confident in both their inner and outer resources. Luthar (1993) suggests that resilient children have considerable intellectual maturity.

Other factors associated with resilience include the finding by Arend, Gove, and Sroufe (1979) that very curious children are more resilient than less curious children. Radke-Yarrow and Brown (1993) associate resilience with children who have more positive self-perceptions. Egeland, Carlson, and Sroufe (1993) and Baldwin, Baldwin, Kasser, Zax, Sameroff, and Seifer (1993) found a relationship between resilience and assertiveness, independence, and a support network of neighbors, peers, family, and elders. In their 32-year longitudinal study, Werner and Smith (1982) found a strong relationship among problem-solving abilities, communication skills, and an internal locus of control in resilient children. As Henry (1999) notes, "Resilient children often acquire faith that their lives have meaning and that they have control over their own fates" (p. 522). Tiet, Bird, and Davies (1998) add that resilient children also have higher educational aspirations, better physical health, and healthier mothers or female caretakers than less resilient children.

In her work on resilient infants and toddlers and the relationship between early signs of resilience and resilience in later life, Gordon (1996) reports the following:

1. Resilient infants and toddlers are energetic, socially responsive, autonomous, demonstrative, tolerant of frustration, cooperative, and androgynous, among other characteristics.

2. Their environments are nurturing, responsive, and indicate a strong bond between the caregiver and the child.

3. Early signs of resilience relate directly to later life resilience and are strongly tied to early indications of an internal locus of control, social skills, and the social support of mothers.

4. Resilience may be enhanced in very young children through social policies and practices that provide social and economic support for the family and improved caregiver education.

Henry (1999) suggests five major themes that derive from her research on resilient children: (1) loyalty to parents, even when they are abusive; (2) the child's desire to perceive the home as normal; (3) the child's attempt to make himself or herself invisible to the abuser; (4) a strong sense of self-value; and (5) the child's focus on the future, with its positive potential for happiness. There are two themes here that should be clarified. The theme of loyalty to parents suggests that even though parents are mistreating the child, the child attempts to understand the reasons for the abuse, making it possible to continue to feel loyalty and love for the abusing parent. The theme of invisibility to the abuser refers to the child's attempt to vacate the home or to hide when a parent becomes abusive. It may also refer to the child's attempt to feel invisible even while being abused. Invisibility allows the child to negate the brunt of the abuse and to feel control over it.

Anderson (1997) believes that the recognition of resilience as an important factor in the mental health of traumatized children came from concerns that children at risk might develop adult pathologies (Byrd, 1994). Anderson (1997) indicates that the term *resilient* originally referred to children who were thought to be "stress resistant" or "invulnerable" because they not only coped with adverse childhood traumas, but they seemed to thrive under very dysfunctional and stressful situations (Kauffman, Grunebaum, Cohler, & Gamer, 1979).

Resiliency research originally tried to discover the characteristics of at-risk children who coped well with stress (Werner, 1989, 1996). Over time, however, resiliency research has focused less on the attributes of resilient children and more on the processes of resilience. As the research has attempted to understand the processes associated with resilience, one important finding suggests that rather than avoiding risks, resilient children take substantial risks to cope with stressors, leading to what Cohler (1987) calls "adaptation and competence."

In a review of the factors associated with resilience to stressful life events, Tiet and colleagues' (1998) findings show that the following have been identified as protective factors that allow a child to cope with stressful events: (1) a high IQ, (2) a high quality of parenting, (3) a connection to competent adults other than the child's parents, (4) an internal locus of control, and (5) excellent social skills. According to Tiet and colleagues (1998), protective factors are primary buffers between the traumatic event and the child's response. When a child's response to stress has a positive effect on the resilient child, whether the risk to the child is low or high, the authors' term this a *resource factor,* although the literature also uses the terms *assets* and *compensatory factor* (Tiet et al., 1998). Tiet and colleagues (1998) also believe that both protective and resource factors are crucial in understanding the way resilience protects people. However, certain situations may make resilience inoperable in even the most resilient people, and current research efforts are attempting to find connections between the type of adverse event (i.e., whether it is controllable or uncontrollable) and its risk factors to resilient people. Tiet and colleagues (1998) write, "To understand resilience, it is essential to identify protective factors that buffer the detrimental effects of risk factors. However, it is also important to identify resource factors because they predict good adjustment at both high and low risk and therefore become critical in the design of preventive efforts" (p. 1191).

Tiet and colleagues (1998) indicate that even resilient children respond inconsistently to stressful events and that another way to look at resilience is to show the relationship between the specific traumatic event and the response. For example, in many of the maltreated children studied for resilience, school-based outcomes have been used that include grades, deportment, and the degree of involvement in school activities. However, Luthar (1993) notes that while resilient children do well on many school-based outcomes, many of these same children suffer from depression. Interestingly, however, even though many of the maltreated children studied showed signs of depression, they still did well on behavioral outcomes measures, including grades and school conduct. Tiet and colleagues (1998) believe that the key reason resilient children cope well with adversity is that they tend

> to live in higher-functioning families and receive more guidance and supervision by their parents and other adults in the family. Other adults in the family may complement the parents in providing guidance and support to the youth and in enhancing youth adjustment. Higher educational aspiration may also provide high-risk youth with a sense of direction and hope. (p. 1198)

This leads one to believe that resilience doesn't negate vulnerability to all outside stressors, but that it provides primary coping mechanisms that permit high levels of functioning even in the midst of emotional side effects, including depression. Rind and Tromovitch (1997) acknowledge this in a controversial review of the impact of child sexual abuse (CSA) on adult functioning by concluding that a child's temperament may affect his or her response to sexual abuse. The Rind and Tromovitch study will be discussed in more detail in Chapter 7 on resilience and child abuse, but in its meta-analysis of studies showing a strong relationship between child sexual abuse and adult malfunctioning, the authors conclude that the effect of such abuse has been greatly overexaggerated. This certainly supports the belief that either resilience is a characteristic that is widespread among many people or the authors have done a gross disservice to the many unfortunate victims of child sexual abuse.

To be fair to Rind and Tromovitch, they do suggest that coping with sexual abuse may have a great deal to do with a number of factors, including the child's temperament and the degree of force used in the sexual molestation. However, a conclusion that child sexual abuse appears to cause damage in just a small number of adults seems highly unlikely. The authors report that the renowned researcher Martin Seligman (1994) believes that CSA is a "special destroyer of adult mental health" (Rind & Tromovitch, 1997, p. 232). In their literature review of studies showing the negative impact on CSA on adult functioning, Rind and Tromovitch's (1997) report that the psychological problems identified by other researchers include "anger, depression, anxiety, eating disorders, alcohol and drug abuse, low self-esteem, relationship difficulties, inappropriate sexual behavior, aggression, self-mutilation, suicide, dissociation, and posttraumatic stress disorder, among others" (p. 232). The authors note that the literature supporting a view that CSA appears to be the cause of these problems, that the problems are generally severe, and that socioeconomic class, education, and other factors do not serve to lessen the impact of the symptoms. According to Rind and Tromovitch (1997), "Results of analyses of the national samples show that such characterizations are exaggerated at the population level. This exaggeration may stem from our culture's tendency to equate wrongfulness with harmfulness in sexual matters" (p. 253). The reader may want to read the original article and compare these findings with those of other researchers who find a great deal of resilience among CSA victims but also social and emotional problems related to the abuse that point to its considerable harm.

In conversations with survivors of the Holocaust, Tech (2003) found the characteristics of those who survived to include a desire for mutual cooperation to cope with survival. This included caring for ill concentration camp inmates, sharing rations that were minute to begin with, and forming "bonding groups" that kept inmates optimistic and positive. Tech also points out that concentration camp inmates who were emotionally flexible were more likely to survive. Inmates who were very traditional in their outlook on life or who felt that they had lost a considerable amount of status were often unable to cope and frequently perished before other, less healthy, inmates did. However, many severely ill inmates who had a positive view of their lives survived against all medical odds. Tech (2003) reports that survivors she interviewed were filled with compassion and sadness and that "conspicuously absent were expressions of hatred or hostility" (p. 345) toward their captors. She writes that even though conditions in the camps were dreadful, "many inmates created for themselves make-believe worlds—a blend of dreams, fantasies, friendships and resistance—as an antidote" (p. 351). Prisoners found these fantasies very gratifying, and "such escapes into fantasy may have improved the prisoners' hold on life. . . . Prisoners created bonding groups which, however illusory, forged links with the past and the future" (Tech, 2003, p. 351).

There are many similarities between the recollections of the survivors Tech interviewed and more scientific studies of survivors of the Holocaust. Baron, Eisman, Scuello, Veyzer, and Lieberman (1996) report that many clinicians who first interviewed survivors of the Holocaust believed that they would be very troubled parents and that their children would suffer from a range of emotional difficulties. However, studies of children of survivors have shown no pattern of maladjustment or psychopathology. Those who have maintained the traditional religious beliefs of their parents have done particularly well socially, financially, and emotionally (Last, 1989). In studies of the development of symptoms of PTSD following a traumatic event, Ozer, Best, Lipsey, and Weiss (2003) report that those most likely to develop PTSD have a lack of psychological resilience, which can been seen as a cluster of prior social and emotional problems that include prior loss, depression, poor support from others, prior traumas, and a family history of pathology. According to Ozer and colleagues (2003),

> It is tempting to make an analogy to the flu or infectious disease: Those whose immune systems are compromised are at greater risk of contracting a subsequent illness. Similarly, this cluster of variables may all be pointing to a single source of vulnerability for the development of PTSD or enduring symptoms of PTSD—a lack of psychological resilience. (p. 71)

What the authors fail to answer is why some people who have had all the earlier signs of coping poorly with a new trauma cope surprisingly well. Most resilient people have had prior traumas and loss, an absence of family support, and episodes of depression but still cope well enough with new traumas to avoid serous social and emotional malfunction.

Perhaps Tiet and colleagues (1998) help answer this question by noting that in their research on resilience, resilient children and adolescents live in better functioning families, receive supervision and guidance from parents or other adults, have higher educational aspirations, and have higher IQs, which the authors believe help in problem solving and in seeking unique solutions to difficult social and emotional problems. However, resilience is often more than just individual attributes and includes external processes or buffers that help increase resilience.

One of the continuing beliefs in the helping professions is that the greater the social and emotional risk to an individual, the more likely pathology will develop. But resilience research suggests that risk factors are predictive of some types of dysfunction for only 20% to 50% of a given high-risk population, suggesting high levels of resilience in the majority of those at risk (Rutter, 1979, 1990, 2003). In contrast, "protective factors," the supports and opportunities that buffer the effect of adversity and enable development to proceed, appear to predict positive outcomes in 50% to 80% of high-risk populations. According to Werner and Smith (1992),

> Our findings and those by other American and European investigators with a life-span perspective suggest that these buffers [i.e., protective factors] make a more profound impact on the life course of children who grow up under adverse conditions than do specific risk factors or stressful life events. They [also] appear to transcend ethnic, social class, geographical, and historical boundaries. Most of all, they offer us a more optimistic outlook than the perspective that can be gleaned from the literature on the negative consequences of perinatal trauma, care giving deficits, and chronic poverty. (p. 202)

In summarizing our current understanding of resilience, Mandleco and Peery (2000) argue that it still is not possible to know which attributes of resilience are most significant for a particular person. They write that "there is often marked variation in an individual's responses to stress, suggesting the presence of any specific factor does not always produce resilience if the person is particularly vulnerable or the adversity too great to overcome" (Mandleco & Peery, 2000, p. 101). The authors continue by noting confusion over the following factors: "(a) the age domain covered by the construct, (b) the circumstances where it occurs, (c) its definition, (d) its boundaries, or (e) the adaptive behaviors described" (Mandleco & Peery, 2000, p. 102). An additional problem with resilience research is that it fails to include a broad population of people by race, gender, age, and ethnicity. It also tends to incorrectly generalize findings to all people experiencing trauma from specific populations, including children and the mentally ill, creating the illusion that we know much more about resilience than can be justified by the evidence. And, according to Mandleco and Peery (2000), the definition of resilience is still vague and continues to affect research results.

Coping With Stress as an Additional Aspect of Resilience

Courbasson, Endler, Kocovski, and Kocovski (2002) define coping as "one's efforts to reduce the impact of a difficult or stressful situation."(p. 35). They go on to say that "this transactional process involves both cognition and behavior" (p. 35). Endler and Parker (1999) indicate that there are three primary styles of coping with stress: task-oriented, emotion-oriented, and avoidance-oriented coping. Task-oriented coping involves attempting to solve or limit the impact of the stressful situation. Emotion-oriented coping involves trying to limit the emotional impact of stress rather than resolve the stressful situation. Avoidance-oriented coping involves using distraction and diversion unrelated to the stressful situation to reduce stress. Courbasson and colleagues (2002) found that a task-oriented approach benefits people under great stress more than the use of other coping strategies and note that "task-oriented coping is associated with problem resolution or amelioration more often than the use of other coping strategies. Alternatively, both emotion and avoidance-oriented coping strategies may exacerbate the problematic situation" (p. 37).

Miller and Smith (2005) suggest that there are different types of stress, each with its own attributes, symptoms, duration, and treatment: acute stress, episodic stress, and chronic stress. These three types of stress are described as follows:

1. Acute stress is the common type of stress we all feel when something goes badly or makes life temporarily more complicated. Acute stress is time limited and goes away when the situation rectifies itself.

2. Episodic stress is experienced by those who place themselves in stressful situations. Being late or continually placing oneself in situations leading to crisis might be examples of episodic stress. People who experience episodic stress often lack the ability to order problems or to deal with them in pragmatic and rational ways, creating situations in which crisis is continual.

3. Chronic stress "is the grinding stress that wears people away day after day, year after year. Chronic stress destroys bodies, minds, and lives. It wreaks havoc through long-term attrition. It's the stress of poverty, of dysfunctional families, of being trapped in an unhappy marriage or in a despised job or career. . . . Chronic stress kills through suicide, violence, heart attack, stroke, and, perhaps, even cancer. People wear down to a final, fatal breakdown" (Miller & Smith, 2005, p. 1).

Coping with stress has been thought to be a dimension of resilience, although there is disagreement in the literature about the definition of coping. Some researchers see coping as a dynamic process, but they measure its existence by considering a person's disposition or by viewing it as something triggered by a life situation (Parkes, 1984). According to this definition, coping is a fluctuating or transitory state. Other researchers see the ability to cope with stress as a permanent and enduring personality trait (Carver, Scheier, & Weintraub, 1989; McCrae, 1984; Parkes, 1986), a definition of coping that sounds much like the definition of resilience. Still other researchers view coping as a set of positive and negative modes of behavior. People with positive coping skills are described as using "more mature, flexible, purposive, future-oriented, reality-based, and metered approaches to combating stressful and anxiety-provoking situations, whereas those with negative coping skills are viewed as rigid, past-propelled, reality-distorting, and generally real adaptive processes" (Livneh, Livneh, Maron, & Kaplan, 1996, p. 503).

Lazarus (1966) believes that coping (1) serves to reduce the impact of harmful events and enables one to maintain a positive self-concept; (2) includes situational factors such as the availability of resources, coupled with individual factors that include one's belief system and other physical and emotional skills; (3) includes an appraisal of a situation and how that situation may affect one's well-being, including the options and limitations of alternative approaches to the situation; and (4) includes very basic options such as seeking more information, asking others how they might resolve a stressful situation, and direct action.

In a slightly different vein, Billings and Moos (1981, 1984) and Pearlin and Schooler (1978) believe that there are three alternative strategies individuals use to cope with stressful situations: (1) attempting to control the negative effects of the situation; (2) trying to modify the seriousness and the meaning of the stressful event; or (3) responding directly by trying to change the stressful event through the use of strategies that may have worked in the past.

Livneh and colleagues (1996) found three active styles of coping that resemble notions of resilience: (1) a style of coping that utilizes planning and seeking help from others; (2) a style of coping that seeks a support group to help with the stressor rather than passively putting it in the hands of fate; and (3) a style of coping that utilizes direct techniques to deal with stressors rather than such indirect techniques as denial or using other activities to temporarily try and forget about the stressor. Interestingly, the authors found that placing a problem in the hands of God or using prayer almost exclusively as a way of resolving a stressful situation was not a particularly effective way of coping and suggested an external locus of control. The more active the coping approach, the better subjects in their study were able to cope.

In determining whether treatment with substance-abusing patients would improve the type of coping approach used, Courbasson and colleagues (2002) treated 71 substance-abusing clients in an outpatient setting 3 full days a week, using anger management, relaxation techniques, stress management, changes in diet, leisure activities, assertiveness training, drug education, goal setting, and help with relationships and intimacy, as well as group psychotherapy using a client-centered orientation. Following treatment, the authors found that therapy had the following impact: (1) Task-oriented coping increased significantly, and consequently there was a large decrease in anxiety and other stress-related symptoms; (2) The use of emotion-oriented coping decreased; (3) The use of avoidance-oriented coping didn't change; and (4) The coping skills used to try to resolve stressful situations improved, resulting in sustained improvement in the clients' psychological distress.

EXAMPLES OF RESILIENT RESPONSES OF TRAUMATIZED ADOLESCENTS

Kristine Schwarz: My name is Kristine. I'm a marriage and family therapist. I work with children, I work teens, I work with children. I work primarily with domestic violence. And I live in California, and we're here working with Catholic Charities on a new project that deals with trauma, which we're going to talk about.

Cliff Mazer: My name is Cliff and I am a psychologist in Atlanta. We're trying to learn about trauma. Every person in this room has experienced traumas in life. Traumas are events that can affect you in negative ways because there are things which challenge a person to be able to keep going. The quality of being able to have bad things happen to you in your life and still be able to keep going is called resilience. Some people have one or two big traumas in their lives, while some people have many traumas in their lives. You would expect that the people that have the most traumas in their lives are the ones that don't survive as well. But it's not always true. In fact, some of the people that have the most traumas in their lives are the people that survive the best and become the most successful people. And that's a very interesting thing. So the question is, Who knows best about what helps a person survive and keep going in life?

The problem with most of the past studies and research is that it's mostly just people in universities making up all kinds of interesting theories. But hardly anybody has been asking you guys how you survived. Hardly anybody has asked you what specifically is it about you that may have helped you to keep going when other people gave up. Sometimes people give up because they get depressed. Sometimes people give up because they just can't handle life. Sometimes people kill themselves. Some people just get killed. That happens. Some people lose a mother. My kids lost their mother; I lost my wife. She died of lung cancer. I have three teenage sons.

All of those things are undeniably bad things. They're undeniably difficult hardships. The question is, Why do people bounce back, and how do they bounce back? What is it about them? What is it about each of you that helps you to keep going? Is it because of who you know? Is it because of who you are? Is it because of certain kinds of strengths you have? One thing we *do* know—it isn't always the strongest person. It isn't always the physically strongest person that survives. Just like on the football field or basketball court, it's not always the tallest player, it's not always even the most accurate player that is the best player. There's something else about those people that makes them as good as they are. So, that's why we're here and that's why we're asking you, and that's what makes you guys special. I'm very respectful of the fact that you came, and I appreciate your coming.

The following examples of resilience are taken from the transcript of a focus group on the nature of resilience, which was held on December 3, 2003, at the Alisos Institute in Santa Barbara, California. The only changes to the transcript were made for readability; some commas and a few bridging words were added, some sentences were shortened, and the group members' responses were numbered. The moderators were Kristine Schwarz, MSW, of the Alisos Institute, and Cliff Mazer, PhD, a clinical psychologist in private practice in Atlanta, Georgia.

THE QUALITIES THAT HELP ADOLESCENTS SURVIVE

Cliff Mazer: When you say who you are, one of the things that's different about this group is that we don't want to know what's wrong with you, we want to know what's right with you. We want to know what you think is a good quality of yours, maybe even one of the qualities. that helps you to be a good survivor. Maybe it helps, maybe it doesn't. But the point is, you probably know a few good things about yourself that you consider to be your better qualities. And I'm not just talking about intelligence. You know, sometimes there're different kinds of intelligence, right? Like, knowing what's going on, like being able to—.

Group member: Like street smarts?

Cliff Mazer: There's a different kind of intelligence, right? There's street smarts, but there are also other qualities, like being patient, being determined, never giving up. There are tons of different qualities. As a matter of fact, you can just throw out a couple of qualities so we know what we're talking about. And then I'm going to ask you questions. The first question I'm going to ask you is, What are the good qualities you have that help you survive?

Group members: (1) Being open and not close-minded; (2) Being able to express yourself and have good language skills to verbalize what it is you're trying to say; (3) Adapting to environments rather than having everything the same way everywhere else you go; (4) I have discipline for myself, I refuse to be a quitter. I can't stand to fail. If I fail, I'd just drop out of school; (5) Compassion; (6) Being mentally strong and physically strong; (7) What I can say about me is, the good part about me is how I understand and never give up whatever challenge I face; (8) Be oriented to the future, not to the past; (9) I used to do bad in school just because, like, thinking about my dad all the time. But I'm over it though. Once I just sit down and think about stuff or I can figure out stuff, I just thought about it. Like, people just kind of go sometimes. You know, everybody gotta go. It's just their time. I give myself an explanation. When I was little I didn't understand why my mom died. As I got older, I just gave myself the explanation that everything happens for a reason. And I believed it, and that's the way I was taught from when I was little. And every foster home that I've been in, they believe that God makes things happen for a home. Now I don't even wonder why my mom died. If I go to Heaven, or whatever, I'll understand why I did when I'm dead; (10) My mother passed in 2001. I really didn't know her that well, but I knew her well enough to know that she loved me. How I dealt with it was a lot of people used to talk to me, and still a lot of people talk to me, and they're telling me, you know, I'm sorry to hear that [your mother died], but stuff happens. So I look at that because that has made me a stronger young man as far as what I used to be. Because now I have to be mature, even though my mom isn't with me anymore; (11) I really like the point that these two made because a lot of people don't understand that living in America is so good, because living other places where people are less fortunate, I mean, people in America don't take that very seriously, I don't think. I mean, what we're going through is not things that they are going through because we read stories about different people, no disrespect, we read different stories from different countries and places in Africa and they are going through torture. I mean, serious torture. And we are not. I mean we go through the things of mom, dad. We're not going through the torture that they go through. So I think many of us need to take the time out to just thank God and realize that even though we've got our trauma, that we are blessed.

HUMOR

Cliff Mazer: Some people who are [resilient] call it having a sense of appreciation and a sense of perspective about things. As bad as you think it is for you, it could be worse. It always could be worse. And that kind of helps us to keep going and to be strong. Is that a true statement for some of you? Can I say something else? You guys are smart, but you're also funny. And I wonder if sometimes keeping a good sense of humor is important, too. To get through life and to get through challenge and trouble, you better have a good sense of humor.

Group members: (1) Crying heals you from the inside; (2) A lot of people put up a front, too. A lot will laugh in front of you, and then go home and cry; (3) I use my sense of humor for little kidding stuff, like, when people talk about me I just make a joke out of it. And sometimes people don't get it. Like, when they talk about me and I make a joke about myself and laugh with them, they don't really get it that I don't think what's happening to me is funny, I just want them not to know how I feel about it. But that's just my way of doing something.

A PAST, PRESENT, OR FUTURE ORIENTATION TO LIFE

Cliff Mazer: Do you tend to be oriented to the future, not to the past? If something bad happened in your past, do you have your mind dwelling on it and staying there in the past?

Group members: (1) I'm not saying that it's all bad to think about the past because my mom died when I was five. And it's still times that I think about my mom, you know, the memories she had of me laughing and laying on the couch and all this stuff. But the thing about it is I get don't stuck on it. If I get stuck on it and I just keep into myself, why did my mom have to die? Why did she leave? Why did she do this? Why did she do that? And that's not going to get me nowhere. It's good to think about the memories, but you can't stay stuck on all the good memories because sooner or later you're gonna say, why did God do this, or why did this happen? And you're going to get stuck. And at one point, you're just not going to be able to push forward for what you want for yourself; (2) I think it's like, if a person's ever been through anything in their life, they should be confident. If they fall or stumble somewhere along the way, or in their future, they shouldn't go back to the past and say, well, look what I've done in the past because the past is only bringing you back to the past. If you try to get to the future, there's no way if you keep looking at all the bad things that happen to you.

RELIGION AND SPIRITUALITY

Cliff Mazer: Another question. Some of you use church as a way of dealing with life. What was it about going to church that may have helped change you?

Group member: I joined the gang. And after that I find out that the only way out of a gang is through death. So I died in Christ. We went to church after a big gang fight, and I guess the sermon was directed towards me. The guy was talking about violence. And this sermon opened up my eyes, and instead of fighting a guy I was mad at, I went up to him and I shook his hand. The Bible has a lot to do with it because there are words in there that express what you feel, and what you think, and what's going on around you. Like, certain passages. If you believe in Heaven, you believe that you can start over, because it tells you that. If it gets inside you, it goes through your head and it's going to stick like a match strike on gas. It lights, and it's a feeling that's inside of you. And that feeling will never leave if you keep it in there.

EMPATHY

Cliff Mazer: They say that people who survive hardship and trauma are people who are optimistic people. And people who are pessimistic and negative don't survive as well. When one of your friends comes to tell you that something bad happened to them, what do you do?

Group members: (1) Listen; (2) Encourage them; (3) Try to give them positive feedback; (4) Say something funny; (5) Try to get them to lighten up. Just laugh or something; (6) Brush it off, because then they're going to look at you and they're going to see, like, that doesn't even affect that person. Then they're going to think, how does that look on me to be bothering that person? That person's stronger than me and they want to build their self up to be like you.

Cliff Mazer: There are different kinds of ways that people can hurt. They can get hurt physically and they can get their feelings hurt.

Group members: (1) I've got something to say, like to add on today. If you get in a fight and you get beat up, then I think it's not a good thing for you to fight anyway, because if you get beat up you're going to say, oh, you're down, you're hurt and that might be how you look at other situations that may not be true. So I don't think it's a good thing for anyway, because I used to think like that; (2) And either way you're going to get talked about. If you whoop somebody's butt, you're going to get talked about and if you get beat up, you're going to get talked about.

Cliff Mazer: It seems like you're saying that fighting in that way is sort of a trap; it's like being a gunslinger, you know. There's always somebody else that wants to have it with you.

Cliff Mazer: Can you name other kinds of situations that make your friends worry?

Group member: I met a girl and we hit it off, I mean, we really did. We became the best of friends. And we never hooked up, but I told her I was always there for her. So she caught me one day and she said, "Me and this guy, we just broke up." I said, "He hurt your feelings," and she said, "Yeah." And she said, "It feels some days like I don't want to live no more." So I had to talk to her about that. So I stopped somebody from killing them self. How'd I do that? Well, first, I made her laugh, just to take her mind off the situation she was going through. Then I got serious with her. I said, "You mean to tell me that this guy is that important for you to take your life?" So I cheered her up and she was like, "Well, when you look at it, he was a dog anyway."

Cliff Mazer: So, actually, you mixed it up. At first you got her laughing, and then you got her serious to give her that perspective. The big picture, like, come on, is it worth killing yourself over?

Group member: A guy can't be that important, you know.

SEEKING OTHERS FOR HELP AND COMFORT

Cliff Mazer: Another question. Who do you go to when you're most stressed out, for help and comfort, to talk?

Group members: (1) God; (2) My momma; (3) My teacher; (4) I go to God first, then I go to my friend.

Cliff Mazer: Do you think it's important that [a person you seek help from] be a certain kind of person, like, compassionate, or loving, or on your level, or someone you can relate to? Or do you think you could get help as good from a book or a manual or something?

Group members: (1) In some ways it is [important], and some ways it's not. Because you can have tough love and you can have love. You can go in a book and find it. Any source that you get it's still the same information; (2) It's better if you get a person because then you'll rely on them, but with a book you'd say, this is just a book. But if a person takes their time to talk to you, you'll really feel like you're special for some reason; (3) If I go through certain situations, I don't always run to the person that is, you know, kind and loving, because there's some situations where I have run to my brother and my brother is not exactly the best person. He's been in jail and been shot. But, I mean, it's just depending on the situation. I mean, you can't always run to the best person that you think will handle the situation. You've got to try different things. You've got to mix up what you do. You've got to trust the difference though; (4) It's good to have a therapist and all. My therapist took me to the fair up there at River Oak. You know, that was the first time that I had talked about my sister, and my grandma, and my family. I sat there and I talked for two hours, just things, just feelings that were coming out. And I still had more to say. But it's good to be able to know that somebody's there, at least one person that you can really sit down, and they'll listen, and hear you out, and give you knowledge.

TALKING ABOUT TRAUMAS AND OTHER BAD EXPERIENCES

Cliff Mazer: What do you think is the hardest thing about speaking about bad experiences and traumas that you've had?

Group members: (1) Being embarrassed that you've gone through it; (2) I don't care what people think about me. You know, I'm not here to please no one. I'm not; (3) Thinking people will see you as a crybaby; (4) Coming up as a young man, I had, still have, a lot of anger inside. But I don't let it show. I used to fight all the time. Every day at school I used to fight. When I was mad, when I fought, that was fun for me because beating a person up gave me an adrenaline rush. And when I'd get through fighting, it's gone. You don't feel, and then you feel sorry; (5) In my situation, I just moved into the house and I made friends, and you've got to explain to them, well, I'm a foster child, my momma died. And it's, like, they don't understand that because they have their mom and their parents, and they don't understand, and they think you're like the outside person.

I like to go in my room and looking at a mirror of myself. I do. The best thing about being a foster child is I go home, and in my room I shut the door and I look at myself in a mirror. And I think about it. I have a mom just like they do. I have a house now, just like they do. I go to school, just like they do, so I'm no different from them.

Cliff Mazer: How can helping adults, like a teacher, counselor, principal, minister, or parent speak to people your age that are trying to get over a bad experience?

Group members: (1) First approach us like they're on our level; (2) This principal I knew once, he was more down to earth with us. He knew what we were going through, and he had more knowledge because he also went through what kids that had the same problem went through, and how they learn to bounce back.

FINDING PEOPLE WHO HELPED

Cliff Mazer: Do you all have memories of somebody during a bad time who helped you? Who are they?

Group members: (1) Ministers; (2) Friends; (3) Teachers; (4) Principals; (5) Peers; (6) A bus driver who died. My grandma talked to me about her because she knew her very well; (7) My mother helped me get through lots of hard times, because my granddaddy died when I was six or five and he gave me anything I wanted. Mostly, I think back and I cry sometimes about it. But my momma tells me that when somebody dies, then it's their time to go to Heaven or Hell. But I've got to be the one to make a good decision so I can go to Heaven and see my grandfather again; (8) Before I got involved with Catholic Charities, I wouldn't care. I'd drop my backpack, throw it down in the hallways, and I wouldn't care. But I had this lady that helped me, my counselor, to understand that you can't go off fighting everybody or anybody who comes your way or looks at you wrong. Because it used to be if you looked at me wrong, I was about to whoop your booty. But now I've gotten to where I kind of think about it and I don't fight.

HANDLING STRESS

Cliff Mazer: So, it's not always a therapist or a psychologist that is able to get through to you at those times when you really need help. It can be sometimes a teacher or a principal, a mother or grandmother. When I think about getting over traumas, one message is that you've got to make changes inside yourself. Another message is you've got to reach out and use the help of other people who can support you. Which message works best for you?

Group member: You've got to mix the two together. You can't expect to do it all with inside yourself. You've got to go to people to help you and you've got to help yourself. If you're not helping yourself, nobody else is going to help you. If you go to someone for help, it would be somebody who's patient enough not to try to drag everything out of you.

Kristine Schwarz: How can you tell when a friend's having a bad experience?

Group members: (1) They stop eating or they eat too much; (2) They can't focus; (3) They sleep too much.

Cliff Mazer: Of all the things that we've been talking about that have to do with stress and trauma and getting over it and that have to do with the change you need to make inside yourself or the help you need to get from other people, is there anything that we haven't mentioned at all?

Group members: (1) You should recommend that they should start reading the Bible every day, go to church and all that stuff, but it can't be forced; (2) Like Jeremiah said in the Bible, it felt like fire on the inside of me. And, well, it was fire shut off up in my bones. It's like a feeling, you know; (3) You could be a Christian and not go to church like you said because if God wants you to see a certain point, He will, I mean, He'll reveal it to you; (4) I mean, you might think that I'm bad at this, but I don't believe in everything that the Bible says because actually half of the stuff, it's like, you know, if you kill yourself you're going to Hell. I'm sorry, I don't believe that because if you're in so much pain, I don't believe it. I'm just saying that I disagree with a lot of stuff that is in the Bible. And, you know, if you don't agree with me, that's fine; (5) I don't think you have to go to church or, you know, praise God every day; (6) It's piece by piece. You could be a Christian and not go to church, like you said, because if God wants you to see a certain point, He will, I mean, He'll reveal it to you.

Summary

This chapter on resilience discusses the many factors that define resilience. The chapter provides definitions of the term *resilience* and the attributes of resilient people. It also discusses the relationship between coping with stress and resilience. A discussion of resilience by youth in crisis provides a way of understanding how traumatized resilient youth understand their unique ways of coping with life stressors.

PART II

How Resilient People Use Culture, Spirituality, and Support Systems to Improve Their Social and Emotional Functioning

Resilience and the Impact of Spiritual and Religious Beliefs on Health and Mental Health

The resilience literature suggests that religious and spiritual beliefs are key elements of resilience. However, members of the helping professions often experience discomfort when clients discuss spirituality and often wonder if there is a role for professionals in the religious and spiritual lives of clients. This chapter will explore the relationship between religious and spiritual involvement and resilience, and the role professionals might take in discussing both issues with clients.

A number of findings suggest the importance of spirituality and religiosity in the lives of people. The majority of Americans indicate that they believe in God (Yntema, 1999), and 7 out of 10 say they attend church or synagogue (Loewenberg, 1988). Religion is regarded as highly important in the lives of older Americans (McFadden, 2000), and active participation in religious and spiritual activities have been shown to positively influence overall health in older Americans (Ellison & Levin, 1998). And as Frankl (1978) reminds us, "Man lives in three dimensions; the somatic, the mental, and the spiritual. The spiritual dimension cannot be ignored, for it is what makes us human" (quoted in Loewenberg, 1988, p. ix).

How best to define the terms *spirituality* and *religion*? George, Larson, Koenig, and McCullough (2000, p. 105) report work done by the National Institute of Aging and Fitzer Institute Working Group (1997) to define spirituality and religious involvement. They found the following elements in the definitions of both:

1. Religious/Spiritual Preference or Affiliation: Membership in or affiliation with a specific religious or spiritual group.

2. Religious/Spiritual History: Religious upbringing, duration of participation in religious or spiritual groups, life-changing religious or spiritual experiences, and "turning points" in religious or spiritual participation or belief.

3. Religious/Spiritual Participation: Amount of participation in formal religious or spiritual groups or activities.

4. Religious/Spiritual Private Practices: Private behaviors or activities, including but not limited to prayer, meditation, reading sacred literature, and watching or listening to religious or spiritual radio or television programs.

5. Religious/Spiritual Support: Tangible and intangible forms of social support offered by the members of one's religious or spiritual group.

6. Religious/Spiritual Coping: The extent to which and ways in which religious or spiritual practices are used to cope with stressful experiences.

7. Religious/Spiritual Beliefs and Values: Specific religious or spiritual beliefs and values.

8. Religious/Spiritual Commitment: The importance of religion/spirituality relative to other areas of life and the extent to which religious or spiritual beliefs and practices serve to affect personal values and behavior.

9. Religious/Spiritual Motivation for Regulating and Reconciling Relationships: Most measures in this domain focus on forgiveness, but other issues may be relevant as well (e.g., confession, atonement).

10. Religious/Spiritual Experiences: Personal experience with the divine or sacred, as reflected in emotions and sensations. (p. 105)

The Impact of Spirituality and Religious Involvement on Health and Mental Health

George and colleagues (2000) analyzed a number of studies attempting to determine the existence of a relationship between religion and health. They found that in 78% of the studies, religious involvement was found to reduce the likelihood of disease and disability. Positive health benefits of religion were particularly noted with coronary disease and heart attacks, emphysema, cirrhosis and other varieties of liver disease (Comstock & Partridge, 1972; Medalie, Kahn, Neufeld, Riss, & Goldbourt, 1973), hypertension (Larson, Koenig, Kaplan, & Levin, 1989; Levin & Vanderpool, 1989), and disability (Idler & Kasl, 1992, 1997). According to George and colleagues (2000), "The strongest predictor of the prevention of illness onset is attendance at religious services" (p. 108). The authors also found a relationship between religious observance and longevity, noting that "multiple dimensions of religion are associated with longevity, but attendance at religious services is the most strongly related to longevity" (George et al., 2000, p. 108).

Among key findings regarding the relationship between religious involvement and positive health and mental health outcomes, Ellison, Boardman, Williams, and Jackson (2001) note the following: (1) There is a positive relationship between church attendance and well-being and an inverse association of church attendance with distress; (2) Frequency of prayer is inversely related to well-being and only slightly positively related to distress; (3) A belief in eternal life is positively related to well-being but unrelated to distress; (4) Church-based support networks are unrelated to well-being; and (5) "There is limited evidence of stress-buffering effects, but not stress-exacerbating effects, of religious involvement" (p. 215).

Gartner, Larson, and Allen (1991) reviewed over 200 psychiatric and psychological studies and concluded that religious involvement has a positive impact on both health and mental health, while Ellison and colleagues (2001) indicate that "there is at least some evidence of mental health benefits of religion among men and women, persons of different ages and racial and ethnic groups, and individuals from various socioeconomic classes and geographical locations. Further, these salutary effects often persist even with an array of social, demographic, and health-related statistical controls" (p. 215).

Baetz, Larson, Marcoux, Bowen, and Griffin (2002) studied the level of religious interest of psychiatric inpatients to determine whether religious commitment has an impact on selected outcome variables, and they report the following results: Frequent worship attendees have fewer symptoms of depression, have shorter hospital stays, are more satisfied with their lives, and have much lower rates of current or lifetime use of alcohol when compared to subjects with less frequent or nonexistent worship attendance. The authors believe that worship may protect clients against greater severity of symptoms and longer hospital stays, increase clients' satisfaction with life, and enhance the quality of life of psychiatric patients (Baetz et al., 2002, p. 159).

Faster and more complete recovery from mental illnesses, substance abuse and/or dependence, and depression appear to be associated with religious involvement (George, 1992). Evidence indicating a relationship between religious or spiritual involvement and recovery from substance abuse is based on studies of Alcoholics Anonymous (AA) and other 12-step programs (Emrick, 1987; Montgomery, Miller, & Tonigan, 1995; Project Match Research Group, 1997). According to George and colleagues (2000), "A central component of these programs is the belief that one has no personal control over the addiction, but that there is a higher power who can help the individual to conduct it" (p. 109). The authors indicate that all of the studies cited are multivariate studies that control for a variety of intervening variables, as well as that longitudinal studies following subjects over a long period of time confirm the existence of a relationship between spirituality and religious involvement and better recovery from mental illness, depression, and substance abuse.

Religion has also been thought to have a positive impact on coping with stressful situations. Spilka, Shaver, and Kirkpatrick (1985) define three roles that religion serves in the coping process: (1) It helps individuals to answer meaning-of-life questions; (2) It offers individuals an increased feeling of control over stressful situations; and (3) It increases individuals' feelings of self-esteem, often by providing them with a source of community and family.

Some Dissenting Views

Although the majority of studies indicate positive benefits from religious and spiritual involvement, there are divergent points of view in the literature. Simpson (1989) found that a sample of Christian Scientists died at younger ages than their peers. Asser and Swan (1998) studied child deaths in families refusing medical care in favor of faith healing and found much higher rates of death. Both sets of authors believe that there are healthy and unhealthy uses of spirituality and religious involvement, but that researchers have thus far been unable to determine precisely what they are and how health and mental health are affected by them. In another dissenting view, Batson and Ventis (1982) write that "there is strong evidence that being more religious is associated with poorer mental health, with greater intolerance of people who are different from ourselves, and with no greater concern for those in need. The evidence suggests that religion is a negative force in human life, one we would be better off without" (p. 306).

Rauch (2003) reports that the proportion of people who say they never go to religious services has increased 33% from 1973 to 2000. To further confuse the relationship between religious attendance and health and mental health benefits, Rauch (2003) quotes theology professor John G. Stackhouse, Jr. as saying, "Beginning in the 1990s, a series of sociological studies has shown that many more Americans tell pollsters they attend church regularly than can be found in church when teams actually count. In fact, actual church going may be half the professed rate" (p. 34). This suggests that the validity of research on church attendance and positive health and mental health benefits may be in some doubt.

Do religious affiliation and spirituality actually answer the most essential questions about life, providing the meaning to people's lives that is considered so important to good health and mental health? Rauch (2003) finds that many people have only a vague notion of the theology of their own religion, and that they are not particularly tolerant of the beliefs of other people. Consequently, Rauch (2003) coined the term *apatheist* to describe the person "who cares little about [his or her] own religion and has an even stronger disinclination to care about other people's" (p. 34).

**A STORY ABOUT AN ABUSIVE RELATIONSHIP
THAT ENDED AFTER A RELIGIOUS CONVERSION**

It's hard for me to tell you exactly why I became involved in an abusive relationship. We had a happy home when I was growing up, and while I never thought of myself as being very attractive and I was painfully shy in high school, still, I don't think I was very different from the other girls I knew. I was also sort of a loner and I was very serious about school. And I was definitely a committed atheist. I thought God was a primitive idea and that organized religion was just another corporation on a smaller scale. All they ever cared about, in my view, was collecting money. Helping people? I don't think so.

I never dated in high school. I'd go to dances and stand on the sidelines while the popular kids danced. Nobody ever asked me to dance until James did, and I have to tell you, it was glorious. James was one those dangerous boys, bad boys we all knew in high school and thought about dating, but some fear factor made that impossible. And rightly so.

James started asking me out. Because my parents didn't approve of me dating and I knew they'd hate James with his fast cars and his ducktail haircut, we began to meet on the side and to make love. He was gentle and exciting, but then, as time went on, he was jealous and started wanting to know where I was. I had to call in and tell him where I was at least three or four times a day. If I didn't, he'd get furious. He never hit me then, but I could just imagine that he would. It paralyzed me with fear. I didn't know what to do and then, of course, I got pregnant. James knew about it and said we had to get married, but I didn't want to get married or have a child. I was just a child myself. My friend Jane and I made an appointment at a clinic to have an abortion, but James found out. We didn't know it but he was following us, and he drove Jane off the road and forced me into the car and beat me up. I lost the baby and was in the hospital for a week. James went to adult court and spent a year in jail.

When he came out, he started following me. I was in college and I'd see him wherever I went. He was stalking me and one night he broke into my room and raped me. He said that I was his property and that if I didn't accept that he was my only love, he'd kill me. I knew he would. Going to classes was impossible and soon my parents came to school and found me so depressed that I hadn't washed or changed clothes in a week. When they found out why, they called the local police and James was arrested again and sent back to prison. During the trial he looked at me in that way where I knew he was going to kill me for testifying against him. That started a long journey of trying to get away from James and meeting other men who seemed nice but were also very abusive.

I met and married a man and had several children with him. I felt so numb during this time that I don't think any of it sunk in. I felt nothing about my husband's abuse and drinking, and if I felt anything for the children, I can't remember. All I felt was this sense that I'd be dead soon and there was nothing I could do about it. I found jobs, I worked, I was successful, and when my marriage broke up, as it had to eventually, I became a workaholic and rose up the ladder at work. I felt miserable and my kids were both having emotional and learning problems. Something had to give.

One of my co-workers, someone I respected, urged me to attend Catholic Mass one Sunday morning. I told her that I thought religion was a fraud and that I could never see myself going to church, but she insisted. She said she'd felt the same way, but as a crisis in her life became more and more severe, she found that going to mass was comforting and said, why not try it, and I did. I thought it was silly and the rituals almost made me laugh. I left feeling very superior and full of loathing for the whole thing, but I went back a second time at the urging of my co-worker, who said it took time. The second time I was touched by how warm people were and how accepted I felt. I mean, at this point in my life,

I felt like a "whore." I really did. I felt I was the "bad seed" to have allowed all these things happen to me, and that I'd let my parents down and myself. To feel good about myself all of a sudden was really a strangely wonderful feeling.

As I began to learn more, I felt increasingly close to the teachings of the Church and found myself slowly becoming involved in church life. As this was happening, I also found that I was a much better mother and that my work excited me. Instead of doing it to occupy time and block out painful thoughts, I was starting to truly enjoy it. And I was very good at my work, so good that I was asked to accept a job, a highly responsible job, in Denver. It meant moving from the east coast to the west with small kids, but I felt strong enough to do it.

I had begun going with a man I'd met at church in Denver, but after a few months I discovered that he was very jealous and had a terrible temper. I stopped seeing him and immediately went for professional help. Even though I was making great strides in life, I seemed to seek out troubled men and wanted to do something about it. The therapy helped a lot and for the first time in my life, I felt clear, not in the Scientology way, but in a spiritual way. I began to greet the day with happiness and enthusiasm. Our family became a happy family and my faith in God and my happiness with the Church made me gloriously satisfied with life. I went through a conversion ceremony, and it was one of the most supremely happy moments of my life. My folks came to Denver and, of course, my kids where there.

I met a man after a while in Denver, also a very committed Catholic. He's a widower and a good man. We went together for a long time, but I was skittish about marriage, given my track record with men. I thought he'd become abusive at some point and it would be like James and my ex-husband all over again. We spoke to the priest and we went to my old therapist to see if we were right together, and we were. I'm now married and I can tell you that it's everything I'd hoped it would be but worried that it wouldn't. I feel joy and happiness now and have come to accept that after all these years it's possible for me to be happy. Yesterday my husband left me a piece of paper right by my purse. It was folded and I thought it was a shopping list or something ordinary like that. When I got to work and remembered it, I unfolded the paper and this is what it said.

> How beautiful are you, my love,
> how very beautiful.
> There is no flaw in you.
> Let me kiss you with the kisses
> of my mouth.
> I am my beloved's and my
> beloved is mine;
> she pastures her flock among
> the lilies.
> Set me as a seal upon your heart
> as a seal upon your arm;
> for love is as strong as death,
> and passion as fierce as the grave.

Many waters cannot quench love
nor can floods drown it.
If we are offered love and turn it away,
we will be scorned.
For it flashes as a fire,
a raging flame. (Song of Solomon)

LESSONS TO BE LEARNED FROM THIS STORY

Some people find that religious involvement mobilizes their coping skills and helps them make healthier decisions in their lives. Finding the right belief appears to have helped this woman discover some useful self-righting abilities:

1. Although she describes a series of abusive relationships, she is optimistic enough to allow the right man to come into her life and healthy enough, as an extra piece of guidance, to have the relationship evaluated by a priest and her therapist.

2. She uses available resources to help her cope, including counseling and the advice of a co-worker.

3. She thinks about meaning-of-life issues and has committed herself to having a joyous life. She sees herself as being in control of her life and is determined to make better decisions. In this way, one could say that she has an internal locus of control.

4. She has a strong value base which comes, in part, from her religious beliefs.

5. She believes in giving back to others and has done this by being involved in church activities, many of which have a social service function and focus on helping others.

6. She utilized friends and social supports to help her deal with an abusive relationship.

7. She took a risk in coming to a new community and leaving support systems that were in place. This risk has paid off well in her life.

Why Religious and Spiritual Involvement May Lead to Resilience

Ellison and Levin (1998) suggest three reasons for the positive impact of religious involvement and spirituality.

1. Control of health-related risks. Some religions have prohibitions against the use of tobacco and alcohol, premarital sexual experiences and other risky sexual activity, and the use of foods that may contribute to high cholesterol and heart problems, as well as strong prohibitions against the use of illegal drugs. The

Mormons, Seventh Day Adventists, and other religious groups with strict prohibitions concerning health-related behaviors are healthier and live longer, on average, than members of other faiths and those who are uninvolved in religion (Enstrom, 1978, 1989; Gardner & Lyon, 1982; Lyon, Klauber, & Gardner, 1976; Phillips, Kuzma, & Beeson, 1980). However, George and colleagues (2000) conclude that strict prohibitions on health-related behaviors only explain 10% of the reason that religious and spiritual affiliations have a positive impact on health and mental health.

2. Social support. Religion may positively affect health because of the fellowship, support, and social bonds that develop among religiously affiliated people. When compared to their nonreligious peers, people who regularly attend religious services report (1) having larger social networks; (2) having more contact with these social networks; (3) receiving more help from others; and (4) being more satisfied with their social support networks (Ellison & George, 1992; Zuckerman, Kasl, & Ostfeld, 1984). Despite this, social support provides only a 5% to 10% explanation of the relationship between religion and health (Idler, 1987; Zuckerman et al., 1984).

3. The coherence hypothesis. A third explanation for the health benefits of religion is that people who are religious understand "their role in the universe, the purpose of life, and develop the courage to endure suffering" (George et al., 2000, p. 110). George and colleagues (2000) call this the "coherence hypothesis" and report that the connection between a client's sense of coherence about the meaning of life and his or her personal role in the universe affects 20% to 30% of a client's health and mental health, largely because it buffers the person from stress (Antonovsky, 1980; Idler, 1987; Zuckerman et al., 1984).

A STORY ABOUT THE IMPACT OF RELIGIOUS DIFFERENCES ON AN INTIMATE RELATIONSHIP

She sits across from me and looks sweetly, lovingly, and overly made up. Not on purpose, not to hide the wrinkles, but to persuade me that she's just the same person she was 4 years ago when the sight of her made me want to leap across the table and devour her. Now all I can think is that she's finishing my sentences for me, with the wrong words.

———————

The following story was sent to me as an example of an emotionally abusive relationship. The story seems less about abuse than about the complex nature of love between two people who share certain religious and ethnic beliefs, but at very different levels of significance. Both people are very successful in their careers, but they have had prior problems with intimate relationships. The story is included in this chapter as an example of how we maintain intimate relationships despite significant personal, religious, and cultural differences.

"Sometimes my life feels . . ."

"Empty," she says.

"No, full of crap."

"The same thing," she says," putting her hand absent-mindedly on her wig.

She's religious. A religious Jewish woman out with an irreligious Jewish guy like me. A wig won't even begin to hide the shame.

"What I'm trying to say is that . . ."

"It's fun being together again."

"For God's sake, Rachel, why don't you . . ."

"Listen to you," she says, and looks up at me.

"Why do you always finish my sentences for me?" I ask.

She puts her hand over her mouth and makes the sign for zipping her lip. God, I'm starting to hate this. Why am I here?

"What I'm trying to say Rachel is . . ."

"That you'd like to keep seeing me on Sundays."

"For the love of Mike, would you stop it?" I yell at her.

Rachel looks away and then back at me. "Why are you so angry at me?" she asks, and I can see little tears in her eyes. Or is it maybe that the mascara is a little loose from the humidity. "You're mad at me, Jake, and you should tell me why."

She's crying now and the words come out as single staccato statements of betrayal. Why did I stop seeing her? Why am I such a cold fish? Why do I make love to her and then drop her like a wet piece of cod? Or is it liver? She never gets American slang right and her English is from somewhere just south of Minsk on the Siberian Railroad. She's beautiful. Little and dark and beautiful. Her smells drive me crazy. The thought of smelling the perfume on her breasts passes by me in a flash. Gulp!

"Because," I say, "just because."

"That's a reason? That's a reason you should give an Orthodox lady who broke every rule in the book to be with you?"

"I didn't twist your arm, did I?"

"No, you were always a gentleman, Jake. You were always so gentle and sweet and loving, and now you aren't, and it hurts."

"I'm sorry if it hurts. I don't mean to hurt you."

"Why are you always so angry with me, Jake?"

"Because."

And I want to tell her that it's this whole Jewish thing, this religious crap with the wigs and the subterfuge and the dishonesty. You go out with a woman, you should be able to let people know it, not meet in secret, in dark corners. It feels illicit. Dirty. It feels like I'm not good enough for her.

"Your mother was in town last month. Why didn't you let us meet?" I ask.

"She wouldn't understand," she says, wiping her eyes with a dainty, gloriously white handkerchief.

"What wouldn't she understand? That we're sleeping together? That we have been for a long time?"

"I shouldn't be. I should be a good Jewish woman."

"But you're not."

"No, I'm not, Jake, and I should think you'd be a little more understanding. You know it would break my mother's heart for me to marry someone who isn't religious."

"While no one, including you, cares about breaking *my* heart, I guess."

"She's an old woman and she's been through hell. She has numbers on her arm from Bergen-Belson. What would you have me do, Jake?"

"Act like a human being, Rachel. Be kind and thoughtful. Treat me with respect instead of acting like I'm tainted because I'm not Orthodox. Don't cringe when I don't show up with a *yarmulke* on. Don't tell me that religious people should only make love when their time is right and the woman is clean, when you and I screw our teeth out all of the time."

"I do it for you, Jake. God knows it hurts inside. I do it because I can't help myself, I feel that way about you. I can't think of anything but you and you get angry at me because I feel that way."

She begins to cry and hides her face with her tiny hands. The lady at the table across from us shakes her head at me.

I put my hand on her arm, but she shakes it off.

"You can be so mean to me, Jake, just so mean and thoughtless. You think that because my English isn't as good as yours that I don't know you're making fun of me, but I do. I don't deserve this from you, Jake. I'm not some fast American woman who knows the score. I wear my feelings on my sleeves and you've hurt me and I won't have it anymore."

She starts to stand up but then crumbles down onto her chair and looks at me, her face covered with wet and runny makeup. It will take her half an hour to get her makeup on right so she can drive back to her little Orthodox ghetto and no one will know that some self-centered, irreligious guy like me has hurt her feelings. And then she stands up, slowly, deliberately picks up her things, turns her back on me, and walks away.

I watch her walk back to her car. She walks with little purposeful steps, and she's sobbing, and I can't stand up and follow her and apologize. I watch her sit in her car where she absent-mindedly hits the horn on the steering wheel with her head. And I watch her drive off, but she just looks past me.

The lady [at] the table next to me looks at me, looks right through my heart. I quickly pay the bill and walk in the opposite direction and almost don't notice the car down the street sitting, waiting, and the woman in the car crying. I walk around the block as if I'm leaving, but when I reach the car, Rachel is still sitting there waiting for me, sobbing, her eyes full of tears and her wig crooked. I open the car door, sit down, and put my arms around her.

"You really are so mean to me, Jake." And I hold her in my arms and wonder what the numbers from Bergin-Belson look like, and if I'm still seeing her because I can't stand the thought of hurting someone whose mother has been tattooed like cattle.

Rachel cries and I look out the window at nothing in particular. It is a beautiful day and like most of our Sundays together, it ends with me holding her and listening to her cry.

LESSONS TO BE LEARNED FROM THIS STORY

This is Jake's story. It's about him, and while it tells us about the many confusing aspects of their relationship, it also shows the conundrum of loving someone who isn't accessible. What should this couple do? The resilient person would probably opt out of the relationship because it has such strong elements of pain. One might think it would have been even better not to have entered into the relationship in the first place. But that's not the way love works, and even the healthiest of us find ourselves in intimate relationships that are painful. What did this couple do that demonstrated resilience in what appears to be a very dysfunctional and hopeless relationship?

1. Jake and Rachel went for therapy to a therapist who worked with highly religious Jewish people. The therapist gave them thoughtful reading material about other couples who had experienced similar problems and also referred them to a group of men and women with similar religious differences.

2. Jake agreed to find out more about Judaism and to accompany Rachel to workshops that would help him understand her Orthodox religious traditions.

3. After a month of therapy, they decided their differences were too great for them to stay together, and they broke up. The break up lasted 3 days, and they recognized that much as they had large religious and cultural differences, they were also deeply in love.

4. They decided to discontinue therapy because it seemed to be driving them apart. In its place, they sat down and rationally charted a course for their relationship. Since Rachel was strongly committed to Orthodox Judaism, Jake said he would learn much more about it, and he did. He agreed to wear a hat in her presence, to keep kosher, and to attend weekend religious services. In the privacy of his house, however, he could do as he pleased.

5. The deeper religious involvement touched him, and his associations with other men in the synagogue blossomed into friendships that allowed Jake to develop a nonjudgmental support group. Several of the men had gone through the same process he was going through and felt great empathy for him.

6. Rachel told her family that they were deeply in love and planned to marry. She hoped they would come to love and respect Jake as much as she did and appreciate that he was working honestly to develop a deeper affiliation with Judaism. With God's help, they would resolve the remaining problems they experienced. Jake, she told her family, was a good man from Orthodox immigrant parents, but he had moved away from his beliefs only to find that he really longed for a spiritual and communal experience.

7. They set up a meeting with the Rachel's mother, her remaining parent. The mother, described by Rachel as a "one tough customer," although ambivalent about Jake's real commitment to Judaism, found that she liked him very much and that she could understand her daughter's reason for loving him. They agreed to continue meeting and to work toward a stronger bond with the remaining family members who still had doubts.

8. Both Rachel and Jake had prior marriages that were, in many ways, deeply problematic. Rachel's former husband, although also Orthodox, was emotionally abusive and unavailable. He and Rachel had three children together, but she did the vast majority of parenting. Jake had married out of the faith, and while he didn't feel that was the cause of the marriage not working, he did feel that his ex-wife's lack of understanding of the messages given first-generation Jewish children by their immigrant parents to succeed at all costs was a primary reason the relationship didn't work. He had one child by the marriage. Both Jake and Rachel had gone many years without finding a suitable mate and were hungry for a relationship. Even though the story Jake wrote was written during a time of crisis in the relationship and seems very negative, both Jake and Rachel felt that the relationship was quite wonderful because it was so giving and loving much of the time they were dating.

9. Jake found that his move toward religion kindled deep feelings inside of him about Judaism and that even before they married and in the privacy of his home, he became a practicing, committed Jew. Rachel found that she was more flexible about his conversion than she thought she would be and delighted in his journey, even though it was sometimes convoluted and confused.

10. Jake and Rachel married after 6 months of working through their concerns. Two years after they married, they report that their relationship is stronger than ever. Their children by their first marriages are able to relate well to one another and to see their parents' happiness as a bond they share.

Should Issues of Religion and Spirituality Be Included in Our Work With Clients?

A good deal of the research reported in this chapter indicates that religious involvement and spirituality may have a positive impact on health and mental health. However, there is disagreement in the literature about whether helping professionals should learn about these issues in their training or discuss either of these issues with their clients. In a study of 53 social work faculty members, Dudley and Helfgott (1990) found that those opposed to a course on spirituality were concerned about its conflicting with the mission of social work, its creating problems stemming from the separation of church and state, and religious and spiritual material in the curriculum conflicting with the personal beliefs of faculty members and students. Sheridan, Wilmer, and Atcheson (1994) asked educators from 25 schools of social work questions regarding the inclusion of religious and spiritual content in social work programs. The majority (82.5%) supported its inclusion in a specialized elective course. In another study, Sheridan, Bullis, Adcock, Berlin, and Miller (1992) surveyed 328 social work practitioners and found that 83% received little training in religion and spirituality during their graduate studies, although a third of their clients discuss religious or spiritual concerns during treatment.

Sheridan (2000) found that 73% of the social workers surveyed had generally positive attitudes about the appropriateness of discussing religion and spirituality in practice. In addition, 43% of the respondents said that religion played a positive role in the lives of their clients, while 62% said that spirituality played a positive role in the lives of clients. Spirituality was reported to play a harmful role in their clients' lives only 12% of the time, while religion was reported detrimental to client functioning 21% of the time (Sheridan, 2000). A majority of the social workers responding said that they had used spiritually and religiously based interventions with clients even though most of the social workers (84%) had reported little or no prior instruction in the use of such interventions. However, over half of the respondents had attended workshops and conferences on religion and spirituality after their professional training was completed.

Amato-von Hemert (1994) believes we should include material on religious involvement and spirituality in graduate training and writes, "Just as we train and evaluate how workers address issues of class, gender, and race, we must maintain our professionalism by training workers to deal with religious issues" (p. 9). Tobias, Morrison, and Gray (1995) say that "today's multiethnic America encompasses a wide-ranging spiritual orientation that is, if anything, diverse" (p. 1), while Dudley and Helfgott (1990) suggest that "understanding spirituality is essential to understanding the culture of numerous ethnic groups that social workers help" (p. 288).

In trying to find a definition of practice that includes religious and spiritual content, Boorstein (2000) reports that a study by Lajoie and Shapiro (1992) came up with more than 200 definitions of transpersonal (spiritual) psychology. However, Lajoie and Shapiro (1992) summarize those definitions by writing that "transpersonal psychology is concerned with the study of humanity's highest potential, and with the recognition, understanding, and realization of intuitive, spiritual, and transcendent states of consciousness" (p. 91). Boorstein (2000) indicates that the differences between traditional psychotherapy and spiritually based psychotherapy are as follows: (1) Traditional psychotherapy is pessimistic (for example, Boorstein quotes Freud as having said that psychoanalysis attempts to convert "neurotic misery to ordinary misery"; p. 413); (2) Spiritually based psychotherapy tries to help clients gain awareness of the existence of joy, love, and happiness in their lives; (3) Spiritually based therapy is concerned with life meaning and not just symptom removal.

A Dissenting View

In a dissenting view of the inclusion of religious and spiritual issues in practice, Sloan and Bagiella (2001) conclude that while interest in the impact of religious involvement and spirituality on health is great, "the empiric support required to convert this interest into recommendations for health practice is weak and inconclusive at best, with most studies having numerous methodological shortcomings. Even if there were methodologically solid findings demonstrating associations between religious and spiritual activities and health outcomes, problems would still exist" (p. 33).

Sloan and Bagiella (2001) point out the following methodological problems in trying to demonstrate a positive relationship between religious and spiritual involvement and improved health benefits: First of all, "we have no idea, for example, whether recommending that patients attend religious services will lead to increased attendance and, if so, whether attendance under these conditions will lead to better health outcomes" (p. 34). Many factors influencing health are beyond the scope of practice. While marital status is strongly associated with health effects, most practitioners would "recoil" at recommending marriage because of its positive relationship to health. Furthermore, "recommending religion to patients in this context may be coercive" (p. 34), since it creates two classes of people: those who comply and those who don't. This may lead to the implication that poor health may be linked to insufficient spiritual or religious involvement. Sloan and Bagiella (2001) conclude that "the absence of compelling empiric evidence and the substantial ethical concerns raised suggest that, at the very least, it is premature to recommend making religious and spiritual activities adjunctive treatments" (p. 34).

In summary, there is compelling evidence that many clients have strong religious and spiritual beliefs that play an important role in the way they cope with social, emotional, and physical difficulties. While many practitioners understand and value the importance of religious and spiritual beliefs, few feel prepared to work with either issue, and most feel that professional education should include content related to understanding and applying knowledge related to spirituality and religious beliefs. However, concerns were raised when faculties were asked how material would be taught given the diverse nature of faculties and student bodies in the helping profession.

Summary

This chapter discusses the relationship between resilience and religious and spiritual involvement. While much of the research suggests a strong relationship between religious and spiritual involvement and better physical and mental health, the research is at a very primitive but encouraging stage of development. Explanations for the positive impact of religious involvement and spirituality are provided. Help in explaining meaning-of-life issues is thought to be the primary reason spiritual and religious beliefs have such a positive impact on people. Two stories show the impact of spiritual and religious beliefs in coping with troubling relationship problems.

CHAPTER 3

Helping Others as an Attribute of Resilience

One of the primary attributes of resilient people is their involvement with others as indigenous helpers who provide social support. Many resilient people are involved in the self-help movement as leaders or participants. In this chapter, I will explore the relationship between resilience and helping others. As Tech (2003) notes in her book on survivors of the Holocaust, "The more accustomed prospective victims are to performing nurturing and cooperative roles, the more likely they are to adapt to changing circumstances" (p. 353). According to Tech, during the Second World War, one partisan group of escaped Jews from concentration camps, the *Bielski Ortiad*, "focused their energies on cooperation, rescue of the oppressed and survival." The survival rate for this group was 95%, as opposed to 20% for those who joined the Russian Resistance movement. "In times of upheaval, in the ruin of traditional society, cooperation and mutual protection rather than combativeness and competition promote greater odds of survival" (Tech, 2003, p. 354).

Indigenous Helpers

Patterson and Marsiglia (2000) report remarkable similarities in the help provided to others by two cohorts of indigenous helpers from two very different geographic locations in the United States. The similarities included offering assistance to family and friends before it was asked for, an attempt to reduce stress in those helped, and a desire to help people strengthen their coping skills. Lewis and Suarez (1995) identify the primary functions of indigenous helpers as buffers between individuals and sources of stress, providers of social support, information and referral sources, and lay consultants. Waller and Patterson (2002) believe that indigenous helpers strengthen the social bond holding communities together and improve the well-being of individuals and communities. Often, indigenous helpers are people who have been able to overcome severe traumas and personal problems. Having dealt successfully with their own life difficulties has given them special abilities to help others.

Robert Bly (1986) suggests that indigenous helpers, or what he calls "People of Wisdom," are known for their expertise in solving certain types of problems. We gravitate to these people because they help us in unobtrusive and informal ways that are often profoundly subtle. Their lack of formal training is offset by their kindness, patience, common sense, and good judgment. According to Bly, people of wisdom provide the support systems in formal and informal organizations that help their co-workers and friends in ways that often have profound meaning to those being helped.

Having seen my father's work with very troubled union members, I came to believe that certain people in the workplace often act as primary buffers for workers by helping them cope with the stressors of life and by resolving crises. I thought these people would be easy to identify and that each organization would have someone whom others would identify as an indigenous helper. By interviewing these helpers, I hoped that I might be able to develop a list of attributes to identify why and how indigenous helpers function as they do. I thought these folks would be excellent examples of resilient people who had overcome adversity and serious traumas in the lives. I've included several examples of indigenous helpers followed by the attributes shared by many of the people I interviewed.

EXAMPLES OF INDIGENOUS HELPERS

Indigenous Helper 1: A good example of a natural helper in an office setting was provided by Sharon Miller, who works in a law firm in San Antonio, Texas. "I work in a highly competitive law office," she said. "You can't trust anyone. If you share anything personal, it gets all over the office and it's used against you in every way imaginable. You can never allow people to think that you're vulnerable or pretty soon you're considered weak. We have a wonderful paralegal who is everyone's friend. She's a great listener, she's honest, and she'd never break a confidence. Everyone shares personal and work-related information with her. She's the office safety valve. If it weren't for her, the place would explode."

The woman Ms. Miller spoke of, an indigenous helper, was asked to share her experiences. She said, "I never thought of myself as anything as grand as a therapist, but it's true that people have been coming to me for advice since I was a child. I grew up in a very troubled home, and I guess I learned to take care of myself in ways that might help others. I've learned over the years that listening well, keeping a confidence, and occasionally making suggestions when people ask for them can have a good effect on people's lives. I don't think of myself as a therapist or anything like that. I guess I just see myself as a good friend who has something to offer. Lots of times the problems people ask me to listen to are so serious that it's clear they need professional help. I'm always sure to suggest that if it's warranted. Other times, people just need a kind person to listen and to remind them that they're good people. It's amazing how seldom we seem to let others know that they're really OK people. Folks just get down on themselves sometimes and they need someone to help them see another path.

"I guess I can trace my desire to help others from my own family life. Both my parents had drinking problems. They were kind people, religious people, but they drank to keep their sadness from overcoming them. I knew my job at home was to keep us all together. I didn't mind and we made it as a family. My parents were always very thankful for the help I gave, and I guess I grew up thinking that while we had serious problems in our home and we had no money because my parents couldn't hold down jobs because of the drinking, that we were blessed with love for one another. We were a religious family and we had a great feeling for God and His gifts. I have a wonderful husband and children, and my parents are good people and we're all close. I feel a lot of love for others and if it shows itself and others choose to use me to talk about their lives, I feel God has blessed me with a gift of caring. How can anyone not want to use that gift to help others?"

Indigenous Helper 2: Oscar Anderson has been involved in the union movement in Kansas City for over 50 years as a teamster. He believes in reaching out to his co-workers and helping them in times of need. On weekends, when many of the men in the union are drinking to excess, he is often helping the men who come to his home to discuss their serious personal problems. Oscar is a nonbeliever in counseling and psychotherapy, but what he does looks very much like therapy, in a rough and unorthodox way. He listens well, offers advice when it's needed, and knows where men can get specialized help. He can be supportive and encouraging as well as confrontational and very directive. Now semi-retired, Oscar had the following to say about helping people on the job:

"Most counselors I know," he said, "never tell people that a lot of what they've done in their lives is good. They never praise people for their hard work or their support for families. They never use humor. All they do is criticize. I see a lot of immature young people at work. It's taken them a long time to grow up. You can't help people grow up over night, it takes time. You've got to listen carefully to what they say, praise them for what they do well, and offer some advice and support for what they don't do so well.

"My parents were immigrant people from Norway. We had a tough life and nobody helped us, but we had great pride and we talked about philosophy and literature at home. My father was a socialist and believed that cooperative living was the only solution to the problems we all encountered. He thought the state should help as much as it could but that in the end, it came down to neighbors helping neighbors. He was a strong union man, but when I was 8, he got killed in a union action by some goons the boss had hired. I was angry about it. I was obsessed with the desire for revenge, and I'd think about finding those goons and killing them.

"The funny thing is that when my dad got killed and I had to take many of his responsibilities over, I started thinking of the people who killed him as symbols of what was wrong with us as a people and I wanted to set an example, like my father, of doing good. I read a lot about the life of Jesus, and about Gandhi, and Martin Luther King had a real effect on me. I decided that my anger was a killing emotion and that by helping, by listening, by being the good man my father was that I'd do much more good for others than if I was full of hate. When I was old enough to work, I joined the same union with the same boss and we built a strong union with love and affection and solidarity. In a sense, we overcame the odds against us and we became a model of how a union could work cooperatively with management. I see others like me in our union and it fills me with joy to know my brothers and sisters in the union understand that when you only care about yourself, you lose the opportunity to grow and expand as a human being and that a belief in something larger than you can lead to great happiness and inner peace."

Indigenous Helper 3: Sam Goldfarb, another natural helper, is a retired manager of a large accounting firm. Sam is originally from Russia but has lived in Minneapolis for 40 years. Someone in his synagogue suggested I talk with Sam because Sam has spent his working years informally helping the members of his synagogue as well as his co-workers. When Sam was interviewed, he was helping to transport an elderly member of the congregation to a doctor's office. Sam is 83 years old.

"You don't go around with a sign on your face that says to come see you if anyone wants to talk," he said, "but you let yourself be around the people who are in trouble. You can tell from their faces and the way they're acting that they're in some trouble in their life. Pretty soon they talk. People love to talk, but only if they feel you won't criticize them. I just listen . . . an old man with an ear and a heart to offer. And when they're done talking, I give them advice, an old man's advice. Sometimes they take it, sometimes they don't. That's life. But most of the time they're grateful to get their problems off their chest."

"You ask why I help others. I grew up in Russia when the Communists took over. Russia was a place of deep anti-Semitism and although many of the early members of the Party were Jewish, it was clear that the Party was full of the same anti-Semitism that had always plagued Russia under the czars. We were lucky. My father knew the score, and we got out just as Stalin was taking over and Russia went crazy with genocide. When we came to America, my father told us that he expected us to make sure that what happened in Russia would never happen in America. This was our home and only by being good to others, by helping when we could, would there be a transformation in the way people treat each other. I've heard it referred to as social capital. Even though we were dirt poor and we had little, we shared what we had and soon, others shared with us too. Soon, our neighborhood which was full of immigrant and racial groups who were supposed to hate each other if you listened to the common wisdom, they were helping each other in every way possible. I stayed with a black family many times when my parents had to work nights. My best friend to this day is Swedish. I began to see as I worked my way through school and I dealt with the anti-Semitism of America that we Jews could hide as we had in Russia and make ourselves invisible, or we could be out front making our mark on the country.

"Many of us became doctors, and social workers, and teachers, and I think it made us a much more giving people. As we gave we got, and I'm convinced that America is a better place because so many immigrants did the same thing. We suffered our tragedies, not by being alone and isolated, but because we lived in a real community where everyone felt our sorrows and gave compassion and support. That's why I help, and because of it, I've been able to deal with my own tragedies, which have been many, and when I feel too sad to give to others, something inside tells me it will help me feel better and, you know what? It does, always."

Indigenous Helper 4: A colleague and friend of mine is a man of wisdom. He teaches history at a local university but has no training in counseling. He had been through three failed marriages, the death of his parents, and the death of one of his ex-wives when a sudden depression sent him to a therapist several years ago, and since then, he's been reaching out to others. This is what he said about the experience: "I think I've always been the perfect academic: Aloof, a bit arrogant, superior, and not very good in handling the feelings of others. My personal life has been a mess and I've gone through periods when I've had serious problems with my children. When their mother died, even though we'd not been married for many years, and yet another relationship was coming to an end, I just got very depressed. I'd always thought these emotional problems were for weak people not strong, tough, resilient people like me, and it was tough on my ego to go for help. Through the process, which took a long time since I was so defensive, I began to understand that my aloofness kept me from experiencing people. My therapist gave me an assignment to be more friendly to other people, particularly people I'd never meet in academia, and this is what I did.

"Most mornings I'd go to a local café for coffee. The local men would often walk by my table and nod in recognition. Sometimes they'd stop and talk to me about my articles in the local papers about immigration. They were the workingmen of America; the plumbers and construction workers, the common laborers and retired railroad workers, the illegal immigrants from Mexico. Their trucks and beat up old cars lined the parking lot outside of the restaurant.

"I have come to value my conversations with these men. Many of them have done badly by women and children, and readily admit it. Some of them are extraordinary people who have done better than most of us. And there are always the men who sit in the back of the restaurant and talk in whispered tones about women. They sound like abusers . . . they sound like children in adult bodies.

"I've learned a lot from talking and listening to the men I meet in the coffee shop. Academics can be pretty disassociated from life, but these men talk like real people, people with flaws, people we all know in our daily lives. When the wives and kids of these men talk to me, [I] get a very sad picture of their behavior. They talk about abuse and neglect, about put-downs, and absences, and mean drinking, and, sometimes, about abandonment. They often describe the impact of insensitive behavior on the women and children who are trying so hard to love their men.

"Sometimes I get a chance to sit with the men and [the] women [in their lives] and listen to them talk about the gender wars they have fought. The men usually sit with their mouths open and often as not say, 'Was I that bad?' Everybody nods their heads. The men have mellowed a lot, so it isn't easy for them to imagine that they've acted so badly in the past.

"Sometimes the men hang around, after the women leave, to assure me that they weren't that bad, but there is an emptiness to their denial; [it] rings hollow. Many times they walk away shaking their heads, angry at me for making them hear so much bad stuff about behavior they'd rather forget. These men who interrupt me as I try and drink my coffee are ordinary men: Men who have had troubles in their lives; men who drink too much, from time to time, and who can be mean and petty; men who regret their past and have done a thing or two that leave them in the night sweats when they wake up from bad dreams; normal men who have made mistakes; decent guys who cared for the baby at night and have provided for families when it was nearly impossible.

"Sensitive men? Probably not. Romantic men? I doubt it. Men who sweep women off their feet with the power and concentration of their lovemaking? It doesn't seem very likely. These men are just regular 'Joes' who need the guidance and the sweet and tender love of a woman: Men who are better when a woman is in their life than when they are alone; men who can hardly navigate the complexities of life and depend on women in ways that seem childlike at times. Men like Roger, a plumber who joins the early morning construction gang at the coffee shop. He sees me sitting in the back reading the paper and comes over to sit with me. Today he complains about his wife. She's too fat, he says. He's lost interest in her. I look over at Roger, who is perhaps 60 or 70 pounds overweight, and I ask if he's looked in the mirror lately. Does he know that his obesity is as off-putting to his wife as hers is to him? He mumbles something derogatory about my mother, but I see him every day and [over time] he looks . . . thinner. When I see him with his wife, they look nice together . . . warm, maybe even tender in the way mature men and women can be with one another. He doesn't thank me for my advice or say how much his life has improved because of my simple advice. All he does is bring his wife over, an attractive woman in her forties, while I drink my coffee and try to read the paper. He beams at me. See how great my wife looks? his smile says. See what a hunk I must be to attract such a great looking lady? It is thanks enough and I smile at their happiness.

"Another guy, Richard, one of the few Black men who sit in the café, morning after morning, complains to me about the way his wife spends his money. 'She's a shopping junky,' he says. 'There's no way she can spend so much money.' He brings her in one morning, a nice, soft-spoken young woman. She talks to me about how difficult it is for a Black family to make ends meet, but Richard is a good husband and father and they make the money go a little further. Richard wants to buy me breakfast. He feels like dancing in the café. His wife has touched a part of his heart with love seeds.

"Denise sometimes comes for coffee and sits with a group of middle-aged women. Some time ago, she and some of the other women at the table began asking me questions about men. I'd listen and, occasionally, I'd offer a suggestion or two. Denise would come back later and tell me how much better her husband was when she'd try little pieces of the advice I'd give her. The ladies were suspicious, but after a while, all of them asked for suggestions about how to understand the men in their lives. Without fail, enough of the suggestions worked so well that I often felt like I was doing therapy in the back seat of the coffee shop. Ladies would come up to me and ask every manner of question.

"For example, Betty Sue wanted to know why her husband had lost interest in sex. I pointed out a few possible reasons, like fatigue from work or anxiety over finances. 'He's a good man,' she said, 'and we used to have a great love life.' All of the women in the group raised their eyes in disbelief and said, 'Sure, sure,' but Betty Sue persisted. There was something really wrong, she thought. So I said to her, why not just say to him something like, 'Honey, it sure used to be nice how we'd spend our time in bed. It would be nice to have that again.' Then I said, see what he says.

"The next day she came back with a big smile on her face. All the ladies at the table were ribbing her. Finally, someone motioned for me to join them. 'He thought I wasn't interested anymore,' she said. 'He thought maybe I was seeing another man, and it was making him crazy.'

"I don't know if I'm doing any good. I'm just a historian, after all, and all I know about therapy is what I've observed in my own therapy and what I've learned in life. It just feels right to reach out to people. The more I think about it, the more I think it makes me the happiest I've ever been to help others. It's what my mother used to call a 'mitzvah' or doing a good deed. Since I've been doing 'mitzvahs,' I'm a lot happier as a person, I can say that for sure" (Glicken, 2005a, pp. 1–3).

Self-Help Groups and Indigenous Helpers

In defining self-help groups, Wituk, Shepherd, Slavich, Warren, and Meissen (2000) write, "Self-help groups consist of individuals who share the same problem or concern. Members provide emotional support to one another, learn ways to cope, discover strategies for improving their condition, and help others while helping themselves" (p. 157). Kessler, Mickelson, and Zhao (1997) estimate that 25 million Americans have been involved in self-help groups at some point during their lives. Positive outcomes have been found in self-help groups treating substance abuse (Humphreys & Moos, 1996), bereavement (Caserta & Lund, 1993), care giving (McCallion & Toseland, 1995), diabetes (Gilden, Hendryx, Clar, Casia, & Singh, 1992), and depression (Kurtz, 1988). Riessman (2000) reports that "more Americans try to change their health behaviors through self-help than through all other forms of professional programs combined" (p. 47).

Kessler, Frank, Edlund, Katz, Lin, and Leaf (1997) indicate that 40% of all therapeutic sessions for psychiatric problems reported by respondents in a national survey were in the self-help sector, as compared to 35.2% receiving specialized mental health services, 8.1% receiving help from general physicians in the medical sector, and 16.5% receiving help from social service agencies. Wuthnow (1994) found that self-help groups are the most prevalent organized support groups in America today. The author estimates that 8 to 10 million Americans are members of self-help groups and that there are at least 500,000 self-help groups in America.

Fetto (2000) reports a study done by the University of Texas, Austin that found that approximately 25 million people will participate in self-help groups at some point in their lives, and that 8 to 11 million people participate in self-help groups each year. Men are somewhat more likely to attend groups than women, and Caucasians are three times as likely to attend self-help groups as African Americans. The number of people in self-help groups is expected to be much higher with the full use of the Internet as a tool for self-help. Participants most likely to attend self-help groups are those diagnosed with alcoholism, cancer (all types), diabetes, AIDS, depression, and chronic fatigue syndrome. Those least likely to attend suffer from ulcers, emphysema, chronic pain, and migraines, in that order (Fetto, 2000).

Riessman (1997) identifies the common functions and purposes of self-help groups as follows: (1) Self-help groups have members who share a similar condition and understand each other; (2) Members determine activities and policies, which makes self-help groups very democratic and self-determining; (3) Helping others is therapeutic for members; (4) Self-help groups charge no fees, are not commercialized, and build on the strengths of the individual members, the group, and the community; (5) Self-help groups function as social support systems that help participants cope with traumas through the supportive relationships between members; (6) Values are projected in self-help groups that define the intrinsic meaning of the group to its members; (7) Self-help groups use the expertise of members to help one another; (8) Self-help group members may find that seeking assistance from the group is not stigmatizing, as seeking help from a health or mental health provider may be; (9) Self-help groups focus on the use of self-determination, inner strength, self-healing, and resilience.

We tend to think of resilience as something uniquely internal to a person, but Riessman (1997) believes that resilience is often a function of a person's social support network. Writing about self-help groups, Riessman provides several explanations of why self-help groups are able to bring out resilience in people who often seem to be highly dysfunctional.

1. Self-help represents among the best defenses against the individuality of a commodity (materialistic) culture.

2. Association around self-help and across conditions produces a degree of race and class mixing that is unusual in our society.

3. The activism of people in self-help organizations offers the resurgence of democratic life among ordinary people in our society, which is crucial if we're to protect and reclaim popular democracy.

4. The people organized in self-help groups have an investment in effective service and can represent a major vehicle for working out and demanding the appropriate role of government in the adequate funding and delivery of services.

5. Members of a self-help group possess social homogeneity and self-determination. Self-determination means that the activity is determined internally by the self-help "unit"—the individual, group, or community. This allows a new dimension of participatory democracy to emerge that is less concerned with issues of control or governance, and more with what the individual or group has to contribute.

6. Paradoxical as it may seem, giving help is the best way of being helped.

7. The self-help approach is built on the inner strengths of the individual, group, or community.

8. The self-help group is one of many forms of social support that enables individuals to withstand crisis, loss of loved one, or alienation. Supportive relationships provide a buffer against stress. They allow the individual to interpret the situation in a different and much less stressful way.

9. The power of self-help rests on a strong belief in experiential learning, the help-promoting properties of the group (its wisdom), and the mental health benefits derived from a cooperative mutual relationship.

10. Self-help programs share an internal focus rather than relying on external interventions by "experts"—teachers, therapists, clergy, or the state. The emphasis is on what's inside the individual or community. This internal factor stands out in a number of other self-help concepts: self-determination, inner strengths, indigenous character, regenerative healing (healing from within), and resilience. (Riessman, 1997, pp. 8–10)

Attributes of Indigenous Helpers

Indigenous helpers use helping processes that most people are comfortable with. They listen, give commonsense advice, and are usually gentle people. As one person interviewed said, "I went for professional therapy and the therapist, right away, had me talking to my dead mother who was supposed to be sitting in an empty chair opposite me. It felt really strange. I was having marital problems but I was supposed to talk to my dead mother? I just couldn't see it. Jim, who is a friend and a very good listener, sat with me at coffee and let me pour my heart out for two hours. He didn't interrupt, was very supportive and calm, and just said that my marriage had come to a point where it was so difficult for me to make a decision that I needed professional help. He was right, of course, but I would have never sought someone out if it weren't for him and ultimately, after a few false starts, like the one I mentioned, I found a good counselor and it saved my marriage."

Indigenous helpers are optimistic. People who seek help from natural helpers often feel accepted, respected, and affirmed. Many people who seek help from indigenous helpers immediately feel more confident in their ability to resolve a problem because the natural helper has defined it in a positive and solvable way.

Indigenous helpers usually learn their helping skills by observing parents or significant adults in childhood. They describe themselves as resilient and rational people who have always been able to resolve their own life problems without needing additional help. Indigenous helpers are usually able to follow their own advice and to lead productive and exemplary lives. It is the healthy lives of the natural helpers that almost always encourages people to seek the helper out.

Indigenous helpers believe in a positive view of people. Almost everyone I identified as an indigenous helper in an earlier work on this subject (Glicken, 1991) expressed a variation on this theme: People are basically good. You should look for the goodness in them and help them use it as a way of dealing with problems in their lives.

Since helpers have no formal training, the approach they use with others is very gentle and fluid. It feels, according to the people I interviewed who have had experience with indigenous helpers (Glicken, 1991), like talking to a dear friend over coffee.

A Story of an Indigenous Helper

My mother used to tell me that a relationship with a good friend was much more important than one with an uninvolved relative. That wasn't the way she said it, of course, but that's the gist of her combination of Yiddish, Polish, English, and the soap opera words of wisdom that defined her philosophy of life.

Throughout those years she suffered from a variety of health problems that ended in long hospitalizations. After the Second World War, when news of the death of all of her remaining family came to us in chilling letters from the Red Cross, she developed a sadness that was very close to the surface and often resulted in what we now would think of as chronic depression. During those years of depression she was lost to us, and I now recognize that I felt she had abandoned us. Another story about my family, which is in Chapter 12 of this book, explores those feelings.

My mother was a lover of soaps. I knew the plots of every soap opera on the radio when I was a kid. When I started telling her what would happen next, however, she gave up on telling me the stories. They were all, it seemed to my 10-year-old mind, about betrayal. Betrayal of wives by husbands, husbands by wives, siblings by siblings, and, in my mother's mind, and worst of all, friends by friends.

To my mother, a friendship was as sacred as a marriage. This was not a gray area issue for my mother. You had a friend or you didn't. A person wasn't a friend one day and an acquaintance the next. A friend was a true and loyal companion who knew what it was like to walk through life in your shoes. A friend felt your pain and knew when you were down and needed help. In some mysterious way, according to my mother, a friend could even read your mind.

Loyalty was everything for my mother. If a friend wasn't loyal, a process not unlike a divorce took place. A friend was there when you needed a friend. You didn't have to spell it out, either. Friends *knew* when they were needed. *They just did.* When I would ask how they would know, she'd shrug and say, as millions of Jewish women have said before and since, "Don't ask." It was a phrase of wisdom that I could not appreciate until I began to say the same thing to my daughter.

When my mother died, I can remember walking through a store and listening to several elderly women talking about her and saying things so sweet and tender that it was all that I could do not to cry. She was the neighborhood helper, you see. Even though she was ill most of the time I was growing up, she always had women over, allowing them to talk about anything, even sex. It was

---

I wrote this story describing my mother and how clear it is to me now that she was an indigenous helper. I hope this story describes the impact she had on me and on others.

shocking to me that my prudish mother, who never said anything bad about any-one and who could only swear in Yiddish (which, as everyone knows, isn't really swearing because the swear words only have assumed and not literal meanings), would allow such talk in our house. And that wasn't all. In our house women talked about alcoholism, domestic violence, child abuse, and even infidelity.

There was an essential sweetness to my mother. She never turned a man away who needed work, always trading fish or hard work for a meal. My friends would come over and feast on chocolate chip cookies so hard we used them as hockey pucks in the winter. They loved her, as did everyone I knew. My school work, which was often miserable and frequently received bad grades, my mother made into the work of a genius. Every paper I brought home was held up by magnets on the refrigerator door. The better the grade, the closer to the middle of the door where the neighbor women could see that this kid they thought was a moron might have some brains in his head yet. Even when she became ill, my mother helped others. "Moishe, take some cookies over to Mrs. Cooper. It would be a shame to waste them." A shame? They were inedible. Even my brother said that her cooking was so bad that when he used to see a sign saying "Home Cooking," or "Mom's Cooking," he used to run like crazy. Still, she gave and always reminded me that giving from the heart, wanting to give, wanting to help—not because it was an obligation, but because it was a burning desire in your heart—this was what made us special as a family. "Sure we're poor, God knows, but we give what little we have. If we don't, how can we be good people? Good people share with others. Good people give back what they've got."

My mother knew that you had to give to receive. When my mother died, the rabbi who spoke at the funeral had never met her, but he said that he'd spoken to her friends and neighbors. She was, he said, a real Jewish woman: tough, tender, and endlessly loyal to her friends and family. When he said that, I knew that no one would ever be that way for me again. She was my mother, but she was also my friend, and I mourned for the loss of both.

LESSONS TO BE LEARNED FROM THIS STORY

In a very special way, my mother's behavior reflected the Jewish imperative that you give to others (*mitzvot*). My father, who I write about in Chapter 12 and who was deeply involved in the labor movement and civic life, acted in a way that reflected the Jewish belief that you deal directly with the social ills of the world and that each of us has a responsibility to make the world a better place (*tikkum olam*). Together, they created a notion of life that was idealistic, benevolent, and caring. These views of life helped my family cope with illness and poverty and led to idealism and optimism during times of real family difficulty. What follows are other lessons in this story.

1. Giving to others helped my mother cope with serious health problems that would have otherwise completely impaired her functioning.

2. The joy and positive regard she received from helping others made her a positive role model for the children in my family, all of whom believe that what you give to others has a positive impact on your life.

3. My mother's compassion and regard for others, even when she was ill, helped my family remain optimistic and tied to the belief that helping others is the highest form of helping oneself. It was the driving force that helped us through very tough times and later had a significant impact on what my brother, sister, and I chose to do with our lives.

4. The idea that a friend is someone who is a loving and involved person, as important and as powerful as family, is an important lesson, one that has never left me and continues to influence the way I deal with life sorrows. Who could manage without friends?

Recently, I was asked to write a memory of a good friend for his 65th birthday. I hope Sam won't mind my including what I said for this book on resilience, because it speaks to the issue of keeping friends through the rocky times we sometimes have and how friendship is like a love affair: difficult, trying, but ultimately, quite wonderful.

At one point in our friendship, Sam and I had a serious misunderstanding that led to an estrangement of almost a year and a half. As it is the custom for Jews before the High Holy Days to try and work out misunderstandings, my friend called and asked that we meet to reestablish our friendship. I agreed, although I did so with a mix of lingering anger at the reason for our estrangement and guilt at letting things go so long and acting, throughout, in a childish and boorish way.

We met in the village in Claremont on one of those perfect late summer, early fall afternoons in Southern California when the air is warm and soft and you can't imagine living anywhere else. We sat for hours discussing what had happened in our lives during the year and a half when we'd not spoken. There was much to discuss and it felt wonderful to have my old friend listen.

I had just had spinal surgery and wondered if I would ever be the same physically. Sam spoke of his family and of his warm relationship with his wife. He told me about new projects and his excitement at writing books he thought would make a real contribution. He spoke proudly of his work with the Advanced Placement exams in history and of his trips to San Antonio to grade AP exams. And he told me about the achievements of his wonderful children and how he and his children were closer to one another than ever. I felt the same thing was happening with my daughter.

I remember thinking that it was pretty astonishing that my friend could stay with me in spirit throughout our time apart and that he could help us repair our friendship. How many friendships do you have in a lifetime, after all? You can't squander a single one.

Just recently, we played tennis together, had dinner at Mediterranean restaurant, and went to a new synagogue for services. It was both the end and the beginning of the yearly cycle of reading the Torah, but to me it felt like the beginning of a new phase in our relationship. We're both on Medicare now, and, say what you will, it makes you ponder your age. I think we both wondered about the future and whether we would be the same healthy and vigorous men we are now the next time the Torah scrolls are unrolled and a new cycle of reading begins.

As for me, I drove home thinking how fragile friendship is and how to have and maintain a real friendship is, in the words of my mother, everything.

A Story About an Indigenous Helper Starting a Self-Help Group

Jack Holden is the leader of a support group for people with chronic depression. Jack has been depressed much of his life and has come to believe that it is a condition he has to live with, much as he would if he had diabetes or heart problems. Jack is a kind and empathic person, and after reading about a support group for depressed people in another community, Jack volunteered his time to organize a similar group in his community. In preparing for this commitment, Jack met with a number of other leaders of various types of support groups in the community and attended meetings of a local volunteer organization in town to get additional ideas. He wrote to a national organization for depressed people asking for assistance in setting up a group. They sent him a kit that explained how one might go about developing a group and included many practical ideas about advertising, screening group members, where to hold meetings, and how to plan an agenda. Jack was able to use free ads in local newspapers and some spot ads on radio and television. Even so, the response was slow and Jack almost gave up. After 4 months, Jack had the names of 10 people who wanted to be part of the group and who were also willing to help in its development.

The group met over a 2-month period, and, much to Jack's delight, they were willing to work hard, entered into some very useful discussions about the mission and focus of the group, and asked Jack to be their leader under the supervision of a helping professional from the community who had agreed to help. Jack read some books on group leadership that the professional had given him, and he attended a weeklong leadership workshop for new leaders given by the national association he had contacted. Jack found both the books and workshop invaluable. During the first several meetings of the new self-help group, the professional observed the group, but after that she assured Jack that what he was doing was just fine. She agreed to meet with him periodically to discuss the group and to enter into a loose supervisory arrangement. She also told Jack that if there was a crisis, he could always call and they would immediately meet to discuss it. They also agreed that if any group member was unwilling to promise not to commit suicide, if suicide came up in discussion, or if group members were concerned about the possibility of a suicide by any group member, that the professional would be contacted and a further assessment would be made by the professional. Thankfully, this has never happened in the 3 years the group has been actively meeting.

Gradually, the group has settled in with about 15 regular members. That's about all Jack thinks he can handle at one time. A few people have left the group because it hasn't worked for them, but others have taken their place. There are 20 people on the waiting list, and Jack is trying to organize another group to be led by one of the current members who has very strong leadership skills. The group meets once a week for 2 hours in the evening. All of the members have suffered from chronic depression for more than 5 years, and all of the members actively see professionals in therapy and are being seen medically to monitor medication. The mission of the group is to offer support, encouragement,

---

This case study first appeared in modified form in my 2005 book Improving the Effectiveness of the Helping Professions: An Evidence-Based Approach to Practice. *To find a more complete description of the research on self-help groups, the reader may want to consult that book.*

help with problem solving, and social events to help group members stay socially active, as well as to disseminate and discuss research information about depression. All the members are responsible for sending one another new articles or research reports via the Internet at least once or twice a month. The group has become so adept at finding new literature that many group members have brought information to their therapists and psychiatrists that was even new to them. The professionals have found that group members who take a very active role in their treatment also do much better in their lives, even though they continue to feel depressed some of the time. For many of the participants, depression is a struggle they have learned to live with through a combination of professional help and the self-help group.

The group believes that it should evaluate whether its work is helpful, and it has developed a testing instrument that measures life functioning in several key areas, including days missed at work; exercise, weight, and blood pressure; number of hours slept each day during the week; and attendance at social events, with reports from spouses, mates, or friends providing a weekly social functioning measure. The instrument also includes a 20-question depression inventory with good reliability and validity called the CES-D (Radloff, 1977). Over time, the evaluation mechanism has shown a gradual improvement in group members' social functioning. The members of the group exercise more, maintain their normal weight, miss fewer days at work, sleep less than they did, and have less depression than before joining the group (as measured by reports from others and scores from the depression instrument). Most group participants have found that even though their depression hasn't gone away completely, they have learned to live with it and get on with their lives more successfully than before.

I observed the group. It is a kind, supportive, and warm group, and many people in it have benefited from Jack's unobtrusive and affirming leadership approach. One group member said, "Jack is so warm and kind, it filters down to the group. People come here and they're pessimistic and hopeless about their depression, but after a few weeks, Jack's optimism is contagious. We all suffer together and depression is an awful thing, but we love one another, we love Jack, and we all live with the hope that we will get better. If Jack left, we'd fall apart. Maybe that's not a good thing to admit, but Jack is the glue that holds us together. I don't mind saying that. He's a wonderful person, and that he suffers from depression like the rest of us makes us love him that much more. There are days when he's too depressed to lead the group and others fill in. We have a buddy system that gives each member another group member to talk to when things get too tough. We go out together for dinner and socialize some. It's like the extended family many of us don't have. We're lonely and isolated people, and having this group is the best thing that's ever happened to me. And I'm glad that we have to maintain our contacts with professionals. It's a safety valve, in my opinion. Depressed people run a high risk of committing suicide. Were it not for the group and the professionals we work with, I couldn't promise not to do it if the feeling came over me really strongly. But the support network we've developed and the professional help keep us from going to extremes, and they give us hope. And for people who feel down most of the time, that's saying a lot."

I asked Jack why he developed the group in the first place. "Part of the reason was selfish," he said, "because I thought it would help me with my depression. Part of it came from wanting to help others. I've learned a lot about handling my depression and I felt like sharing it with others. I know that some people have biochemical depressions from birth maybe, but most of the people in group have had awful things happen to them, mostly when they were kids, but not always. We have people in group who were raped or assaulted as adults and they've developed depressions.

"In my case, I was pretty badly abused by my father and brother when I was a kid. I did fine in school and I had outlets, but underneath it all, I was a very sad kid. When I left home, the sadness just got worse. I had no friends and I felt very isolated and lonely. I started going to church near my home and, I don't know . . . it was uplifting. It gave me a sense of who I was. I started helping the church with legal issues and soon people were coming to me with legal questions that were almost always personal issues. I took some counseling courses and I felt good about myself when I was helping. It lifted the depression.

"I won't kid you and say that I don't have very dark moments, because I do. And I won't tell you that since I started the group my life is always happy, because it isn't. But when I help others, when I'm in the group, I feel transformed, like I'm somebody else, and it makes me very happy, almost giddy. I came out of this horrible torture that I endured as a kid, I became educated, I tried to be a good person, and in my own thoughts about myself, it's amazing I've done so well. I'm happy to give back. How else can I make any sense out of what was done to me? It's a way of eliminating what happened because I didn't turn into the mess my father and brother did. I can't imagine a better way to share my gratitude for whatever God gave me to cope with the abuse than to give to others" (Glicken, 2005b, pp. 269–271).

Summary

This chapter on indigenous helpers and self-help groups offers some hopeful evidence that people involved in self-help often experience an increased level of resilience. Helping others seems to be an effective way of helping oneself. Self-help is generally supportive in nature and usually provides an affirming and positive approach to problem solving that emphasizes natural healing, support, and group affiliation.

CHAPTER 4

The Powerful Helping Impulse of Our Cultural Heritage

Examples From Three Ethnic Groups

Resilience in Latino/as[1]

The term *Latino/a* is used in this chapter to represent a group with a shared language and some similar customs and traditions; however, the terms *Hispanic* and *Chicano/a* are also used in the literature to describe people from Cuba, Latin America, Mexico, and Puerto Rico. Hernandez (1990) notes that while three disparate groups of Latino/as (Cubans, Puerto Ricans, and Mexicans) identify very different systems of beliefs related to political orientations, government involvement in their lives, and the extent of discrimination they face in the United States, over 70% of Americans feel that the three groups are "very or somewhat similar."

Stressors in the lives of Latino/as, particularly newly immigrated Latino/as, include poverty, illegal status, poorly paying jobs, lack of health care, unfamiliarity with the culture and the many laws and social customs, and not being welcome in this country even when they have a legal right to be here. This immediate sense of alienation and the unfamiliar rules and regulations of American life often place Latino/as in situations that test individual and family resilience. As the Surgeon General (Satcher, 2001a) notes in a report on the importance of understanding culture when social and emotional problems exist,

> Their [Latino/as] per capita income is among the lowest of the minority groups covered by this Supplement. Yet there is great diversity among individuals and groups, depending on factors such as level of education, generation, and country of origin. For example, 27 percent of Mexican Americans live in poverty, compared to 14 percent of Cuban Americans. Despite their lower

average economic and social standing, which place many at risk for mental health problems and illness, Hispanic Americans display resilience and coping styles that promote mental health. (p. 1)

How Latino/a Cultures Cope With Social and Emotional Problems

More traditional and newly immigrated Latino/as often do not directly seek treatment for social or emotional problems (Rogler & Malgady, 1987). Velasquez, Arellano, and McNeill (2004) believe that there are several reasons why Latino men, in particular, don't seek professional help:

1. "Psychotherapy is for *jotos* or *maricones* (homosexuals), or *viejas* (old women)" (p. 180). From an early age, the message given to Latino men is to be strong, be tough, and take it like a man.

2. "Psychotherapy is only for people who are mentally ill or *locos* (crazy)" (p. 180). Latino men often believe that their problems originate with other people (their children, spouse, boss, friends) and that only people who have internal problems that originate inside of themselves need help.

3. "Psychotherapy is simply chatting with somebody" (p. 180). Many Latino men believe that problems that affect one physically (anxiety, depression, headaches, feelings of tension) should be dealt with by seeing a physician who can at least prescribe medication.

4. "Psychotherapy will simply open up problems that cannot be resolved" (p. 181). These problems may not only lead to a male feeling vulnerable and inadequate but they may worsen if not discussed with others.

When Latino/as have a problem they cannot solve on their own, they often first discuss it with extended family members or *compadres,* the close friends who baptize their children and who play such an important role in Latino/a culture. Latino/as experiencing stress may also seek help from priests or religious figures, in the form of direct advice and suggestions. Elderly people, particularly women, represent wisdom in the Latino/a culture, and they may also be contacted before a professional is seen.

When the problem becomes unsolvable and somatic complaints result, Latino/as may seek help from the family doctor. The use of medication to relieve the crisis would be considered an acceptable form of treatment at this stage of coping with the crisis situation. Complaints at the emotional level might be confused in the person's mind with physical difficulties. Problems with anxiety, for example, might be thought to originate in the stomach, and the person might first attempt to get medical relief for the stomach ailment.

The family doctor plays a vital role in the treatment of people in crisis. In many parts of Latin America and Mexico, as well as in the United States, the family doctor may prescribe an anti-depressive or anti-anxiety medication but tell the person that it is for the treatment of a physical ailment. This deception is not considered unethical, since it offers some relief and may decrease symptoms. Without counseling, however, the problem may move back and forth in severity. In this respect, the crisis may have an extremely long duration.

Congress (1990) says that the following elements are necessary ingredients for professional work with more traditional Latino/a clients: (1) *confianza*: the development of basic trust of the worker by the client; (2) *personalismo:* the worker's personalization of the service, permitting latitude in what the client wishes to discuss at the moment and thus increasing the responsiveness of the client to treatment; (3) *respecto:* the worker's belief that respect is intrinsically a function of all interactions with another person and that it forms a significant part of all crisis work with the Latino/a client. Without respect from the worker, the client will probably disengage from treatment.

In the Latino/a community, there is a considerable imperative to be strong even in the midst of a crisis. One way to promote clients' strength in the midst of crisis is to praise their accomplishments, particularly those related to the extended family. Another way to encourage Latino/a clients to discuss their feelings is to say, "I know that you've experienced much heartache and that you don't feel that your family appreciates you. How would you like your family to treat you differently?" The discussion prompted by a client's response to this question might touch on the core reasons for the crisis. Another useful approach is to ask clients how they taught their children to handle the issue of respect for a parent, since this issue is key to how parents view their children and, ultimately, how successful they have been with their children.

The Importance of Cultural Metaphors (*Dichos*) in Latino/a Life

In Latino/a culture, proverbs or *dichos* assume considerable importance and are often used to cope with difficult problems. Zuniga (1992) says that *dichos* are actually metaphors that traditionally have been used in treatment and classifies therapeutic metaphors as

> 1) major stories that address complex clinical problems; 2) anecdotes or short stories focused on specific or limited goals; 3) analogies, similes or brief figurative statements or phrases that underscore specific points; 4 relationships metaphors, which can use one relationship as a metaphor for another; 5) tasks with metaphorical meanings that can be undertaken by clients between sessions; 6) artistic metaphors which can be paintings, drawings clay models or creations which symbolize something else. (p. 57)

Glicken and Garza (1996, 2004) have identified several commonly used *dichos* which serve to facilitate resilience. *Sentir en el alma,* for example, translates literally as "to feel it in your soul," but it is used to mean to be terribly sorry. *Con la cuhara se le queman los frijoles* translates literally as "even the best cook burns the beans," but its popular meaning is that everyone makes mistakes. *Entre azul y buenos noches* translates directly as "between blue and good night," but in use it means to be undecided. *A la buena de dios* may translate literally as "as God would have it," but its common meaning is as luck would have it. *No hay mal que por bien no venga* translates as "there is nothing bad from which good does not come," or it's a blessing in disguise. Another *dicho* used to facilitate resilience, *la verdad no mata, pero incomoda*, means "the truth doesn't kill, but it can hurt." And yet another *dicho* with relevance for resilience is *al que no ha usado huaraches, las correas le sacan sangre*, which loosely translated means, "he who has never worn sandals is easily cut by the straps," or it's difficult to do things that one is not used to. And finally, as Zuniga (1992) notes, for the client in a deteriorating relationship which might end in termination, the *dicho* of *mejor sola que mal acompanada* might be used. Roughly translated, this *dicho* means "it's better to be alone or unmarried than to be in a bad relationship."

A Focus on Feelings

Feelings are highly valued in Latino/a culture. One way Latino/as assure each other that they are being empathic with one another is to say that they will communicate together, *de corazon a corazon,* or heart to heart. In Mexico, this concept of a close personal relationship in which true feelings can be communicated has various levels of understanding. It is sometimes associated with the process called *el desague de las penas,* or unburdening oneself. It is what North American therapists call venting, and good friends or close relatives might encourage loved ones in crisis to share their feelings, heart to heart.

Velasquez and colleagues (2004) note that Latino/as may use Spanish idioms to indicate emotional states. These may include terms such as *embrujado,* which suggests that someone has cast a spell on the person; *encabronado,* which suggests extreme anger at someone, with potential to harm that individual; *flojo,* which suggests apathy, lethargy, and fatigue; *loco de remate,* which indicates that a person is becoming mentally ill; and *latoso,* which suggests that a person is developing a physical or emotional problem that may require care by family members and has become a "pain in the neck" as a result.

Cultural Issues That Affect Latino/a Resilience

Considerable credence is given to the significance of dreams in Latino/a culture. Dreams are considered omens, or predictors of the future. Dreams provide answers to problems. While many Latino/as ascribe specific meanings to dreams or make interpretations of them, others may ask a person's own interpretation of a dream or wonder what the dream would be like if the person finished it. Resilient people often interpret dreams in a highly positive way and see their future in ways that may be far more optimistic than is warranted given the reality of their lives. This is sometimes called "wearing a mask" or being Pollyannaish, but it often serves to make people facing serious social problems endure.

As an example, I supervised a master's thesis in which two of my MSW students went to Chiapas, Mexico, to determine whether the civil unrest in the area had created high levels of depression among the women living near the battle zones. My students found a very high level of resilience, measured both by a depression inventory (the CES-D) and in interviews. The women felt a need to be strong, to keep their families together, to console one another, and to keep their cultural traditions alive. The level of depression in these women was lower than that found in the general population of Mexican women. While the situation was often dire and loved ones were being killed, the women used humor, fun, and religion to keep themselves going. Their religious beliefs were highly individualized to suit their personal circumstances, and while they denied using folk healers when they felt depressed, the folk healers my students spoke to said business was booming since the onset of civil unrest. The folk healers used a number of techniques of treatment, which included letting people vent and providing encouragement and support, positive *dichos* (which they often wrote down for their clients), and herbs and folk remedies that were felt to be effective with depression. My students described their work as rough psychotherapy, with considerable attention paid to culturally impactful language and a focus on client strengths.

Altarriba and Bauer (1998) report that resilient Latino/as prefer to think in the present, with the past and the future of minor importance in problem solving and decision making. Resilient Latino/as prefer to be openly expressive in their behavior, but they may defer to the authority of family members and professionals on some occasions. In a report on mental health and culture, the Surgeon General (Satcher, 2001b) notes the following strengths that provide resilience to Latino/as in crisis:

a) strong family involvement and loyalty; b) a deferential approach to family members that emphasizes respect and harmony in family interactions; c) beliefs that suggest acculturation into mainstream American life; d) a desire to maintain cultural traditions; e) the ability to function well in both mainstream American culture and Latino cultures; f) strong identification with ethnic and cultural traditions, values, and beliefs within Latino cultures; g) traditional gender roles that fit comfortably into harmonious family life yet strong roles for women in the family and the community; h) accepting change and modern life when it becomes apparent that such change will improve one's life; i) a style of relating that is highly personal yet one that emphasizes an empathic and caring approach to people; j) a high degree of spirituality that demonstrates an appreciation and acceptance of the need to be at one with others and with notions of the deity; k) an inner strength that responds with strength, hard work, and resilience when confronted with racial barriers and class prejudices; l) a willingness to use political and community strategies to change life when barriers arise. (p. 2).

A STORY OF HOW A RESILIENT LATINA COPES WITH LIFE

I grew up in a mining town not far from the U.S. border. My father was a mining engineer, and because of his status with an American company, I had the opportunity to go to an English speaking school with the children of American workers. I was an enthusiastic student and did well in school. On my 18th birthday I was raped by one of my teachers and became pregnant by him. No one believed that he had done such a thing until he did the same thing to several other girls. By then it was too late, and I immigrated to the U.S. and had my baby here. I felt shamed and demoralized. The rape left me feeling very troubled about relationships and sex.

I met a man who said that he would love me even though the child wasn't his. We married, but our marriage was an unhappy one. I had ambition and wanted to go to college while he wanted me to stay home and have babies. He was very jealous and often accused me of being unfaithful. Later on, he would beat me when he was drinking. I thought American Hispanic men were different, but it was the same thing as in Mexico with the jealousy and the need to dominate.

We had two children together before the marriage completely dissolved. It was very difficult, but I went back and got my college degree and then my graduate degree in education. I've had many supportive people in my life and some special people who helped when I was down. I have an optimism that many people find Pollyannaish, but it works fine for me. When I'm down, and there have been many reasons to feel down, I've sought therapy. Most therapists know nothing about Hispanics and it's been frustrating to find a good one. I have a wonderful physician and he's been very helpful when I'm depressed or anxious. My sister lives nearby. She's younger and much more socialized into American life. She's been a big help. She's very tough but tender. Her life, like mine, has not been a bed of roses. We see our parents a lot. . . . [They] are still in Mexico. They have it bad, and my brothers and sisters and I all help out. My children have no feeling for Mexico and are so thoroughly Americanized they have lost all contact with their culture. Nothing I do makes them interested, and it's because they think we Mexicans are somehow inferior and they don't want to think of themselves that way. But I keep trying and hope they'll see the beautiful things I grew up with in Mexico: the passion, the ability to laugh and have fun when times are tough, the sharing with others when you have something to share, the concern about helping. Someone called it a cooperative lifestyle, and I guess that's what I remember most: how willing people were to help out.

My children have had it rough. They all have good values but have not been ambitious or valued education as I did. Maybe their father's influence has been negative in those areas. They work hard, but their choice of women is often very bad, perhaps as bad as my choice in men. Men find me attractive and I'm always being hit on for dates. It's usually about sex so I don't take it personally, but once in a while an honest man comes along and it's very good. I'm very insecure and sometimes I drive men away with my need for assurances. I suppose I'm also very jealous. I try and keep disturbing thoughts about the people I date out of my head, but that isn't always possible.

I feel deeply about the people I work with and am not a very good bureaucrat and often have problems at work. That's OK. After what I've been through, being helpful to people is more important than sucking up to bosses. My father had to do that in Mexico, ingratiating himself to people who thought Mexicans were the lowest of the low, and all it got him was poverty, ill health, and no recognition for his hard work.

You asked me to tell you why I'm resilient. I don't know if I am all the time. I get depressed and anxious a lot and I have to see doctors for help, but it never stops me from going to work or taking care of my children. If I am resilient, I think it's because I'm very angry at what happened to me when I got raped and the way people treated me. I just don't want the bastards to win. If I give up, if I stop fighting, then I lose and they win. And I also think God has wonderful things for me to do and that He's been looking out for me when times are the toughest. I wouldn't want to let Him down since He never let me down when I asked for His help. In my religion, we believe in a personal God. God is alive inside of me and I can talk to Him whenever I need to. And my family has it tough, but with education and my work has come power. I believe the power I have to help them will make a statement to other Mexican women like me who go through rough times. It will say, "You can make it: You're strong, and tough, and beautiful, and don't give up, because if you give up, we all suffer."

LESSONS TO BE LEARNED FROM THIS STORY

This remarkable Latina was a former student of mine. Her desire to achieve and her perseverance in the face of numerous health and family problems always struck me as remarkable examples of resilience. She is one of the people I always think of when the issue of resilience arises. The following are the major lessons about resilience from her story:

1. The storyteller does not dwell on the rape or her subsequent abusive marriage, traumatic as both were, but brings up her children with strong values and has personal ambition.

2. She uses education to achieve financially and educationally in life and to empower herself and her family.

3. Empowerment and achievement in her career have brought her independence and the ability to help her parents in Mexico.

4. She sees her unwillingness to give up as a positive example for other Latinas.

5. She has remained close to her extended family and they, in return, have been supportive and positive.

6. She is strongly in tune with God and feels His presence inside of her.

7. Even though her life has had many moments of difficulty, she isn't bitter.

8. She fights for her clients even though she says it sometimes gets her into trouble at work. She is proud of not being a good bureaucrat and puts helping her clients before her own survival in organizations.

9. She values her cultural heritage and hopes that her children will one day recognize the wonderful things about Mexico that made her early life so happy. In many ways, these early life experiences in Mexico have been her anchor and serve to help her cope with the traumas she's experienced in adult life.

Resilience in African Americans

Discrimination continues to be a key factor in the lives of Black Americans. As the Surgeon General (Satcher, 2001b) notes in describing challenges faced by African Americans,

> The overwhelming majority of today's African American population traces its ancestry to the slave trade from Africa. The legacy of slavery, racism, and discrimination continues to influence the social and economic standing of this group. Almost one-quarter of African Americans are poor, and their per capita income is much lower than that of whites. They bear a disproportionate burden of health problems and higher mortality rates from disease. Nevertheless, African Americans are a diverse group, experiencing a range of challenges as well as successes in measures of education, income, and other indices of social well-being. Their steady improvement in social standing is significant and serves as testimony to the resilience and adaptive traditions of the African American community. (p. 23)

When African American clients seek help for stress-related problems or traumas, the help may be less than adequate.

In a report on race and mental health, the U.S. Surgeon General (Satcher, 2001b) notes that the cultures of clinicians and the way services are provided influence diagnosis and treatment. Service providers, according to the report, need to be able to build upon the cultural strengths of the people they serve. The Surgeon General's report notes that "while not the sole determinants, cultural and social influences do play important roles in mental health, mental illness, and service use, when added to biological, psychological, and environmental factors" (p. 1). In trying to understand barriers to treatment that affect ethnic and racial minorities, the Surgeon General says that the mental health system often creates impediments that lead to distrust and fear of treatment and deter racial and ethnic minorities from seeking and receiving needed services. The Surgeon General adds that "mental health care disparities may also stem from minorities' historical and present day struggles with racism and discrimination, which affect their mental health and contribute to their lower economic, social, and political status" (Satcher, 2001b, p. 1).

In an earlier report on mental health, the Surgeon General wrote,

Mental illness is at least as prevalent among racial and ethnic minorities as in the majority white population. Yet many racial and ethnic minority group members find the organized mental health system to be uninformed about cultural context and, thus, unresponsive and/or irrelevant. With appropriate training and a fundamental respect for clients, any mental health professional can provide culturally competent services that reflect sensitivity to individual differences and, at the same time, assign validity to an individual's group identity. Still, many members of ethnic and racial minority groups may prefer to be treated by mental health professionals of similar background. (Satcher, 1999, Chapter 8, p. 4)

Whaley (2001) is concerned that Caucasian clinicians often see African Americans as having paranoid symptoms that are more fundamentally a cultural distrust of Caucasians because of historical experiences with racism. He believes that the diagnostic process with African Americans tends to discount the negative impact of racism and leads to diagnostic judgments about clients that suggest they are more dysfunctional than they really are. This tendency to misdiagnose, or to diagnose a more serious condition than may be warranted, is what Whaley calls "pseudo-transference." Whaley (2001) believes that cultural stereotyping by clinicians who fail to understand the impact of racism leads to "more severe diagnoses and restrictive interventions" (p. 558) with African Americans. Whaley's work suggests that clinicians may incorrectly use diagnostic labels with clients they feel uncomfortable with, or whose cultural differences create some degree of hostility, which casts doubt on the accuracy of diagnostic labels with an entire range of clients. This concern suggests the subjective nature of the diagnostic process in general, and the *DSM-IV* in particular.

Laszloffy and Hardy (2000) believe that as long as racism occupies such a significant role in everyday life, it cannot be completely eliminated from therapy unless therapists carefully examine what they say to clients, what they do with clients, and what they really believe. In validating the need for cultural and racial sensitivity, Pena, Bland, Shervington, Rice, and Foulks (2000) write, "In work with African-American patients, the therapist's skill in recognizing when problems do or do not revolve around the condition of being black could have serious implications for the acceptability of treatment, the development of the treatment alliance, and in psychotherapy, the accuracy of interpretations" (p. 14). The authors report that each of these variables has a significant impact on treatment effectiveness and outcome and that therapists with limited awareness of the significance of race in their interactions with clients may experience problems in "listening empathically" and actually understanding clients' conflicts that are directly related to race.

Franklin (1992) believes that all therapy must recognize the invisible factor of racism, which provides messages, starting in childhood, that Black males "lack value and worth and [denies the] African American full access to life's amenities and opportunities" (p. 353). Franklin (1992) also believes that the African American male's sense of invisibility damages his self-esteem because of constant messages that that he is unacceptable.

Constant assaults on his self-esteem lead, in turn, to feelings of anger and internalized rage. To cope with these indignities, African American men devise various strategies and behaviors [including] immobilization, chronic indignation, acquiescence, depression, suicide or homicide, and/or internalized rage. (p. 353)

Poussaint (1993) notes that "since the 1970s, Black people have been made aware of the serious strains in Black male-female relationships by Black female writers who examined issues of racism and sexism from their own racial and gender perspective" (p. 86). The author reports that perceptions by Black women of abusive, disrespectful, and demeaning treatment by Black men are countered by Black men who complain that Black women have condescending and superior attitudes toward them and that they feel devalued. Black men and Black women face difficulties in relating to one another because gender issues are compounded by racism and "the subordinate roles of Blacks in American society. Sadly, Black men and women themselves harbor racial stereotypes about each other" (p. 89). Poussant (1993) believes that if these tensions aren't dealt with,

this estrangement threatens our very survival. Not only is the Black family damaged but the unity of the Black community is at stake. Every Black woman and man has a responsibility to do their share in bringing an end to this internecine warfare. The future of our people, and our children's welfare today, is endangered by our stubbornly refusing to compromise. We need to begin to show more love and respect for one another. We are in a state of crisis and the time to act is now! (p. 89)

To resolve these tensions, Poussant (1993) suggests the following guidelines for Black men and women: (1) acknowledging sexist behaviors, including lack of respect for women and the need for psychological and physical dominance, as well as acknowledging the reverse sexism of viewing Black men as losers; (2) exploring the reasons for competitive feelings toward one another and making certain to avoid of one-upmanship; (3) analyzing attitudes toward interracial romance and, painful though the subject might be, understanding that everyone has a right to select his or her own mate; (4) being more empathic toward shared concerns about racial discrimination affecting both Black men and Black women; (5) listening to one another and hearing mutual concerns about life; (6) emphasizing the positive qualities of Blacks and identifying Black couples who model positive behaviors that Black men and women may emulate; (7) controlling anger, put-downs, and verbal and psychological abuse; (8) treating one another with respect and dignity; (9) avoiding the use of sex and money to manipulate or control partners (pp. 88–89).

Lawson and Sharpe (2000) propose similar guidelines for helping African American men and women following a divorce. The authors propose a way of helping that (1) promotes culturally competent patient-provider relationships in which clinicians are aware of the social marginality, discrimination, and economic inequities that divorced African American men face; (2) develops compassion and awareness for the emotions that African American men may not openly show but which are deeply felt, such as grief over the loss of a relationship (this also suggests screening for symptoms of depression and anger); (3) respects the ambivalence African American men feel for the helping process and remembers the many past and present examples of how badly these men have been treated by the medical and psychiatric communities; (4) encourages alternative approaches to practice that utilize spirituality, family, support networks, and client strengths; (5) promotes community education and encourage public concern for the vitality of the African American family and for African American men; (6) provides services in alternative locations, including churches, employment benefit programs, sports arenas, and community health centers; (7) utilizes self-help groups for the purpose of mutual support and acceptance by other African American men experiencing divorce; (8) influences social policy changes by training more culturally competent practitioners who are sensitive to the needs and concerns of African American men; (9) works to encourage legislation that permits flexible property division, child custody, and economic support policies.

How Resilient African Americans Cope With Life

According to Manheimer (1994), religious participation is a good predictor of happiness among older African Americans, with social activities related to church attendance contributing most to their life satisfaction and personal adjustment. Haight (1998) agrees and indicates that in her own study of the spirituality of African American children,

> available empirical evidence suggests a relationship between socialization experiences emanating from the African American church and a number of positive developmental outcomes. For example, Brown and Gary (1991) found that self-reports of church involvement were positively related to educational attainment among African American adults. In an interview study of African American urban male adolescents, Zimmerman and Maton (1992) found that youths who left high school before graduation and were not employed, but who attended church, had relatively low levels of alcohol and drug abuse. In a questionnaire administered to African American adults (Seaborn-Thompson & Ensminger, 1989), 74 percent responded "very often" or "often" to the statement, "The religious beliefs I learned when I was young still help me." On the basis of data from the 1979–80 National Survey of Black Americans, Ellison (1993) argued that participation in church communities is positively related to self-esteem in African American adults. (p. 215)

Winfield (1991) describes a longitudinal study of valedictorians and salutatorians who graduated from public and private high schools in Illinois. She believes the study provides insight into the factors that increase the success of students of color in the transition from high school to college. The stories included in the study indicate that these students needed to overcome extreme external obstacles to attain high standards of achievement, and that they did it through persistence, determination, and hard work. They relied on peers, indirect role models, and the rewards of interpersonal engagements and community service to reinforce their already strong motivation.

In describing resilience in the African American community, the Surgeon General's report on mental health indicates,

> Adaptive traditions have sustained African Americans through long periods of hardship imposed by the larger society. Their resilience is an important resource from which much can be learned. African American communities must be engaged, their traditions supported and built upon, and their trust gained in attempts to reduce mental illness and increase mental health. Mutual benefit will accrue to African Americans and to the society at large from a concerted effort to address the mental health needs of African Americans. (Satcher, 1999, Chapter 8, p. 5)

Majors and Billson (1992) provide the following nine dimensions of African American resilience through cultural expressiveness:

1. Spirituality: an approach to life as being essentially vitalistic rather than mechanistic, with the conviction that nonmaterial forces influence people's everyday lives;

2. Harmony: the notion that one's fate is interrelated with other elements in the scheme of things so that humankind and nature are harmonically conjoined;

3. Movement: an emphasis on the interweaving of movement, rhythm, percussiveness, music, and dance, all of which are taken as central to psychological health;

4. Verve: a propensity for relatively high levels of stimulation and for action that is energetic and lively;

5. Affect: an emphasis on emotions and feelings, together with a special sensitivity to emotional cues and a tendency to be emotionally expressive;

6. Communalism: a commitment to social connectedness, which includes an awareness that social bonds and responsibilities transcend individual privilege;

7. Expressive Individualism: the cultivation of a distinctive personality and proclivity for spontaneous, genuine personal expression;

8. Oral Tradition: a preference for oral/aural modes of communication, in which both speaking and listening are treated as performances, and cultivation of oral virtuosity - the ability to use alliterative, metaphorically colorful, graphic forms of spoken language;

9. Social Time Perspective: an orientation in which time is treated as passing through a social space rather than a material one, and in which time can be recurring, personal, and phenomenological. (p. 55)

Gordon (2000) reports that resilient African American adolescents have strong motivation, have environmental support, place an emphasis on extracurricular activities, and have high achievement goals. In addition, these students have robust cognitive motivational patterns and are firm in purpose and outlook. Reis, Hebert, Eva, Maxfield, and Ratley (1995) studied cases of African American students who achieved in urban schools. The authors found that achieving students have a network of high-achieving friends. They also found that successful students support the concept of grouping in honors and advanced classes, have supportive adults in their lives, and participate in multiple extracurricular activities. High-achieving females usually choose not to date, have a strong belief in self, and have resilience to negative factors as well as a strong identity with racial and cultural factors. The authors found that high-achieving students have periods of low achievement and found no relationship between high achievement and poverty, divorce, or other family dynamics. Finally, Reis and colleagues found evidence of a desire to finish high school and enter college in over 1,100 African American youth who were involved in athletics, and they suggest that for this population of youth, success at athletics is one way to show resilience and success.

Burt and Halpin (1998) suggest that while African Americans have shared a challenging history, they have also demonstrated a remarkable collective resilience. Resilience themes that emerge from Burt and Halpin's work include the following: (1) Contemporary African American college students are strongly influenced by their families and community; (2) African Americans' positive relationships with other cultural and ethnic minorities as well as with White Americans significantly affect the degree of their resilience as individuals; (3) Strong racial and ethnic identity has a positive impact on resilience; (4) Students who understand Black history have better African American identity development; (5) The types of resilient behaviors that lead to school success for African American adolescents are those that build social identity, friendships, and social support networks.

Wyatt (2004) writes that "for Black youth, establishing a strong spiritual core can support the development of a healthy identity to effectively cope with the oppressive challenges in their lives" (p. 1). She notes that students with high levels of spirituality have (1) a positive outlook about themselves; (2) active coping patterns; (3) an affirmative relationship with God; (4) a sense of belonging to a community; (5) confidence in their ability to solve their own problems; (6) honesty in their relationships; (7) the ability to work hard to accomplish a task; (8) leadership qualities; (9) the ability to work cooperatively; (10) the willingness to share their material possessions with others; (11) the ability to give and receive affection and care; (12) the perception that others were willing to help them; (13) the perception that others were willing to protect them; (14) enjoyment in the company of others; and (15) respect from others.

Williams (1992) believes that we often fail to see resilience in Black men and suggests that in order to see their real strength, we need to (1) acknowledge the positive behaviors and achievements of Black men; (2) not use labels in describing their behavior, as such labels are often the racial labels that historically have been applied to Black men; (3) stop bashing Black men and applying sexual stereotypes to them that many Black men feel are racist; (4) value rather than criticize the Black experience; and (5) support the Black family and community by recognizing that they live in a broader context where they are valued and contributing members.

A STORY ABOUT ABANDONMENT BY A FATHER

My dad left us when I was about ten. I don't remember much about him, but my mother said he was a real son of a bitch and that he used to beat up on her and on us a lot because he was into the booze. Funny, but I don't remember any of that. Neither does my sister. For 20 years I had this anger in me over what he did. I'd listen to my mom, watch her as she got old and alone, think that he was responsible for how poor we were, and just hate the hell out of him for what he did. I mean, how do you just up and leave a family?

So anyway, I got married and about 5 years into the marriage, damned if I didn't do the same thing. I'm not proud of myself, mind you, but it happened. My wife was just dumping on me all of the time. Nothing I did was good enough. From morning to night, all I ever heard was how bad I was. I had my fill of it and, one day, I just took off.

Well, it got me to thinking about my dad and I started looking for him. I found him through the V.A. It wasn't easy, but finally, I got his address and phone number. He was living up in Bakersfield, which is a pretty easy drive from where I was living. I figured I'd drive up and back in the same day, see him, tell him off, and leave. I ended up staying three days. He was happy to see me and made me promise to go back to my wife. He said he'd tried going back to my mom a number of times, but she wouldn't let him and that he'd written us or called me and my sister, but she stopped the letters and the calls. He told me he always felt guilty about leaving, but he was just a young man and not very good at talking things through. And he mentioned the stuff my mom was doing to him like her nagging and her putting him down until he didn't feel like a man anymore. It sounded pretty familiar. He told me he never drank or abused anyone.

I went back home and confronted my mom. She admitted to me that he was telling the truth, but that her feelings were hurt so she made up the story about him never contacting us. She said he paid child support for a long time. I asked how she could do such a thing, said it had a bad effect on me for a long time. She shrugged her shoulders. "Men are all shits," she said. "What difference did it make?"

"Well, it made a difference to me," I said, "and I'm gonna get to know him," which is what I did. He's no perfect man, that's for sure. But he's a good man and he's someone I feel proud to call my father. We do a lot together now. We like the same things, how about that? I see him every week or two. He's almost ready to retire and he may move down here to be closer, or my wife and I may move up there. It depends on where the work is. My dad just set up a trust fund for my daughter so she could go to college. He wants me to go, too. He thinks I'm smart enough and said he was gonna take some courses. "Never too old to learn," he said.

It goes to show you how wrong you can be when you listen to someone else tell you about your dad. I should've found out for myself a lot sooner. It would have saved me from being so mad all these years. I bet there are a lot of men out there who have the same problem.

ANOTHER STORY ABOUT ABANDONMENT

My brother and I were running wild after my old men left us. Why we didn't end up in jail is beyond me. My mother became an alcoholic after he left. Went through men like they were going out of style. Married six times before I left high school. I hated the son of a bitch for what he did to us.

One day I was back from the service visiting my mom. We couldn't find the guy she was living with at the time. We went looking for him and finally found him in the barn where he'd hung himself. There he was, twisting in the wind, dead as hell. My mom just looks at him and says to us, "Another son of a bitch bites the dust." That's what she said to me and my brother. We both looked at her. I think we were thinking the same thing at the same time.

My brother went looking for my dad and found him in some nursing home over in Napa where he'd gone to live after he left my mom. He said my mom was the most difficult woman he'd ever known, that she was drinking before he left, and that she was going through men right and left. We couldn't believe him because we thought that he was making it up to make himself look good, but he told us to make a few phone calls to people who knew them when they were still together, and gave us some names, and we called. It was an eye opener. He was telling the truth.

You don't go from hating the guy who left you to loving him, but I feel better about myself now. I thought he left us because he hated me and my brother. It didn't occur to me that it was all about my mom. To me, she was a saint for having kept us together after he left. I could never see her doing anything wrong to anyone. It sounds strange, given the drinking and all the men, but that's the way I felt. I still do, for that matter. I see my dad once in a while. We don't have much to say to each other. I see him out of respect and to remind myself that you need to have a relationship with your dad, even if it isn't a good one.

I read about the fighter George Foreman who said that not knowing about his father put him in a terrible rage. He didn't find out about his father until he was 26 and his father had long ago passed away. I remember reading that he had this awful anger in him, and he said there is rage in the boy who doesn't know anything about his dad. He doesn't know where he comes from and his dad doesn't know anything about him. It's got to have a bad effect. He said that he wanted to hurt people because of the teasing he got because he didn't know who his father was. . . . I know that a lot of Black kids feel the same way about themselves. A big part of life is missing and we don't know what to do to make up for it.

I used to listen to the guys at work talking about their dads. They'd say some pretty hateful things about them—you know, their drinking and meanness—but pretty soon, they'd be telling you these great stories, and a lot of us, some of the Black guys, too, we'd just smile and nod but inside, we'd be dying because the guys who helped make us left, and we never knew anything about them or, I guess, about why they left and whether it was . . . because of us. I know that a lot of Black men are angry at themselves because if the person who's supposed to love you leaves, it must mean he doesn't love you, and then, can you really love yourself? I wonder.

Lessons to Be Learned From These Stories

These stories suggest many elements of resilience in two men who might have chosen more troubled paths, but didn't. The following elements of resilience appear in both stories:

1. The importance of finding out the truth about one's family history is apparent in both stories. Finding the truth and reestablishing relationships with long-absent fathers helped both men become more self-accepting.

2. Even though both men came from troubled families with angry mothers, women who felt abused by their husbands' abandoning them and their children, the men in these stories thought their mothers were wonderful beyond measure and used that sense of having a positive parent to help them cope with life.

3. When the men found their fathers, rather than dwelling on their anger, they focused on feelings of loyalty and optimism. Through the developing relationships with their fathers they began to see themselves in more positive ways.

4. Both men learned about themselves by pursuing their fathers. Rather than giving up and continuing to define their fathers in very negative ways, they sought their fathers out and came to their own conclusions about what sort of men they were and the circumstances that led to their fathers' leaving. Having closure on the relationships with their fathers helped these men to move on in their own lives.

5. Both men are thoughtful and introspective. Even though each one has his own relationship problems, they both used the absence of their fathers in their childhoods to help reunite them with their spouses.

6. In the first story, the father encourages his son to go to college. The father says that he himself plans to take courses, that it's never too late. And it's never too late to grow as a person or to right troubled directions in life.

Resilience in Ethnically Traditional Asian Americans[2]

This section concerns Asian Americans who are part of ethnically traditional Asian cultures. These individuals often face challenges to their resilience because of the strong pull they feel between their desires to assimilate and to continue to be loyal to their families and cultures. They may also experience discrimination, particularly if they are new immigrants to America, and they may experience the high expectations of parents for success in school and work as a form of family protection should the family experience difficulty. As we will see, traditional Asian cultures often stress family identity over personal identity, which, in some cases, creates challenges to resilience in otherwise well-functioning people. Immigrants from Southeast Asia are particularly at risk and experience

> PTSD [posttraumatic stress disorder] decades after fleeing their country of origin. Specifically, trauma experiences may include any of the following events: threats of mass genocide; torture; witnessing torture; being forced to commit atrocities; death; loss of family members; persecution; rape and sexual violence; starvation; dangerous escapes from their home countries; and extreme hardship in refugee camps.
>
> In the U.S., refugee women may also encounter psychological challenges in the resettlement process. Not only have they undergone forced migration and loss of family, community, and social support networks, but once in the U.S., they may be faced with living in a foreign culture and environment with little or no resources or emotional support. To compound the difficulty of the situation, as a result of unemployment or underemployment of refugee men, women may be forced to work to help support the family. Ironically, whereas men may experience downward mobility, women may experience upward mobility because of increased occupational opportunities in the U.S. as compared with their country of origin. However, changes in gender roles due to resettlement frequently create conflicts between refugees' cultural values and those of the resettlement country. This in turn changes the family dynamics and places severe pressure on traditional marriage and family relationships. (Chung & Bemak, 2002, p. 111)

In describing challenges faced by Asian Americans, the Surgeon General writes,

> Asian Americans and Pacific Islanders (AA/PIs) are highly diverse, consisting of at least 43 separate ethnic groups. The AA/PI population in the United States is increasing rapidly; in 2001, about 60 percent were born overseas. Most Pacific Islanders are not immigrants; their ancestors were original inhabitants of land taken over by the United States a century ago. While the per capita income of AA/PIs is almost as high as that for whites, there is great variability both between and within subgroups. For example, there are many successful Southeast Asian and Pacific Islander Americans; however, overall poverty rates for these two groups are much higher than the national average. AA/PIs collectively exhibit a wide range of strengths—family cohesion, educational achievements, and motivation for upward mobility—and risk factors for mental illness such as pre-immigration trauma from harsh social conditions. (Satcher, 2001b, p. 35)

The Collective Self

Hsu (1983) describes the core American national character as "rugged" individualism, which he defines as the intrinsic and unquestionable values of self-containment, autonomy, self-reliance, and self-determinism—characteristics implying that the person who possesses them takes responsibility for self before taking responsibility for others. The Asian worldview values social collectivism: a social order that is essentially family based and interpersonally or collectively oriented. This worldview is primarily explained by the versions of Confucianism, Buddhism, and Taoism that have been incorporated into the various Asian cultures. Ino (1985a, 1985b, 1987, 1991) and Ino and Glicken (1999, 2002) call this worldview the "collective self."

Confucian philosophy and ethics are concerned with the virtue of the individual as exemplified by his or her participation in appropriate social relationships that lead to social harmony at all levels of society. The Chinese concept of *jen,* or human-heartedness, expressed through social conduct that is strictly prescribed, characterizes the five essential relationships between (1) sovereign and subject (superior and subordinate), (2) parent and child, (3) older and younger brothers, (4) husband and wife, (5) and friends. *Li,* or social propriety, is to be shown in all interpersonal relationships to facilitate and sustain social harmony (Herbert, 1950). Filial piety is central to Confucian thought and practice.

In Asian thought, pragmatism is valued over idealism and the focus of life activity is the present time. Furthermore, unlike the Western notion of being the master of one's own fate, the Asian belief is that one is not in ultimate control. The person is always an integral part of the larger encompassing universe that has authority over the individual.

Taoism differs from Confucian pragmatism in its concern with the metaphysical and mystical: the cosmic process of Tao, or the Way. The person, an integral part of the cosmos, follows the principle of *Wu-Wei,* or nonaction, which means that he or she should always act in accordance with nature and not against it. The notion that nature heals and the human (medicine) assists suggests the belief that nature and not the person has ultimate authority over the course of a person's existence (Chang, 1982). In Taoism, therefore, the person is not in complete control of nature, nor of his or her destiny.

Buddhism concerns itself with the Four Noble Truths: (1) the truth (or fact) of suffering; (2) the origin of suffering; (3) the end of suffering; and (4) the path [leading] to the end of suffering. Enlightenment is achieved by following the Noble Eightfold Path, which includes accurate knowledge and correct actions that lead to the effective or "right" development of the mind. Concentration and meditation are mental processes that help lead to the development of the "right" mind. Buddhism stresses seeking enlightenment through the avoidance of desires suggesting ignorance and teaches the idea of eternal life through rebirth. Proper deportment and social conduct, ancestor worship, emotional restraint, loyalty, and respect for others in the present life have implications for the quality of one's next life (Chang, 1982; Gaw, 1993).

In Asian cultures, dynamic social harmony is the major social rule governing all meaningful interpersonal relationships (Ho, 1987). It requires varying degrees of social cooperation, adaptation, accommodation, and collaboration by all individuals in the social hierarchy. In the Asian social hierarchy, social roles are based more on family membership and position, gender, age, social class, and social position than on qualification and ability. However, there is a basic belief that age, training,

and life experience are associated with wisdom and competency, although deference and respect from an individual in a subordinate role requires that the person
in a superior social position care for that individual.

The Importance of Family and Social Harmony

The formal idea of family in Asian society extends family identity and membership
backward in time through all of the ancestors in the male family line, continuing
on to the present time, and then on to those future descendants who have yet to
appear (Lee, 1996). One's sense of family is not time bound or limited to only those
important kin who are living. While the father is the head of the nuclear family
household and is responsible for the family's economic and physical well-being, he
still shows deference and loyalty to his father and older brothers, as well as to his
mother and older sisters. Elders in the father's extended family are also respected.
The mother is included in the extended family of her husband. As a mother, she is
the "emotional hub" of her nuclear family of creation, responsible for nurturing her
husband and their children. While wielding tremendous emotional power and
often acting as the relational and communication link between father and children,
she, nevertheless, has little public power and authority and defers to her husband,
his mother, and the elders in her husband's extended family.

In Asian society, self-restraint and stoicism, inhibiting disruptive emotional
expression, conscientious work to fulfill one's responsibilities, heightened social
sensitivity, and other-directedness all contribute to maintaining social harmony.
However, a person's breech of social obligation or duty can potentially damage the
social harmony of the family, group, or larger community. The person's significant
others will express the loss of confidence in his or her ability to fulfill obligations to
the family or group through the mechanism of shaming that person.

From an Asian perspective, the prescribed forms of interpersonal interaction are
intended to preserve dynamic social harmony by minimizing direct conflict and
social discordance. Communication, as an aspect of social interaction, is highly
contextual and tends to flow downward from superior to subordinate, often in the
form of directives. Both verbal and written communications are indirect, in the
passive tense, and at times may appear convoluted. Furthermore, much of the communication is nonverbal, where the conduct of the superior and not the content of
the message is most meaningful. These principles of Asian communication styles
serve to maintain vital social harmony in any interpersonal interaction.

The Asian socialization process develops highly differentiated adult individuals
with mature levels of deep emotional interdependency and strong feelings of role
responsibility and obligation. But within the context of Asian social reality, physical distress may appropriately exemplify psychosocial distress (Root, 1993). For
instance, a therapist can view an Asian American client's gastrointestinal disorder
as a normal expression of psychological stress over an intense interpersonal conflict
and not necessarily as a "symptom" or indicator of the client's inability to cope with
psychosocial conflict. To alleviate the physical symptom may be an appropriate
treatment for a relational conflict over which the client has no control.

When Asian Americans' Resilience Fails

Asian Americans, as a group, tend to seek help from mental health professionals only when all other more familiar and usual coping strategies, interpersonal resources, resiliencies, and safer avenues of help have been exhausted. Despite the underutilization of existing services, many Asian American mental health professionals believe that there is a significant unmet need for appropriate mental health care (e.g., Furuto, Biswas, Chung, Murase, & Ross-Sheriff, 1992; Gaw, 1993; Sue & Morishima, 1982; Uba, 1994). In a study of nonpatient Southeast Asian Americans, Gong-Guy (1987) estimated that 14.4% of the sample needed inpatient mental health services and 53.75% could benefit from outpatient care, in comparison to corresponding 3% and 12% rates in the general population.

Several reasons explain the discrepancy between perceived need and overall service usage, including the following: (1) the Asian conception of mental health and mental illness and their management; (2) the strong Asian stigma and shame attached to seeking "out-of-the-family" assistance for emotional problems; (3) the inappropriateness of Euro-American mental health care approaches for Asians; (4) shortages of culturally sensitive mental health professionals; and (5) socioeconomic barriers (Sue & Morishima, 1982; Uba, 1994).

Asian Americans will often seek mental health services only after they are in serious emotional crisis. They will have first exhausted their usual and then their atypical coping strategies and will have sufficiently "overridden" their deeply felt sense of shame and humiliation at breaching family privacy and "loss of face" by seeking help from outside the family. The Asian client who is experiencing the emotional "disequilibrium" of a crisis situation is most responsive to outside assistance (Golan, 1978; Roberts, 1990). However, the same client is also very vulnerable to outside influences, leaving him or her concerned about the possibility of worrisome miscommunication and misinterpretation of the need for mental health services by family, friends, and the Asian community.

When an Asian American client seeks mental health services, the client is already emotionally disengaged or estranged from family and significant others because the usual collective Asian social support system has failed to remedy the problem or conflict. Because of strong feelings of shame, or a collective need to protect the family and/or significant others, the client may be withdrawn and isolated. On the other hand, if the family seeks help for one of its members, then the family has exhausted its own strategies for discreetly helping the family member and must now, regrettably, seek outside assistance and risk considerable shame.

The high level of stigma associated with intractable emotional problems and mental disturbance has its origin in the strong Asian belief in emotional toughness and resilience. In the view of the Asian community, an individual can endure hardship and overcome personal problems through individual perseverance, hard work, stoicism, and the avoidance of morbid and disturbing thoughts and feelings.

Issues That Test Resilience

Asian American clients often exist in at least two, if not more, interacting significant social worlds—the collective-based social world of their Asian identified families, religions, and communities and the individual-based social order of the larger American society. To understand the collective part of the Asian American self, one must first understand the way individual conduct affects the Asian family. And here, family takes on a very broad level of importance, as in many Asian countries family provides the client with a sense of identity that may affect every aspect of life from birth to death. Family is a concept that includes a large, extended group. What an individual does in Asian societies has broad consequences, for it may affect the way the family is viewed by the larger community.

Asian Americans face several life crises that may test resilience, including bicultural identity development, significant non-Asian relationships, significant loss, expulsion from family, and dysfunctional families of origin. In the following section, several common life circumstances are explored. There are also examples of resilient clients in crisis and descriptions of the way these clients were able to resolve seemingly intractable problems with some help.

Bicultural Identity Development: For second- and later-generation Asian Americans, the multicultural socialization process may result in a mix of self-identities that are, at times, conflictual and contradictory. For example, an Asian immigrant may possess a basic sense of collective self and yet have very acculturated and assimilated attitudes and behaviors and even claim conscious "allegiance" to the mainstream American way of life. At best, bicultural Asian American self-development can result in resolvable internal psychic confusion and an affective commitment to some form of multicultural self. At worst, it may develop into critical intrapsychic disorganization and instability of self. The strength and durability of the client's individual self depends on how psychosocially sound his or her other significant family members are and the internal consistency of family interrelationships.

Significant Non-Asian Relationships: Asian Americans who have an essential collective self will naturally seek collective as opposed to individualistic relationship involvement with those who become a part of their significant social world. However, the individual may not always be conscious of these needs and they may be unaware of who can best fulfill them. Consequently, Asian Americans may become socially involved with others in an apparently assimilated and acculturated fashion. Serious interpersonal conflicts can arise when two people with very different self-dynamics and accompanying interpersonal needs attempt to create a deep, fulfilling, and intimate bond.

A Story About James and Lisa, a Bicultural Couple

When they first sought help, James was a 41-year-old Sansei (third-generation Japanese American) who had been married for about 2 years to Lisa, a 35-year-old Anglo American. Lisa was very unhappy with the marriage and frustrated that they had not been able to effectively communicate with each other about her unhappiness. Whenever she tried to initiate a conversation about the marriage, James avoided discussing their problems, saying only that their marriage was good and that they just had to work harder at it. He had consistently rejected her earlier requests that they talk to a counselor. James felt very embarrassed about sharing their marital problems with a stranger. While Lisa's family was aware of their marital problems and tried to be supportive, James did not want to disclose their marital problems to his family. As Lisa became more adamant about separating, James became more desperate to save the marriage and finally agreed to join Lisa for five treatment sessions.

When they came for treatment, Lisa was friendly, self-assured, worried, and verbally expressive. James, on the other hand, looked tired, disheveled, tense, constricted, and depressed, and seemed to be on the verge of tears. Separately, both denied that there was any serious physical risk to either James or Lisa, although Lisa was worried that James might be physically affected by what was occurring. They acknowledged that they still cared very deeply for each other, despite the serious marital stress, and that there was more disappointment than animosity in their feelings about the marriage. The short-term goal of the marital counseling, agreed upon by the couple, was to help James better deal with the stress of their marital problems and to do some preliminary exploration to help identify the reasons for their conflicts.

In the course of the five sessions, James began to feel more emotionally stable. He was receiving considerable support from his older brother and his wife as well as from two close friends. Major sociocultural differences were uncovered which neither James nor Lisa thought were present. While James identified himself as "all American" and highly assimilated into mainstream America, his core self was collective rather than individualistic in origin. His own Nisei parents, who seemed as "American as apple pie" and only spoke English at home, had raised James and his older siblings in a traditional Japanese way. Even though James had mostly non-Asian friends throughout his life, he developed a "thick" layering of individualistic self that he actualized in his social relationships, but which concealed a core collective-self base. With Lisa, as he settled into a secure married life, he began to relax his defenses, allowing the needs of his collective self to emerge and seek fulfillment. James had a very traditional view of marriage and was critical of Lisa for not understanding, even though he had failed to explain the traditions of his culture sufficiently for Lisa to recognize that he expected Lisa to defer to him and place his needs above hers. There were many other unspoken expectations of Lisa that James had not explained but felt Lisa should understand and respect just because she was his wife.

By the end of the five sessions, both Lisa and James realized that they had entered into a much more complex marriage than either had imagined. They agreed that they needed to talk further with a marriage counselor and accepted a referral to another therapist who was culturally sensitive to both Asian and Euro-American ways of being. James left treatment feeling much more in touch

---

This story is a modified version of a case that first appeared in a book I wrote on men (Glicken, 2005c). The couple, James and Lisa, were interviewed several years after the following case was written. Their comments appear at the end of the case.

with the traditions of his culture and felt ready to enter into a dialogue with Lisa to explain and process those traditions. Lisa left treatment recognizing their cultural differences and agreeing to learn much more about the traditions that had shaped James, but uncertain that she could meet all of James's needs. Both were impressed with the process, which they described as positive, and which James noted, "helped me understand not only the problems my cultural heritage created in our marriage, but many of the positives in those traditions which I have a deep appreciation for. It also confirmed my feelings for Lisa and helped me realize the hard work she had done to maintain our marriage. What I thought would be an embarrassing experience turned out to be very touching and I'm grateful to Lisa for not giving up on me" (Glicken, 2005c, pp. 268–270).

An Interview With James and Lisa

Author: Could you tell me how things are going in your marriage 2 years after our initial discussion?

James: I think they're going well, but we still have moments when our cultures collide with one another. The good thing is that we discuss it and usually the problem is dealt with on the spot.

Lisa: I agree, and I think James has come a very long way since we first began experiencing difficulty in our marriage.

Author: How so?

Lisa: He realizes the conflict between his traditional views and mine and prefaces discussions with a description of his views and wonders how we can resolve the opposing points of view. Usually there isn't a problem.

Author: Can you give me an example?

James: Yes. Last week we went to some friends' house for dinner. They are a mixed cultural marriage like us, only the wife is Asian and the husband is Anglo. Anyway, we could see that the cultural differences between them were causing a lot of conflict, so we discussed the process we used to resolve problems with them. They were very taken with the dialogue we used to explain how we were handling things.

Lisa: Another example concerns my in-laws, who have been superficially nice, but still don't accept me. James has come to my defense, in a very gentle way, to remind them of my accomplishments and to let them know that we are very much in love and that it is a lasting love. I can tell his parents are impressed and accept his defense of me in a way that makes them, and me, feel very proud.

Author: How would you rate the quality of your marriage [now], as opposed to when we first chatted several years ago?

James: It's much tighter emotionally. We have fewer disagreements and we are enjoying each other in a way that feels really good.

Lisa: I think there is much about James's culture that is beautiful and easy for me to like. That's helped. James's explaining things to me has made me

> realize the tough position he often feels between his culture and the broader one we mostly live in. I admire how James is able to navigate both cultures so well. But more than that, I think we discovered that we're both resilient, capable people and that with some help and a lot of self-work that we were able to make a promising but troubled marriage really work well. I think we're in much better shape than before and I think, as James says, we really enjoy each other.

Significant Loss: For the Asian American who has an important established relationship with someone, the loss of that person, through either death or the dissolution of the relationship, has profound implications for the integrity of his or her collective self. The process of mourning and grieving the loss of that individual and the subsequent emotional reconstitution entails a major psychosocial reconstruction of the collective self. When there is a major loss through death, all Asian cultures have their distinct rituals and practices to help with the healing process of collective-self reintegration. This reaffirms the integrity of the collective self for all parties and helps them continue on in life. In the extreme case, a crippling loss may so severely threaten the integrity of the person's collective self, and desire to live, that he or she cannot imagine living on without the lost other. When this type of person is unable to experience emotional collective-self support from others, he or she may be at serious risk for suicide.

Family Expulsion: In Asian tradition, the son never truly leaves his family of origin. The family he establishes becomes incorporated into the continuous family line as the next generation. Generally speaking, the daughter leaves her family of origin only when she marries, relocates to her husband's family of origin, and establishes a new collective self incorporating his significant family members. Her bond of loyalty and duty to her own father and mother is "transferred" to her husband and his mother. If the son or daughter is "disinherited" or cast out from the family for some perceived travesty by the family before the right developmental time, this can cause a serious emotional collective-self fragmentation and a deep sense of self-loss.

Dysfunctional Asian American Family: A dysfunctional traditional Asian American family is one in which the significant adult family members are incapable of managing their role responsibilities and obligations and cannot provide a sufficient level of care and appropriate child rearing to promote the development of a healthy collective self. Occasionally, this includes promoting a confusing, contradictory experience of self without any inherent coherence and psychosocial integrity, or imposing family roles and responsibilities on its member that are self-destructive. When this takes place, a family-level therapeutic intervention is called for.

Summary

This chapter discusses resilience in three prominent ethnically diverse groups: African Americans, Latino/as, and Asian Americans. The chapter notes the impact of racism and discrimination and the many complex issues related to ethnically sensitive practice. The stories that are included in the chapter indicate resilience, and discussion of the lessons to be learned from each story are included to provide examples of resilience in the way storytellers coped with traumas in their lives.

Notes

1. Some of the material on Latino/a resilience appearing in this chapter was first presented as a paper by Mina Garza, MSW, and me in 1996 at the California Conference for Latino Social Workers and also appears, in modified form, in Glicken (2004a, 2005c).

2. A portion of the material on Asian American resilience in this chapter was initially published in S. M. Ino and M. D. Glicken (1999), "Treating Asian American Clients in Crisis: A Collectivist Approach," *Smith College Studies in Social Work, 69*(3), 525–540 and in S. M. Ino and M. D. Glicken (2002), "Understanding and Treating the Ethnically Asian Client: A Collectivist Approach," *Journal of Health and Social Policy, 14*(4), 37–48. I want to thank the editors of both journals for permission to reprint some of that material for this chapter.

PART III

Examples of
Resilience Across Areas
of Psychosocial Difficulty

CHAPTER 5

How Resilient People Cope With Substance Abuse

The Extent of the Problem

In 2004 data provided by the U.S. Department of Health and Human Services (2005) from a national survey, an estimated 120 million Americans age 12 or older (51% of this age group) reported being current drinkers of alcohol. About 54 million (22.9%) participated in binge drinking at least once in the 30 days prior to the survey, and 15.9 million (6.7%) were heavy drinkers. The prevalence of current alcohol use increased with increasing age, from 2% at age 12 to 70.9% at age 21. About 10.7 million persons age 12 to 20 (28.8% of this age group) reported drinking alcohols in the month prior to the survey interview in 2004. Of these, nearly 7.2 million (19.3%) were binge drinkers and 2.3 million (6.2%) were heavy drinkers. About 1 in 7 Americans age 12 or older in 2002 (14.2%, or 33.5 million persons) drove under the influence of alcohol at least once in the 12 months prior to the interview.

In the 2004 survey (U.S. Department of Health and Human Services, 2005), an estimated 19.5 million Americans, or 8.3% of the population aged 12 or older, had used illegal drugs the month before the survey was taken. Marijuana was the most commonly used illicit drug, with a rate of 6.2%. Of the 14.6 million people who reported using marijuana, about one third, or 4.8 million persons, used it on 20 or more days in the month before the survey was taken. An estimated 2 million persons (.9%) were current cocaine users, 567,000 of whom used crack cocaine. Hallucinogens were used by 1.2 million persons, with users of Ecstasy numbering 676,000. There were an estimated 166,000 current heroin users and about 6.2 million persons, or 2.6% of the population age 12 or older, were current users of psychotherapeutic drugs taken non-medically. An estimated 4.4 million used pain relievers, 1.8 million used tranquilizers, 1.2 million used stimulants, and .4 million used sedatives. Among youth in the 12 to 17 age group, 11.6% were current illicit drug users. The rate of use (20.2%) was highest among young adults (18 to 25 years old). About 11.0 million persons were driving under the influence of an illicit drug during the year before the survey. This corresponds to 4.7% of the population age 12 or older. The rate was 10% or greater for each age from 17 to 25.

A survey conducted by SAMSHA, an office of the U.S. Department of Health and Human Services (HHS, 2000b), found that 14.5 million Americans age 12 or older were classified with drug and alcohol dependence or abuse, amounting to 6.5% of the total population. *Alcohol Alert,* a publication of the National Institute of Alcohol Abuse and Alcoholism (2000), reports that more than 700,000 Americans receive alcoholism treatment, alone, on any given day. Using HHS data, Kann (2001) notes that the use of alcohol and drugs continues to be one of the country's most pervasive and serious health and mental health problems. Substance abuse is a leading cause of car accidents, homicide, suicide, and HIV infection and AIDS, and it contributes to crime, poor workplace productivity and accidents, and lower educational achievement.

The cause of substance abuse and the reasons for such high numbers of people experiencing the problem is complex. In women, substance abuse has been linked to dual diagnoses, childhood sexual abuse, panic and phobia disorders, eating disorders, posttraumatic stress disorder, and victimization (Backer & Walton-Moss, 2001). Substance abuse in men appears to be caused by the early use and addiction to alcohol, parental use and acceptance of alcohol and drugs, problems with family bonding and family conflict, ease in obtaining alcohol, a high level of peer use of alcohol, and positive peer attitudes toward alcohol and drug use (Backer & Walton-Moss, 2001). Factors that appear to affect both men and women include rebellious behavior against parents, gaining peer acceptance by drinking to impress peers, and self-treatment through use of alcohol and drugs for mental health and/or academic problems (Grant & Dawson, 1997). Interestingly, substance abuse rates appear to be similar across many cultures and nations. England, Canada, and Australia, for example, all report addiction rates that are nearly the same as that of the United States, suggesting that there is a genetic factor to substance abuse. I recently asked Becky Jackson, a long-time addiction therapist and writer about addictions across cultures and countries, about the cross-cultural similarities. In a personal interview held October 14, 2005 in Palm Springs, California, Ms. Jackson told me that

> while certain cultures have taboos against alcohol and alcohol dependence and have low rates of alcohol abuse (Jewish, Arabs, and certain Southeast Asian groups come to mind), when you look at drug abuse data, they often offset low alcohol addiction rates. Consequently, a number of people in the field believe there is a genetic component to substance abuse.
>
> An example of this may also be found in the high rates of alcoholism in children of alcoholics. I don't think this can be explained entirely by saying that children imitate parental behavior or that when parents use alcohol to relieve stress, children do the same thing, although this may be true to some extent. It's also true that certain traumas such as rape, sexual molestation, and assaults may increase the use of alcohol and drugs and lead to substance dependence. Generally speaking, I believe that the similarities in the rates of substance abuse across cultures suggest a genetic predisposition to abuse substances or an addictive tendency that may be organic in origin.

When you speak to enough alcoholics, you hear a familiar story: They immediately felt wonderful when using alcohol for the first time or they [couldn't] stop drinking [after] the first time they [tried] alcohol. The more they use, the better they feel and the more addicted they become. Most people who experience alcohol early in life either get sick, don't like the taste, or find it unappealing. That alcohol abusers have a very different initial reaction to alcohol tells me that alcoholism has a highly organic component. It may be triggered by stress, but it's there, nonetheless. This is why AA and other 12 step programs teach people that they are powerless over their addiction. Just saying you will stop often repeatedly fails. The benefit of 12 step programs is that they are spiritual and they provide the alcoholic with a support group and mentor. In otherwise isolated people who often fail in life, these three aspects of treatment can have a powerful positive impact and lead not only to changes in drinking but to significant changes in the way people live their lives.

In a book I wrote about childhood violence (Glicken, 2004b), a drug and alcohol abuser (whom I called Mr. R.) reinforces the notion of a genetic component to addiction when he describes his initial experience with alcohol:

After basic training in Texas, we were shipped to a little air base in the cow and oil town of Casper, Wyoming. To that point, I had never had a drink of alcohol. My life was about to undergo a major change. On our first leave into town, I accompanied a group of older guys to a bar. I was small for my age and looked about fifteen years old at that time. Casper wasn't a strict kind of town when it came to the law. Desperate to be manly, I ordered the most macho sounding drink on the menu, a Salty Dog. My first drink was like magic. I quickly had another. The magic increased. All my fears and insecurities seemed to disappear. I felt like Mike Hammer in a Mickey Spillane novel, my favorite reading at the time. I asked all the women to dance and insulted their companions. I couldn't drink enough. What a marvelous freedom, from self, this alcohol. No wonder my father said it was the devil's greatest tool. It was the greatest fun in the world! I wanted to call home to say I had found the solution to my problems; however, I knew intuitively that would not be the thing to do. Sometime during that night, I entered a blackout. I awoke the next day in my bunk, mouth and eye both cut and bloody. My head hurt like hell and I was on disciplinary routine. None of that mattered because I'd found a freedom from my shyness, my fears, and my inhibitions. I couldn't wait to go drinking again. (Glicken, 2004b, p. 161)

The Research on Resilience in Coping With Drug and Alcohol Abuse

Granfield and Cloud (1996) estimate that as many as 90% of all problem drinkers never enter treatment and that many end the abuse of substances without any form of treatment at all (Hingson, Scotch, Day, & Culbert, 1980; Roizen, Cahalan, Lambert, Wiebel, & Shanks, 1978; Stall & Biernacki, 1989). Sobell, Sobell, Toneatto, and Leo

(1993) report that 82% of the alcoholics they studied who terminated their addiction did so by using natural recovery methods that excluded the use of a professional. In another example of the use of natural recovery, Granfield and Cloud (1996) report that most ex-smokers discontinue their tobacco use without treatment (Peele, 1989), while many addicted substance abusers mature out of a variety of addictions including heavy drinking and narcotics use (Snow, 1973; Winick, 1962). Biernacki (1986) found that addicts who stop their addictions naturally use a variety of strategies, including breaking off relationships with drug users, removing themselves from drug-using environments (Stall & Biernacki, 1989), building new structures in their lives (Peele, 1989), and using friends and family to provide support for discontinuing their substance abuse (Biernacki, 1986). Trice and Roman (1970) believe that using self-help groups with substance-abusing clients is particularly helpful because such groups tend to reduce personal responsibility, with its related guilt, and help build and maintain a support network that assists in continuing the changed behavior.

Granfield and Cloud (1996) studied middle-class alcoholics who used natural recovery alone, without professional help or self-help groups. Many of the participants in their study felt that the "ideological" base of some self-help programs was inconsistent with their own philosophies of life. For example, many felt that some self-help groups for substance abusers were overly religious, while other self-help groups were invested in a disease model of alcoholism and consequently viewed alcoholism as a lifetime struggle. The subjects in the study by Granfield and Cloud (1996) also felt that some self-help groups encouraged dependence, and that associating with other alcoholics would probably make recovery more difficult. In summarizing their findings, Granfield and Cloud (1996) report that the respondents in their study discounted the use of self-help groups because they saw themselves as "efficacious people who often prided themselves on their past accomplishments. They viewed themselves as being individualists and strong-willed. One respondent, for instance, explained that 'such programs encourage powerlessness' and that she would rather 'trust her own instincts than the instincts of others'" (p. 51).

In further support of the importance of natural healing, Waldorf, Reinarman, and Murphy (1991) found that many addicted people with supportive elements in their lives (a job, family, and other close emotional supports) were able to "walk away" from their very heavy use of cocaine. The authors suggest that the "social context" of a drug users' lives may positively influence their ability to discontinue drug use. Granfield and Cloud (1996) add to the social context notion of recovery by noting that many of the respondents in their sample had a great deal to lose if they continued their substance abuse. They note that the subjects in their study "had jobs, supportive families, high school and college credentials, and other social supports that gave them reasons to alter their drug-taking behavior," and add that "having much to lose" gave their respondents "incentives to transform their lives" (p. 55).

O'Connor, Cayton, Taylor, McKenna, and Monroe (2004) report a unique project in Oregon where released felons from state prison are involved in a statewide program that includes the use of chaplains and over 1,300 volunteers. Most of the released felons have drug- and alcohol-related problems that, to a large extent, have led to their acting out behavior and confinement in prison. The program takes into account the fact that at least half of the released felons consider themselves actively involved in religious or spiritual practices, and over 90% indicate and interest in spiritual and religious involvement. Once released, the felons in the program meet in circles comprised of five to seven highly trained community volunteers who provide transitional support and behavioral accountability to the high-risk offender who volunteers to be the core member of a treatment circle in his or her community.

> The circle members meet once a week with the offender, and one member of the circle calls or meets with the core member each day for the critical first year following release. "The circle members are trained in the dynamics of criminality and substance abuse and how to provide a system of support and accountability that differs from, but augments, any correctional treatment or supervision provided by corrections professionals. (p. 74)

The authors report that this approach has been particularly effective with high-risk felons and that recidivism in this group has fallen 30%, with reduced substance abuse one of the primary reasons for the reduction in re-offenses.

Writing about the strengths perspective and the treatment of substance abuse, Moxley and Olivia (2001) note that recovery requires the client and the clinician to focus on the meaning of life and the higher purpose that binds us all together. The authors write, "Nothing in life effectively helps people to survive even the worst conditions as the knowledge that one's life has meaning. A salient challenge is to ensure that individuals articulate their own perspectives concerning what the transpersonal means to them" (p. 259). In defining transpersonal aspects of resilience in resolving problems with substance abuse, Moxley and Olivia (2001) write,

> The purpose of any human being is to fulfill a life goal that is constructive and vital to the advancement of humankind, of the environment, and of the universe.
>
> The absence of opportunity induced by discrimination, stigmatization, and social marginalization can set conditions in which a career of chemical dependency can become a likely alternative.
>
> People can gain insight when they come to understand the forces influencing their chemical dependency and when they realize that while they can blame these forces, they must also confront them and overcome them.
>
> The transpersonal domain reminds people that nothing in life [as] effectively helps [one] to survive even the worst conditions as the knowledge that one's life has meaning. (p. 260)

In a further example of resilience, Fleming and Manwell (1998) report that people with alcohol-related problems often receive counseling from their primary care physician, or nursing staff in the physician's office, in five or fewer standard office visits. The counseling consists of rational information about the negative impact of alcohol use, as well as practical advice on ways of reducing alcohol dependence and the availability of community resources. Gentilello, Donovan, Dunn, and Rivara (1995) report that 25% to 40% of the trauma patients seen in emergency rooms may be alcohol dependent, and that a single motivational interview at or near the time of patients' discharge reduced drinking levels and readmission for trauma during 6 months of follow-up. Monti, Colby, Barnett, Spirito, Roshenow, and Meyers (1999) found that 18- to 19-year-olds admitted to an emergency room with alcohol-related injuries who received a single feedback session on their drinking "had a significantly lower incidence of drinking and driving, traffic violations, alcohol-related injuries, and alcohol-related problems" (p. 993). Clearly, the many substance abusers who cycle off substances either on their own or with almost minimal help are able to use their inner resources to reduce their abuse of alcohol and drugs.

The effectiveness of brief counseling sessions suggests that many substance abusers have inner resources that help them cope with drug and alcohol abuse. Hanson and Gutheil (2004) reinforce that short motivational interviews are effective, particularly with older adult substance abusers. They note that before help is sought and used effectively, older adult substance abusers go through several phases: (1) the contemplation stage, in which they are ambivalent about change and, while open to it, weigh the benefits and costs; (2) the preparation stage, in which they have made a decision to change their substance-abusing behavior but no action has been taken; (3) the action stage, in which they "make lifestyle changes that are more obvious and acceptable to others. For example, problem drinkers may try to abstain from all alcoholic beverages for at least one week and keep all medical and social services appointments during that time" (p. 369); (4) the maintenance stage, which begins after they have sustained behavioral change for around 6 months, and in which their change efforts focus on strengthening and consolidating gains, preventing relapse, and living healthier lifestyles. Maintenance is a lifelong process with no clear endpoint. In the case of problem drinking, a great deal of movement occurs back and forth across stages. Relapse frequently happens, and, when it does, individuals may return to any of the earlier stages before eventually eliminating the problem behavior permanently (Hanson & Gutheil, 2004, p. 370).

In considering the processes of natural healing, Granfield and Cloud (1996) report that substance abusers who cycle off substances without additional professional or self-help assistance build new social support systems to replace the old ones that reinforced a culture of substance abuse. In the new social support systems,

> these respondents built new support structures to assist them in their termination efforts. They frequently reported becoming involved in various social groups such as choirs, health clubs, religious organizations, reading clubs, and dance companies. Others from this group reported that they returned to school, became active in civic organizations, or simply developed new hobbies that brought them in touch with nonusers. Thus, respondents built new lives for themselves by cultivating social ties with meaningful and emotionally satisfying alternative communities. (p. 55)

Interestingly, the authors indicate that even though subjects in their study made attachments to new social support systems and to communities, they hid their substance abuse from others, believing that if people knew about their past, it would affect their new relationships. Whether this is the way resilient people deal with addictions is difficult to say, since addiction is a stigmatizing issue in our society, but it does contradict the approach used in AA (in which members identify themselves as alcoholics in meetings) and cause one to question whether there is in fact a strongly genetic component to substance abuse.

A STORY OF FAMILY RESILIENCE AND ALCOHOL ABUSE

There was a lot of emotional abuse in my family, like name-calling and really bad put-downs. My dad used to come home from work and have five or six drinks and start calling all of us "morons" or "retards." As he'd drink more, he'd tell us we were worthless and that none of us had any spunk and that we were all useless. My sister was homecoming queen, and he said she probably won because she was "screwing" most of the guys at school. I was a National Merit Scholar, and he said that I probably cheated my way through school and that anyone who was so dumb could never get to be a scholar without cheating.

It wasn't long before we all started using alcohol because it was there in the house. I have a wonderful brother and sister and we were all drinking by sixth grade, and I mean heavy drinking. It didn't stop us from doing well in school or being popular, but we had serious drinking problems by high school. I know for a fact that my brother was drunk when he played in the state high school basketball championships. He was voted outstanding player and told me later that by the time the awards were given out after the games, he'd vomited twice and was seeing double. My sister was using amphetamines to stay awake at night and study. We all wanted to get out of the house so badly we could taste it, and we all were drunks by 18.

I was the oldest and I got a scholarship to a small private school in Iowa. Two years later, my sister joined me and then my brother joined us a year after that. We lived together and took care of each other. We knew we had alcohol and drug problems and we just helped each other stop. My brother and sister are remarkable people. They went through college and did very well, even though we all had to work nights and weekends just to afford tuition. We volunteered to help other people who had drinking problems in school and some of them even came to live with us for a while. My sister went on to become a doctor and is successful and happily married. My brother and I are attorneys and are in partnership.

We've not been so successful in relationships. Both of us have been married twice and are now single. We talked about it, and we concluded that we both seem to get involved with very passive and submissive women who are much like our mother. She did very little to stop our father's abusive behavior, but she modeled our notion of women and I guess we're stuck with a bad model. We've both been in therapy for help with relationships and that's been very useful. None of us drink or even think about drinking.

How did we stop drinking? By forming our own support group at college and by being our best friends. We were there for each other when we felt like

This story was told to me, and what I wrote was approved by the storyteller.

backsliding into drinking again. We also acted as sounding boards with one another for our failures, our fears, and our anger. We're all still pretty angry at my father. He died last year, but before he died, he wrote us a letter apologizing for his bad behavior. We never responded and he died alone. I know that wasn't kind of us, but sometimes you have anger that doesn't go away, and mine won't and neither will theirs. We talk about it and think that what we did was adolescent, but none of us feels guilty. He took our childhoods away and he didn't deserve our love for doing it. Maybe I'll think differently when I'm older. I have two children and they're wonderful. I've never said a cross word or been negative with them. I know the harm it can do. Who wants to repeat the mistakes of your own father?

One last thing. We all became involved in religion when we left home. We went to different churches but, to this day, we're involved. We talked about it in college and all of us felt that we needed fellowship and to think about what life meant to us. There's a strong chance that when you grow up in an abusive home that you become cynical about life. I think religion has helped that from happening, and I think our love for each other has cycled over to a love of people. I feel it in church and no matter how badly my week goes, when I'm in church, this wonderful feeling of peace comes over me.

Am I happy? I think so, most of the time at least. I have my bad days when I beat myself up for one thing or another, but then it dawns on me that I'm using the same words our dad used, and in no time, I stop. I remember that I've been a good man, a successful man, and a much better man than my dad could ever have hoped to be. It gives me solace to know that I've been strong enough to overcome what might have been a disastrous drinking problem, and that I've been a good person. When you think about it, that's what counts most—being a good person.

LESSONS TO BE LEARNED FROM THIS STORY

There are a number of ways the storyteller and his brother and sister display positive signs of resilience. They include:

1. The ability to remove themselves from the abusive home life they were experiencing, establish their own support system by living together, and help one another, as well as the mutual support they gave one another, are all signs of resilience.

2. They all found solace and life meaning through religious expression and by helping others.

3. They used their energies and intellects to succeed socially and vocationally, and although they do not always have happy personal lives, they do have meaningful and successful careers. Like many abused children, they did very well academically and in extracurricular activities and used that success as a way of counteracting their father's abusive behavior and their mother's passivity.

4. They managed to make themselves invisible during the times they lived at home, avoiding their parents to the extent possible. When they left home, they managed to negate their abusive father's effect on them by removing him and his influences from their lives. Some might think that their response to his death was harsh and dysfunctional, but it did serve a purpose: It highlights a problem that still needs to be resolved. One hopes that with time they will be able to do this.

A STORY OF A BASEBALL PLAYER AND ATTORNEY JAILED BECAUSE OF DRUG AND ALCOHOL ABUSE

I am a former attorney and professional baseball player who became an alcoholic and spent 3 years in prison for fraud. I used my position of trust as an attorney to steal nearly a quarter of a million dollars from my clients. I took the money from a trust fund and used it to live beyond my means. I lost my good name, my career, and my freedom. I nearly lost my family and my life. Today, I am a drug and alcohol counselor working with addicts to help them recover from the debilitating effects of addiction that brought so much damage to my life. Few suspected back then that I had a substance abuse problem. Fewer still could have foreseen the good that ultimately arose from such unseemly circumstances.

My fall from the height of success to the despair of addiction and imprisonment was a breathtaking plunge. I grew up in a normal family and although we never had a lot of money, my life abounded with great opportunities. Most of the opportunities came from sports, but I also excelled in school. In fact, I did well enough in baseball and in the classroom to attend UC Berkeley on a full athletic scholarship. After a stellar collegiate career, I played professional baseball in the New York Yankees organization. I loved baseball, but Berkeley left me with some pretty serious aspirations. Ultimately, I decided that I wanted to be a trial lawyer. I quit pro ball after two seasons to attend law school at UCLA where I grew up, and then moved to Oregon where I built a successful law practice. Progress in my early life appeared seamless; each step seemingly led to the pinnacle, and life there looked promising in all directions.

How did the wheels come off the cart? Not because I was a victim. There is no villain in my story to whom I can self-righteously point the finger of blame and say, "You caused me to go astray." The circumstances of my childhood, while certainly not perfect, did not create some wellspring of hate, bitterness, and discontent. My parents weren't abusive. I didn't fall prey to some childhood trauma. My basic needs were never denied. I suffered no debilitating emotional ordeal. Quite the contrary, I led an enviable, even privileged life. Not privileged in the sense of money, but rather the privilege of talent, opportunity, and achievement. No one held me back or down, or stood in my way; rather, all the significant adults in my life supported and encouraged me to fulfill my potential.

My early years were by no means untouched by difficulty. My parents divorced when I was 10, a grievous wound that I would long suffer. And my dad drank. I didn't realize how much he drank until late in my high school years. I spent every other weekend at his apartment across town, and it eventually got to the point where it seemed that all he ever did was drink. But he never got abusive, belligerent, or maudlin. He just drank until he couldn't talk, and then he'd fall asleep. I didn't really know what an addiction was. If my family had a history of addiction, I had no knowledge of it. Yet despite the divorce and my dad's drinking, it seemed to me that I had it pretty good. My parents loved me, took interest in my life, and expected me to make something of myself.

Despite my relatively stable youth and a growing list of accomplishments, I became an alcoholic. I didn't have a problem with drinking until my mid-20s. Before then, I drank socially, occasionally to excess but always (at least for a time) wiser. However, during my third year as a lawyer, I encountered a problem that I couldn't handle on my own. I was given an assignment to try a case that I didn't think I could handle, and I panicked. Then, in my frenzied search to overcome panic, I discovered that alcohol blunted my fear and anxiety. So great and irrational did my panic grow about being in court that I have since come to believe that I was having a nervous breakdown. The whole affair left me shell-shocked, but I thought I had the answer: As long as I could drink and control my anxiety and fear, I would be OK.

I didn't know it then, but I had stepped onto a slippery slope. At first the slope fell ever so gently away. In fact, you might even say it rose up to greet me, because it worked. It took away the anxiety and fear that gnawed at me each time I had to face the courtroom. It was then that I came to view alcohol as my salvation.

At first I thought I had control over my drinking. I drank the night before court appearances so I could calmly prepare my case, and so I could fall asleep and be rested for court. But, as time passed, I lost control over how often and how much I could drink. Alcohol now controlled me. My life became a chaotic mess, but I didn't see that the culprit was booze; rather, I thought booze was the only thing that shielded me from the pain of an increasingly chaotic life. Eventually, my drinking would help create a climate of moral and ethical decay where all that mattered was making sure my needs were met, regardless of the cost.

Notwithstanding my apparent promise as a young man and a solid record of accomplishments as an adult, alcohol's fleeting medicinal effects exacted a terrible price. As my life crumbled around me, I chose to take money from my client trust account to prop myself up and to maintain my appearance as a successful attorney. Eventually caught, I had to stand before the judge as he pronounced sentence over a life gone terribly wrong; the once unbounded promise all but destroyed by the despair of addiction. I had taken the gifts I'd been given and squandered them. Alcohol did not cause me to steal money from my clients, but it fostered the moral corruption and ethical deterioration that led to a criminal life. And yet, as I listened to the judge explain my just fate that day, I heard evidence of something gone right and the promise of an eventual reunion. The judge told me that "there has been an ongoing transformation of the inner man that is worthy and admirable. I honestly believe you have the ability to be a wonderful person and a wonderful father, and I honestly believe that your rehabilitation efforts are sincere."

I quit drinking when I got caught. I quit drinking because the pain it caused finally outweighed the fear of giving it up. More importantly, I entered treatment and started attending AA meetings. I entered treatment because I knew if

I didn't the judge would throw the proverbial book at me. Oddly enough, once I got there, I found out just how much I belonged. I committed myself to the process; I wanted to make recovery part of the fabric of my life.

By the time of my sentencing, the judge saw something of the renewed hope and promise that began because I quit drinking and stared to reclaim my life. But recovery isn't easy. When I finally "hit bottom" the options looked bleak. I could dry up and blow away like so much refuse, or stand up and fight for my life. I chose to fight for my life.

I spent 3 years and 1 day in prison for my crimes, but today I look upon my experiences as life restoring. Prison proved to be an unexpected experience. I expected my life to be in danger, so it came as no surprise that I lived in a cell-block that housed murderers (several of whom I would share a cell with). At the same time, I worked in a prison treatment program that trained me to teach alcohol and drug education to other inmates. For 2 years I taught inmates the dangers of alcohol and drug use. That training led to an opportunity to work as counselor and teacher for a County Drug Court Program in Oregon, an adult felony diversion project. More importantly, it gave me a chance to give back what was so openly given to me in my own treatment program and in the meeting rooms of AA.

Today, my recovery program remains the sustaining force in my life. It has allowed me to live courageously in the face of anxiety and fear. My recovery program has also taught me that I am a caretaker over the state that constitutes life. Ironically, I worked in a profession where I could have been a true servant to my clients. But as a lawyer, I abused my position of trust, seeking only to get what I could for myself. Today, although I can't practice law, I have found true meaning and purpose in my life because I now embrace my role as caretaker. Whereas I once did what I had to do for my clients in order to get money, I now endorse my duties as caretaker: To my clients at drug court; to my wife and kids; to my employers; and now, finally, to myself. I have even written a book about my experiences as a lawyer and addict. It may never be published, but the experience of writing it has made me a better counselor and teacher.

My life today is far from perfect; only my response has changed. I still experience anxiety and fear of daily living, but today I don't have to drink over it. Instead, I am able to accept anxiety and fear as a natural and normal part of living. The journey that began when I quit drinking proved hard yet well worth the effort. Every couple of months, drug court holds a graduation ceremony for those who have successfully completed its rigorous requirements. Those who graduate have spent almost 2 years of their lives struggling to overcome addiction. I have now been there long enough to have played a significant role in the success of at least some of the graduates. On those occasions when a graduate thanks me publicly for what I have done on his or her behalf, I am filled with gratitude for God's mercy and grace.

Lessons to Be Learned From This Story

We often think that people who steal and then blame it on their drinking would have stolen anyway and that the behavior indicates a character flaw. I asked Becky Jackson about this. "It's true," she said, "that we use the term *dry drunk* to describe people who aren't drinking anymore but whose fundamental personality is that of an alcoholic who tends to blame his or her problems on something other than their own bad choices in life. I don't think this is the case with our ex-lawyer. His conversion seems genuine and his story is much like many stories I've heard from alcoholics in recovery. He shows believable remorse, he's helped other alcoholics, he knows he has a life-threatening problem, he's come out of a horrible personal tragedy much better and more self-aware than ever, and he seems to have learned a great deal about himself.

"Most nonaddicts fail to understand that addictions are compulsions and once they are full-blown, they carry people into behaviors for which they are deeply ashamed. There are many things I would like to know about his life, including the support systems he had in place when the problem began and whether his wife and family were aware of his behavior. I wonder if he had a spiritual direction and if he had a mentor to talk to when problems were developing. I also wonder why he chose to be a litigator when it obviously set off a great deal of anxiety to appear in court, and I wonder why he doesn't see a connection between his father's drinking and his own. Nonetheless, I think the storyteller shows great resilience in overcoming the alcoholism, the time spent in prison, and the difficult readjustment to life without the profession he was trained in. His spiritual direction, his work with other alcoholics, and his selfless life are all indicators that he is coming to grips with who he is and that he will be a much better person because of it. That to me is certainly a positive indication of his attempt to overcome his drinking and the repercussions in his life that it caused."

A STORY ABOUT AN ADOLESCENT SUBSTANCE ABUSER

Jason began acting in a strange way when he reached 16. There was nothing I could put my finger on, and I thought it must have to do with adolescence and being rebellious. I'd been rebellious as a teenager, so for 6 months it didn't really hit me that he had a problem. Then I was contacted by the police. Jason had been picked up for drunk driving and had injured himself and wrecked our new car. My husband and I were shocked. We were churchgoing people, a little naïve, and never thought Jason would do such a thing. And boy, were we angry and full of righteous indignation. We went to the hospital and reamed him out, took his keys to the car away, and grounded him until the coming of the ice age. What we didn't see was the hurting young man inside and the fact that he had some serious emotional problems. You wonder why you don't see the problems until you have a crisis, but maybe we weren't looking too hard. Jason's drinking caused problems in our marriage, and within 6 months, my husband and I were separated and Jason was in therapy that didn't seem to be going anywhere.

He was getting drugs from people at school and on the streets and stealing money from my husband and me. Now that we know the pattern of adolescent drug and alcohol use, we know that it's a pretty typical pattern. All this time he was deteriorating badly and so were we. I blamed it all on my husband's

The following story was told to me by a parent whose adolescent son had begun abusing drugs and alcohol. I wrote the story.

aloofness and the fact that he was facilitating Jason's substance abuse. I mean, he actually bought Jason a car after his accident, and when Jason went to live with him, his father treated him more like a buddy than a son. My husband blamed me because he said I was treating Jason like an inmate in a prison and questioning everything he did like I was the warden. I think he was right. I was scared, hurt, and ashamed. We live in this wonderful place with houses worth millions of dollars and you want people to think the best of you. Even the idea of an alcoholic kid made me cringe.

I know Jason hated me during that period of time because I was so strict. He went to therapy and we all joined a support group for parents who have alcoholic kids. It was demeaning at first. I hated it. I came up the hard way, and the thought of all these privileged kids complaining about their parents made me mad as hell. I wanted to slap every single one of them for whining so much. And then one session I heard something that really affected me. One of the parents was telling her daughter how much trouble she'd caused the family. I looked over at Jason and he was crying, and so was his dad. And then I started crying, too. We just held each other for a long time. My husband and I reconciled, and we started having family talks. They helped all of us. We talked about everything, even very private things. Jason didn't think that we loved him. He thought I was always disappointed in him and that my standards were so high, he couldn't ever achieve them. My husband said that he felt the same way. It hurt, you know. I'd come up the hard way from poor parents and I was very demanding of myself, and it affected everyone, my perfectionism and my drive. It forced me into therapy. I don't know how we made it during the 2 years we went through treatment and relapse, and more treatment, but we did. We had supportive friends, a group of people we went to church with, and, most of all, a deep faith that we could make it, and we did.

A few years later, Jason was in college and doing great. He's going to be an architect just like his father. Anyway, he wrote me this wonderful letter, and it said that he always thought of me as a great mom, even in the worst of times, and he knew he wouldn't have made it were it not for me. I know that sounds corny, but it just made me cry. I'd begun to think I was a terrible mother and that all the problems we had during that period of time were because of me.

LESSONS TO BE LEARNED FROM THIS STORY

I asked our storyteller to tell me why she thought they were doing so well when at the time they all seemed so unlikely to improve. She told me the following:

1. They made it because of friends, their faith in God, and their deep and abiding desire to be successful. Her husband had also come up the hard way and saw Jason's problem as a failure that would destroy all the progress he had made in his life if it weren't resolved. He was motivated to help, as was his wife. They put their pride aside and did what was necessary to resolve the problem.

2. The main thing that helped was the support group and the professional therapy they all received, including, at one point, family therapy. It helped to reach a deeper level of understanding about how they all contributed to Jason's problem and how unsuccessful they'd been as a family before Jason's substance abuse problem became known to them. Like many young alcoholics, Jason had been drinking since he was a child—he had been taking liquor from his parents from the time he was 8 years old. Although he was often drunk in the evenings while they watched TV, his parents were unaware of his condition. The therapy helped the family members see how much they were either ignoring or missing in each other's feelings and behaviors. Both parents felt miserable in their marriage, but they had never discussed it until Jason's problem led to their separation and forced them to seek help.

3. Jason's mother began to read the material they were bringing home from the support group. It motivated her to find out much more about family problems and therapy. She even took a psychology class on family dynamics to help her better understand her own family, and it helped.

4. Although she was angry at her husband for leaving and for facilitating Jason's drinking, she never said anything critical to Jason about his father. Instead, she went directly to her husband and tried to make him see that buying presents for a deeply troubled child was like trying to buy love. He was shaken by this perception, and it was then that the family immersed itself in trying to get help and doing the sometimes difficult work of changing the family's behavior.

5. She spoke to friends and to co-workers she trusted. To her amazement, many of them had children who had experienced substance abuse problems, and although these parents had been appalled and hurt, they did the hard work necessary to get better, and it helped. Almost all of the children were fine and doing well. It was for her the single most motivating experience, since it gave her hope.

6. She discovered that the aloofness she had always felt with others had distanced her from her son, and even though he said he dreaded the chats, she talked to him a great deal about all aspects of his life. She also shared information about her early life that was eye opening to him. He never knew that she had grown up in a very poor abusive family or that her father left when she was 7 and had never come back. Jason thought he had died. She told him how painful it had been, and how she blamed herself for her father's leaving and thought that there must be something wrong with her to have driven Jason's father away. She also blamed herself for Jason's drinking. Jason held her and started crying and assured her it wasn't that at all, it was the feeling he had that he wasn't a good enough son and that he'd never make his parents happy. They agreed then to keep up a dialogue and to talk about feelings and perceptions until they were clear about how they felt about each other. For her part, she had never loved anyone as deeply as she loved her son. And until he was born, she thought herself incapable of love. Jason was so touched by what his mother said that he couldn't talk for a long time and then went to his room and cried.

7. The coping mechanism Jason's mother used most was the sense that it would all work itself out and that, in the end, the family would be better because of what they went through. And, as she had hoped, they *were* better, and it was the most wonderful experience to be in a happy and loving family.

A Story About Recovery From Substance Abuse: Mr R. Changes His Life

By the end of 1986, my drinking and drug use had taken a heavy toll. Physically, I was in serious trouble. In February of 1987, I ended up in the hospital. My body had given up. I was in a state of incomprehensible demoralization at the age of 46. I had no new plans to try, no more diversions to implement. Just about everything I had worked for was gone, or soon would be. I felt totally defeated, as if I had been at war with life and now had finally lost. There was some element of relief involved in this frame of mind.

I was discharged from the hospital with the instructions to never drink or use drugs again unless I wished to die. It was suggested I seek out Alcoholics Anonymous as a resource. I remember the few meetings my probation officer had me attend in the early 1970s, and the losers and idiots I remembered there. Was I now of that class myself? It was a crushing thought. However, I had nowhere else to turn. I began my journey into sobriety with AA as an angry, fearful, and resentful man. I did not immediately feel at home in AA as some do. I fought it as I had fought everything else in life for so long. But I didn't drink. It became clear to me over those first six months of sobriety that if I were to remain sober, it would require the greatest effort I had ever mustered for anything. I was desperate to remain sober and believed, without reservation, that to drink again would be the end of me. Thoughts, serious thoughts of suicide, came and went again. The trick was to learn to live life on life's terms, not my own.

When I was a boy of perhaps 10, I examined the notion of The God that ruled our home. I decided that if God was like my father, I wasn't interested. I described myself over the years as an agnostic. I didn't know if there was a God or not, and, frankly, I didn't care. It made no difference in my life either way. I also had a great loathing for churches and what I called church people. And now, here I was in a program that required me to acknowledge a higher power and adopt the notion of spirituality. What a bind to be in. The great thing was that I met others in the program that had felt as I did, and they managed to make things work over time. I acknowledged AA as my higher power and it seemed to work, as I remained sober.

Earlier in this chapter, I briefly described Mr. R. (Glicken, 2004b), a drug and alcohol abuser, and his first experience with alcohol. This next section describes his recovery.

About eight months after I got sober, I found employment facilitating DUI classes. I would teach five to eight classes a week and found that I derived a great sense of reward from that activity. I actually enjoyed working with people. Who would have thought? I returned to school at the local community college and, like so many other recovering people, began taking courses in the chemical dependency program. When I had been sober approximately 12 months, I also began working part time at a nonprofit short-term residential program serving those with mental illness in crisis. I found I enjoyed working with the mentally ill more than with substance abusers. Then I found that many of the mentally ill also had substance abuse problems. It was a wonderfully challenging population of people.

After an incident in which I abused yet another woman, it occurred to me that though AA was keeping me sober and my life was progressing in good directions, if I were to ever have any hope of having a healthy relationship with a female, I needed to try some professional help. I was referred to a female psychologist in Austin who agreed to work with me. And so began my journey in therapy. She seemed to know just how fast I could go and always kept me challenged. At times she suggested I take a short break and that was also helpful. She took considerable time to educate me on women's issues and how women think differently than men. I began to understand something about women's values and needs. To me, it was amazing stuff. Then came the day after about six months when my insurance ran out. I wanted desperately to continue but was unable to pay for the full cost alone. My therapist told me not to worry. She stated she had a strong belief in me and what I was doing and usually had one client she worked with without charge. She would keep going with me as long as it was productive. I have to say that of the many beneficial things that came from my almost two and a half years with her, her belief in me was the single most impacting event. I had always had so little belief in myself, and been such a terrible disappointment to so many, that to have a person, especially a woman of her status, express belief in me, was huge. When I reflect back over the years since then, that one thing still stands out.

I recall a time when in an effort to express my gratitude for her caring and skills, I blurted out that I would, if needed, protect her, kill for her. She laughed and said, "If you want to do something for me, then please go love someone, and you might try starting with yourself." Obviously, I never forgot that either (Glicken, 2004b, p. 169).

LESSONS TO BE LEARNED FROM THIS STORY

There is much in Mr. R.'s story that suggests the presence of a great deal of resilience in the midst of some behavior most of us would find difficult to accept. And yet, in the end, I think that he made great strides as a person. The fine, resilient, principled person I knew would have made his family proud, I believe, because resilience isn't a constant, and when it counted most, Mr. R. demonstrated the capacity to love and to help others in a selfless way that can be described as resilience in its highest form.

Summary

This chapter on resilient people coping with substance abuse noted the high rates of alcohol and drug abuse in America. Although a variety of emotional problems may lead to substance abuse, there is reason to believe that substance abuse also may have a strong genetic component. Research on self-healing and short-term treatment was included. Four stories and lessons to be learned about how resilient people cope with substance abuse were also included in the chapter.

CHAPTER 6

How Resilient People Cope With Mental Illness

The Extent and Impact of Mental Illness

In this chapter I will present evidence that people who have episodes of mental illness are much more resilient than we often think, and that notions of mental illness as a lifelong, unchanging condition that never improves and that leaves people functioning in confused and nonproductive ways are incorrect. Many people who experience mental illness overcome the problem and go on to lead productive and successful lives.

This is not to downplay the prevalence of mental illness or the seriousness of the symptoms. Druss, Marcus, Rosenheck, Olfson, Tanielan, and Pincus (2000) report that about 3 million Americans have an emotional condition that affects their ability to work or to seek educational opportunities. Approximately 1% of the population develops schizophrenia during their lifetime and more than 2 million Americans suffer from the illness in a given year. Although schizophrenia affects men and women with equal frequency, according to the National Institute of Mental Health (NIMH), the disorder often appears earlier in men than in women, usually in their late teens or early 20s in men and in their 20s to early 30s in women (NIMH, 1999). The NIMH (2001) estimates that over 2 million Americans experience the symptoms of bipolar disorder each year. Those symptoms include distorted views and thoughts, a lack of will to live, labile emotions that often seem out of control, and difficulties with cognition (Jamison, 1995).

A 2005 editorial in the *Economist* describes the state of mental health in America:

"Every generation," cautions Howard Goldman of the University of Maryland School of Medicine, "thinks it's more stressed out and souped up than the rest." True indeed. But more and more Americans are seeking help for mental problems, and many are doing so younger. One study, conducted among students at a large midwestern university, showed a dramatic increase in mental-health problems reported by college students: the number seeking help for depression doubled, while the number with suicidal tendencies tripled. Another study found that 5.5 million more Americans were taking prescription drugs for mental-health problems, or problems of substance abuse, than was the case only five years earlier. ("Stressed Out and Traumatized," 2005, p. 84)

About one in five Americans now suffers from a diagnosable mental disorder. The National Institute of Mental Health (2001) estimates that more than 13% of Americans—over 19 million people between the ages of 18 and 54—suffer from anxiety disorders, 9.5% from depressive disorders, and millions of others from conditions ranging from posttraumatic stress disorder (PTSD) to schizophrenia and bipolar disorder (Glicken, 2005b).

Markowitz (1998) reports that people with mental illness are "more likely to be unemployed, have less income, experience a diminished sense of self, and have fewer social supports" (p. 335). Part of the reason for this finding may be a function of the stigma attached to mental illness. "Mentally ill persons may expect and experience rejection in part because they think less of themselves, have limited social opportunities and resources, and because of the severity of their illness" (Markowitz, 1998, p. 343). Markowitz also notes that the impact of anticipated rejection on the mentally ill person is largely caused by "discriminatory experiences" in which the person observes an employer perceiving potential problems based solely on a diagnostic label and not on the person's actual behavior. This perception of rejection compounds the person's feelings of low self-worth and depression.

Writing about the prevalence of mental illness in America's universities, Butler (2005) notes that a survey done of the professional and graduate programs at the University of California in Berkeley found that 10% of the students were having serious emotional problems. A similar study at two law schools found that 63% of the students had higher levels of depression 2 years into their programs than they did when they started. The study's coauthor, Lawrence Krieger, says, "Students come to law school as quite highly motivated, idealistic, happy people, and then it crashes" (Butler, 2005, p. 47). Students' feelings of well-being and life satisfaction declined significantly over time, the study found, while nearly every negative emotion increased. According to Krieger, "Everything went in the wrong direction" (Butler, 2005, p. 47).

Furr, Westfield, McConnell, and Jenkins (2001) report that 53% of their sample of college students had experienced depression since beginning college, with 9% reporting that they had considered committing suicide since beginning college. MIT (Massachusetts Institute of Technology) has experienced the suicide of a student each year for the past 15 years. The University of California system "expects" an average of three suicides a year per campus. These figures do not take into account students who commit suicide off campus or drive while intoxicated and depressed and have single car fatalities.

Traditional Treatments of Mental Illness: A Research Review

It is clear that traditional treatments for mental illness have had questionable results. In a study of treatment attrition for problems related to mental health, Edlund, Wang, Berglund, Katz, Lin, and Kessler (2002) found an attrition rate of 10% by the 5th visit, 18% by the 10th visit, and 20% by the 25th visit. Factors influencing attrition included concerns about treatment effectiveness and discomfort with the mental health treatment process. Explaining these two client treatment concerns, Edlund and colleagues (2002) write:

> Results of our analyses of patients' attitudes about mental health care should raise at least two concerns. First, a large proportion of respondents believed that mental health treatments are not effective. Patients who held such a belief were significantly more likely to drop out of treatment. These findings suggest that clinicians should spend additional time and effort to educate their patients concerning the effectiveness of mental health treatments. In our recent study of mental health advocacy group members, we observed that receiving such education from providers was critically important in facilitating patients' acceptance of their treatments. Second, respondents who reported feeling uncomfortable in mental health care were substantially more likely to drop out than patients who reported being comfortable. A likely explanation for this finding is that expressing greater discomfort with mental health treatment is a marker of perceived stigma or other psychological barriers. (Edlund et al., 2002, p. 850)

Manfred-Gilham, Sales, and Koeske (2002) studied social and vocational barriers to participation in treatment for mentally ill patients as reasons for treatment attrition. The researchers concluded that the more realistically workers prepared clients for barriers they might encounter in the community, the more likely clients were to continue on with their treatment regimen. The authors write, "We have some evidence from Kazdin et al. (1997) that therapists' perceptions of barriers predicted client treatment continuation more strongly than did the client's own self-report" (p. 220). Manfred-Gilham and colleagues (2002) also note that there is a strong link between the strategies used by workers to prepare clients for barriers in their lives and the clients' ability to deal with those barriers.

Using a computerized literature search to determine the impact of psychosocial interventions with the mentally ill, Bustillo, Lauriello, Keith, and Samuel (2001) found that family therapy and assertive community treatment helped prevent psychotic relapses and rehospitalization. However, the authors report that these two treatments have no consistent impact on "pervasive" psychotic symptoms, social functioning, or the ability to obtain and sustain employment. For mentally ill people, social skills training may lead to improved social skills, but Bustillo and colleagues found no evidence that it prevented rehospitalization, relapse into psychotic behavior, worsening of psychopathology, or improved employment status. Employment programs that place and train mentally ill clients appear to help these clients obtain competitive employment. Some studies, according to the authors, show a decrease in delusions and hallucinations in mentally ill people as a result of cognitive behavioral therapy. Personal psychotherapy may, according to Bustillo and colleagues, also improve social functioning.

Evidence of Resilience in People Diagnosed as Mentally Ill

Chronicity as an Incorrect Notion

Carpenter (2002) suggests that mental health services have been developed with the belief that mental illness is a chronic disease requiring continual care and supervision. She notes that the fourth edition of the *Diagnostic and Statistical Manual of Mental Disorders* (*DSM–IV*; American Psychiatric Association, 1994), like earlier editions, indicates that schizophrenia will result in progressive deterioration and cautions readers that complete remission of symptoms is rare. But research evidence fails to support the notion of long-term chronicity in patients diagnosed with mental illness. For example, Carpenter (2002) reports that most people with a diagnosis of schizophrenia or another serious mental illness experience "either complete or significant remission of symptoms, and work, have relationships, and otherwise engage in a challenging and fulfilling life" (p. 89). In a study of over 500 adults diagnosed with schizophrenia, Huber, Gross, and Schuttler (1975) found that over one fifth of the sample experienced complete remission and over two fifths experienced significant remission of symptoms. In a 40-year follow-up study, Tsuang, Woolson, and Fleming (1979) found that 46% of those diagnosed with schizophrenia had no symptoms or had only nonincapacitating symptoms. The Vermont Longitudinal Study (Harding, Brooks, Ashikaga, Strauss, & Breier, 1986a, 1986b), a 20- to 25-year follow-up study of former state hospital patients, found that 72% of the people diagnosed with schizophrenia had only slight or no psychiatric symptoms. Despite these very optimistic findings, Carpenter (2002) writes,

> The premise of chronicity continues to be widely accepted in the mental health system, and dismal prognoses continue to be communicated to people with psychiatric disabilities (Kruger, 2000). These prognoses leave little room for a sense of hope on the part of those labeled with mental illness and, as such, may become a self-fulfilling prophecy (Jimenez, 1988). The consumer-survivor recovery movement has sought to restore that hope with an innovative perspective on the meaning and course of psychiatric disability (Kruger, 2000). (p. 89)

The Consumer-Survivor Recovery Movement

Carpenter (2002) defines the consumer-survivor recovery movement as one that assumes people with psychiatric disabilities can and will recover. Recovery is defined as a process of achieving self-management through increased responsibility for one's own recovery. This process is aided by the sense of hope provided by the professional, family, and support systems of the person with psychiatric disabilities. In further defining the movement, Carpenter (2002) says, "The consumer-survivor definition of the experience of psychiatric disability is as much about recovery from the societal reaction to the disability as it is about recovery from the disability itself" (p. 90). Anthony (1993) believes that recovery from mental illness is aided by what he calls "recovery triggers," one of which is sharing with patients, their families, and the community the research indicating that many people with psychiatric problems do, in reality, recover. Another trigger involves information about the availability of services and treatment options such as self-help groups and alternative treatment approaches. Using an assessment approach that focuses on client strengths also helps in recovery and is a strong antidote to the medical model that perceives the person with mental illness to be pathological and often ignores significant growth and change. The experience of Nobel Prize winner John Nash (Nasar, 1998), who had a gradual remission from many years of mental illness, is a reminder that people change with time and that remission of symptoms, if not outright cures of mental illness, are often possible.

Chinman, Weingarten, Stayner, and Davidson (2001) suggest that one way of improving treatment results and decreasing relapses is through the mutual support of mentally ill clients. According to the authors, mutual support groups reduce hospitalization rates, the amount of time spent in hospitals, symptoms, and days spent in the hospital. They also improve quality of life, self-esteem, and contribute to better community reintegration of clients with severe psychiatric disorders (Davidson, Chinman, Moos, Weingarten, Stayner, & Tebes, 1999; Kyrouz & Humphreys, 1996; Reidy, 1992). Mutual support groups provide acceptance, empathy, a feeling of belonging to a community, necessary information to help in the management of social and emotional problems, new ways of coping with problems, and examples of role models who are coping well. Chinman and colleagues (2001) report that "mutual support also operates through the 'helper-therapy' principle that suggests that by helping one another, participants increase their social status and self-esteem (Riessman, 1965, p. 220)."

Chinman and colleagues (2001) indicate that there is growing evidence that, in addition to mutual support groups, consumer-run services may prove to be very effective in helping clients cope with their mental illnesses. They write that studies found that

> consumer providers are sometimes better able to empathize, to access social services, to appreciate clients' strengths, to be tolerant and flexible, to be patient and persistent, to be aware of and respond to clients' desires, and to be able to create supportive environments which can foster recovery and the restoration of community life (Dixon, Krauss, & Lehman, 1994; Kaufman, 1995). Other studies found that a consumer-run case management service yielded equivalent outcomes to those generated by a conventional case management team (Felton, Stastny, Shern, Blanch, Donahue, Knight, & Brown, 1995; Solomon & Draine, 1995). (Chinman et al., 2001, p. 220)

Writing about the treatment of severe depression with psychotic overtones, O'Connor (2001) states that we often fail to recognize that what keeps people severely depressed is their view of their depression as ongoing, untreatable, and hopeless. These self-definitions reinforce the depression and keep it from improving. To help his patients cope, O'Connor (2001) provides them with aphorisms about depression that he believes serve as a way of changing long-held beliefs about their depression and about themselves. While cognitive in nature, the aphorisms O'Connor provides are also strengths based. These aphorisms are "assertions about the nature of depression and recovery from it, which help patients move toward taking an active role in questioning how the condition affects them" (p. 507).

Family and Spousal Resilience

Families of mentally ill people have often been vilified or seen as a negative in both the development and care of mentally ill clients, but Enns, Reddon, and McDonald (1999) found that family members of hospitalized psychiatric patients were very much like other families and saw themselves as having a high degree of resilience in coping with the multiple problems associated with a loved one's illness. Enns and colleagues (1999) believe that the family of the mentally ill person should be seen as a resource in the treatment of the mental illness, and they write that the findings of their study suggest that

> family members of patients with a mental illness rate themselves at least on par with the general population in many areas of support and family functioning. For example, participants reported comparable levels of satisfaction with internal family processes such as task accomplishment and role performance, when compared to the general population, and indicated they were more likely to acquire social support, and to utilize members of their immediate family for support. (p. 136)

In a study of resilience in spouses of hospitalized psychiatric patients, Mannion (1996) found that spouses experienced feelings of both burden and resilience, but that their resilience was greater than that of family members or friends. Spouses have a need to be appreciated and supported for their commitment to hospitalized spouses. Mannion (1996) writes,

> Overall, this survey supported the concept that the experience of having a spouse with mental illness can involve both burden and resilience. Personal resilience was more evident than either family or consumer resilience, a trend which could be explored in future studies. [The findings] suggest that spouses have a profound need to have their contributions and sacrifices, as well as those of their children, validated by others. Might the process of having one's contributions and sacrifices acknowledged and credited by others represent a method of transforming burden into a source of gratification, thereby enhancing resilience? (p. 136)

A Story of a Spontaneous Remission From Mental Illness

When I was a 23-year-old college student, I suddenly began having some very strange symptoms and I was diagnosed with Schizophrenia, Undifferentiated Type [*DSM-IV* Code No. 295.90; American Psychiatric Association 1994, p. 289]. I had no prior history of mental illness and no one in my immediate family had ever experienced mental illness. I was under a great deal of pressure preparing for the oral defense of my master's thesis in oceanography. How I did in my orals would determine whether I would be accepted into a prestigious doctoral program, which is the key to a successful career in my field. I remember walking home from the library and suddenly feeling confused. I didn't quite know where I was or how to get home. Everything seemed foreign to me like I was someplace I'd never been before. My friends told me later that I became really withdrawn and seemed unemotional and almost robot-like. It was pretty scary. One minute I was fine, and the next minute I felt so confused and afraid I could hardly move my body.

My symptoms got worse and my major professor walked with me to the university counseling center where the diagnosis of Schizophrenia, Undifferentiated Type was given by a psychiatrist on staff. I wasn't considered a danger to myself or to others and so I wasn't forced to go to a hospital for an evaluation, but I wasn't able to continue with my studies, and I was placed on antipsychotic medication and I was seen in a day program in the local community hospital. As my symptoms worsened, I was sent to a private inpatient hospital where I stayed for almost 4 months. Even though I was pretty heavily sedated, I can remember the time I spent in the hospital, and I know that my symptoms included mild hallucinations, social withdrawal and isolation, and some delusional thinking in which I talked about a presence that was about to kill [me].

After about 2 months, with my symptoms getting worse every day, I suddenly started to feel better. I was able to attend counseling sessions and contribute to the discussion. I realized that I interacted well with the other patients and the staff, and I can remember hoping that I could return to school. Six months after the symptoms came on so fast, I was able to return to school, with no other problems a year and a half after the onset [of the illness] (Glicken, 2005b, pp. 193–194).

An Interview With the Storyteller

Author: How would you explain the reason you got better so quickly from what is often thought to be a very long-term problem?

James: I don't think I was psychotic. One day I was walking home from school and I suddenly had the most ominous feeling that I was going to die. It had never happened to me before and it was frightening. I withdrew from people. Some days I couldn't talk. I was aware and conscious of everything taking place around me. I don't think I had any hallucinations, but maybe I did. It was more

---

This story first appeared in modified form in my book on evidence-based practice (Glicken, 2005b). I asked the client if I could interview him regarding his thoughts about spontaneous remission. The interview follows the story.

that I felt a presence nearby and that it would do me great harm. Maybe I was overstressed from school pressure, but I don't think so.

Author: The onset was that fast?

James: Yes. One minute I was fine and the next minute I was scared out of my wits. It took many months for the fear to go away and for me to be able to talk to anyone. When I began to get better, it seemed to happen all by itself. It was like a cloud lifted and suddenly I was well again.

Author: To what do you attribute the remarkable change you experienced?

James: I doubt if the antipsychotic medications helped, and I'm certain that therapy didn't help at all. There were some very kind professionals who were really nice to me and many wonderful patients who sat with me when I was really frightened. I don't think I was psychotic. I really don't think it will ever happen to me again, but if it does, I certainly have a better handle on what to do about it.

Author: Did you do any research on spontaneous remissions in situations like yours?

James: I did quite a bit, in fact, and I asked some mental health people as well. The major answer is that we still don't know enough about brain chemistry or the reasons for the sudden onset of symptoms of mental illness. I ended up thinking that my problem was a combination of life stressors and a biochemical condition that resulted in symptoms that appeared to be psychotic-like, but most likely were not.

Author: What do you think produced the symptoms?

James: I talked to maybe 8 to 10 patients who had symptoms like mine and then got better quickly. I wonder if this false psychosis was some opportunistic disease that attacks when the body is least capable of resisting. I was under extreme pressure to do well in my orals. My father is a professor at a famous university and he'd put me under a great deal of pressure to succeed. My schoolwork took away from any social life and I was using a combination of sleeping pills and Xanax to cope with anxiety, and a little meth to give me energy. Maybe this all contributed to my illness and maybe it didn't. I'm just not sure.

Author: Have there been any social repercussions from your illness?

James: The worst part of the problem has been the stigma. I don't know how many letters I had to write before I could return to school. I've already been turned down for a doctoral program that showed so much interest in me before my illness. I've had to lower my expectations for my doctoral degree. I'll be going to a good school but not a prestigious one.

Author: Might that be the better choice after what you've experienced?

James: Do you mean is it better because it'll be less stressful and I won't run the risk of getting crazy again?

Author: Sorry, that came off badly, but yes, that's what I meant.

James: That's one way of looking at it. But look, if I'd had mono or pneumonia or any physical illness that made me too sick to go back to school, would you say the same thing?

Author: No, I suppose not. I'd figure once you were well that you wouldn't have any more health problems.

James: That's the way I feel about what happened to me. It's this belief we have that once you're mentally ill, even if you aren't, you're always going to be seen as being mentally ill. And the absence of stress is going to make me less likely to backslide? I don't think so. I'm a healthy young guy with my future ahead of me, and this one incident, that I think was really a misdiagnosis to begin with, has changed the way people see me. I resent it.

Author: You think it was a misdiagnosis?

James: Absolutely. I went into the literature and guess what I found out? Some people have psychotic-like symptoms because of bad drug interactions. No one checked on my drug use, but in addition to Xanax and Ambien for sleeping, I was also taking methamphetamine. I was trying to have a high level of functioning and then to calm down when I needed sleep.

Author: Did you tell your doctors about the drugs you were taking?

James: Yes, I did. I've known people who get pretty paranoid on meth and that's what I think was happening. When they diagnosed me with a mental illness, I was shocked. I mean, we live in a drug culture and I thought the doctors would know about street drugs and what they do, but apparently they didn't. Or maybe they thought it was kinder to say that I was mentally ill instead of a drug user. I don't know. I *do* know that I'm a healthy, tough, successful man and I wasn't crazy and I won't be in the future.

Author: Did you continue taking Xanax, Ambien, and meth while you were in the day program and then the hospital?

James: I took all three drugs plus some antipsychotic meds that really made me very confused and lethargic. When I went to the hospital, rather than taking me off everything and letting me heal naturally, they put me on different antipsychotic drugs that made me feel even goofier. They also took me off Xanax, Ambien, and meth. After a while, I learned to tongue my meds from the other patients, and after a few weeks, when the drugs stopped affecting me, my symptoms started to go away. It took me a while to convince the staff that I was well, but that's what happened to me.

Author: So, to summarize, you took responsibility for your own treatment. Once you saw the negative impact of the drugs you were taking and felt that they might be responsible for your conditions, you got much better.

James: Absolutely. And from the other patients I met I think we all feel the same way. Give us more responsibility in our own treatment. Treat us like adults. Let us test out alternative treatments, and be aware that as a group, we know a lot more about what works and what doesn't than the staff.

Author: This is a book about resilience. Do you feel that you're a resilient person?

James: I do. I overcame a bad moment in my life. I'm optimistic about the future, and I've had long talks with my dad about the pressure he was putting on me. He's agreed to be more supportive. I'm living a much more thoughtful and less stressful life, and I feel great empathy for the people I met in the hospital. I'm a volunteer now, and it gives me a lot of joy to work with people who are going through what I went through. It hurts me to see them in such pain, and the positive view I have of life is a sign of optimism to them. I hope it tells them that they'll get better. They get so few of those messages that I feel like I'm a ray of sunshine, you know, a little corner of hope. It's the first time I've been able to see myself really engaged with people. For a scientist, it's a pretty great feeling.

A Story About Long-Term Emotional Problems

I suppose you could say that I've had emotional problems from an early point in my life. When I was 5, I began self-mutilating myself by cutting my arms. My parents were very upset, but they didn't send me for professional help. My father was a psychologist in a large medical center, and I think he was embarrassed about the whole thing and thought that my seeing someone would reflect badly on him. I think I was reacting to a family system where I felt left out. After the self-mutilating episodes, I was left out by my family even more, although my father loved me and I was his favorite. My mother seemed continually hostile toward me, and maybe she was jealous of the relationship I had with my dad. My two sisters just ignored me. After some tough times in early adolescence and some acting out on my part, I was sent to a boarding school. Getting away really helped, and I was able to get my bachelor's degree from an excellent private college and go on and complete a doctorate in English. My goal was to teach or become a writer.

My relationships with men have been troubled. I guess I find wounded men, and maybe I have such insecurity inside that I think that's all I'm worthy of. Or maybe I compare men to my successful and loving father and put too much pressure on them. In any event, it's been a constant sorrow for me. I had a serious car accident which led to problems on my job and two nervous breakdowns. Since then I've been in therapy and I'm on medication under the supervision of a psychiatrist. Therapy and the meds have been a lifesaver. I had injuries that required long surgeries and convalescences, and I've been unable to work at a job. I've been very wise with money and have made excellent decisions about houses which I've sold and make good money on. My sisters have also been very supportive and we now enjoy a wonderful relationship. Maybe the death of my parents allowed that to happen.

I've begun my lifelong desire to write and have had success at selling stories, and now I'm working on a romance novel. My agent is very optimistic about selling it. I'm surrounded by wonderful friends, although I wish there was a man in my life. It's one of those things that makes me sad sometimes, but I'm always optimistic. I've always had great animals in my life, and my current dog is just amazing and gives me lots of joy. He's very sensitive to my moods and knows when I need him to be close to me.

I know that I'm easily upset and I try and live my life in a way that produces the least amount of stress. I also consider myself spiritual and interested in gaining knowledge. I read and attend as many lectures on interesting subjects as I can. I live in a community where something wonderful goes on almost everyday which I try and attend.

I think I'm resilient in many ways, but I also know that I'm prone to being easily upset when things go badly. I could give you lots of psychiatric diagnostic terms for my condition, but the reality is that I function at a high level, I'm a good and honest person, I don't hurt other people, and while I think I'm wounded in many ways, I've come through bad times and held myself together. It's been many years since I had my nervous breakdowns, and I'm proud that I've kept myself going as well as I have given the added stress of medical problems and surgeries brought on by the car crash I was in (a semi-trailer swerved into my car lane, killing the man in car behind me and badly injuring me). I've been in severe pain a good deal since, but I've learned to manage it by biofeedback and exercise.

I've always loved reading, and I go to books and research articles about my condition whenever I'm feeling really down. You could say I've sort of become an expert about myself. I try and live a spiritual life and to give to others, but I confess that often I'm pretty self-centered and self-involved. Many of the men I've dated have told me that and I have no reason not to believe it's so. My friends hint about it too, but they also think I'm a kind and generous friend and all of them reach out to me when I'm feeling down. I do the same for them. I know that sometimes my thinking isn't very clear, and I feel confused about how to handle problems in my life that most people are able to deal with easily. I don't think I'm at all religious and I'm not certain that I believe in God. What kind of God would give me the kinds of problems I've had to deal with?

I just read what I wrote and I want to say another thing. My therapist has been an important person in my life. I think it's one thing to tough out life problems by yourself, which I think is what's meant by being resilient, and quite another to have a guide, coach, cheerleader, friend, and ally to help you do whatever you can't quite do for yourself. My therapist is wise, and patient, and supportive, even when I make mistakes. I think a lot of us who have gone through pretty serious emotional problems do well with support. If I could say anything to the professionals you're writing this book for it would be to remember that we may do bizarre things, but we're human beings with emotions and needs and ambitions. Using terms that imply craziness or abnormality are just smoke screens to say you can't help us because of your own biases or limitations. I've been helped, and I know the person who helped me is an exceptionally competent professional and also a wonderful human being. I hope that helps, Morley. There are other things about my story that I wanted to add, but you said to keep it short and not so personal that I could be identified, and I've tried to do that. Thanks, Morley. Writing about my experiences makes me feel even more that I'm a resilient person and that my parents would be proud of what I've accomplished and the person I am today.

Summary

This chapter discusses the prevalence of mental illness in America and the often stigmatizing effect the label of mental illness has on patients. This stigma frequently inhibits improvement in the condition and may affect employment opportunities and further social and financial possibilities in a person's life. Two positive findings suggest that resilience may be part of the reason some people improve from episodes of mental illness without relapse and that patients helping one another may provide a self-help treatment with a very positive impact. One story suggested the way in which mental illness may respond to treatment and the possibility of spontaneous remission of the symptoms. A second story included a self-appraisal, and readers may wish to mull over whether they agree with the story teller.

CHAPTER 7

How Resilient Children Cope With Abuse

Lambie (2005) reports that approximately 5 million cases of suspected child abuse were reported to Child Protective Services (CPS) nationally in 2000. By 2003, 2,400 children were found by CPS and the courts to be victims of abuse each day. Nationally, each week, CPS agencies receive more than 50,000 reports of suspected child abuse, but estimates indicate that for every child whose abuse is reported, there are five more children whose abuse goes unreported (Prevent Child Abuse America, 2003). According to Lambie (2005), over 18,000 children a year suffer permanent injuries as a result of child abuse.

Miller (1999, p. 32) indicates that the following are common symptoms of children who have been abused: high levels of anxiety and hypervigilance, causing the child's nervous system to constantly be on alert; irritability, denial, and intrusive thoughts that sometimes create panic attacks; nightmares with themes of violence that are similar to their abuse; impaired concentration and memory lapses; withdrawal and isolation; acting out; repetitive play; self-blame; belief in a foreshortened future, that is, where they will only live a short length of time; regression, periods of amnesia, and somatizing the trauma into physical illnesses that include headaches, dizziness, heart palpitations, breathing problems, and stomachaches.

Similar problems have been noted in adult survivors of child abuse, but additional common symptoms in adults include substance abuse; difficulty in maintaining intimate relationships; prostitution; severe psychosomatic disorders; abusive behavior; violent crime; depression; bipolar disorder; psychosis; anxiety and panic disorders; and a host of problems that suggest the inevitability of almost anyone who has been abused as a child suffering severe consequences.

In the classroom, abused children are 25% more likely to repeat a grade, and 75% of all high school dropouts have a history of abuse or neglect (Sechrist, 2000). Long-term harm caused by child abuse may include brain damage, developmental delay, learning disorders, problems forming relationships (interpersonal and social difficulties), aggressive behavior, depression, low academic achievement, substance abuse, teen pregnancy, sexual revictimization, and criminal behavior (Lambie, 2005). Lambie goes on to note,

> The more immediate effects include feeling helpless, hopeless, and ashamed. Victims may feel unworthy of having friends and fearful that their "family secret" will be revealed; therefore, they may isolate themselves and withdraw. Such students may have increasingly pessimistic feelings about themselves, leading to decreased self-worth, self-blame, guilt and shame, as well as negative feelings about their own bodies (Russell, 1999). In some cases, these destructive feelings about "self" can manifest in self-mutilation. Other abused students may develop perfectionist tendencies and focus on overachievement as a form of escapism by concentrating on areas that may provide them with some sense of control (e.g., school success) (Horton & Cruise, 2001). This type of perfectionism may be accompanied by anxiety and inflexibility. (p. 256)

Pollak (2002) found that abused children are highly sensitive to signs of anger in facial expressions. As a result, they tend to see maladaptive intentions in others when none may exist and may act on their misperceptions in a variety of incorrect ways: anger, withdrawal, fear, and flight.

As we know, however, many children who experience abuse are able to cope with it in admirable and even heroic ways and have made the adjustments necessary so that they demonstrate behavior that is well within normal limits. In a highly controversial article, Rind and Tromovitch (1997) suggest that the impact of child sexual abuse (CSA) may be much less than we think. They write,

> Our goal in the current study was to examine whether, in the population of persons with a history of CSA, this experience causes pervasive, intense psychological harm for both genders. Most previous literature reviews have favored this viewpoint. However, their conclusions have generally been based on clinical and legal samples, which are not representative of the general population. To address this viewpoint, we examined studies that used national probability samples, because these samples provide the best available estimate of population characteristics. Our review does not support the prevailing viewpoint. The self-reported effects data imply that only a small proportion of persons with CSA experiences are permanently harmed and that a substantially greater proportion of females than males perceive harm from these experiences. Results from psychological adjustment measures imply that, although CSA is related to poorer adjustment in the general population, the magnitude of this relation is small. Further, data on confounding variables imply that this small relation cannot safely be assumed to reflect causal effects of the CSA. (p. 253)

Most helping professionals believe that child abuse ultimately results in serious emotional problems in childhood and adulthood unless it is treated early in the abuse cycle. But there is still a great deal to learn about treating the various forms of child abuse. In a book review of *The Treatment of Child Abuse,* edited by Robert M. Reece (2000), Lukefahr (2001) concludes that there is still a lack of specific and effective treatments for the victims of child abuse. Kaplan, Pelcovitz, and Labruna (1999) report that the effectiveness of treatment for children who have been physically and sexually abused "has generally not been empirically evaluated. In a review of treatment research for physically abused children, Oates and Bross (1995) cite only 13 empirical studies between 1983 and 1992 meeting even minimal research standards" (p. 1218). Delson and Kokish (2002) indicate that while conventional wisdom suggests early treatment of child abuse, in their study, "self-esteem did not improve and actually deteriorated over time in many of the victims, regardless of treatment" (p. 1). The authors go on to indicate that "the best predictor of improvement was adequate maternal and family functioning. It may be that supportive social services and counseling for care givers would prove more effective than direct counseling for victims, at least in terms of short term adjustment" (p. 1).

Resilience in Abused Children

A consistent finding over the last 20 years of resilience research is that most children from highly dysfunctional families or very poor communities do well as adults. This finding applies to almost all populations of children found to be at risk for later life problems, including children who experience divorce; children who live with stepparents; children who have lost a sibling; children who have attention deficit disorder or suffer from developmental delays; and children who become delinquent or run away. More of these children make it than don't (Brown & Rhodes, 1991), including children who grew up in substance-abusing or mentally ill families (Werner, 1993), and those who have experienced multiple risks. Rutter (1990) found that half of all children who grow up in high-risk families in which severe traumas take place overcame adversity and achieved good emotional and social development.

Masten (2001) believes that resilience is part of the genetic makeup of humans and that it is the norm rather than the exception. "What began as a quest to understand the extraordinary has revealed the power of the ordinary. Resilience does not come from rare and special qualities, but from the everyday magic of ordinary, normative human resources in the minds, brains, and bodies of children, in their families and relationships, and in their communities" (Masten, 2001, p. 229).

If we are to accept these findings and those of Rind and Tromovitch (1997), and there are a number of professionals who are particularly concerned about the accuracy of the Rind and Tromovitch findings, then one possible reason is that some victims of abuse and other traumas do well because they are resilient (Masten, 2001). Anderson (1997) says that the recognition of resilience as an important factor in the mental health of traumatized children came from concerns that children at risk might develop adult pathologies. Anderson (1997) indicates that the term *resilient* originally referred to children who were thought to be "stress resistant" or "invulnerable" because they not only coped with adverse childhood traumas, but they also seemed to thrive in very dysfunctional and stressful situations (Kauffman, Grunebaum, Cohler, & Gamer, 1979).

If resilience plays such an important role in coping with abuse, what might be the coping skills developed by resilient children? Henry (1999) says there are five major reasons that help to explain resilience in children who have been abused: (1) Resilient children are loyal to their parents and try to understand the reasons for the abuse; (2) They normalize the abusive environment so that it feels as similar to the home environments of other children as possible; (3) They create a sense of the invisibility and control by leaving the home or hiding when their parents become abusive; (4) They value themselves even when being tormented by others; and (5) They have a vision of the future suggesting that the abuse will end at some point because they will leave the abusive environment and start a new life.

Resiliency research originally tried to discover the characteristics of at-risk children who coped well with stress (Werner, 1989). In a review of the factors associated with resilience to stressful life events, Tiet, Bird, and Davies (1998) found that higher IQ, quality of parenting, connection to other competent adults, an internal locus of control, and social skills have been identified as protective factors that allow children to cope with stressful events. The authors called protective factors in children associated with resilience "primary buffers" between the traumatic event and the child's response. In summarizing their work on resilient youth who have experienced serious life traumas that include maltreatment, Tiet and colleagues (1998) write,

> In conclusion, resilient youth tend to live in higher-functioning families and receive more guidance and supervision by their parents and other adults in the family. Other adults in the family may complement the parents in providing guidance and support to the youth and in enhancing youth adjustment. Higher educational aspiration may also provide high-risk youth with a sense of direction and hope. Although IQ had no impact in youth at low risk, youth at high risk who have a higher IQ may cope better and therefore avert the harmful effects of adverse life events. (p. 1198)

Other factors associated with resilience include the finding by Arend, Gove, and Sroufe (1979) that very curious children are more resilient. Radke-Yarrow and Brown (1993) associate resilience with children who have more positive self-perceptions. Egeland, Carlson, and Sroufe (1993) and Baldwin, Baldwin, Kasser, Zax, Sameroff, and Seifer (1993) found a relationship between resilience and assertiveness, independence, and a support network of neighbors, peers, family, and elders. In their 32-year longitudinal study, Werner and Smith (1982) found a strong relationship between problem-solving abilities, communication skills, and an internal locus of control in resilient children.

Over time, however, resiliency research has focused less on the attributes of resilient children and more on the processes of resilience. This new emphasis in the research suggests that rather than avoiding risk, resilient children take substantial risks to cope with stressors, leading to what Cohler (1987) calls "adaptation and competence." Henry (1999) points to a spiritual element of resilience and writes that "resilient children often acquire faith that their lives have meaning and that they have control over their own fates" (p. 522).

However, resilient children often respond inconsistently to stressful events, suggesting that another way of looking at resilience is to show the relationship between the specific traumatic event and the response. Luthar (1991) did this and found that while resilient children do well on many school-based outcomes, a large percentage of these children suffer from depression. Although depression was evident in many of the maltreated children studied, the children still did well on behaviorally oriented outcomes measures such as grades and school conduct (Luthar, 1991), leading Luthar to conclude that the difference between resilient and nonresilient children is only behavioral and that both groups suffer emotionally. According to Luthar (1993), one reason resilient children do well behaviorally is that they have more intellectual maturity than nonresilient children, which permits them to develop successful strategies to cope with their abuse and still do well in life. However, Garmezy (1983) found that the more intelligent children are, the more highly sensitive they are to their situations, and the more likely they are to experience stress, in comparison to less intelligent children experiencing the same situations. Both Garmezy and Luthar believe that resilient children do better in life but may still suffer many debilitating emotional problems as adults.

In her work with abused children, Anderson (1997) suggests the benefits of a positive perspective in assessing the behavior of children who have been sexually abused. She believes that the focus of work should be not on the damage done to the child but on the survival abilities of the child to cope with the abuse. What this suggests is that practitioners must look for themes of resilience in the "survival stories" of abused children and help those who have been abused to recognize the active role they played in surviving the abuse. Perhaps, as Anderson (1997) suggests, "the psychological scars will never disappear completely; however, focusing on the child's strengths and resiliency can help limit the power of sexual abuse over the child" (p. 597).

Henry (1999) believes that practitioners often miss an essential point with abused children: The way these children cope with the abuse is actually "the strength that enables them to survive in an unsafe environment" (p. 519). Henry concludes that the behaviors such children develop as they cope with abuse provide important pieces of information that can assist practitioners in helping the children. Rather than viewing coping behaviors as dysfunctional or pathological, Henry believes that we should try and understand these children's ways of dealing with extraordinarily traumatic experience and to be supportive of and positive with the children regarding their efforts. Workers who view the abuse as necessarily damaging will look for dysfunction and focus on what the children are doing wrong. From the children's point of view, they are doing the best they can and should receive support for their often heroic efforts. According to Henry (1999), the work we do with maltreated children should focus on solving problems rather than on finding fault with the children's adaptation to their maltreatment.

Anderson (1997) acknowledges that the professional literature often looks for an association between child maltreatment and emotional problems. She gives as an example the observation that many maltreated children use wishful thinking or daydreaming to emotionally distance themselves from the abuse. Rather than seeing such coping mechanisms as dysfunctional, Anderson suggests that we recognize the children's coping strategies as strengths and not as impediments or dysfunctions.

 Henry (1999) points out that children are willing to give parents many opportunities to correct their abusive behavior. In addition, through their actions, play, and approaches to problem solving, children provide many ideas about the way they survive cruel and abusive life events. In working with adults who care deeply about them, abused children find their feelings about the sorrow and distresses they've endured validated, and from that pain and the sorrow of their lives, they find meaning in their maltreatment, as well as joy and comfort in the way they have persevered, survived, and become stronger. In further stressing the use of a positive approach with abused children, Anderson (1997) writes,

> It is essential to formulate specific and clear guidelines for treatment that center on survival abilities because gathering this information helps children to take pride in their accomplishments. Rebuilding self-esteem and pride is extremely important for children who have been sexually abused because the trauma permeates their identity and may leave them lacking in feelings of self-worth. (p. 593)

A STORY OF A CHILD COPING WITH ABUSIVE PARENTS

 You talked to me two years ago when you were writing another book, but you never asked me to write anything about myself. I was 13 when you talked to me. I am 15 now. I still live with this great family since I left home, but I see my folks a lot and they're doing much better now. My dad has stopped drinking, but every once in a while he goes on a binge and then the case manager won't let me see him. My mom is still pretty mad about life and she can be—you know—sarcastic a lot. She thinks I caused them a lot of trouble because I wrote a story about what they were doing to me and it got them into trouble with the police and the welfare people. I feel sorry about that, but maybe I should tell my story like it happened in some kind of order. That's what my foster father says, and he's an English teacher and the father of my best friend.

 My parents drank a lot, and when they drank, they could be very mean. Maybe when I was 4 or 5, I knew when they were going to be mean and I'd try and hide or I'd go to a friend's house. My dad was an accountant then, and I think he was one of the smartest people I ever knew. But when he drinks, he gets really angry and mean. My granddad (his father) was the same way as my dad. He could be really nice, but when he drank, he was mean and he'd swear at me and sometimes he'd hit me. I never could figure it out. I thought drinking was supposed to make you happy or silly. I got to be good at knowing when my dad was drinking too much and I'd get out of the way as fast as I could. If

---

The case that forms the basis for the following story first appeared in Glicken (2004a). The current story is an updating of that case, is written by the child rather than by the author, and comes 2 years after the initial interview took place.

I didn't, I'd get hit or punched. I guess I was able to believe that he loved me even when he hurt me, because I could see how nice he was when he wasn't drinking. I figured if he'd just stop drinking, then he'd be the nice guy I sometimes saw.

My mom was different. She was always mean, even when she wasn't drinking. [I knew that] she was abused as a girl because she'd tell me the stories pretty often, and then she'd say how much better my life was and then she'd hit me, or pinch me, or put my hands in really hot water. I still have some scars from the things she did to me. The drinking just made her madder, and when she wasn't hitting me or calling me names like "stupid" and "dip shit" and stuff like that, she'd hit my dad and they'd have these bad fights.

A lot of the time when they were drinking and I knew I was going to get hit, I used to hide in the basement until they fell asleep. While I was down there, and maybe I started hiding from them when I was 4 or 5, I found these books with stories. I watched the TV programs that helped you learn about your letters, and I could even read some by then. There were hundreds of stories and I started to read them. I was pretty slow at first, but then when my reading got better, I could read pretty fast for a kid. Reading was wonderful. The stories made me forget all the fighting, and I could see a whole different world than the one I lived in at home. My friend's dad was an English teacher. When he found out I was reading, he gave me more books to read, and we'd talk about them. I think he knew about my parents from his son, and I think he was trying to make up for what was going on in my home. He was a very smart man and when we'd talk, I'd just want to read more stories. He asked me if I ever wrote things and I said no, that I never did. So he encouraged me to write and I began to write stories about my parents and the fighting and all. I guess they were pretty awful stories because after reading one (maybe I was about 11), he called the child welfare office and now I'm living with my friend and his mom and dad.

It's wonderful at their house. They're really good to me. I see my mom and dad a lot and they still love me in their own way. I know I won't be able to live with them, but they're my parents and I still love them. My dad has pretty much stopped drinking and lives by himself. Sometimes he still goes on binges, but I know he's trying. There's some chance that I might live with him, but the social worker said that we had to be sure that he'd stopped drinking for at least a year before we could consider that. But we do a lot together, and he's a very smart man, and he knows lots of interesting things. The last time I saw him he started to cry about how bad he was as a dad. I don't know, to me he always seemed like he was trying to be nice, but he had a lot of crazy stuff inside of him because of what his dad did to him. And being an alcoholic, from the stuff I've read, is a tough thing to change. At least that's what I think.

I never felt too close to my mom, and I still don't. But I've learned from her that if you blame other people for your problems, you never do anything to change them. She hasn't learned anything from my leaving the home. She thinks it's my fault and still believes that she was a great mom. She doesn't remember any hitting, or putting my hands in hot water, or any of the stuff she did to me. I guess I love her but I don't really like her much.

You asked me how I turned out so well. I don't know. I do really well in school. I like sports and I think I'm pretty popular, but I have my days when

I don't like myself much. My foster dad says I get the "blues" and he lets me listen to these old blues singers from the South, and boy, one of them, Robert Johnson, he must have had the blues really bad because he sounds like I feel sometimes. I think my dad was a good guy when he wasn't drinking. He helped me feel loved and I could forgive him for drinking. My granddad, even though he could be mean, the summers I spent with him and my grandma were pretty great. Books and reading saved my life. I learned that you could escape from the things that were happening at home and into another world. My friend's family helped too, and I spent a lot of time at their house even before I went to live with them.

I've never believed much in God. If there was a God, He wouldn't let stuff like I went through or what happened to my mom ever happen to little kids. I *do* believe in being a good person, though, and I try to help other people. I volunteer at the hospital on the ward that takes care of kids who've been abused so bad they have to be in the hospital to mend, and I go to a couple of groups for kids like me who have been abused. I tried counseling once, but the counselor wasn't very good and she kept insisting that I should be a lot sicker than I was and that, sooner or later, all the things that happened to me would end up hurting me, making me depressed, or a drunk or something. I think she sucked, and she was wrong. The groups I go to think just the opposite; that we're special because we took so much abuse and turned out so well. And I guess I'm proud that I turned out so well. Maybe the counselor was right and sometime, when I'm an adult, I'll be screwy, but I don't think so. What do you think?

Lessons to Be Learned From This Story

This remarkable young man had many reasons not to persevere, and yet he does and does so remarkably. In the following section, the lessons learned from this story are noted, along with some supportive information from resilience researchers.

1. Very early on, the storyteller learned to protect himself from his parents' abusive behavior while still feeling loyalty to his parents. This is what Tiet and colleagues (1998) call "protective factors" and what Henry (1999) sees as an example of how children can make themselves invisible to their abusers while still being loyal to them.

2. The storyteller sees the dysfunctional behavior of his parents in a rational way by noting the early harm done to both parents by their families, and he is forgiving. It has probably helped him to see that his grandfather's drinking affected his father and that his father grew up in abusive environment. Henry (1999) points out, and the storyteller's story confirms, that children are willing to give parents many opportunities to correct their abusive behavior.

3. Our storyteller knows it's unlikely that either of his parents has the emotional capacity to allow him to live with one of them, but he sees them often and has begun to have a good relationship with his father. He is endlessly optimistic while maintaining a realistic view of his family. He hopes for a great deal, but expects little.

4. He does well in school and has goals for himself that provide a positive view of his abilities and the way they might be used in the future. These coping skills and the rational way he views his family may exist because of his significant intellectual and emotional intelligence.

5. He has a negative view of the counseling he received, but a positive view of the support groups he has attended. This is often the case because support groups focus on positive behavior, while treatment sometimes focuses on psychopathology.

6. He had the good fortune, or the wisdom, to choose an exceptional foster family to live with. If he chose them, it shows a significant ability, especially in someone so young, to recognize a nurturing and positive environment.

7. His early discovery of reading gave him a healthy escape from his maltreatment. While some might argue that losing himself in reading might have produced a very introverted individual, this doesn't seem to be the case at all. The positive response to his reading from the man who became his foster father may be partly responsible for this.

8. He recognizes that he has bad days. His foster father has helped him see that many other people suffer from the "blues." In listening to someone who has suffered from the blues sing so powerfully about his feelings, he has found a model of how one can feel down, but hopeful, and even use sadness for extraordinary creative purposes. He certainly doesn't romanticize depression but, rather, sees it as a possible result of his maltreatment.

9. He recognizes his anger at his mother and tries to interact with her, but he believes that she hasn't changed. This grounded understanding of his mother helps him to deal with her without letting her behavior affect him too badly. One might suggest, however, that as he begins to date and develop intimate relationships, a negative view of the parent of the opposite sex might result in difficulties and could point to the need for help.

10. He doesn't believe in God, but he does helpful things for others and lives a caring life. Ambivalence about God isn't terribly difficult to understand in a child who has been badly abused. The more important issue is his active role in helping others and living a socially responsible life. Some would suggest that his behavior indicates the existence of strong spiritual feelings and beliefs.

A STORY OF A RESILIENT CHILD COPING WITH ADULTHOOD

I'm 33 now, two years older than when you interviewed me for another book. You might recall that my mother sexually abused me when I was a child. It's certainly had a negative effect on me, and while I was a very good student and went on to complete a doctorate, I suffered from ongoing depression, confusion, and a fear of intimacy.

The case presented here first appeared in Glicken (2004a). The current story is an updating of that case written by the subject rather than by me and comes 2 years after the initial interview took place.

There were two major issues I was dealing with when we spoke last. One was that I was going through tenure and didn't think I'd get it because I was confused about how to handle university politics. The other was that I was beginning a relationship with a lady I loved and I didn't think I could be sexual with her. I'm happy to say that I've resolved both problems. I not only got tenure and a promotion, but there's talk about me becoming departmental chair. I found out that most people in the department think that I'm fair-minded and understanding, and they trust me. I never knew that and it comes as a surprise, but a nice one. As for my relationship, we're engaged, and with the help of some great therapy, we're doing fine with sex. Even great.

When I was a kid, I learned to put what was happening to me aside and to try not to think it mattered. I knew my mother was probably mentally ill and that my father wouldn't help. He was glad that she was spending time with me instead of him. So I got on with my life and I tried to make my home life a forgettable nightmare. I left home as soon as I could, got some therapy, and went on and finished my education. I'm proud of my achievements, and I know there's something special about me that's allowed me to deal with a pretty sick experience.

I think I would have been a lot better if I'd had therapy when I was a kid and if someone had taken me from my home and put me in a good foster home. I had no relationship with my father, and my mother was either in the hospital or molesting me. I coped by excelling at school and by focusing on my dream to be a teacher. I spent as much time as I could away from home and at school, and joined every club and organization in school I could find just to stay away from home. When my mother started molesting me, I had this fantasy that it was something she did out of a great love for me. It made me feel superior to my father—real Oedipal stuff I suppose. But as I grew older, I started hating her. Maybe the molestation started [when I was] 4 or 5 and ended with her permanent hospitalization for mental illness when I was 14. I never saw her again. I lived with my dad for a while, and then I went to live with my mother's sister and her husband. They were kind enough, but they treated me as if I had a disease they didn't want to get. I think at some level they knew what my mother had been doing to me, [and] felt guilty enough to let me live with them through high school, but didn't want to get too close because they thought I was partly responsible for my mom's behavior.

Who did I hate the most? I hated my father for not stopping the abuse and for not protecting me. I hated my mother too, but my father knew what was happening and he did nothing. As I found out in therapy, that's not very unusual. I hated them both, but I didn't feel the need to punish them, and I used what I could at home to keep me going. I read and loved films and plays and ballet. I often wondered if that meant I was gay, but the thought of sex with a man was even more disgusting than [the thought of] sex with a woman, so I figured I wasn't gay. I dated but I was never intimate. Well, once. I got really drunk in college and had sex with this girl I knew. I felt nothing. I felt numb and detached. I thought about a school assignment all the time we were having sex just so it wouldn't make me sick.

As I achieved as an academic, I also began to experience intense feelings of loneliness and a desire to be close to someone, excluding having sex. Everybody thought I was this swinging single guy because I dated so much, [but it was] lots of first dates. What they didn't know is that I didn't go out a second time because I was afraid that it would end in sex.

[Two years ago] I had begun seeing someone and it was pretty wonderful. I told her I didn't believe in sex before marriage and, bright woman that she is, she said I was full of, well, full of it. She wanted to know what gave. We were way beyond the point where we would normally have been sexual, and she loved me but was confused about why weren't being physical. So one night I told her and a torrent of emotion came out of me and I cried and figured she'd leave, but she didn't. She said that what we had together was much too good to let go and that we should go to a therapist and get it worked out.

I was pretty skeptical at first. I've had my therapy experiences and they're fine if you talk about superficial things, but I was doubtful that anyone could help us with a sexual problem so overwhelming that I could hardly think about sex without getting physically ill. I won't bore you with the details, but the therapist did a lot of what he called "sensate focusing" where we'd be together naked but not do anything sexual. My fiancée is a very beautiful woman and it didn't take long for nature to take its course. We began to make love and it was sublime, it really was. And it still is and it's getting better. I'm going to be a father in 7 months, so we're speeding up the wedding date. I'm not inviting my parents. Maybe that's childish of me, but they hurt me pretty badly when I was a kid and I like the idea of having them out of my life. My fiancée says I'm being vindictive, and maybe I am, but hating someone can be a very liberating emotion. The Italians have a saying that having one person to hate is better than having a lot of friends. Maybe not, but right now and until God let's me stop hating so much, I'm happy and I've come a long way in my life. I've always trusted that God would get me out of the mess I was in and, thankfully, He has.

What do I think helped me cope with my childhood? I think being able to block out the bad things that were happening and focus on the good. Having done well in school and being well liked by my peers helped a lot. I've read about how children who are being abused try and become invisible. By being away from home much of the time, I think I tried to do exactly that. I also hated my parents and, I'm sorry, but hate can be a powerful force for getting you to change your life. It made me want to get as far away from them as I could and to be successful so I'd never ever have to rely on anyone again. I had a couple of friends in school who were being physically abused (I was too ashamed to tell them about my abuse), and it helped me [to] see what wonderful people they were. We've stayed good friends and they're doing well. They saved me along with some teachers who took an interest in me. I don't think we should ever forget how important teachers are in the lives of troubled kids. Maybe I was also blessed with intelligence and the ability to see things clearly. I believed in God and knew He'd protect me from harm. I went to a lot of different churches, but I've become a Catholic and I feel very happy about it. My fiancée is Catholic. We get joy out of practicing our religion. I'm going to be a father and I pray to God I'll be a better father than mine was and that I'll listen, be supportive, and love my child with all the pent-up love I've been saving for just this very time in my life.

LESSONS TO BE LEARNED FROM THIS STORY

Why didn't our storyteller seek help to end the molestation when he was a child? It's a question people often ask when children are silent about being sexually abused. Anderson (1997) provides an excellent answer:

> Somehow as children they not only endure the sexual abuse but find ways to go on with their lives. They have the burden of not revealing that anything has happened to them (Maltz and Holman, 1987). This prevents them from seeking assistance, and they are left to develop strategies for surviving the trauma on their own. Their capacity for self-repair takes tremendous energy, preventing them from accomplishing important developmental tasks. Because their survival abilities are overshadowed by the trauma, these strengths may be overlooked during treatment if the practitioner limits the definition of resiliency to the exhibition of competency. (p. 595)

The depression and sexual and intimacy concerns we might have expected from his history did, in fact, develop. Might therapy as a child have helped lessen his adult problems? Not if the therapist focused on what was wrong with him, according to Anderson (1997), who writes, "A pathology focus encourages practitioners to perceive clients as having some disorder or deficit that creates negative expectations about their potential to address the stressors in their lives" (p. 597). Instead, Anderson suggests that by building "on the positive aspects of the self that helped the child survive trauma, we open up creative ways to work with children who have been sexually abused" (p. 597). Here are the lessons one might learn from the storyteller's version of his resilience to sexual molestation by his mother:

1. The storyteller made himself invisible and stayed away from home as much as possible. He had dreams about the future, which supports Henry's (1999) findings that resilient children have a future orientation. He knew that he had some problems as a result of his abuse and sought help, although he describes much of it as being superficial. Keep in mind that therapy is only as "in depth" as the client wants it to be, so we can't know for certain if the superficiality of the therapy was because he chose not to self-disclose completely or because the therapists weren't skilled enough to help him.

2. Even as a child he sought out people who would be supportive. This is exemplified by the friends he made with other abused children and by his peer relationships. He carried his ability to make friends into his professional life, and it brought him success in his academic job and, through a relationship with his supportive and understanding fiancée, brought him intimacy. Together, he and his fiancée have worked to resolve his concerns about sexuality. Finding the right person to love isn't necessarily something that happens, but that it happened to him shows that he is capable of excellent judgment when dealing with others.

3. He has a caring and mature relationship with God. Unlike the former storyteller, he doesn't blame God for his situation and is thankful that his religious beliefs helped him cope as well as he has.

4.   He says he hates his parents. One would like to think that resilient people don't feel hate for their abusers, but his hate is grounded in the sense that having left his former life, it no longer exists. In a sense, this is the ultimate example of becoming invisible. Perhaps he will make amends with his parents once he becomes a parent, but it might not happen (and it often doesn't). We shouldn't frame this as pathology but, rather, as a coping mechanism. We should understand and accept it as his way of dealing with an untenable situation. Anderson (1997) points out that the professional literature often fails to differentiate behavior used to cope from dysfunctional behavior. Hatred of parents, while certainly not an emotional response we would like to see in our clients, clearly helps the storyteller now and should be seen in the context of coping rather than dysfunction.

5.   He has days when he's depressed and, like many resilient people, he may respond inconsistently to stressful events. Even though he has depression and self-doubts, like the children Luthar (1991) identifies as resilient, he still performs well at work and educationally. It's important to remember that many resilient people achieve in life but never quite master happiness or self-fulfillment. This makes them no less resilient and, ultimately, it just reinforces their humanity.

Factors Predicting Resilience in Abused Children

Mandleco and Peery (2000) have organized the internal and external factors supported by the research literature to affect resilience in children (p. 101). The authors note that internal factors include biological and psychological factors, including cognitive abilities, personality traits, the ability to relate to others, health, and genetic factors. Their list of external factors includes family life, parenting, community resources, and factors outside the person that help people acquire resilience. The sections that follow use the notion of internal and external factors influencing resilience to summarize the attributes we associate with resilient children.

Biological Factors

Resilient children are often healthy, have few childhood illnesses, have higher energy than the average child, and frequently have physical strength, good coordination, and endurance. Family histories of resilient children note very limited occurrences of hereditary or chronic illness. An infant with an easygoing temperament may become a child who is predisposed to develop resilience. Once developed, such a temperament is a positive factor in mediating stress. Males are more vulnerable to risk of physical and emotional problems during and after infancy than females and suffer more chronic problems than females throughout the life cycle.

Psychological Factors

Cognitive capacity includes intelligence and the way people solve problems, or what has been referred to as "emotional intelligence." Resilient children score higher on educational achievement and scholastic aptitude tests and have better reading, communication, and reasoning skills than nonresilient at-risk children. Emotional intelligence includes introspection and impulse control. As Mandleco and Peery (2000) suggest, "These children carefully think about and phrase their answers before responding, instead of immediately replying" (p. 102).

Coping ability is a process rather than an attribute, and it includes positive responses to frustration, challenge, and stressors and may include "curiosity, perseverance, seeking comfort from another person, or protesting, and perhaps is the best external manifestation of *resilience*" (Mandleco & Peery, 2000, p. 103).

Personality characteristics consistently associated with resilient children include positive descriptions of self and others. Such attributes as good self-esteem, self-awareness, self-understanding, an internal locus of control, optimism, motivation, and curiosity have been associated with resilient children. Many resilient children use religion and spirituality to maintain a positive approach to life since faith provides a sense of coherence. Curiosity is another internal characteristic of resilient children. Radke-Yarrow and Brown (1993) report that resilient children living in a number of high-risk situations often found that having considerable information about their situation increased their understanding of stress-producing situations and events. Resilient children also appear to be more empathic, sensitive to others, well liked by peers, respectful, and to have a positive response to authority and adults.

Factors Within the Family

We may not be able to describe the homes of abused children as organized and structured home environments, but such environments seem to be related to resilience. By extension, parental practices that are consistent and equitable are also associated with resilience. Brooks (1994) indicates that parents of resilient children provide nurturing, confidence-building, and emotionally positive relationships with their children. Resilient children often have a strong relationship with at least one family member, who acts as a stable role model. This family member is often identified by resilient children as their mother. Relationships with siblings that are characterized by mutual warmth and protectiveness are especially helpful to at-risk children.

Factors Outside of the Family

Supportive peers and adults outside of the family may provide at-risk children with friendship and direction and help these children to view the future in a positive way. Supportive adults may include teachers, family friends, religious leaders, and therapists. Schools, churches, synagogues, youth organizations, and after-school programs are important for at-risk children and adolescents. Schools may provide caring adults and an environment where abused children can succeed. The relationship between at-risk children's family life and rich outside life may result in resilient children who respond positively to their communities and are caring and involved citizens.

In determining which characteristics of resilient people are most significant, Mandleco and Peery (2000) caution that the influence of a specific component may "vary, interact differently and operate directly or indirectly over time in a particular child's situation. However, little empirical evidence suggests a significant percentage of the variance in predicting *resilience* can be accounted for by any one variable alone" (p. 110).

Summary

This chapter discusses resilience in abused children, noting that even children who do well on many behaviorally oriented measures sometimes suffer negative emotional consequences of having been abused, including depression and low self-esteem. The attributes of resilient children were presented and two cases were discussed showing resilience in an adolescent victim of physical abuse and an adult victim of child sexual abuse by his mother. Lessons to be learned were noted.

CHAPTER 8

How Resilient People Cope With Life-Threatening Illness, Disabilities, and Bereavement

This chapter discusses resilience in people who have life-threatening illnesses or who have experienced the painful death of a loved one. A number of authors have noted that serious illness and bereavement bring with them a desire to resolve important life issues. Kubler-Ross (1969/1997) believes that coping with life-threatening and terminal illness often leads to life-changing growth that focuses on the meaning of life. Frankl (1978) writes, "Even facing an ineluctable fate, e.g., an incurable disease, there is still granted to man a chance to fulfill even the deepest possible meaning. What matters, then, is . . . the stand he takes in his predicament . . . the attitude we choose in suffering" (p. 24). Many patients with serious and terminal illnesses "find that the beliefs and values they have lived by no longer seem valid or do not sustain them. These are the ingredients of a spiritual crisis, the stuff of spiritual suffering" (Hardwig, 2000, p. 29).

As I will point out with the stories presented in this chapter, resilient people have entirely unique ways of coping with life-threatening illness. The story presented in the section on coping with serious illness is an example of a woman with breast cancer explaining how she has coped with her illness.

Coping With Serious Illness

Hardwig (2000) believes that the medical care system often makes important treatment decisions without truly consulting the terminally ill patients. The use of pain-killing drugs often limits the dying patient's ability to think clearly and to effec-tively resolve important life issues. Because family members may find it difficult to let loved ones die naturally, they may ignore the patient's wishes and may utilize intru-sive life supports and treatments that interfere with the patient's ability to find closure on long-standing family issues. The lack of closure often affects the family's ability to cope with the patient's death and may complicate and prolong bereavement.

Caffrey (2000) believes that the emphasis on the reduction of anxiety and depression in dying patients through overmedication (palliative care) often dimin-ishes resilience and limits the patient's ability to finish unfinished business. Blundo (2001) found that encouraging collaboration between terminally ill patients and the medical staff resulted in "patients reordering their priorities, spending more time with family, and experiencing personal growth through the very fact of having had to cope with their traumatic loss or illness" (p. 486). In a similar, but tragic, finding, Richman (2000) reports that patients with nonempathic physicians "were more likely to consider euthanasia or doctor-assisted suicide" (p. 485).

In summarizing successful coping strategies used by seriously and/or terminally ill patients, Livneh (2000) suggests the following strategies:

1. Problem-Focused/Solving Coping and Information Seeking: These strategies refer to resolution of the stress and anxiety of illness through information gathering, focused planning, and direct action taking. These approaches have had positive effects on global mental health (Chen, David, Thompson, Smith, Lea, & Fahy, 1996), have lead to decreased levels of depression and anxiety (Mishel & Sorenson, 1993), and have increased vigor (Mishel & Sorenson, 1993).

2. Fighting Spirit and Confrontation: These strategies are described as accept-ing a serious and perhaps life-threatening diagnosis while optimistically challenging, tackling, confronting, and recovering from the illness and have been linked to longer survival among people diagnosed with cancer (Greer, 1991) and to decreased scores on anxiety and depression (Burgess, Morris, & Pettingale, 1988) and to decreased emotional or psychological distress (Classen, Koopman, Angell, & Spiegel, 1996).

3. Focusing on Positives: This group of coping strategies (which includes positive restrcuturing and positive reframing) has been associated with psy-chological well-being (Ell, Mantell, Hamovitch, & Nishimoto, 1989), lower emotional distress (Carver, Pozo, Harris, Noriega, Scheier, & Robinson, 1993), and increased vigor (Schnoll, Mackinnon, Stolbach, & Lorman, 1995).

4. Self-Restraint: This strategy refers to personal control to cope with the stresses of a serious or terminal disease and is a predictor of lower emotional distress (Morris, 1986) but may also lead to a reduction of quality-of-life among sur-vivors of such illnesses as cancer (Wagner, Armstrong, & Laughlin, 1995).

5. Seeking Social Support: Seeking support and assitance from others has been linked to decreased emotional/psychological distress (Stanton & Snider,

1993), better psychosocial adaptation (Heim, Valach, & Schaffner, 1997), and a greater perceptions of well-being (Filipp, Klauer, Freudenberg, & Ferring, 1990).

6. Expressing Feelings or Venting: While the evidence is mixed, two studies show decreased depression (Chen et al., 1996) and better emotional control (Classen et al., 1996) when venting of feelings takes place. The negative aspect of this coping strategy is that angry patients sometimes allienate loved ones and the professional staff, which may lead to increased feelings of depression and loss of social supports [for] patients.

7. Using Humor: Carver and colleagues (1993) found that the use of humor resulted in decreased emotional distress among people with cancer.

8. Finding Increased Life Meaning: Many writers discuss the potential for increased meaning of life as a result of serious or terminal illnesses. McClain, Rosenfeld, and Breitbart (2003) found that high levels of spirituality in dying patients led to hopefulness that resulted in a more cooperative relationship with the treatment team, improved resolution of long standing emotional problems, and the desire to live longer. Finn (1999) believes that spirituality leads to "an unfolding consciousness about the meaning of human existence. Life crises influence this unfolding by stimulating questions about the meaning of existence" (p. 228). Balk (1999) suggests that three issues must be present for a life crisis to result in spiritual changes: "The situation must create a psychological imbalance or disequilibrium that resists readily being stabilized; there must be time for reflection; and the person's life must forever afterwards be colored by the crisis" (p. 485). Kubler-Ross (1969/1997) believes that terminal illness often leads to life-changing growth and new and more complex behaviors that focus on meaning-of-life issues, while Greenstein and Breitbart (2000) write, "Existentialist thinkers, such as Frankl, view suffering as a potential springboard, both for having a need for meaning and for finding it" (p. 486).

A STORY OF A RESILIENT WOMAN COPING WITH BREAST CANCER

I am so lucky! I am the one who found my cancer.

I found it one spring evening, while nursing my son. A perfectly round lump, the size of a small marble, smooth and hard and anchored deep within.

I went to two different doctors and consulted a surgeon. I had a mammogram, and an ultrasound. Each time, I was pronounced "healthy." [I was told,] "It's just a cyst, nothing to worry about."

I am so lucky. It didn't go away. I insisted on its removal. After my biopsy, the surgeon assured my husband, "It's nothing. Looks like a cyst."

I am so lucky. The lab report was conclusive.

I had cancer.

I am so lucky to learn, early on, not to rely on "experts" to divine my body and its intelligence.

I am so lucky to have rediscovered my own voice, whose insistence and volume saved my life.

I am so lucky to learn that "they," the outside voices, could not save me or even help very much. In this disavowal, I found the power to engage life and death, loss and gain, with an expanded range of freedom and fascination. They said, "How sad she has to lose a breast, a terrible sacrifice she has to make to live."

I observed, "What a relief it is to lose a body part and yet still feel completely whole. I understand now, I am not a body, but something more."

They said, "She's going to lose her active lifestyle, her professional tenure."

I observed, "What a privilege it is to stare out the window, for hours, at trees dancing in an autumn storm. See how they embrace their destruction with grace and guile, knowing spring waits just beyond its bluster."

They said, "She's bald, one-breasted, she can't think, she can't even care for her children. How tragic."

I observed, "Years of striving to obtain worldly power, to maintain appearances, and to craft an identity, never even got me in the neighborhood of "happy." I found it lying alone in a bathtub, bald, maimed, and brain-dead. It was a feeling of being held and loved beyond measure. Because I had nothing to give the world, I could at last hold it and something else beside."

They said, "Thank God it isn't me!" I giggled and thought, "Thank God it is me! I am so lucky."

FURTHER THOUGHTS OF THE STORYTELLER

I think what I'm trying to illustrate in my "story" is that when confronted with a crisis you have a choice: experience it consciously or unconsciously. The conscious experience requires you to suspend others' ideas about what is happening to you and for you to own it for yourself. You discover, unwrap, and judge it; it is your gift to open.

The conscious experience requires you to forgo opacity in any form (drugs, alcohol, anger, cynicism, judgment, denial, etc.), and to stand naked in the flame of your suffering until its secrets are revealed. The conscious experience contains within it a belief that something that is you and not you has brought forth this experience to you for a purpose. The conscious experience requires faith, patience, and a burning desire to be intimate with God and yourself.

LESSONS TO BE LEARNED FROM THIS STORY

I met this remarkable young woman at a study group on the biblical figure Job. I was taking the course because I believe that it's a story about resilience, and I hoped it would help give me another perspective for this book. The group leader kept mentioning this woman's traumatic experience and, after class, I asked her about it. This very moving story was the result of our conversations outside of class and her willingness to share her experiences for this book. I have since had the unfortunate experience of having several good friends develop breast cancer. Instead of saying the obvious, which never conveys what you really think and the pain you know your friend must be in, I gave both friends this story. They told me later that they were very touched, and they both said that it, more than anything anyone had said to them, helped them cope with their cancer. My friends are doing very well, I'm happy to say.

1. The storyteller has taken control of her life. She has confidence in her own judgment, even when it differs from that of experts.

2. The storyteller finds sublime meaning in her cancer. How significant that she finds the cancer as she's nursing her child and concludes that she has gained more from the experience than she has lost.

3. A great deal of the meaning I get from this story is the need to trust your instincts and to retain a positive skepticism regarding professional opinions. That is to say that resilient people don't deny what a professional might say about their health, but they also trust their own knowledge about their bodies and compare it wisely to what medical professionals tell them.

4. It seems to me that having to cope with a life-threatening illness has allowed the storyteller to go to a much more existentially meaningful place in her life. The experience has made her more introspective and much more aware of fundamental questions pertaining to her life. She no longer finds superficialities such as outer beauty as important as inner strength and inner peace.

5. While most people would think of cancer as intrusive and even repugnant, she thinks of her cancer as uniquely hers. This sense of uniqueness helps her develop a positive approach to its containment and treatment. She feels that she is a partner with her body in the resolution of the problem and that what she says about her cancer to herself will help her get, and stay, well.

6. She thinks the cancer has brought her closer to herself and to others. It's done her a favor, perhaps, in prioritizing what is most important to her at a time in her life when the demands of child rearing, marriage, and career seem to have left her feeling estranged from herself and life's purpose. The illness has given her a relationship with herself and with life that she'd never had before. For many less resilient cancer victims, the illness may have just the opposite effect, serving to confuse and derail hopes and aspirations and resulting in confusion rather than clarity about life's meaning.

COPING WITH SERIOUS ILLNESS: ANOTHER VIEW

Two weeks after my tenth birthday, on the joyous occasion of St. Patrick's Day, I was diagnosed with diabetes. Back then, the average life span of those with Type I Diabetes was 27 years. If anyone had informed me at the time that I would only live 17 more years, things might have turned out differently. But no one told me that. The message from that very first day was this: You are strong, you will handle this, and you will survive. And I have.

The nurses who helped me learn the ropes of diabetes gave me the power to control my own diabetes. They gave me blood sugar diaries, they taught me how to give my own shots, and they showed me how to use a sliding scale for insulin shots. Most of all, they said, "Do not let diabetes define you."

The following discussion of coping with a serious illness was written by my daughter, Amy Glicken (2002, p. A15), and describes her way of coping with childhood onset diabetes.

People living with chronic illnesses are reminded every day of their differentness from those who are healthy. They are reminded in small ways: the newspaper headline that touts a new cure, being asked by security to remove your pager (which is actually an insulin pump), a low blood sugar reaction after yoga class. So, we exert our power over the small things. We say, "I have diabetes," rather than, "I am a diabetic," lest we become little more than a label. We say the words out loud when other people won't. We proudly display our medication on our nightstand. We educate the mother who is worried about her child developing diabetes simply because he eats too many carbohydrates. We take pride in knowing our blood sugar count, or our chances of survival when other people walk through the world ignorant of their mortality.

With new technologies like blood sugar monitors, human insulin, and continuous insulin pumps, having diabetes is no longer a death sentence. Having diabetes is, rather, an impetus to stay healthy. An impetus to not let it beat us. An impetus to make our short time here on Earth meaningful.

After having diabetes for fourteen years, it has become more than a chronic disease for me, more than a steady companion; diabetes is very much a part of who I am. Diabetes is not a burden, nor is it a crutch. It is just a disease that I, and millions of others, live with every moment of every day. When we face the fact of surviving with diabetes, as many have to face the fact of surviving with cancer, or HIV, or heart disease, we find strength in our uniqueness; we find strength in our ability to share our knowledge with others; we find strength in our ability to control our illness rather than letting it control us. I live with diabetes as though it were my troubled child—a lot of work and occasionally painful, but in the end, oddly beautiful and uniquely mine.

Coping With Bereavement

According to Balk (1999), bereavement is the loss of a significant person in one's life that can result in long-lasting physical and emotional problems, including fear and anger, sleep disturbances, substance abuse, cognitive difficulties, and uncharacteristic risk taking that may significantly affect relationships with others. Jacobs and Prigerson (2000) warn that bereavement sometimes develops into a complicated or prolonged grief lasting more than a year. The symptoms of complicated grief include intrusive thoughts about the deceased, numbness, disbelief that a loved one has passed away, feeling confused, and a diminished sense of security. Prolonged grief may be unresponsive to interpersonal therapy or to the use of antidepressants.

Stroebe (2001) points out a number of problems with the grief work usually done to treat prolonged bereavement. She suggests that there is limited empirical evidence that resolving grief through therapy is more effective than resolving it naturally, as well as that resolving prolonged bereavement is complicated by culture, religion, gender, and socioeconomic class. "There is no convincing evidence that other cultural prescriptions are less conducive to adaptation than those of our own" (Stroebe, 2001, p. 854). Stroebe is also concerned that traditional treatment of grief seems primarily concerned with prolonged grief and lacks the precise definitions useful for research studies, so that the researcher must ask, "What is being worked through? In what way?" (p. 855).

In trying to resolve the problem of clearly defining grief and grief work, Stroebe (2001) says the following questions need to be answered: (1) What are the coping skills that allow some people to cope with loss while others don't? (2) What are the differences between normal and prolonged grief? (3) What are the primary reasons that some people resolve their grief in natural ways while others experience complicated and prolonged bereavements? (4) Is an existential approach to grief work where meaning-of-life issues are dealt with any more effective than focusing on removal of grief-related symptoms? (5) Do those who seem to resolve their grief naturally and in a normal period of time experience their grief later, and, if so, is it a more severe grief than that of those who experience prolonged grief?

Coping With the Death of a Loved One

Piper, Ogrodniczuk, Joyce, and McCallum (2002) studied the relationship between the expression of positive affect in group therapy and favorable treatment outcomes for complicated (long-lasting) grief. The authors found a strong positive correlation between these two variables in a number of the therapy groups they studied and believe that a positive affect (including smiles, nods in agreement, sympathetic looks) creates optimism in the person and has a positive effect on others in the group. Piper and colleagues also found that a positive affect in clients correlates well with a cooperative attitude and a desire to do the work necessary to resolve the complicated and traumatic grief they are experiencing. This was true regardless of the type of treatment that was offered, and no difference in effectiveness was seen between cognitive behavioral approaches and interpersonal approaches. Client affect rather than the approach used was the overriding factor in successful resolution of prolonged grief, according to the authors.

Jacobs and Prigerson (2000) report that self-help groups are an effective adjunct treatment to professional therapy because they "offer the inculcation of hope, the development of understanding, social supports, a source of normalization or universalization, and a setting to learn and practice new coping skills" (p. 487). Raphael (1977) studied a 3-month psychodynamically oriented intervention for high-risk, acutely traumatized widows during the first stages of grief. The author defined high risk as the lack of support by a social network, the suddenness or unexpected nature of the death, high levels of anger and guilt, ambivalent feelings about the marital relationship, and the presence of other life crises related to or predating the death of a spouse. The predating life crises were often financial or work related, or involved children, substance abuse in the deceased spouse, or marital infidelity. When compared to the control group, the treatment group had better general health, was less anxious and depressed, and had fewer somatic symptoms.

Marmar, Horowitz, Weiss, Wilner, and Kaltreider (1988) compared two treatment groups, one in brief psychodynamic therapy and the other in a self-help group, and found that those in both treatment groups experienced diminished stress and improved social functioning. However, improvement in grief-related symptoms began at the end of treatment and continued on thereafter, making the researchers wonder whether the improvement was caused by the treatment or was a delayed response to grief that would have taken place in time, with or without treatment. Sireling, Cohen, and Marks (1988) compared a group receiving "guided mourning" with a control group instructed to avoid cues that might bring about memories of their grief. The treated group had a reduction in grief-related distress and physical problems that was maintained for up to 9 months in follow-up studies.

Because of their concern that traumatic grief should be considered a separate diagnostic category because of it's unique set of symptoms, Jacobs and Prigerson (2000) call for the development of a specific therapy for the treatment of grief. By specific therapy, they suggest one that "focuses on separation distress and relevant elements of traumatic distress and that addresses several tasks (such as educating about the nature of these types of distress), helps individuals to cope with the distress, and mitigates the distress using variety of strategies" (p. 491).

To help provide diagnostic guidance for the assessment of prolonged grief, Jacobs and Prigerson (2000) suggest using the following list of symptoms lasting more than 2 months and having significant negative impact on social functioning: (1) frequent attempts not to remember the deceased; (2) feelings of hopelessness, meaningless, and futility; (3) a sense of emotional detachment and numbness; (4) feelings of shock; (5) difficulty accepting the death of a loved one; (6) difficulty imagining their lives without the presence of the deceased; (7) a lost sense of security; (8) assuming the physical and emotional symptoms of the deceased person, including negative behaviors; and (9) considerable signs of anger and bitterness toward the deceased (p. 496).

In writing about ambiguous loss or loss where the death of a loved one is never confirmed (as in kidnappings, soldiers missing in action, etc.), Abrams (2001) indicates that to cope with ambiguous loss, individuals and families must (1) confront the change in their situation; (2) be able to hold something meaningful of the past while letting go of that which is not in the present; (3) learn that the situation may not change, but what they are hoping for can change; (4) make sense of the loss; (5) maintain a degree of hope; and (6) be active and connected to others. Abrams writes, "Central to the ability to make sense out of the loss is the ability to maintain hope, to find some way to change, and to construct a meaningful narrative" (p. 284). In explaining why some families cope better with ambiguous loss than others, Abrams suggests that understanding individuals' resilience may be the key to understanding their ability to cope with unresolved death. He notes, "Clearly, some family members have greater inner and outer resources probably due in part to genetic endowment, intergenerational forces, role in the family, relationships with family and friends, early life experiences, quality of nurturing, and social supports" (Abrams, 2001, p. 286).

A Story About the Death of Family Members

My daughter died of a brain tumor in 1991. It was a sudden thing. One day she was a healthy and vital girl of 11, and 5 months later, she was bald and emaciated and her eyes had a hollow look. She cried herself to sleep from the pain she had to live with and the chemo. When she finally died, it felt like a blessing, but I fell apart and began to drink heavily. I suppose I was so caught up with my own pain that I didn't realize that Edward, my husband, was in deep unrelenting mourning. One day he went out in the fields of our farm, took a shotgun with him, and blew his brains out. I thought he was going hunting, and I can remember being happy that he was able to get out of the house while I was still in bed grieving and drinking to the point of numbness.

When they told me about Edward, I think I went a little insane, and they hospitalized me for several months. I was in a state where I was aware of what was happening around me but unable to respond. It felt like being paralyzed. You want to move your legs, you tell your brain to move them, but they don't move at all. And I felt responsible. Edward had been dealing with depression, and when Mara got sick, he was really very suicidal. Once he drove our truck off the road and hit a tree. I knew he shouldn't have a gun with him, but my brain was as paralyzed as my mouth. I just didn't have the energy to say or do anything.

A month after I was released, my father died. He had an aneurism and it caused a stroke. He was a young man. Not even 60. Three people dead in several months. The thoughts that go with death are so strange. When my daughter died, all I could think was I'd never have a grandchild. I found myself crying for the unborn child I'd never know. When Edward died, I thought, well, your life is over and you'll never have another man in your life. You'll sleep alone. When my father died, I figured I had offended God in some way and that I was paying the price for being bad, somehow. I began reading the Bible and it gave me solace. And even though I hadn't ever been much of a Jew, I found myself driving to a city 30 miles away to a small synagogue and going to Friday and Saturday services. It was very foreign to me and at times I thought to myself, this is very silly, this need for religion, but it helped.

I now have a strong faith, and in the lonely days when it all comes back and I feel depressed and isolated, I find that going online and talking to other people who have lost loved ones and turned to Judaism has been a blessing. I have a friend online (we've never met in person) who tells me that death can have its own spiritual rewards because it makes you know how sacred life is and makes you live your life with much more meaning. I can't be certain that my life has more meaning. I still live on the farm. Maybe it's a mistake to live alone on a farm, but it keeps me going, and sometimes, when I'm feeling close to God as I work in the fields, I even feel at peace. The work enters my body, seeing the things I've planted grow. The barren earth becomes alive with crops and other people will enjoy the bounty I've helped to create. Maybe I'm kidding myself, but perhaps this is what God wanted me to do—to take death and, from the sorrow I feel, create new life.

This story was told to me, and I've written it in my own words.

LESSONS TO BE LEARNED FROM THIS STORY

It's difficult to understand how anyone could cope with this series of family deaths and do as well as the storyteller. But this assumes that she is doing well. She admits to having depressed days and to feeling sad over the loss of her family and the inability to cope with the death of her daughter. But she survives, in a fashion. It seems that her religious beliefs have helped and that she feels she's doing what God expects of her. What follows are lessons we can learn from the story:

1. Grief can cause very serious emotional responses. In her case, a life-threatening alcoholic binge and deep despair.

2. Her way of coping is to be as grounded in her daily routines as possible. She tells us that she puts one foot forward at a time and gets on with life.

3. She wants to help by growing crops that will bring joy to others. This seems a very healthy and positive desire, given what she's been through and given her experiences with death and dying. In Judaism, doing *mitzvot,* or good deeds, is often seen as a positive way of coping with tragedy and despair. Helping others is thought to be the key to helping ourselves.

4. The storyteller has experienced a psychological numbing that permits her to deal with her grief and to complete daily life routines.

5. She has an explanation for God's role in her life. Meaning-of-life issues seem very important to her.

6. When people who have lost loved ones are able to go on, to put one step in front of the other, to do the mundane daily tasks that permit them to get through the day intact, it takes a great deal of emotional strength regardless of whether grief is prolonged or the numbness and detachment are signs of depression, as some readers of the story have suggested. One of the most traumatic events in life is random violence of the type she experienced with the suicide of her husband. The October 2002 *Harvard Mental Health Letter* reports a study conducted at the University of California in San Diego in which 132 randomly selected patients seen by family doctors completed an interview and questionnaire describing traumatic events in their lives, including combat, natural and human-made disasters, violent rape, abusive behavior, and assault. Almost 70% of the sample had experienced at least one traumatic event. Of the sample, 20% currently had PTSD, 29% had major depressions, and 8% had both. PTSD was most likely to occur in those who had experienced several types of traumas, particularly those who had been assaulted. Seventy percent of the patients with current or lifetime PTSD said that violence was their worst traumatic experience.

Coping With Disabilities

Finn (1999) reports that there are as many as 24 million Americans with a severe disabling condition. Finn indicates that, nationally, "there are an estimated

1.7 million people with disabilities who are homebound and an additional 12.5 million who are temporarily homebound. There also are many caretakers of disabled and elderly people who are essentially homebound as a result of their responsibilities at home" (p. 220). Finn goes on to say that a number of social and emotional problems develop from being "alienated" or "socially quarantined" from the larger society, including depression, loneliness, alienation, lack of social interaction, lack of information, and lack of access to employment and cites Braithwaite (1996), Coleman (1997), and Shworles (1983) as supporting his assessment (Finn, 1999, p. 220). In a study of the impact of physical and emotional disabilities, Druss, Marcus, Rosenheck, Olfson, and Tanielan (2000) write that

> combined mental and general medical disabilities were associated with high levels of difficulty across a variety of functional domains: bed days, perceived stigma, employment status, disability payments, and reported discrimination. These findings may best be understood by the fact that co-morbid conditions, unlike either mental or general medical conditions alone, are most commonly associated with deficits spanning several domains of function. In turn, respondents with deficits across multiple domains have few areas of intact function available to make up for their existing deficits. The uniquely high levels of functional impairment associated with combined conditions speak to the potential importance of integrated programs that can simultaneously address an individual's medical and psychiatric needs. (p. 1489)

Finn (1999) studied the content of messages sent by people with disabilities using the Internet as a form of group therapy. He found that most correspondents wanted to talk about their health and about specific issues of treatment and quality of care but that, overall, the correspondents acted as a support group helping others cope with emotional, medical, and social issues. These issues included "highly technical descriptions of medications, procedures, and equipment to subjective accounts of treatment experiences. There also was considerable discussion of interpersonal relationship issues such as marital relationships, dating, and sexuality" (p. 228). Finn (1999) reminds us that many disabled people are home bound and that the Internet becomes an important part of the communicating they do each day. This is particularly true for homebound people who may also have difficulty speaking or hearing.

A CASE STUDY OF JACK, A MAN COPING WITH A DISABILITY

Jack Phillips is a 52-year-old professor of engineering who was injured in a car crash that left him unable to walk without the help of a walker or a wheelchair. Jack is depressed and is seriously thinking of physician-assisted suicide. His

---

Parts of this case first appeared in a book I wrote on evidence-based practice (Glicken, 2005b, pp. 203–205). The case has been modified for use in this book.

personal physician has recommended that Jack seek help for the depression, but Jack has been too depressed to even consider it. During one of his visits to the hospital for an overall evaluation, a hospital social worker dropped by his room to chat. The social worker sat and listened to Jack talk about the "mess" he'd made of his life and how his disability was just another example of "what a loser I am."

Talking to the social worker seemed strangely comforting, and when she suggested that they continue talking the next day, uncharacteristically, Jack agreed. Jack hates the feminizing way helping professionals make him feel and described what it felt like going to a marital counselor when his marriage fell apart. "I felt like someone lobbed off my balls, which is pretty funny because that's exactly what's happening to me now that I can't walk." The social worker was much more understanding than the marital counselor had been, and Jack felt she wasn't going to make him feel weak. As Jack continued seeing the worker on a biweekly basis, he shared his life disappointments with her. She listened and observed that he was being very hard on himself because she felt that Jack had done amazing things in his life. Jack wasn't so sure he agreed and wondered if the worker was just trying to placate him. The worker assured him that she didn't believe placating ever worked, but it certainly wouldn't work with a highly intelligent man like Jack. As Jack thought about their conversations, he began to realize that he'd been successful in many small and large ways, but that he had an inner voice, the voice of his father, that kept insisting that he'd been a failure. Gradually, the inner voice changed and Jack felt that he was starting to see what the worker meant. He also felt better physically.

Jack decided that he would return to teaching, even though it would be tough for him to get to and from work. He thought he would be a much more considerate teacher than he had been before his illness. He also decided to talk to everyone he had stopped talking to because of real or imagined conflicts. This included many of his colleagues and family members, who, he felt, had hurt him over the years. As Jack began to talk to old friends and members of his family, he felt elated at being able to resolve old hurts. The people he spoke to felt the same way and said that they had missed Jack and were happy to have him back in their lives.

Jack made it through the semester and, with a good deal of help from his doctors and continued support from his social worker, through the following semesters. As time went by, Jack developed a support network that consisted of estranged friends, family members, former students, and many of the disabled people he'd met in the hospital during his treatment. During one of their infrequent sessions, Jack told the worker, "You saved my life. I was full of bile before we started talking and now I feel a strange sort of happiness and contentment. I think I've made a difference in people's lives the past year. I think I'm happier because I was able to get rid of a lot of the toxic feelings I had inside. You always treat me with respect and you acknowledge my intelligence. It made me want to do as much for myself and for others as possible. I owe a lot to you for helping me put my anger and depression to constructive use."

In describing her work with Jack, the worker said, "Like many disabled patients, Jack was very angry. He had his mind set on suicide because he felt so helpless. He'd always thought he had control over his life and now, for once, he didn't. Helping him see his strengths, respecting his anger, encouraging his need to finish unfinished business, and watching his transformation from an angry and resentful person to a loving and kind person has been a very special experience for me. I see it often when people search for closure that includes resolving old conflicts and animosities.

"One of the main helping approaches I used with Jack was behavioral charting. We found several articles in the literature about people who had dealt with serious disabilities by charting their progress each day through their physical rehabilitation and then during their jobs and personal lives. We devised goal attainment scales with realistic expectations. Given Jack's engineering background, he liked the idea that he could assist his treatment by maintaining good health habits and that diet and exercise might have a very positive impact. He created an elaborate chart that measured a number of different variables such as calorie and fat intake, sleep, how long it took to dress and shower, fatigue at certain hours of the day, and the times when he needed to rest. After a while, he could tell that he actually felt better then he did at the beginning of the charting.

"The anticipation of meeting goals had a positive impact on him physically and emotionally. He gained weight; he enjoyed the taste of food, whereas before, he hardly noticed what he ate. And his teaching, which he evaluated after every class, was far better than it had been before his disability. He put time and energy into it. Before his accident, he'd become cynical and dismissive about teaching. The charting also helped him understand how the disability was affecting him and tapped sources of resilience he didn't realize he had. He knew that mornings were his best time and arranged his schedule to teach in the morning. He found that he sometimes became depressed at night and decided that meeting friends and family for dinner helped lessen his depression. The end result was a happier, healthier, and more fulfilled person. I see real value in helping disabled people. And I forgot to mention that he finished a book he'd been trying to write for years. It's become a well-selling book whose proceeds go to his family and to several charities he supports. These are all significant achievements, and they hopefully point out the benefits of working with the disabled. We shouldn't deny them the opportunity to grow and expand anymore than we would clients with other types of problems. In Jack's view, he grew more in the last year of life than he had in the previous twenty."

JACK'S BEHAVIORAL CHART

The following goals represent a partial list of the more than 40 goals Jack developed in his behavioral chart. He sought to

1. Bring his weight back to his pre-accident state. He achieved 80% of the goal.

2. Walk or use a wheelchair to travel at least a mile a day. He surpassed this goal by averaging 2 miles a day.

3. Improve his teaching and move from receiving an average student rating of 2.5 on a 5-point scale to a 4.0. He surpassed this goal, with his last set of classes evaluated at a 4.8.

4. Improve sleeping from an average of 2 hours a night to at least 6 hours. Because pain from the accident often kept him awake, he slept an average of 5 hours a night, but napped in the afternoon for another hour.

5. Have dinner or attend a social or family event at least two times a week. He surpassed this goal by increasing his social activities from less than once a month before the accident to five times a week.

6. Use biofeedback and other behavioral techniques to reduce his pain and dependence on painkillers. At the start of the charting, Jack was averaging eight Vicadin a day, but eventually he was able to take only two when his pain was very intense.

7. Use positive feedback and supportive statements with friends, family, students, and treatment staff. Jack went from no supportive or positive statements (most of his statements were neutral or negative) to more than 40 positive statements a day. Examples included words like "Thanks," "That was really helpful," "That was well done," "I really appreciate what you did for me," and so on. Silences were considered neutral statements, and negative statements included those Jack typically used to make, such as, "Stop being such an incompetent jerk," "When are you going to learn to do things right?" and "How can anyone so stupid do this kind of work?"

8. Work continuously on his book, which had gone from no writing in 2 years to 2 hours each day, and ended in the completion of the book. His students helped with references and editing, but the book went from a very muddled half-done book to a completed and well-praised book in a year.

9. Finish unfinished business. Jack made a long list of people he wanted to see and apologize to for past hurts and misunderstandings or just reconnect with, like old friends and colleagues whose company he missed. Jack had been very reclusive before seeing the worker, but eventually saw everyone on his list at least once and sometimes more. He added names to the list when it became apparent he would finish it fairly easily.

10. Read a serious book, see a serious play or film, and\or attend a play, musical, or lectures at least once a week. In fact, he went from doing none of these to doing many cultural activities at least three or four times a week, often with friends and family.

11. Make an attempt to involve himself in the civic life of the community. Jack was selected to be an unpaid consultant to the city's engineering department. Before this, he never involved himself in civic activities.

12. Try and involve himself in the religion he'd turned away from when he began to sour on life. This was a less successful activity than some of the others he undertook, but he did attend Sunday services most Sundays, and while they didn't move him much, he liked meeting friends and neighbors and joining them for meals after services were completed.

Summary

This chapter discusses coping with serious and terminal illness, disabilities, and bereavement. It is suggested that these states can best be dealt with if people are permitted to use their usual coping mechanisms, and that collaborative relationships between patients and medical personnel can result in clients' having a more cooperative relationship with medical staff, the ability to finish unfinished business, and an enhanced ability to cope with grief over loved ones who have died. In addition, material is included that explores the research on coping with terminal illness and bereavement. Stories are provided, followed by discussions of what we can learn from them.

CHAPTER 9

Resilience in Older Adults

Aging is often a very stressful process for many people, one that challenges a long history of resilience. Health problems, loss of loved ones, financial insecurities, lack of a support group, a growing sense of isolation, and lack of self-worth are common problems among older adults that lead to the serious symptoms of anxiety, depression, and substance abuse. The prevalence of anxiety disorders has usually been thought to decrease with age, but recent findings suggest that generalized anxiety is actually a more common problem among older adults than depression. A study reported by Beekman, Bremmer, Deeg, van Balkom, Smit, and de Beurs (1998) found that anxiety affected 7.3% of an elderly population compared to depression, which affected 2% of the same population. Lang and Stein (2001) estimated that the total number of older Americans suffering from anxiety could be in excess of 10%. Since many anxious elderly people do not meet the criteria for anxiety found in a number of research studies, the prevalence of anxiety-related problems in the elderly may be much greater than has been assumed, perhaps as high as 18%, and constitutes the most common psychiatric symptom experienced by older adults (Lang & Stein, 2001).

Depression is also a serious problem among older adults. In a study of older adults, Blazer, Hughes, and George (1987) found that 8% had symptoms of depression or other disorders serious enough to warrant treatment. They note that 5% to 15% of older adults in acute health care facilities had depression, while 25% of residents in long-term care facilities had symptoms of depression that are not captured in current descriptions of depression (Blazer, 1993). Wallis (2000) reports a depression rate of 6% in older adults, nearly two thirds of whom are women, and notes that depression is prevalent among those in an older population because it often accompanies the loss of loved ones, health problems, and the inability to live independently. According to Wallis, 75% of older adults in long-term care have mild to moderate symptoms of depression. Casey (1994) reports a study that found the rate of suicide among adults 65 and older almost double that of the general population. The completion rate for suicide among older adults was 1 in 4, as compared to 1 in 100 for the general population (Casey, 1994), suggesting that older adults are much more likely to see suicide as a final solution rather than a cry for help. Older adults who commit suicide often suffer from major depression, alcoholism, severe medical problems, and social isolation (Casey, 1994). Mills and Henretta (2001) indicate that more than 2 million of the 34 million older Americans suffer from some form of depression, yet late-life depression is often undiagnosed or underdiagnosed.

Hanson and Gutheil (2004) report that while older adults consume less alcohol and drink less often than younger adults, many suffer from alcohol-related difficulties. Earlier-onset problem drinkers account for two thirds of all older adults experiencing alcohol-related difficulties. Later-onset problem drinkers develop alcohol-related problems after age 50 and are less likely than earlier-onset drinkers to have alcohol-related physical problems like cirrhosis or mood and thought disorders. Hanson and Gutheil (2004) report that estimates of later-life alcohol abuse problems range from 5% to more than 15% of the elderly population, or 2.5 million older adults.

Anxiety, depression, and misuse of substances among older adults frequently coexist with physical manifestations that include chest pains, heart palpitations, night sweats, shortness of breath, essential hypertension, headaches, and generalized pain. Because physicians often fail to diagnose underlying symptoms of anxiety and depression in older adult patients and are embarrassed to think that an older adult is abusing drugs and alcohol, the emotional component of the symptoms is frequently ignored. Definitions and descriptions of anxiety used in diagnosing younger patients often fail to capture the unique stressors that older adults must deal with, or the fragile nature of life for older adults as they attempt to cope with limited finances, failing health, the death of loved ones, concerns about their own mortality, and a sense of uselessness and hopelessness because their roles in life have been dramatically altered with age and retirement.

Although the problems of anxiety, depression, and substance abuse among older adults seem increasingly problematic, this chapter describes resilient older adults who experience many of the problems related to aging without experiencing serious pathology or dysfunction.

Coping With Problems Related to Aging

In their research on successful aging, Vaillant and Mukamal (2001) state that we can identify the predictors of longer and healthier lives in individuals before they reach the age of 50 by using the following indicators: parental social class, family cohesion, major depression, ancestral longevity, childhood temperament, and physical health at age 50. Seven variables indicating personal control over physical and emotional health, which are also related to longer and healthier lives, include alcohol abuse, smoking, marital stability, exercise, body mass index, coping mechanisms, and education. Vaillant and Mukamal (2001) conclude that we have much greater control over our postretirement health than has been recognized in the literature.

For the purpose of understanding what is meant by successful aging, Vaillant and Mukamal (2001) identify the following indicators: (1) Although elderly people taking three to eight medications a day were seen as chronically ill by their physicians, those in this group who were deemed to be aging successfully saw themselves as healthier than their peers; (2) Elderly adults who age successfully have the ability to plan ahead and are still intellectually curious and in touch with their creative abilities; (3) Successfully aging adults, even those over 95, see life as being meaningful and are able to use humor in their daily lives; (4) Aging successfully includes individuals' remaining physically active and continuing activities (walking, for example) that were used at an earlier age to remain healthy; (5) Older adults who age successfully are more serene and spiritual in their outlook on life than those who age less well; (6) Successful aging includes individuals' caring for continuing friendships; creating positive interpersonal relationships; feeling satisfaction with their spouses, children, and family life; and assuming social responsibility in the form of volunteer work and civic involvement.

In a study of the relationship between the ability to cope with stress and physical and emotional well-being in women 65 to 87 years of age, Barnas and Valaik (1991) found that women with insecure attachments to their adult children had poorer coping skills and lower levels of psychological well-being than women with positive attachments. The same finding regarding the relationship between a person's well-being and the quality of that person's attachments was evidenced in a sample of women with a mean age of 20 and a sample of women with a mean age of 38. Both groups with poor attachments suffered more anxiety and depression and were seen by friends as being more anxious than women in both groups with positive attachments. These findings led Barnas and Valaik (1991) to conclude that insecure attachments produce poorer coping skills that lead to more vulnerability to stress across the life cycle. The authors define attachment as relationships of affection that are formed throughout the years and are not necessarily limited to a child's bond with his or her parents.

Robert and Li (2001) argue that despite a common belief in the relationship between socioeconomic status (SES) and health, research actually suggests a limited relationship between the two variables. Rather, there seems to be a relationship between community levels of health and individual health. Lawton (1977) suggests that older adults may experience communities as their primary source of support, recreation, and stimulation, unlike younger adults who find it easier to move about in search of support and recreation. Lawton and Nahemow (1973) believe that positive community environments are particularly important to older adults who have emotional, physical, or cognitive problems. The need for healthy and vital communities is especially relevant for older adults who have health problems that limit their mobility. A tragic example of the impact of unhealthy communities is the Chicago heat wave of 1995 in which 739 older and less mobile people died. The reason for the very large death rate is that many elderly and less mobile people were afraid to leave their homes and to be exposed to environments they felt were dangerous and unsafe (Gladwell, 2002). In explaining why she was afraid to leave her home even though she was literally dying of heat prostration, one elderly lady said, "Chicago is just a shooting gallery" (Gladwell, 2002, p. 80). Furthermore, Chicago had no emergency system for helping elderly and less mobile people. So many people died during the heat wave that

> callers to 911 were put on hold. . . . The police took bodies to the Cook County Medical Examiner's office, and a line of cruisers stretched outside the building. The morgue ran out of bays in which to put the bodies. The owner of a local meat-packing firm offered the city his refrigerated trucks to help store the bodies. The first set wasn't enough. He sent a second set. It wasn't enough. (Gladwell, 2002, p. 76)

Rather than thinking in terms of a relationship between individual SES and health in an aging population, Robert and Li (2001) suggest three indicators of healthy communities that relate directly to individual health: (1) a positive physical environment that provides an absence of noise, traffic, inadequate lighting, and other features of a community that may lead to functional loss in older adults; (2) a positive social environment that includes an absence of crime, the ability to find safe environments to walk in, and easy access to shopping; and (3) a rich service environment that includes simple and safe access to rapid and inexpensive transportation, the availability of senior centers, and easy access to meal sites.

After studying the impact of natural disasters on a population of elderly adults demonstrating predisaster signs of depression, Tyler and Hoyt (2000) indicate that elderly adults reporting high levels of social support had lower levels of depression before and after a natural disaster. They also report that "older people with little or no social support, perhaps due to death of a spouse and/or loss of friends, may have a more difficult time dealing with life changes and, as a result, are particularly vulnerable to increases in depression" (p. 155).

But, overall, Pearlin and Skaff (1996) note how remarkable it is that so many older people cope so well with life stressors. Solomon (1996) reports that specific personality characteristics are highly related to successful coping in older adults. The characteristics most likely to show a positive relationship between successful coping and aging are "flexibility, adaptability, and a sense of humor as well as financial, social, and organizational skills" (p. 48). Solomon also indicates that the ability to find meaning in crisis situations instead of just being able to manage them is a critical aspect of coping. Butler, Lewis, and Sunderland (1991) suggest that coping is enhanced in older adults who are able to shift their priorities to accommodate change, while Solomon (1996) believes that people's sense of mastery is closely related to their ability to cope with stressors related to aging. She identifies two personality factors that are particularly related to coping in older adults: "1) the ability to interpret success in controlling past hardships as evidence of competence to master current hardship, and 2) the ability to shift priorities from areas where a measure of control has been lost to areas where control may still be maintained" (p. 48).

Rowe and Kahn (1998) define successful aging as including the following three components: (1) good health and a low risk of disease and disability (good health includes regular exercise, a healthy diet, and regular check ups); (2) high mental and physical functioning (this suggests that in healthy aging, people are intellectually active and stimulated); and (3) an active engagement with life and a strong system of social support. The authors believe social supports are very important in maintaining successful aging and provide the following reasons: isolation is a powerful risk factor for poor health; social support—such as emotional, physical, and personal contact—has direct positive effects on health; social support can buffer or reduce some health-related effects of aging; and social support helps protect one against the stresses of life. Rowe and Kahn (1998) believe that it's never too late to reverse bad health habits, and they provide the following examples of good health practices in older adults:

1. Physical activity is the crux of successful aging. Physical activity includes aerobic activity such as walking, dancing, and gardening and more strenuous activity like weight training (or weight lifting).

2. Diet and exercise helps reduce weight, the chances of having heart disease, and colon and rectal cancer; reduces the effects of diabetes, arthritis, and osteoporosis; and helps to increase strength and balance which helps to reduces falls.

3. Fitness cuts our risk of dying. Older women who exercise are 20% less likely to die than those who were sedentary.

4. The risk of heart disease falls as soon as one stops smoking. After 5 years of cessation, an ex-smoker is not much more likely to have heart disease than a non-smoker.

5. Smoking cessation results in reduced chances of heart disease, increased lung capacity, and decreased blood pressure.

6. Active mental stimulation and keeping up social relationships with friends and family also helps to promote physical ability.

7. Older people can sustain, perhaps even increase, their mental functioning by reading, through word games and mental exercises, and by engaging in stimulating conversation.

Late Life Depression: The Case of Primo Levi

Primo Levi was the remarkable author of books about the human spirit and the Holocaust, including the books *The Periodic Table* (1975/1995b) and *If Not Now, When?* (1982/1995a). As a young man, Levi was imprisoned for a year in the notorious Auschwitz concentration camp, a subject he wrote about with great humanity and sensitivity. Many think his books about the concentration camp experience are among the best examples of human beings' ability to deal with incredible trauma. In his mid-60s, at the height of his recognition as a writer, Levi suffered a serious and unrelenting depression. He was ill with prostate problems and he was finding writing increasingly difficult.

Describing his depression, Angier (2002) writes, "The real pit of his depression had begun. It was so bad that he had lost interest in everything and didn't want to see anyone" (p. 706). Elsewhere, she tells of a letter written to a friend in which Levi says, "I am going through the worst time of my life since Auschwitz, maybe the worst time in my life because I am older and less resilient. My wife is exhausted. Forgive me for this outburst" (p. 708). Later, he called his doctor and said, "I can't go on" (p. 731). Moments after talking to his doctor, he walked outside the apartment where he had lived most of his life, stood at the railing of the staircase, perhaps paused for a moment, and then jumped five stories to his death. Trying to understand his decision to commit suicide, Angier (2002) writes,

> He just needed to get out and really thought he might walk downstairs. He opened the door and found himself outside. It wasn't the light and air he had dreamed of, but it was a deep void. I think he looked for [his wife] to stop him, then he leaned (over the railing of the staircase) and looked, but she wasn't there; and he let go. (p. 731)

Angier (2002) believes that Levi's suicide was a private decision. "Auschwitz caused him guilt and shame, and torment about human evil; but he contained these in decades of writing and talking, and with the knowledge that he had done everything he could to right them. What we suffer from most in the end is our own private condition. It was his own private condition that killed Primo Levi" (Angier, 2002, p. xx).

While we can never know Levi's reason for committing suicide, his example might help us understand the complex nature of aging and the inability of even highly resilient people to cope with serious deteriorations in physical and emotional health. However, according to Waern, Runeson, Allebeck, and Beskow (2002), late life suicides are often explained by failing health, aloneness, changing cognitive abilities, family deterioration, and death of loved ones. The primary reason for elder suicide, however, is a severe late life depression that is unresponsive to treatment (Waern et al., 2002).

In studies of Holocaust survivors such as Primo Levi, researchers Baron, Eisman, Scuello, Veyzer, and Lieberman (1996) report that survivors who were aware of their ethnic identities and cultural heritage were less vulnerable to emotional traumas. Newman (1979) suggests that religious beliefs were beneficial to survivors and that religious beliefs provided many survivors with a feeling of personal control that helped give meaning to the concentration camp experience.

Angier (2002) describes Primo Levi as a highly assimilated Jew who wrote little about the Jewish experience in the death camps but wrote, more specifically, about the human experience. She believes that he told us very little about himself in his books and was often aloof from people, even people he knew well. "He very rarely betrays his feelings, and almost never has negative feelings—this is the first and most important thing everyone notices in his great books about the Shoah [Holocaust]" (Angier, 2002, p. xv). Angier further believes that Levi was a deeply conflicted man and that the "torments" of his experiences in the death camps, which he tried to cope with by living a highly rational life (he was also a well-known chemist), began to fail him. As Levi aged, the conflicts he saw in other parts of the world (like Cambodia), which paralleled his Holocaust experience, "at slowly diminishing intervals rose up and dragged him under" (Angier, 2002, p. xix).

Does this mean that a lack of strong religious beliefs prevented Levi from coping with his Holocaust experiences? No. Having worked professionally with Jewish Holocaust survivors, I've known many survivors who were religious and many who had deep hostility toward religion. What I think defines the survivors who lead successful lives is an inner strength that shows itself as a resilience of the spirit. Does that resilience sometimes change with age? Yes. Baron and colleagues (1996) note that clinicians were highly pessimistic about the survivors they were seeing who had just been released from the death camps. They believed that survivors were severely maladjusted and, as one measure of their maladjustment, would make poor parents. The children of survivors, they reasoned, would also show major maladjustments (for example, hypervigilence, the inability to form attachments, irrational fears, depressions, etc.). But as Baron and colleagues (1996) note, "Children of survivors have shown no pattern of maladjustment or psychopathology in most research" (p. 513). Perhaps this demonstrates that resilient people can perform many socially successful functions, such as parenting, and still suffer episodes of depression similar to that of Primo Levi.

Many of the survivors of genocide from Europe, Cambodia, Bosnia, Latin America, Africa, and elsewhere, while strong and resilient, also show a core of sadness and pessimism about life. Some experience debilitating depressions at various times in their lives, and one is strongly inclined to believe that disappointment and regret often result in pessimism, depression, and a loss of hope later in life. Clearly, Levi's late life depression parallels the experience of many elderly people in a society that doesn't know, and perhaps doesn't want to know, how best to help people cope with aging.

A STORY OF RESILIENCE IN AGING

I'm going to be 70 this summer. It kind of shocks me to think I'm 70, because in my mind, I think of myself as a very spry 30-year-old. Given the fact that I have cancer of the uterus in remission, I guess every year I live is a blessing. I've had a tough life in many ways. I left home when I was 18 because my parents were quite demanding and sometimes they could be mean and disregard my feelings. Even though I was a National Merit Scholar, my self-esteem was low and I passed on the opportunity to go to our local college in the Mid west and began a secretarial job in Los Angeles. At some point early on, I became involved with a marine drill sergeant who was abusive and alcoholic. I had a daughter by him, and she is 45 now and has never met her father. It's taken its toll on her and she has very low self-esteem.

After that, I married another alcoholic, who was also probably bipolar, and had a child by him. When my second husband couldn't work anymore, and we had divorced because of his illness and his drinking, he would park his car a block away from my house so he could see our daughter on her way to and from

This story was told to me, and I wrote it with the approval of the storyteller.

school. One morning, when my daughter was in 7th grade, she went to see him and found him dead. It was hard on all of us, and my heart goes out to my daughter, who never really knew her father when he could be a really wonderful person, before the illness made him too sick to work or to be a parent.

Even during my disastrous marriages, I've worked hard, raised my children, done well at work, and managed to move from the inner city of Los Angeles to a beautiful condo complex in San Diego.

In the past few years, I've had three major surgeries and radiation for cancer. I also have painful arthritis problems and am unable to use pain killers because the blood pressure medications I've taken over the years have affected my kidneys and liver. I've always been very quiet and unassertive, but after two bad marriages, cancer, and a very tough life, I've begun to stand up for myself. It's a powerful feeling, and I get better at it every day. I volunteer my time at a variety of places, and I continue to work part time, from my home, for a group of doctors. The doctors work in Los Angeles and send me my work by UPS or by fax. I'm very happy that they think enough of me and my work to have continued employing me after I moved to San Diego. I'd really like a little more work, but I appreciate my free time in this lovely San Diego environment, which I spend reading and enjoying my many friends. Both my daughters live nearby, and while they have their own problems, we enjoy a wonderful relationship. My oldest daughter and I have had our differences, but living in the same community allows us to see each other often and we've begun to have a much better relationship.

I have very high blood pressure and worry about my health sometimes, but, thank God, I have excellent medical care and have been healthier in the past 3 years, since I moved from the inner city of Los Angeles to San Diego, than I've been in many years. And I enjoy my life. My brother and I just went on a cruise to Mexico, and my daughters are always inviting me to concerts and shows. This summer we'll do a cruise to Alaska together. Even though I have little money beyond what I receive from my social security and part-time work, I don't feel that I ever deny myself the things that are most important to me, like concerts, Broadway shows, and the theater. I sing in a chorus and volunteer at the local branch of the library, and that's given me a great deal of pleasure. I'm also on the condo complex board of directors where I live and have met many lovely people since I moved here that I count as friends.

You asked if I think I'm resilient, and I guess the answer is yes. I don't really think of myself as being unusual, but I suppose I've always been able to deal with many stressful and painful things in my life and never feel so down that I can't get on with my life. That isn't to say I've not had difficult times when I've felt depressed or anxious, because I have. When I couldn't understand something that was going on in my family or in my life, I always read or talked to people I thought would help me understand it better. I had some very good friends when I was growing up who helped me cope with my home life, which could be difficult because we were dealing with a lot of poverty and illness. And I always had school to feel good about myself, since I was a very good student. Even though I lacked confidence and felt insecure, I did well in school, but it never dawned on me that I was capable until I got older. And I think I've been a happy and content person, for the most part. My parents were poor, working-class immigrants, and we had a very difficult life. There was never enough money, and we all had to work from a pretty early age to buy our own clothes. No one helped us learn to become confident people and we pretty much had to make our own way in life.

Last year I went to my 50th high school reunion, and I was surprised to find out that everyone thought we had a lot of money. We were dirt poor, but I guess our home was filled with laughter, food, and music and we probably were doing a lot better emotionally than my friends' families. My parents never gave my brothers or me a chance to feel sorry for ourselves, even though we had plenty of reason. Instead, we were told that we needed to work hard, do well in school, and be successful, because nobody would take care of us. If we wanted to survive, we'd have to depend on ourselves. And they were right. No one has ever taken care of me or helped me in my times of need. I've had wonderful friends and my brothers have been a support sometimes, but mostly, I've done it on my own. It wasn't fun and I missed out on many things that other people have in their lives, like love and intimacy. But I've survived when other people haven't, and I've been a good person. I've been honest, and helpful to others, and spiritual. I've always been there to help out in organizations, and I believe that what you give to others is what you ultimately end up giving to yourself.

I don't think I'm religious, but I love the idea of being with people in a spiritual community. I think I have some dear friends who represent my spiritual community. And while I wish I'd married well, had more money, and lived a more glamorous life, mostly I'm content and thankful that God gave me a good mind, a lot of skills, and a toughness that's allowed me to make it through some bad times when other people might have folded and given up. It's where you end up in life, not where you start. I wouldn't trade where I am right now for anything or with anyone.

LESSONS TO BE LEARNED FROM THIS STORY

The storyteller notes that even though her life has had many disappointments, including abuse and alcoholism in her marriages, that she's been able to persevere through all of the tough times. She believes that much of her resilience is based on what she learned from her parents, whose philosophy was to never give up and to get on with life no matter how badly things went. I have listed below the reasons she coped so well with adversity and the lessons about resilience we can apply to our work with clients.

1. The storyteller has moved to an environment where she is surrounded by natural beauty and is close to her children. This has allowed her to heal from her many physical problems in a warm and caring environment where she has many close friends.

2. She is grounded in the present and the future. While the past has been painful, she's willing to look at it rationally and she doesn't use past failures to feel regret or to feel sorry for herself. In fact, she has few regrets.

3. Her biological family could be difficult and she honestly describes the behavior that led her to leave home, yet she doesn't blame them for her early marital problems and sees the many positives in her home life that gave her messages of resilience.

4. As she's aged, she's also become more assertive and self-secure. She finds the need to stand up for herself a positive and believes it's a certain sign of improved emotional health.

5. She gives to others, is involved in a number of organizations as a volunteer, and believes that giving to others enriches her life.

6. She stays involved with cultural events and believes that it's important to be socially active and to do what you love as a way of aging well.

7. She continues to work and enjoys her work.

8. Although she has had a number of illnesses, she views herself as being healthy.

9. She sees herself as emotionally tough and believes that the early messages she received from her parents, emphasizing survival and strength, have helped her cope well with adversity.

A CASE STUDY OF RESILIENCE IN A DEPRESSED OLDER MALE

Jake Kissman is a 77-year-old widower whose wife, Leni, passed away a year ago. Jake is emotionally adrift and feels lost without Leni's companionship and guidance. He has a troubled relationship with two adult children who live across the country and has been unable to turn to them for solace and support. Like many older men, Jake has no real support group or close friends. Leni's social circle became his, but after her death, her friends left Jake to fend for himself. Jake is a difficult man, who is prone to being critical and insensitive. He tends to say whatever enters his mind at the moment, no matter how hurtful it may be, and then is surprised that people take it so badly. "It's only words," he says, "what harm do words do? It's not like smacking somebody." Before he retired, Jake was a successful salesman, and [he] can be charming and witty, but sooner or later, the disregard for others comes through and he ends up offending people.

Jake's depression shows itself in fatigue, feelings of hopelessness, irritability, and outbursts of anger. He doesn't believe in doctors and never sees them. "Look what the "momzers" (bastards) did to poor Leni? A healthy woman in her prime and she needed a surgery like I do. They killed her, those butchers." Jake has taken to pounding on the walls of his apartment whenever noise from his neighbors upsets him. Complaints from surrounding neighbors have resulted in the threat of an eviction. Jake can't manage a move to another apartment by himself, and someone from his synagogue contacted a professional in the community who agreed to visit Jake at his apartment. Jake is happy that he has company, but angry that someone thought he needed help. "Tell the bastards to

This case first appeared in a book I wrote on evidence-based practice (Glicken, 2005b, pp. 227–229). The case is included here because it describes treatment with an older male who is both resilient and difficult. Jake's story will hopefully help the reader understand that even resilient people can be difficult, and that treatment, if done right, can enhance resilience.

stop making so much noise and I'll be fine. The one next door with the dog, shoot her. The one on the other side who bangs the cabinets, do the same. Why aren't *they* being kicked out?"

The therapist listens to Jake in a supportive way. He never disagrees with him, offers advice, or contradicts him. Jake is still grieving for his wife, and her loss has left him without usable coping skills to deal with the pressures of single life. He's angry and depressed. To find out more about Jake's symptoms, the therapist has gone to the literature on anger, depression, and grief. While he recognizes that Jake is a difficult client in any event, the data he collected helped him develop a strategy for working with Jake. The therapist has decided to use a strengths approach (Glicken, 2004a; Saleebey, 1992; Weick, Rapp, Sullivan, & Kisthardt, 1989) with Jake. The strengths approach focuses on what clients have done well in their lives and on using those strengths in areas of life that are more problematic. The approach comes from studies on resilience, self-healing, and on successful work with abused and traumatized children and adults.

Jake has many positive attributes that most people have ignored. He was a warm and caring companion to Leni during her illness. He is secretly very generous and gives what he has to various charities without wanting people to know where his gifts come from. He helps his children financially and has done a number of acts of kindness for neighbors and friends, but in ways that always make the recipients feel ambivalent about his help. Jake is a difficult and complex man, and no one has taken the time to try and understand him. The therapist takes a good deal of time and listens closely.

Jake feels that he's been a failure at life. He feels unloved and unappreciated. He thinks the possibility of an eviction is a good example of how people "do him in" when he is least able to cope with stress. So the therapist listens and never disagrees with Jake. Gradually, Jake has begun discussing his life and the sadness he feels without his wife, who was his ballast and mate. Using a strengths approach, the therapist always focuses on what Jake does well and his generosity, while Jake uses their time to beat himself up with self-deprecating statements. The therapist listens, smiles, points out Jake's excellent qualities, and waits for Jake to start internalizing what the therapist has said about him. Gradually, it's begun to work. Jake told the therapist to go help someone who needed it when [his] anger at the therapist became overwhelming. Jake immediately apologized. "Here you're helping me and I criticize. Why do I do that?" he asked the therapist. There are many moments when Jake corrects himself or seems to fight an impulse to say something mean-spirited or hurtful to the therapist, who recently told him, "Jake, you catch more flies with honey than you do with vinegar." To which Jake replied, "So who needs to catch flies, for crying out loud? Oh, I'm sorry. Yeah, I see what you mean. It's not about flies; it's about getting along with people."

Gradually, Jake has put aside his anger and has begun talking to people in the charming and pleasant manner he is so capable of. The neighbors who complained about him now see him as a "doll." Jake's depression is beginning to lift and he's begun dating again, although he says he can never love anyone like his wife, "but a man gets lonely so what are you supposed to do, sit home and watch soap operas all day? Not me." The therapist continues to see Jake, and they often sit and quietly talk about Jake's life. "I was a big deal once. I could sell an Eskimo an air conditioner in winter. I could charm the socks off people. But my big mouth, it always got in the way. I always said something that made people mad. Maybe it's because my dad was so mean to all of us, I got this chip on my shoulder. Leni was wonderful. She could put up with me and make me laugh. When she died, I was left with my big mouth and a lot of disappointments. You want to have friends; you want your kids to love you. I got neither, but I'm not such an "alte cocker" (old fart) that I don't learn. And I've learned a lot from you. I've learned you can teach an old dog new tricks, and that's something. So I thank you and I apologize for some of the things I said. It's hard to get rid of the chip on the shoulder and sometimes it tips you over, that big chip, and it makes you fall down. You're a good person. I wish you well in life."

DISCUSSION OF THE CASE

Most of the treatment literature on work with older depressed adults suggests the use of a cognitive approach. Jake's therapist felt that the oppositional nature of Jake's personality meant that he would reject a cognitive approach. Instead, a positive and affirming approach was used that focused on Jake's strengths, because "most depressed patients acutely desire the therapist's approval, and it is an effective therapist who gives it warmly and genuinely" (O'Connor, 2001, p. 522). While much of the research suggests the positive benefits of cognitive therapy, the therapist found the following description of cognitive therapy to be at odds with what might best help Jake. Cognitive treatment attempts to change irrational thinking through three steps: (1) identifying irrational self-sentences, ideas, and thoughts; (2) developing rational thoughts, ideas, and perceptions; and (3) practicing these more rational ideas to improve self-worth and, ultimately to reduce depression (Rush & Giles, 1982). While this approach might work with other older clients, the therapist believed that Jake would take offense and reject both the therapy and the therapist, finding them preachy and critical.

Instead, the therapist decided to let Jake talk, although he made comments, asked questions to clarify, and made connections that Jake found interesting and oddly satisfying. "No one ever said that to me before," Jake would say, shaking his head and smiling. "You learn something new everyday, don't you?" The therapist would always bring Jake back to the positive achievements in his life, which Jake would initially toss away with comments like, "That was then when I paid taxes, this is now when I ain't gotta penny to my name." Soon, however, Jake could reflect on his positive achievements and began to use those experiences to deal with his current problems. In discussing the conflict with one of his neighbors, Jake said, "Maybe I should bring flowers to the old hag. Naw, I can't bring flowers, but she's no hag. I've seen worse. What about flowers? Yeah, flowers. Down at Vons I can buy a nice bunch for a buck. So it costs a little to be nice. Beats getting tossed out on my keester." Or he would tie something he had done when he was working to his current situation: "I had something like this happen once. A customer complained to my boss, so I go over and ask her to tell me what she's mad about so I can fix it, and she does, and it gets fixed. Sometimes you gotta eat a little crow." As Jake made connections, and as he began to trust the therapist, this process of self-directed change reinforced his sense of accomplishment and led to a decrease in his depression. It also led to a good deal of soul searching about how he had to make changes in his life now that his wife was gone. "So maybe I should stop feeling sorry for myself and take better care. What do you think?"

A CASE STUDY OF A DEPRESSED OLDER FEMALE WITH A SUBSTANCE ABUSE PROBLEM

Lydia Holmes is currently a 68-year-old retired executive assistant for a large corporation. Ms. Holmes had a long, successful, and happy career moving up the ladder in her company to one of its most important and highly paid positions. She retired at age 65 in good health, and wanted to travel and spend more time with her grown children and her grandchildren. A year earlier, still in good health and happy with her decision to travel, Lydia experienced the beginning signs of depression and an addiction to Vicodin, a pain killer she had been prescribed for lower back pain. Alarmed, since she had never experienced prolonged depression before, but reluctant to tell the doctor about her addiction to pain killers, she saw her gynecologist during her annual physical examination and shared her symptoms with him. He immediately referred her to a psychiatrist who placed her on an anti-depressive, told her to stop using the pain killers, and urged her to consider therapy. Since she had no idea what was causing the depression, and thought that it might be something biochemical related to aging and the discontinuation of hormone therapy for symptoms of menopause, she decided against therapy and stayed with the anti-depressant.

There was little relief from the medication, nor was she able to discontinue the use of illegally obtained pain killers. A second visit with the psychiatrist confirmed the need for therapy and a change in medication. The second medication made her fatigued and lethargic. After an additional month of feeling depressed, she saw a clinical psychologist recommended by her psychiatrist.

Lydia was very pessimistic about therapy. She had known many people in her company who had gone for therapy and who had come back, in her opinion, worse than before they'd entered treatment. She also thought therapy was for weak people and refused to see herself that way. When she began seeing the therapist, she was very defensive and kept much of the problem she was having to herself. The therapist was kind and warm and didn't seem to mind at all. This went on for four sessions. On the fifth session, Lydia broke down and cried and described the awful feeling of depression and her confusion about why someone who had never been depressed before would experience such feelings. The therapist asked her if she had any idea why she was experiencing depression now. She didn't. All she could think that might be relevant was that she had been an active woman all of her life, and since her divorce at age 55, she had put all of her energies into her work and her children, but [she] now felt as if she was of little use to anyone. She was bored and thought it had been a mistake to retire.

This case first appeared in Glicken (2004a, pp.197–199) and is updated here with a recent interview with the client and her therapist.

The worker thought this was a very good theory and suggested that she might want to explore the possibility of going back to work, perhaps part-time at first, to see if she liked it. She returned to her old company, worked part-time in a very accepting and loving department where people were genuinely happy to have her back, and found that, if anything, the depression was increasing. Alarmed, she contacted the therapist and they began the work that ultimately led to an improvement in her depression.

The therapist felt that Lydia had put many of her intimacy needs aside when she was divorced. She had not had a relationship since her divorce and felt bitter and angry at her ex-husband for leaving her for a younger woman. She had no desire to date or to form intimate relationships and said, repeatedly, that her good female friends were all she needed in her life. It turned out, as the therapist helped Lydia explore her past, that Lydia was given large responsibilities to manage her dysfunctional family when she was a child. Never having learned about her own needs, Lydia took care of people and now wondered who would take care of her as she grappled with depression and aging. Her very good friends found it difficult to be around her when she spoke about her depression. Increasingly, she felt alone and unloved. Her children were busy with their own lives and she didn't feel it was right to ask for their help. The therapist arranged for several family meetings and her children were, as Lydia predicted, sympathetic but unwilling to help in more than superficial ways. The recognition that her family didn't care about her as fully as she cared about them validated feelings she had not expressed to the therapist that her family and friends were not the supports she imagined them to be and that, in reality, she was very much alone in life.

This realization led to a discussion of what Lydia wanted to accomplish in treatment. Of course, improving the depression was foremost in Lydia's mind, but she also wanted to make some changes in her life. She expressed interest in social activities and accepted the therapist's suggestion that she join a self-help group for depressed older people going through an adjustment to retirement. Attending the group helped Lydia realize that she was a much healthier and optimistic person than many of the severely depressed people in the group. She also made several friends who turned out to be true friends, one of whom was male. While the relationship didn't become intimate, they were able to have companionship, to travel together, and to attend events. Lydia found his company very comforting and supportive. She joined a dance group and, through the group, also made several friends. She began to date and experienced a type of intimacy with the man she was dating that she hadn't known in her marriage. In treatment, she focused on what she wanted in her life and how to use her highly advanced cognitive skills to achieve those goals. The depression began to lift as her social and personal lives improved.

While Lydia was not forthcoming about her drug addiction and claimed that she was no longer using Vicodin, several motivational interviews with her therapist led to her seeking help by joining a self-help group using the 12-step approach. In the motivational interviews, the therapist applied the following description of the motivational interview reported by Hanson and Gutheil (2004):

Motivational interviewing is a brief, focused, client-centered, collaborative practice approach designed to elicit behavioral changes by helping alcohol- and drug-involved clients (and their partners) identify, explore, and resolve ambivalence (Miller & Rollnick, 2002). It consists of two phases—phase 1 in which motivation for change is built, and phase 2 in which commitment to change is strengthened. Motivational interviewing facilitates change by evoking cognitive dissonance, usually between the current problem behavior (for example, excessive drinking) and the client's self-image, aspirations, or perceptions (Glasner, 2004). By selectively applying motivational interviewing tactics, professionals help clients recognize the adverse consequences of addictive behaviors and move from the precontemplation and contemplation stages toward preparation and action. (p. 368)

There are moments when she is still depressed, but the therapist believes these are more biochemical and situational than serious signs of depression. She continues to work with the psychiatrist on finding a better way to manage her depression biochemically. After 6 months of trial and error, they found a medication and dosage that worked well for her. She continues to work part-time and recognizes the primary reasons for her depression and continues to work on those reasons with her therapist. Her addiction to pain killers gradually lessened, but she admits that when she feels lonely and "out of sorts," she uses over-the-counter medications for pain because of their sedating effect on her.

DISCUSSION OF THE CASE

Lydia is not unlike many older adults who find that retirement brings with it the painful realization that they are often alone in life. Depression isn't an unusual end result of this realization. Lydia is a highly successful woman with many strengths. The one thing she could not easily do is to seek help, a not uncommon condition in people who have cared for others throughout their lives with little thought to being cared for themselves. The therapist stayed with Lydia during her moments of denial and rejection of help and allowed Lydia to go at her own pace. Once Lydia confirmed her painful depression and explained why she thought it was happening, the therapist supported her theory, which led to a helping agenda that Lydia could accept. Like many parents, Lydia recognized that her children were only marginally involved in her life. This was difficult for Lydia to accept and felt hurtful to her in the extreme. However, Lydia now realizes that her children have resented her intrusiveness in their lives since her divorce. They saw her as looking to them as a way of filling her life, without their asking for or wanting her involvement in their lives. The reaction of her children made Lydia realize that she was using her children to satisfy her intimacy needs before and after her divorce and that they resented it. She continues to discuss her children with her therapist, and Lydia and her children grapple with their confused feelings.

Once again, Lydia feels in control of her life and, highly intelligent and insightful woman that she is, sees that rebuilding her life is important at this point in time. She has moved to another self-help group of more highly functioning people and feels a kinship with them. Her relationships with her male friends have blossomed, and she realizes that the anger she had toward her husband limited her ability to allow men into her life. The new feeling of comfort she has with her male friends has made her aware that many men find her interesting and attractive, and she is experiencing the pleasant sense of being in demand as a friend and companion. She values her male friends and sees in them the true friendships she wasn't always able to have before therapy began.

I spoke to Lydia about her experiences in treatment. She told me, "I think I'd been a bit depressed since my marriage started to fail. To cover it up, I was busy every second of the day. I'd work all day and then go to every play, musical event, and function I could find, usually with friends. My relationships were very superficial, so it came as no real surprise that my friends weren't there for me when I became really depressed. The first thing I realized after retirement was that I had free time that I'd never had before. I filled it with everything I could find, but still I had time on my hands. At some point, I didn't know what to do with myself. It was clear to me that my kids felt confused about having me around, but I talked myself into thinking they needed me and I didn't pick up the signs of their unhappiness over my frequent calls and visits. When the depression hit, I knew I needed help, but I talked myself into believing it was hormonal. I knew better, but I just didn't want to accept that I was depressed because I was living a depressing life.

"My therapist was pretty amazing. She let me babble on and not ever get to the point, until I finally had nowhere to go with my feelings and just fell apart in her office. She involved me in determining the issues we would work on. She was very supportive and encouraging and always seemed to be able to see things in a positive way. In time, I guess I began to see things more positively. The groups I went to run by other depressed people and people with drug and alcohol problems really made a difference in my life. I've made some very good friends through the people I've met in group. They're not superficial people and they care about me. I've stopped bugging my family, and I don't need to be busy every minute of the day. I have moments when I'm depressed, but it's not like the depression I had when I began therapy. That depression felt like I was falling down a black hole and I'd never get out. My therapist made me realize that I had lots of skills to manage my depression, and the discussion about my life gave me an opportunity to see that I had never really asked anyone to give back to me, emotionally. I think my husband got tired of my always giving even when he didn't need anything. He'd ask what he could do for me and I'd never know what to say. I think he started to feel irrelevant. I now have a relationship in which we give equally, and while it sometimes feels wrong to even ask, I'm getting a lot better at it. Would I have gotten better without therapy? I doubt it very much. Medication helps a little, but it's no magic cure. Therapy pretty much saved my life. For those people like me who have been self-sufficient and capable all their lives, I just want to say that it's OK to ask for help when you need it. I still feel tough and competent, but I also know that my toughness has limits."

Summary

This chapter discusses resilience in older adults. Depression and anxiety sometimes exist in high numbers with older adults because of health, financial, and social support problems. Descriptions of characteristics of resilient older adults are provided as well as early life attributes that may predict resilience as people age. Stories are included in the chapter that suggest resilience in older adults. One of the stories is a case demonstrating that even resilient older adults may benefit from treatment.

CHAPTER 10

Resilience in Gay, Lesbian, Bisexual, and Transgender (GLBT) Individuals

G ay, lesbian, bisexual, and transgender people have an obvious set of traumas confronting them throughout the life span. Being homosexual or having doubts about one's actual gender in a society that is homophobic and moralistic can have profound repercussions, which may include experiences such as bullying in school, gay bashing, family rejection, job discrimination, and hate crimes. These repercussions begin early in life and continue throughout the life span. Many homosexual and bisexual people suffer severe depressions as a result of homophobia, and there is a higher rate of suicide in the homosexual and bisexual populations than in the population at large. While our society has moved to protect sexual orientation from legal discrimination, such discrimination occurs in great numbers, and the hidden and not so hidden conduct of all too many among us who bash and persecute homosexual and bisexual people is a remnant of a long history of persecution of these groups. But before going any further into this chapter, let's first be clear about the way the term *sexual orientation* is used here.

The American Psychological Association (2005) defines *sexual orientation* as an "enduring emotional, romantic, sexual, or affectional attraction toward others. Sexual orientation exists along a continuum that ranges from exclusive heterosexuality to exclusive homosexuality and includes various forms of bi-sexuality" (p. 1).

In considering the development of identity and whether it suggests potential for emotional risk and reduced resilience, Elizur and Ziv (2001) describe the same-gender identity processes as follows:

1. Self-Definition: The realization of same-gender feelings against the background of self and others' expectations for the development of heterosexuality breaks one's sense of belonging to a "reality" shared with the

social-familial environment. The consolidation of an alternative identity narrative requires the working through of denials, pressures to conform to family expectations and the majority culture, internalized and external heterosexism, and fears of real and imagined consequences.

2. Self-Acceptance: The development of acceptance helps to depathologize one's sense of self and to consolidate a positive gay identity. This is both an inner cognitive-emotional evolvement and an interpersonal process. Contact with others who share one's gender orientation is usually the primary means of developing self-acceptance. It helps to overcome the sense of isolation and stigmatization, and provides self-accepting role models. The sharing of one's identity with heterosexuals may complement the growth of acceptance.

3. Disclosure: This is an evolving process that encompasses both leaps of disclosure and continuous dialogues with others, during which the identity narrative is repeatedly reshaped and enriched with new meanings. Supportive relationships with other persons of same-gender orientation, feelings of acceptance by heterosexual significant others, including the family, and the level of tolerance and safety within one's social-cultural context influence the strategy and goals of disclosure. (p. 131)

Harassment, Homophobia, and Vulnerability

Human Rights Watch (2001) indicates that there are media and research reports that GLBT (gay, lesbian, bisexual, and transgender) individuals experience high levels of antigay harassment, abuses, and violence. *Transgender* refers to those individuals who are male or female but regard themselves as actually being of the opposite sex. The reports may lead people to believe that only GLBT people experience antigay harassment, but adolescents targeted for harassment in public schools are mostly those *assumed* to be homosexual. In fact, of the 5% of a school population in Seattle (Seattle Youth Risk Survey Results, 1995) who experienced antigay harassment, only 20% of the students were actually gay, demonstrating how homophobic behavior can affect heterosexual as well as homosexual adolescents.

From descriptions about their lives in public schools, it is clear that many GLBT youth feel alone and are fearful of being hated if others discover their sexual orientation. Many of these asolescents have no one to talk to about their feelings, desires, and problems. They usually don't know of peers who are gay or lesbian in their schools or neighborhoods. A Canadian Public Health Association study (Health Canada, 1998) of youth living in large and small communities indicated that "GLB youth almost universally experience a sense of isolation . . . [this happens to be] the most relentless feature in the lives of most gay, lesbian and bisexual youth. And the isolation is more profound than simply social and physical: it is also emotional and cognitive" (pp. 4–5).

SAMSHA (2001), a branch of National Institute of Mental Health writes, "Gay, lesbian, and bisexual youth experience significantly more violence-related behaviors at school and have higher rates of suicide attempts" (p. 1). The report continues, "Active homosexual and bisexual adolescents had higher rates of suicide attempts in the past year (27%) compared to youth with only heterosexual experience (15%). Students with same-sex experience were significantly more likely to be threatened with a weapon, to have property stolen or deliberately damaged, and to not go to school because of feeling unsafe" (p. 1). In describing the harm done by homophobia, Bidstrup (2000) writes,

> There are the obvious murders inspired by hatred. In the U.S., they number in the dozens every year. Abroad, the numbers run to the hundreds to thousands, no one knows the precise number for sure, as in many countries, the deaths of homosexuals are not considered worth recording as a separate category.
>
> But there are other ways in which homophobia kills. There are countless suicides every year by gay men and lesbians, particularly youth, which mental health professionals tell us are not the direct result of the victim's homosexuality but actually the result of how the homosexual is treated by society. When one lives with rejection day after day and society discounts one's value constantly, it is difficult to maintain perspective and realize that the problem is *others'* perceptions not one's own, which is why suicide is several times as common among gay men as it is among straight men.
>
> Perhaps the highest price is paid by youth. The young person just emerging into adulthood who has begun to realize that he is different, and the difference is not approved of, finds acceptance of self particularly difficult. This is especially true when others perceive the young person as different, and persecute him as a result, with little effort made by authority figures to stop the torment. This is why gay youth commit suicide at a rate of about seven times that of straight youth. Yet it is surprising how often homophobes actually try to prevent intervention by teachers in the schools. (pp. 2–3)

According to Elizur and Ziv (2001), GLB youth are at much greater risk than the general population of youth for "major depressions, generalized anxiety disorders, conduct disorders, substance abuse and dependence, suicidal behaviors, sexual risk-taking, and poor general health maintenance (Fergusson, Horwood, & Beautrais, 1999; Lock & Steiner, 1999; Safren & Heimberg, 1999)" (p.125). The authors believe that sexual minority status is a significant risk factor for GLB adolescents' physical and mental health. Elizur and Ziv (2001) indicate that estimates of suicide attempts by GLB adolescents, for example, are far above adolescent norms: ranging from 30% to 42%.

Regarding adults, Elizur and Ziv (2001) note that available evidence indicates that gay, lesbian, and bisexual individuals are at greater psychological risk than the general population. This is the result of these sexual minority groups' experiences with stigma, discrimination, and violence, as such experiences predict psychological distress and dysfunction. Elizur and Ziv (2001) write that "GLB survivors of hate crimes suffer from posttraumatic stress reactions and other negative mental health consequences that are often exacerbated by societal heterosexism" (p. 130). In addition, gay men experience HIV-related symptoms and AIDS-related bereavement, which also contribute greatly to their emotional distress. However, in all other ways, the authors found the psychological adjustment of stigmatized and nonstigmatized sexual minority samples to be the same.

In fact, disclosure of sexual orientation to families has been repeatedly found to be a risk factor for GLB youth (Savin-Williams, 1998). Those who had disclosed their sexual orientation reported verbal and physical abuse by family members and acknowledged more suicidality than those who had not "come out" to their families (D'Augelli, Hershberger, & Pilkington, 1998). Therefore, it is not surprising that many youth tend to hide their sexual orientation, coming out first to peers and only later to siblings, mothers, and fathers, respectively (Savin-Williams, 1998). Full disclosure to parents, if it occurs, takes place after years of struggling with same-gender attractions.

Theuninck (2000) describes two primary sources of stress in the lives of GLBT individuals. External stressors include events that are largely independent of a person's perception of them, such as physical and verbal insults and abuses. Internal stressors include internalized homophobia and the perception of a society that discriminates against gay, lesbian, bisexual, and transgender people. Through internalized homophobia, Theuninck suggests that some GLBT individuals come to believe that homosexuality is illegitimate, a sickness, a moral weakness, a defect, or a deformation of self. This belief may lead to intense self-loathing, according to the author. Theuninck (2000) also believes that because of stigma, GLBT people come to fear that their sexuality will become known and that the ever-present possibility of their being attacked or discriminated against in the course of daily life will increase.

GLBT Resilience

While they accept the concept of resilience in GLB individuals, Rouse, Longo, and Trickett (1999) believe that homophobia and gay bashing have an extraordinarily negative impact on these individuals' lives. They write that GLB adolescents, in particular, need love, care, and support from parents, educational personnel, close family friends, and other adults in the community, as well as from their peers. "People, opportunities, and atmospheres all add to the resilience equation. A resilient personality is not sufficient. It takes the person and his or her environment" (Rouse et al., 1999).

Although many families may initially reject a family member whose sexual identity they reject, Savin-Williams (1998, 2001) found that families can add to the resilience of GLB youth because families evolve and may shift positions in an attempt to develop strategies to fight social stigma. The authors report that family support and assistance is a buffer for GLB adolescents against the mental health problems associated with verbal abuse and gay bashing. The authors also report that the comfort of parents with the sexual identity of a GLB adolescent is a predictor of the adolescent's comfort with his or her sexual identity. Smith and Brown (1997) found that when individuals' disclose their sexual identity to their parents, there is an initial crisis, following which family relationships often improve and, in some cases, improve to a better level than before the disclosure.

Elizur and Ziv (2001) report that "following a particularly stressful adolescence, many GLB adults appear to make a rebound toward greater mental health and to achieve a level of psychological adjustment on par with heterosexual comparison groups, even though they continue to face unique stress factors" (p. 130). A significant aspect of their later resilience is explained by family acceptance. In a study of gay men, Elizur and Ziv (2001) found support for the following propositions:

(a) supportive families are more likely to be accepting of gay orientation; (b) family support has an effect on gay men's psychological adjustment that is partially mediated by family acceptance; and (c) the effects of family support on identity formation and family knowledge are fully mediated by family acceptance, while the effect of family acceptance on identity formation is partly mediated by family knowledge. Consistent with the resiliency model, these results suggest that families can play a positive role in the life of gay men, even in societies with traditional family values. As for identity formation, the acceptance of same-gender orientation by family members appears to be a particularly meaningful form of support. (p. 135)

While GLBT and heterosexual persons alike develop their identities by struggling with issues that may be painful, the denial, ambivalence, and outright rejection of sexual identity experienced by GLBT individuals increases the potential of rejection by their families and communities. Resilience can be reinforced when clients deal with feelings of "otherness" through self-exploration, discussions with others having similar issues, and, certainly, through therapy. As the following story demonstrates, supportive parents and therapy can be very effective in helping clients with minority sexual orientations resolve their feelings of "otherness."

A STORY ABOUT A FIRST AWARENESS OF BEING GAY

I think most gays are in some form of denial when they begin to suspect that they are gay. I mean, it's just about the worst thing that anyone can be for most teenaged guys. I was not only in denial, I but I was homophobic. I played high school football and the worst thing you could say about someone was that they were "queer" or a "fag." I said that to a lot of guys and kept the fact that I was having intense sexual fantasies about some of the guys on the team to myself. It was scary that I might be found out. I'd see guys in school who were very effeminate (we might say swishy now) and I'd tell myself that wasn't me, I wasn't one of those little sissy guys who looked and talked like a girl. I was an athlete and very macho. Still, the feelings I had for guys were very intense, and I can remember having a crush on one of my teammates and feeling very foolish about it. A guy! It was disgusting. I started buying magazines with pictures of really buff men in them, and masturbating to the pictures. I guess most of my friends were doing the same thing to pictures of women. It was my dad who found the pictures and asked me to chat about them.

I told him that the pictures were for training so I could figure out the sort of body I wanted, but my dad wasn't buying it. Neither was I. Pretty soon I was blurting out all this stuff about how guys turned me on and how awful that made me feel. He wondered if girls also turned me on and I said, no, that they didn't. So we went to a counselor who specializes in this sort of thing, and while I didn't want to be gay, and I mean I'd have done anything not to have been, I was, and I had to accept it.

It took 2 years of therapy and participating in some groups I went to with guys like me who were realizing they were gay, and hating it, for me to have my first sexual experience. It was wonderful and terrible and repulsive and sweet. I mean it was wonderful, and it made me realize that I was gay and that it was just the way it was. If I accepted it and enjoyed the experience, I could be like anyone else. I could love someone, I could enjoy sex, and I could even be part of a couple.

I'm ashamed to say I never told my friends in high school. I went to a college where no one from my school went. I met some great people, men and women who were gay, and I learned a lot about how gays are as different in many ways as heterosexuals are. My mom and dad were wonderful about it. When I brought my first serious love relationship home for Thanksgiving, they were as excited about it as if it was a girlfriend. My brother, on the other hand, has been a jerk and makes snide comments about it, but screw him; he's always been a jerk. About 2 years after I started going to college, I told a few of my good friends from high school that I was gay, and they treated me like I had leprosy. It's OK. I'm glad I've been open about it. I know people who marry and have kids but are as gay as I am. It only leads to hurt feelings to be in denial. I belong to a gay church, and it's wonderful, and I've become involved in gay politics. I've been out drumming up support for gay marriage, which I think is something that will happen sooner than later.

Do I wish I'd been heterosexual? You bet. It would have made my life easier. Am I comfortable with my gayness? Not entirely, but I'm getting there. I think gay people internalize negative stereotypes about gays that leave us with poor self-concepts. Do I think I could change and become straight? Of course not. I think you have to accept who you are and like yourself. My dad said something when we were having these long chats about being gay. He said that he always hoped for a strong, healthy child with great values, and in that way he couldn't have asked for anything more than what he got in me. He said that my being gay meant nothing to him because the son he loved was me and it didn't matter, my being gay, and he meant it.

Many of my friends have had bad experiences with their fathers when they came out. I know a number of guys who were disowned by their fathers and haven't seen them in years. I remember reading a story about a guy who was going to his parents' house to tell them that he was gay. He came from a very traditional culture and he figured that when he told them, he'd be disowned. He went into the house and began to bring up the subject, but his parents kept avoiding it until he finally realized that they'd known all along and loved him, and that actually telling them that he was gay would break the facade, the charade they were playing, so they had this nice chat about the weather. His folks said they had a nice girl for him to meet and would he come for dinner that Sunday, and he did. He didn't want to change the rules of the game they were playing and, in that way, everyone maintained their integrity.

I don't know if I like that story or not, but it's what you often hear. I'm pleased I didn't have to go through that sort of dishonesty and that I could be honest about it all. I think it made accepting myself a lot easier.

LESSONS TO BE LEARNED FROM THIS STORY

For adolescents, discovering and disclosing a gay, lesbian, bisexual, or transgender sexual identity can be very challenging experiences. The strong support of others, like the storyteller's father, therapist, and groups, can help adolescents to cope with these experiences. This is what we can learn from the story:

1. The storyteller is fortunate to have a father he trusted who was sensitive and caring and helped him deal with his initial anxiety about being gay. The storyteller sought professional help, with the support of his father, which helped him deal with his negative feelings about being gay. As resistant as adolescents can be about therapy, his willingness to enter into long-term therapy and become involved in groups with other gay young men having difficulty dealing with being gay are very positive signs of resilience.

2. He has exceptionally supportive parents. While coming out is sometimes difficult because of the strong negative reaction of parents, the storyteller has parents who have been supportive and loving, and it's helped him cope.

3. He took his time before he had a sexual experience, and by that time, he was certain about his sexual orientation and felt comfortable with himself.

4. He feels confident that hiding one's gayness will lead to difficulty. This is a very mature and accurate perception on his part. Caldwell (2004) reports that once married gays and lesbians come out about their sexual orientation, about two thirds of the marriages end within 2 years. "Some estimates put the number of gays and lesbians who have or have had a straight spouse at around 2 million nationwide. However, with recent advances for gay rights, many married gay men are coming out and leaving their wives" (p. 56). However, as Caldwell indicates,

> There's a big price to be paid for coming out and ending a marriage. "A lot of times there is anger from the spouse and the children, and that has to be repaired over time," says Joni Lavick, director of mental health services at the Los Angeles Gay and Lesbian Center. "But at a certain point many of these men overcome their own internalized homophobia and can't live a lie anymore. The pressure of keeping a secret is so great that dealing with what is going to happen is less toxic than staying in the closet." (p. 56)

5. The storyteller has developed a support group and uses a gay church congregation for affiliation and spirituality.

6. He told old friends about his sexual orientation. While many were not accepting, he felt that coming out to his close friends was the appropriate thing to do, showing that he acts from a high level of moral and ethical principles.

7. Although he says that his brother has been a "jerk" about his sexual orientation, the storyteller isn't fazed by it and continues to have a close relationship with other members of his family.

A Story About Coming Out

When I was growing up, I remember thinking that I'd never like to be married because I'd be married to a boy. Boys were great and I played a lot with them, but the idea of a romantic love with a boy seemed sort of repulsive. I knew for sure that I preferred girls by the time I was an adolescent. Not that it was easy for me to talk about, because it wasn't. I grew up in a very traditional Catholic home, and the idea of the oldest daughter being gay, it would have never flown. So I dated guys all through high school and, being attractive, I guess, I had a lot of dates, none for more than a time or two. Making out was out of the question, and word got around in high school that I wasn't about to put out, so I never got asked to the prom or anything like that. It incensed my father, who thought that I was being a good girl, and in our Catholic family, not being sexual before marriage was considered a positive quality. He was angry for me because he thought the guys were ignoring me because I wasn't easy.

The truth was that I was having romantic fantasies about other girls and women. I had crushes, and I knew from reading that I was probably gay. I hate the word *lesbian*. It sounds like a disease. I tried to talk to my mother about it when I was around 15, but she was mortified and sent me to a priest who was even more mortified and told my father. My father hit the ceiling and sent me to a convent school out of town. There were other girls who thought they were gay like me, and it was where I had my first romantic and sexual experiences. The experiences were good and bad. Girls can be as shitty as guys when it comes to love and sex, and it took me some time to understand that there were female predators out there. But once I understood that and began to choose wisely, I've been very happy being gay. I mean, it's what I am. Unfortunately, I've been estranged from my family and it hurts. I want to go home for Christmas and be with my family, but there are always excuses why I can't come home. Aunt Mary needs my room, or Cousin Ann is getting old and needs to be with us.

I found a priest who does family reunifications and we met with my entire family. My father cried all through the meeting and wouldn't touch me. It was awful. He kept asking why God had done this, and wasn't I a good enough Christian to know right from wrong and what the Bible says about unclean acts? To me it's not unclean, it's beautiful. Who are they to say such things? I went for therapy and it helped me a lot. I began to see it as their problem, not mine, and I kept the door open, but they didn't walk through it.

I'm in graduate school now, studying to be an architect. It's all I ever wanted to be. I had this fantasy of designing a house for my folks. Maybe I will some day. Right now, I'm not in a relationship, but I have good male and female friends, and I'm comfortable with who I am. It hurts sometimes when my family seems so down on me, but recently my father wrote me a letter. I'd won an award for a design I did for a small affordable house, and he said in his letter that he was very proud of what I'd done and that his heart was opening, through prayer, and he wanted to come, with my mom, and see my school and spend a weekend with me. He said to bring anyone I wanted to, I guess meaning a girlfriend. I'm not in a relationship right now so I brought two gay friends, a guy and girl, but said nothing about them. You could tell all through dinner that my folks were very confused. Were they or weren't they gay?

At the end of the weekend, which was great, my dad said he wanted to see me at Thanksgiving and Christmas and that my room was mine and always would be. It took almost 10 years for that to happen and, while I was in a lot of pain, I thank God it happened and we now have a real relationship. It feels wonderful. You should always keep the door open and you should be optimistic, I guess, and you should know if you're gay that things like what happened to me are bound to happen. We're a very oppressive society toward people who are different.

LESSONS TO BE LEARNED FROM THIS STORY

As is apparent from the story, and as Elizur and Ziv (2001) suggest, families can both hurt and heal. Because a family initially has a strongly negative response to the disclosure of a family member's gay, lesbian, bisexual, or transgender sexual identity doesn't mean that the relationship cannot improve. The following list provides descriptions of what can be learned from this story:

1. Elizur and Ziv (2001) write that "coming-out to family is not a panacea, and it is neither good nor bad in itself. Rather, it is the quality of one's decision-making, the unfolding of disclosure as a process, and the fit between the configuration of disclosure and the familial/social environment that has repercussions for the consolidation of one's identity and psychological adjustment" (p. 128).

2. As Beeler and Diprova (1999) suggest, people who go through the process of coming out need to develop appropriate strategies. Therapists and friends can help develop such strategies, but the main consdieration is that the individual's attempt to discuss sexual identity with parents and significant others should be done in a way that is authentic. The storyteller was clearly authentic in her attempts to discuss her sexual identity with her parents and others.

3. Even though the storyteller's parents were unresponsive to her attempts to discuss her sexual orientation with them and were, in fact, judgmental and rejecting, she left the door open to a family reunification. While it took almost 10 years to happen, it *did* take place, and she and her family are in the process of healing old wounds from their earlier rejections. This is clearly an example of a resilient person's optimism and unwillingness to give up.

4. Kline (1998) suggests that as important as healthy family support may be to the acceptance of self, even more important is the consolidation of gay identity that helps people discuss their sexual orientation with family and friends in a way that fosters support and acceptance. Our storyteller used the available literature and her own inquisitive nature to confirm for herself that she was gay. Once having confirmed and accepted that she was gay, she accepted herself in the face of considerable rejection and family withdrawl.

5. Our storyteller disclosed her sexual identity to others, but Savin-Williams (1998) found that disclosure often brings with it verbal and physical abuse from family members. Many youth keep their sexual orientation a secret and, unlike our storyteller, who shows great resilience, their "full disclosure to parents, if it occurs, takes place after years of struggling with same-gender attractions" (Elizur & Ziv, 2001, p. 131).

A Story About Confronting Homophobia

Kids can be very cruel, and they were very cruel to me when I was growing up. I was the scapegoat for every homophobic impulse anyone had when I was in school. I was beaten up a number of times, and everything from having my locker trashed to having people put signs on my back that said "Queer Here" and "Beware of Fag" was done to me by the time I was 14. I didn't think I was gay, and so it hurt all the more. I didn't think I was different from any of the other boys in school.

I started reading about gays when I was still in grade school. I was surprised to read that the descriptions of gay people were precisely what I felt about myself. I know it sounds naïve, and maybe I was in denial, but what I felt about myself was what I thought everyone felt. By adolescence I knew that was complete nonsense and I could accept that I was gay, but the bullying and taunting were just making me miserable.

My folks were working-class people, not very sophisticated, and my dad told me to fight back, and I did. I hit a kid so hard, a kid who was taunting me about being gay, that he was put in the hospital for observation. When the principal found out why, he seemed very embarrassed. I was suspended for a while but, believe me, the taunting and bullying stopped. I've never been one to think that gays should take gay bashing lightly. I don't. You listen to what other people say about you passively, and pretty soon you start believing it. What *crap* that is! I'm a gay guy with an MBA. I'm smart and able. I love my country and I'm a good person. To hell with letting others tell you what you're supposed to believe about yourself.

My gay friends are intimidated by gay bashing. Well it *is* dangerous and scary. So we've taken up self-defense, and when anyone bothers us, the stereotype of sissy men or girly boys, as our governor likes to call us, goes right out the window. You have to be tough to act tough, and while I see myself as a gentle person and I haven't hit anyone since that kid in high school, I have an inner belief that I can defend myself. It gives me a persona that even the dumbest homophobe knows means business. I hate the idea of gays feeling weak. It damages your self-esteem.

My partner is a very tender guy. He's very emotional and he hurts when others hurt. He was in a bar with me a few weeks ago and someone said something so homophobic and full of malice, I thought I'd explode. My partner, who can bench press 350 pounds, just quietly told him that bashing was a sign of deep insecurity and rather than striking out against others because it made him feel more secure and powerful, to look inside so he could see the hurting, unloving person, full of sexual identity confusion and denial about his own attrac-tion to gay men. I know it's pretty common stuff, but he said it in a way that took this guy back. Pretty soon the guy was telling my partner about his abusive dad and how his dad hated gays because he needed someone to hate, and the guy apologized. It was pretty terrific, that moment, and I cherish my partner for having the strength to be calm rather than getting angry. Where would that have led?

Maybe straights know that homophobia kills, but it's so engrained in men and in the culture to fear us, that it's a real burden. I get depressed when I find out that there's been yet another gay killing. Isn't it enough that AIDS has almost done us in?

I wonder why homophobia is so strong in our culture. And I think it must have something to do with religion and the animosity religions have toward homosexuality. I also think that many men in our society worry about their masculinity and fear they won't cut it when it comes to being a man. The notion of machismo just seems extraordinarily homophobic, and it's a concept that exists in every culture I know about. I wonder how many men, in their insecure and sometimes failing attempts to be real men, turn their anger at themselves outward so they can feel superior when inside they ache with inse-curity. I don't know, but we gays are just like everyone else. If you got to know any of us, you'd see we don't have a secret society that's intent on world domination.

I have a Jewish friend who told me that the club he'd just joined arranged a tennis match. The guy he played began talking about the World Zionist Conspiracy and, as an example, how Jews had ganged up on him when he ran for public office. My friend walked off the court and told the owner of the club about him. The owner just shrugged, so my friend contacted many of the Jewish members (there were a lot), and they insisted that the guy be kicked out of the club or the owner risked losing their membership. Maybe that guy still believes in an international Zionist conspiracy, but at least he knows what happens when he's publicly anti-Semitic. I sense that the same thing operates with gays, that there's some primitive belief that we're contagious and that we carry the seeds of world destruction. It just can't be good for young gays to grow up with homophobia, and I, for one, think the professional community has done all too little to combat it. I hear about counselors and therapists who go mum when clients say homophobic things. Being silent in the face of such bile only rein-forces it. I agree with that 60s statement: If you aren't part of the solution, you're part of the problem.

LESSONS TO BE LEARNED FROM THIS STORY

The consequences of homophobic bullying are serious. To underscore this fact, Hawker and Boulton (2000) write, in their meta-analysis of the subject, that it is clear that "peer victimization [is] most strongly related to depression." The results of their analysis suggest that "victims of peer aggression experience more negative affect, and negative thoughts about themselves, than other children [do]" (Hawker & Boulton, 2000, p. 451). This is what we can learn from the story:

1. Bullying in school led the storyteller to depression and a sense of isolation. The storyteller shows a rare ability to deal with the bullying he received by understanding its source and by reading about homophobia.

2. He understands that certain male behaviors, often called machismo, are sometimes associated with homophobia. In defining machismo, Baca Zinn (1980) writes that it is "the male attempt to compensate for feelings of internalized inferiority by exaggerating masculinity" (p. 20). Mirande (1979) describes the behaviors associated with machismo: "The macho male demands complete deference, respect and obedience not only from his wife but from his children as well" (p. 479). Perhaps the term *machismo* is more easily understood as "traditional." Explaining machismo in this way, Chafetz (1974) writes, "The masculine sex role for [traditional men] is generally described by reference to the highly stereotyped notion of machismo. In fact, a strong emphasis on masculine aggressiveness and dominance may be characteristic of most groups in the lower ranges of the socioeconomic ladder" (p 59). But to attribute homophobia only to this group of men is a mistake. Homophobia is present in a number of men and women who are well educated, are sophisticated, and would never think of themselves as "traditional."

3. The story of his partner's resolution of a homophobic encounter suggests a very evolved way of dealing with anger, one the storyteller admires and respects. Although he sounds fairly belligerent, he has elegant ways of coping with his anger.

4. He understands that his level of achievement in life and the homophobic responses he endures are quite separate from his self-identity as a person. He has a very positive opinion of himself and tells us, "You listen to what other people say about you passively, and pretty soon you start believing it. What *crap* that is! I'm a gay guy with an MBA. I'm smart and able. I love my country and I'm a good person. To hell with letting others tell you what you're supposed to believe about yourself."

5. He doesn't believe in being passive in the face of homophobia, and he remarks, "I hate the idea of gays feeling weak. It damages your self-esteem." While he isn't confrontational to the point of actually fighting, he does believe in being physically and emotionally strong as one important way of coping with homophobia. And he understands the origins of homophobia, which makes him not only strong but also knowledgeable.

6. He accurately criticizes the helping professions when he comments that therapists often let clients share homophobic feelings and beliefs without trying to change those beliefs. Sandage and Hill (2001) agree, and they suggest that modern psychology has no model of the civic virtues that promote healthy individual and community behavior. In fact, they believe that much of psychology and perhaps most of the helping professions have no models for the positive values that should be stressed with clients or for the necessary constructive social behaviors that will lead to an increased sense of social responsibility and a healthier community life.

Summary

This chapter discusses the resilience of gay, lesbian, bisexual, and transgender individuals. The stories included here exemplify the difficult issues facing GLBT individuals, including homophobia, coming out about their sexual orientation, and family rejection. Homophobia is a serious problem that results in gay bashing, depression, and higher levels of suicide among GLBT individuals. Clearly, much of the difficulty faced by GLBT individuals can be explained by external pressures and attitudes that are sometimes internalized by GLBT clients and may challenge their resilience. A more accepting and understanding society would go a long way toward reducing psychosocial problems experienced by GLBT individuals in America.

CHAPTER 11

How Resilient People Cope With Loneliness, Isolation, and Depression

Why Resilient People Sometimes Experience Loneliness, Isolation, and Depression

We often think that resilient people are stress-resistant and that feelings of depression and loneliness are inconsistent with resilience, but these assumptions aren't always true. While resilient children and adults do very well on behavioral measures of life functioning and success, they often do well in the midst of prolonged depressions, and it is important for us to better understand this situation. Masten (2001) suggests that although some children may be resilient in many ways and have self-righting capacities that permit them to cope with very difficult life issues, this does not make them invincible, and they need to be provided with healthy and positive social and educational environments at school, in the community, and at home that permit growth. When this fails to occur, the resilient child may still experience success and achievement, but may experience them in the presence of depression.

Kramer (2005) believes that a person may move from resilience into depression many years after a trauma has been coped with successfully. "Depression," he writes, "is not universal even in terrible times. Though prone to mood disorders, the great Italian writer Primo Levi was not depressed in his months at Auschwitz" (p. 53). Kramer continues,

> I have treated a handful of patients who survived horrors arising from war or political repression. They come to depression years after enduring extreme privation. Typically such a person will say "I don't understand it. I went through _____" and here he will name a shameful event of out time. "I lived through

that and in those months, I never felt *this.*" *This* refers to the relentless bleakness of depression, the self as hollow shell. Beset by great evil, a person can be wise, observant and disillusioned and yet not be depressed. Resilience confers its own measure of insight. (p. 53)

Masten and Coatsworth (1998) suggest that the literature on resilience has helped us understand why some youth succeed despite poverty and other at-risk situations. The authors describe the protective functions that foster resilience, but they wonder if the concept of resilience has made us disregard the life difficulties and hardships of many resilient and nonresilient youth and the eventual emotional side effects of abuse, poverty, and life in very troubled environments.

Some researchers have assumed that resilience is a quality that only "stress-resilient" people possess (Wyman, Cowen, & Work, 1999). These researchers' view holds that resilience is a unique personality trait rather than a fairly universal capacity to withstand trauma that is strengthened by environmental protective factors. But what happens when resilience is assumed without additional concerns for protective factors that permit resilience to continue? Three incorrect consequences may develop: (1) The idea of "invincible kids" may be assumed, which encourages the belief that since some children succeed, regardless of the stress they face, those who fail must be at fault; (2) The erroneous belief may be held that once children are deemed to be resilient, their resilience will last throughout the life span; and (3) Because resilience is taken for granted, we may neglect to develop the necessary social policies, practices, and clinical interventions to bolster the resilience of at-risk people, particularly youth, to prevent unwanted side effects like depression.

The Prevalence of Depression

A Canadian study using data from the National Population Health Survey indicates that the highest rates of first onset of depression (1.4%–9.1% of the population) occur among young adults (ages 12 to 24), and lower rates (1.3%–1.8%) occur among people age 65 or older (Patten, 2000). Similar data are noted by the National Institute of Mental Health (NIMH; 2001), which reports that in any given 1-year period, 9.5% of Americans, or about 18.8 million American adults, suffer from a depressive illness. The economic cost of this disorder is high, but the cost in human suffering cannot even be estimated. Depressive illnesses often interfere with normal functioning and cause pain and suffering, not only to those who have a disorder but also to those who care about them. Serious depression can destroy family life as well as the life of the ill person.

Fifteen percent of those diagnosed with mood disorders commit suicide, and fully two thirds of all suicides are preceded by episodes of depression (Bostwick & Pankratz, 2000). People with depressive disorders have three times the number of sick days in the month before the illness was diagnosed than their co-workers who did not suffer from depression (Parikh, Wasylenki, Goerung, & Wong, 1996). Depression is the primary reason for disability and death among people ages 18 to

44 (Murray & Lopez, 1997). Pratt, Ford, Crum, Armenian, Gallo, and Eaton (1996) followed 1,551 study subjects without a history of heart disease for 13 years. Subjects with major depressions were 4.5 times more likely to have serious heart attacks than those without major episodes of depression (Pratt et al., 1996). Supporting these data, Kramer (2005) writes,

> Depression is associated with brain disorganization and nerve cell atrophy. Depression appears to be progressive—the longer the episode, the greater the anatomical disorder. Nor is the damage merely to the mind and brain. Depression has been linked with harm to the heart, to endocrine glands, to bones. Depressives die young—not only of suicide, but also of heart attacks and strokes. Depression is a multisystem disease, one we would consider dangerous to health even if we lacked the concept of "mental illness" (p. 52).

The Nature of Loneliness and Depression

Definitions of Mood Disorders

The fourth edition of the American Psychiatric Association's diagnostic manual, *DSM-IV* (APA, 1994), indicates that mood disorders include Major Depressive Disorders lasting two weeks or more with evidence of symptoms of depression; Dysthymic Disorders in which depression has lasted more than two years with more depressed days than non-depressed days; Bi-Polar Disorders where both depression and mania may be event at a severe level and where one or both symptoms may cycle back and forth; and Cyclothymic Disorders where depression and mania cycle back and forth, but not at the same levels associated with Bi-Polar Disorder (AMA, 1994, p. 317). The common bond among these various disorders is an impact on mood that suggests intermittent to long-term depression, or cycling between very high manic stages and very severe depressions. It is also possible that some mood disorders may have psychotic features, as is sometimes the case with Bi-Polar Disorder or very severe depressions. However, such features are often not evident, and psychosis is only suggested for those clients demonstrating psychotic behavior and not by the *DSM-IV* term *Mood Disorders*.

Definitions of Loneliness and Isolation

Uruk and Demir (2003) indicate that loneliness is generally thought to be associated with negative feelings about social relationships. They define loneliness as "an unpleasant experience that occurs when a person's network of social relationships is significantly deficient in either quality or quantity (Peplau & Perlman, 1984)" (p. 179). Uruk and Demir (2003) continue their definition of loneliness by saying that it is "the psychological state that results from discrepancies between one's desire for and one's actual composition of relationships" (p. 179).

Although loneliness can be emotionally distressing, it is also a signal that something needs to be done to increase one's social network. Uruk and Demir (2003) report a high correlation between parents who have little time to spend with their children, or fail to form attachments with their children, and the development of loneliness in adolescence that often continues into adulthood. They also believe that feelings of loneliness are signals to adolescents and young adults to improve their social network and to develop friendships and intimate relationships.

Stober (2003) believes that loneliness often stems from feelings of self-pity. The author found that self-pity correlated highly with the following personality characteristics: neuroticism, depression, an external locus of control, anger, rumination, ambivalent-worrisome attachments, and reactions to stress related to relationships. Joiner, Catanzaro, Rudd, and Rajab (1999) believe that loneliness stems from a lack of pleasurable engagement and, as a result, a painful disconnection from trying to engage. In other words, people seek social contact, fail, and disengage from others in a way that adds to their feeling of failure and ultimately ends in reinforcing their sense of loneliness. Joiner and colleagues call this the "bedrock" of loneliness.

Weiss (1973) distinguishes loneliness due to emotional isolation from loneliness due to social isolation. Emotional isolation appears in the absence of a close emotional attachment (often related to a lack of parental attachment), while social isolation appears in the absence of an engaging social network (often related to a lack of peer support, friendships, and close social networks). Relationships with parents and relationships with peers constitute the two different social contexts in which loneliness develops. Rubin and Mills (1991) believe that loneliness develops when a pattern made up of social anxiety, lack of dominance, and social isolation results in peer rejection and negative self-perception. Olweus (1993) suggests that when children blame their own incompetence for negative social experiences with peers that result in rejection, the end result is often social withdrawal, feelings of isolation, and depression. Rotenberg, MacDonald, and King (2004) found considerable evidence that loneliness correlates highly with lack of trust, particularly in young women. Rotenberg and colleagues note,

> As we expected, the relationship between loneliness and trust is stronger for girls than it is for boys. The trust measures accounted for 57% of loneliness for girls but only 18% of loneliness for boys. These patterns are consistent with the hypothesis that if girls do not believe or rely on their same-gender peers to keep intimacies confidential and to fulfill promises then they are cut off from their preferred and prevalent form of interaction (i.e., same-gender close-peer networks) and therefore are highly prone to loneliness. Finding this pattern with girls and not with boys also is consistent with the notion that girls are more inclined to establish a network of close peers than are boys. Close peer networks may be normatively expected for girls, and thus they may be distinctly at risk for loneliness because they demonstrate both low trust beliefs in same-gender peers and low levels of reciprocal trusting behaviors with peers.
>
> These findings have implications for social functioning during adulthood. Women have larger intimacy networks than do men and, therefore, the observed association between loneliness and trust beliefs in same-gender peers may be stronger for women than for men during adulthood as well. (p. 235)

It is natural to assume that depression and loneliness may be interrelated since most depressed people experience feelings of severe loneliness and social isolation. Powell, Yeaton, Hill, and Silk (2001) studied the effectiveness of treatment with clients experiencing long-term mood disorders. They concluded that self-help groups were very important providers of positive management of mood disorders because social support forces otherwise lonely and isolated people to interact with others, often at a fairly intimate level. In considering demographic issues as a predictor of the ability to cope with mood disorders, Powell and colleagues failed to find any specific indicator other than the level of education, which, they believe, is an important aspect of dealing with mood disorders. Surprisingly, daily functioning was inversely related to the number of outpatients' contacts, which suggests, according to the authors, that as people improve, they see less need for professional help. Support from families and friends also failed to predict outcomes.

Since early detection of depression is essential in people's learning to cope with feelings of loneliness and depression, Duffy (2000) reports several important predictors of depression:

> A family history of major affective disorder is the strongest, most reliable risk factor for a major affective illness. Other factors associated with affective disorders include female sex (risk factor for unipolar illnesses), severe life events and disappointments, family dysfunction, poor parental care, early adversity, and personality traits.
>
> Based on the current state of knowledge, emphasis on identifying and treating mood disorders as early as possible in the course and particularly early-onset (child and adolescent) cases and youngsters at high risk (given a parent with a major mood disorder) is likely to be an effective strategy for reducing the burden of illness on both the individual and society. (p. 345)

Duffy (2000) also reports beginning evidence that brief, family-based psycho-educational interventions decrease the negative impact of parental mood disorders on children and improve family functioning in mood-disordered children. Individual treatment and family psycho-educational interventions in adult bipolar patients often decrease relapse rates and improve overall family functioning. Duffy notes that while early identification of children at risk of mood disorders is necessary, "the most effective strategy for reducing the burden of illness on individuals and society is not clear" (p. 346). However, the serious impact of mood disorders on individuals and their families, and the high risk of suicide, justify a need to develop new and more effective interventions. In the meantime, early interventions that utilize education, identification of family members who are at risk, and family interventions may decrease the seriousness of the condition and reduce the fears and misconceptions of family members. Harrington and Clark (1998) indicate that early intervention through the use of appropriate medications and mood disorder therapies may actually reduce the severity and reoccurrence of adolescent mood disorders.

The Treatment of Loneliness and Depression

In a very negative view of treatment effectiveness with severely depressed clients, O'Connor (2001) says that most depressed people receive care that is "superficial, inadequate, and based on false information" (p. 507). He also notes that close examination of most treatments for severe depression suggests that they are inadequate (Mueller et al., 1999; Solomon et al., 2000) and that most assumptions about the treatment of depression turn out to be untrue. Those assumptions include the belief that the newer antidepressants are effective, that cognitive psychotherapy helps most patients, and that most patients can recover from an episode of depression without lasting damage (O'Connor, 2001, p. 507).

Remick (2002) found psychotherapy to be as effective as antidepressants in treating mild to moderate depressions and dysthymic disorders. The author found little support for a commonly held belief that a combination of drug treatment and psychotherapy was more effective than the use of either approach alone. Cognitive behavioral therapy and interpersonal therapy appeared to be the most effective psychotherapy approaches with mild to moderate depressions and required 8 to 16 weeks for maximum benefit (Remick, 2002, p. 1260).

Stark, Rouse, and Livingston (1991) compared cognitive-behavioral therapy (CBT) with nondirective, supportive therapy in the treatment of highly depressed children. Following the end of treatment and 7 months posttreatment, children receiving CBT had fewer depressive symptoms in interviews and on the Children's Depression Inventory than children receiving supportive treatment. Brent, Holder, Kolko, Birmaher, Baugher, and Roth (1999) obtained the same results using CBT with adolescents. However, in work with depressed adults, the positive impact of CBT was not observed (Elkin, Shea, Watkins, lmber, Sotsky, and Collins, 1989). Chambless and Ollendick (2001) found five studies showing a certain amount of improvement in depressed adults receiving CBT. One study they report on is that by Peterson and Halstead (1998), who used CBT in an abbreviated group therapy form in 6 sessions rather than the typical 20 sessions. The average reduction in depressive symptoms after 6 sessions was 37%, although the degree of gain made and the length of follow-up were not described. Blatt, Zuroff, Bondi, and Sanisolow (2000) compared the effectiveness of CBT and interpersonal therapies with that of antidepressants and clinical management, as well as with the effectiveness of a placebo and clinical management. They found no differences among treatments at posttest, but in 18 months of follow-up, both groups receiving psychotherapy rated their life adjustment significantly better than clients receiving only medication or a placebo.

Writing about the treatment of severe depression, O'Connor (2001) states that we often fail to recognize that what keeps people depressed is their own view of their depression as ongoing, untreatable, and hopeless. In time, people's cognitive definitions of their depression become self-definitions that reinforce the depression and keep it from improving. To help his patients cope with their depressions, O'Connor (2001) provides them with aphorisms about depression, which he believes they can use to change their long-held beliefs about their depression and about themselves. These are some examples of O'Connor's aphorisms: "(1) If

I change what I do, I can change how I feel; (2) Change can come from anywhere; (3) I am more than my depression" (p. 517). These aphorisms are "assertions about the nature of depression and recovery from it, which help patients move toward taking an active role in questioning how the condition affects them" (p. 507). O'Connor believes that "aphorisms [are] statements that perform an action simply by being spoken" (p. 512).

A Story About Loneliness and Isolation

I think people who grow up in very troubled families never quite get the hang of intimate relationships. In my family, we were so busy surviving poverty and the illness of my mother that none of us really mastered the ability to be loved or to love someone in return. My father's favorite saying was that it was better to be home by yourself reading a good book than to be out with bad friends. Of course, he considered all my friends to be bad, so I spent my childhood reading books and being pretty much alone.

People sometimes think I'm arrogant when what I *really* am is shy and introverted with moments of grandiosity where I can act like I'm the greatest thing since sliced bread. Basically, I'm pretty withdrawn, and I don't think people react well to me. I'm never invited to dinner by colleagues, or asked out for coffee, or any of the things that tell me others find me appealing. Sometimes it's very hurtful to me. Even so, I've been very successful at work and have risen quite high in my chosen field. I experience loneliness after work and on weekends. It can be a killer. I've tried everything, including going to as many social functions as possible to fill my time, but I feel even more alone and isolated. It's hard to explain being lonely when you're around people.

I've gone for therapy, of course, but most of the time it's so superficial and completely misses the mark that it ends up hurting me more than helping. You go to a therapist, and in a way it's like falling or not falling in love. I mean you have expectations, and when they're not met and you've put in so much time and energy to get another person to listen, maybe even *like* you a little, and they don't, it's like having a knife stuck in your heart.

I went to a therapist who was highly regarded by my ex-girlfriend. Maybe it was a mistake to see this particular therapist because the therapist and my ex-girlfriend's best friend were business partners. All through my therapy I had the feeling the therapist was telling her partner about me and her partner was then talking to my ex-girlfriend. I confronted my therapist about it and she was very angry and denied it. I would write summaries of our treatment, which she didn't read, and then I wrote a story with a lot of transference stuff in it and I knew she hadn't read it and called her on it.

Every once in a while I meet a lady and we enjoy a brief moment or two before the relationship ends. I'm seeing someone now and, knowing it's going to end sooner or later, I take the nights we spend together and I think of them as a collection of fine wines, or beautiful paintings, or wonderful memories—her mature body silhouetted against the moonlight, the strength of her legs, the loveliness of the nipples on her breasts. I know she's going to see me for what I really am and get rid of me. And then, instead of having the warmth of her companionship, I'll be alone again.

I fight feeling down all the time. I force myself to get up in the morning and go to work. Sometimes I can go for months and the beauty of the work I do feels like an endless poem. It's the happiest time for me, and I feel like Superman leaping tall buildings in a single stride. But when that moment passes and the work feels like bricks on a wall that won't fit together, a curtain falls over me and I'm in turmoil.

I don't think there's an easy answer to loneliness and, believe me, it's everything it's cracked up to be. It hurts like hell. You asked me how I cope and the best answer I can give is that I force myself to. I'm not at all religious, but I believe in God and I think that He meant for me to do something special. He's given me gifts for which I feel grateful. I don't believe He's made me lonely or that the problems in my early life are insurmountable. I believe that I can overcome those obstacles. So I keep on truckin' and out of a week, 2 days are sublime, 2 days are miserable, and 3 days are neutral. I don't think that's so bad. I worry that when the 2 miserable days become 3 or 4, that I won't make it anymore, but until then, I feel lucky that I've achieved so much in my life and that I'm physically healthy and, to some extent, even happy.

I don't think there's any magical answer to loneliness. You keep on trying, you don't allow yourself to feel too sorry for yourself, and you take each day as it comes. I know those are clichés, but sometimes there's truth in a cliché, and as someone who was raised on the messages my mother got from the soap operas, I truly believe that sometimes the Tooth Fairy takes your lost dreams and replaces them with gold.

Lessons to Be Learned From This Story

What happens when people who are otherwise quite successful in many aspects of their lives are unable to shake severe feelings of loneliness and develop interesting and sometimes elegant ways of coping that suggest significant degrees of resilience? This story deals with that issue.

Loneliness really *is* everything it's cracked up to be. The storyteller's description of the therapy he received supports O'Connor's (2001) view of treatment with depressed clients as "superficial, inadequate, and based on false information" (p. 507). O'Connor notes that many assumptions held by professionals regarding the effectiveness of antidepressants and short-term cognitive therapy are not true, and that the belief "that most patients can recover from an episode of depression without lasting damage, on close examination, turns out not to be true at all" (p. 507).

The storyteller relates his lack of ability to seek and find intimacy to problems in his early life with his family that were brought on by his mother's illness and poverty and by a father whose messages encouraged isolation. And yet he perseveres and achieves even in the midst of despair. The following are some of the primary reasons for the storyteller's ability to cope with life while experiencing isolation and loneliness.

1. He believes that he has something important to accomplish in life and that God has given him a role, as yet undefined, to do something special. Perhaps this is a spiritual aspect of the client's search for life meaning that gives him an inner-directedness that permits him to achieve even in the midst of despair.

2. He gets great satisfaction from his work when it goes well. For this individual, work can is a hedge against painful feelings of aloneness and insecurity.

3. He is very self-directed and believes that he has control over his isolation and loneliness. An internal locus of control is a positive sign in our storyteller, as it is in anyone who is experiencing loneliness and isolation, because it tells us that he will seek appropriate help from others if his emotional life becomes too painful.

4. While he indicates that his father made it difficult for him to develop friendships, he doesn't blame his parents or his early life experiences for his problems in achieving friendships, companionship, or intimate relationships. Not blaming others is a considerable a sign of resilience.

5. He has an optimistic and positive view of the future and believes that he can overcome his problems. Optimism bodes well for his attempts to alleviate the problems of isolation and loneliness.

6. Even though he has a negative opinion about therapy, he has tried it, which shows a recognition of the need to seek help when painful inner feelings become overwhelming. Knowing when you're unable to resolve problems by yourself and recognizing your need of outside help are signs of maturity and self-awareness. Even though he isn't positive about the benefits of therapy, he uses it when necessary, and we can assume this means that he is hopeful that it will work for him if the therapist is right.

A Story About Loneliness in the Company of Others

We're sitting at a restaurant with the unlikely name of The Fig Tree. For reasons I don't fully understand, I keep calling it "The Fig Leaf." Maybe the lust I have for the woman with me has something to do with it. She has a soft Texas accent and one of those names that only someone from Texas could ever have. Emily Anne Jennifer or Pamela Ellen Anne. The restaurant is romantic and moody, but our waiter keeps flitting in and telling us irrelevant things about the food meant to ingratiate himself to us. He pronounces everything wrong and knows nothing about the foreign languages he uses to describe the food we will eat. Emily Anne is beside herself with joy and engages him in meaningless chatter about the chef and asks if he knows someone by the name of Billy Edward.

"This is so beautiful," she coos. We're sitting behind a waterfall and my jacket is getting wet. She looks at me and, for the first time in the night, I'm sure we'll end up in bed. It's been a thousand years since I've made love to anyone and the thought scares me a little.

This story was sent to me by a colleague. It was originally titled "Pumpkin Eaters" and is followed by a self-analysis.

She reaches over and touches my hand. I like her cool skin. I'll bet her body will be smooth and soft to the touch. I'm sweating. And then she begins to tell me about her babies and the "troubles." We sit facing one another and she tells me about her miscarriages and her C-section. I'm looking concerned, but all I want to do is tell her that she's breaking the magic spell. Talking about miscarriages and dead babies isn't what you want to listen to on a first date. I glance at the lady sitting at the table next to us with the absolutely good sense to wear a low-cut dress. I can't make out anything about Emily Anne's body other than to imagine the probable scars she carries and the fact that making love to her may lead to an exploration of the pathways of each and every one of them.

"February is the worst month," she says, and being two days from Valentine's Day, she adds, "except . . . for meeting you." I try to smile, but it feels off-center and not convincing. "Everyone dies in February," she says, "and whenever I go through the month, I get depressed." They serve our salads as she tells me about her February curse. The waiter lingers over us and tells us about the dressing the chef has prepared, especially for us. It tastes like glue.

After she tries her salad and tells the waiter that it flies on the wings of a dove, she starts telling me how she explained her last miscarriage to her six-year-old son. "Mommy had a nice little brother inside of her just for you," she says, "but he couldn't quite tell us that he was hurting and we missed the signs and now he's in heaven with your granddad." The little boy ponders the news and wonders if granddad will like him when he goes to heaven, since his brother has already been there with him and has a head start. It's one of those questions I wish she'd answered, but she only moves on to the next chapter of this first date litany of bad February luck.

After the miscarriage, she decides that if she can't have a baby, she'll adopt. But her ex-husband isn't keen on adoption and has an affair. Her family disowns her because the birth mother is high on pot most of the time. Emily, however, loves the pregnant girl like her own daughter and feels a spiritual kinship. "But that baby died too," she says sadly, taking bites of her salad with the dressing the chef prepared especially for us that tastes like glue. The man at the table next to us kisses the woman in the low cut dress on her cheek and runs his hand over her breast. He smiles at me. She smiles at me too, but Emily Anne is oblivious and continues on with her story about early death and babies falling into heaven. I wonder how many other men on first dates have heard this same story.

She found another pregnant girl and they had a beautiful child, Troy. He's beautiful, but Emily's husband left and Troy is hyperactive and causes scenes at school. He is beautiful, but he likes killing birds, and he goes volcanic sometimes and it takes her hours to calm him down. She has a sad look on her face. They bring the main course and she describes the birthing mother. "She looked enough like me to be my sister," she says. "I talk to her sometimes in my dreams."

The birds of the South gather round the tree next to us and coo. Emily Anne has a blissful look on her face. "I didn't know it could be so painful to have children," she says, glancing away from me. "I don't have anything left except for the children," she says, and watches the couple next to us. They look wonderful together, svelte, and handsome, and fashionable. "I don't like to talk about it," she says, and then before dessert and tea and the little gummy delicacies they leave on your plate with the bill so high it makes me dizzy, she tells me that she loved someone very much but it didn't work out. "I tried, but we are only human," she says, and wipes a tear from her eyes. "Yes we are," she says to no one in particular and looks vaguely at the people passing by.

I listen on and we walk home after dinner holding hands and putting our arms around one another. When we get home, she wonders if we'll sleep together and almost cries when she tells me she's scared. And we do, we do sleep together, and it is tender and loving and everything works. How can you ever know what a night of dead babies will bring? Maybe the couple next to us went home and fell right asleep, but out of Emily Anne comes a passion I can't quite believe, and we make love like two Pumpkin Eaters in a Pumpkin Patch reserved for older lovers and those of us whose hearts are heavy with the death of babies.

THE STORYTELLER'S SELF-ANALYSIS

My colleague who wrote the preceding story provided the following response to questions I asked about the story. "You asked me to send something about resilience, which means, I guess, that you think I'm resilient. Thanks, old friend, but frankly I feel pretty beaten up by life. Yeah, I can hear you telling me how much I've achieved and how amazing I am, and sometimes, I even believe it myself. Mostly, I think I've been an unhappy person for as long as I can remember. I've been married four times and each woman has made me feel lonelier than the next. They all told me how detached I was. I believe them. Sometimes I can't feel a thing. The marriages end, I feel nothing, and then I go on to another poor soul who tries her best, it ends, and again I feel nothing. For 6 months after my last marriage, I bought a house but couldn't get up the energy to buy a bed or a sofa, so I slept on a bed roll and sat on a milk crate.

"About the story I sent you. I don't know why I wrote it. Maybe it's about loneliness and detachment and coming together for a brief moment with someone you're prepared to hate but end up being astonished by. Maybe it's also about the pain people carry around that they have to share with absolute strangers because they can't find solace elsewhere. Maybe it's about the women I choose and the fact that I've given up on meeting anyone really good for me, as if that person even exists. Maybe, old friend, it's about all of us older guys who achieve at such a high level and end up alone to face another hopeless night in bed with confused thoughts of ending it all.

"I think loneliness is a killer. You try to engage with others and you try to be intimate, but some force inside makes it impossible. You're forever holding back and pretty soon other people don't want you around because they get nothing from you. You're like the wall or the rug. Most nights I drink myself to sleep trying to figure it out. I've gone for help and it doesn't make a difference. I know I'm successful, I know I've achieved, I know people envy me for my accomplishments, but what am I left with? Another empty house to come home to, a lonely meal without company, 4 hours of drinking and TV, and if I'm lucky, sleep without nightmares. It's really unconscionable of God to make me so resilient and never give me happiness in return. When the time comes, I'm going to tell Him that to His face. And that's the truth, Morley, it really is."

Summary

This chapter about loneliness, isolation, and depression provides reasons that social isolation sometimes leads to depression. Reasons are given in the chapter for some resilient people's experience of loneliness and depression. These reasons include the lack of social support needed to maintain resilience and delayed reaction to traumas that may have occurred many years earlier, such as the experiences of people dealing with state-conducted terror and concentration camps. In addition, there are two stories in the chapter that deal with loneliness. One story is followed by an analysis by me, and the second story is followed by an analysis by the storyteller.

CHAPTER 12

Family Resilience

The Changing American Family

Many aspects of family life in America have dramatically changed during the past 50 years. An article in the June 2003 issue of *Pediatrics* entitled "The Changing American Family: A Report of the Task Force of the American Academy of Pediatrics" reports the following data on family life in America: (1) The majority of families in America now have no children younger than 18 years of age; (2) People are marrying at an older age, and the highest number of births occurs in women over the age of 30; (3) From 1970 to 2000, the percentage of two-parent families with children decreased from 85% to 69%; (4) Twenty-six percent of all children live with a single parent, usually their mother; (5) The rate of births to unmarried women has gone from 5.3% in 1960 to 33.2% in 2000, and the divorce rate, while slowing, is still twice as high as it was in 1955; (6) The median income of female-headed households is only 47% of the median income of married-couple-headed families; (7) The number of children living in poverty is now five times higher in female-headed families than in married-couple-headed families.

While the concept of family is still well thought of in America, when social issues arise such as youth crime and lowering educational achievement, we tend to blame the family for problems experienced by children, while at the same time looking to the family for solutions. The final report of the American Assembly ("Strengthening American Families," 2000) suggests that changing social conditions in America have not only weakened families but have also overstressed many families, resulting in increasing numbers of troubled families and, with it, increasing numbers of malfunctioning children and adolescents. The idealized notion of the traditional family with one parent working and another staying at home and caring for the children has been replaced by a reality in which families are unable to succeed economically without both parents working, latchkey children are home alone for long periods of time after school, the amount of family violence is increasing, and children are poorly supervised—with their parents believing that as long as they clothe and feed the children and provide housing, anything that goes wrong with the children is the result of malfunctioning social institutions such as schools. This is why schools have increasing responsibility not only to modify poor social behavior but also to provide values, teach about relationships and intimacy, and in many ways, act as surrogates for missing, chaotic, and poorly functioning parents.

The social and economic pressures on American families have increased in many ways. For example, time is more limited when family time includes the time it takes parents to get to work and back. This travel time also lengthens the family's day. In addition, working parents responding to a number of forces may find their family life complicated by the use of child care that places children in environments a distance from their homes and that may place children at risk of influences that compromise family values and result in incompatible approaches to discipline. The article in *Pediatrics* mentioned earlier ("The Changing American Family," 2003) includes the following statement: "In public opinion polls, most parents report that they believe it is more difficult to be a parent now than it used to be; people seem to feel more isolated, social and media pressures on and enticements of their children seem greater, and the world seems to be a more dangerous place" (p. 1541).

A Small Sample View of Family Life in America

Several years ago I asked four of my graduate social work classes to describe any problems they were having with their families of origin. Of the roughly 80 students in the classes, everyone was experiencing problems. Many of the men in the class had not spoken to their brothers in years. One woman in the class said that she'd not spoken to her mother since 1989 when, at the funeral of her son who had died in a car crash, her mother said, "You've got three other children, a husband, and plenty of money, but look at me. I'm alone, and poor, and nobody cares about me anymore."

Another woman in my class said that she'd not spoken to her brothers and sisters in 15 years, until the thought of growing old by herself motivated her to seek closer relationships with her siblings. They still have, she said, an "uneasy" relationship. Another student said that he and his three brothers have not spoken to each other in more than 10 years, and that even when their father died, they refused to speak to one another at the funeral. Another student described his two brothers, whose relationship is filled with long-held animosities, as unable to be civil to each other. The younger brother complains that the older one is such a know-it-all that it makes him angry to even be near him. The older brother accuses the younger one of torpedoing the relationship with his constant attacks on the older brother's intelligence. The younger one is college educated, while the older one put his younger brother through college at the price of being denied his own education. The older brother complains that he's never been thanked for the help he gave. The younger one says that he has never had a day go by when the older brother hasn't demanded that he acknowledge the help he received. Every encounter between the two brothers is a set of subtle put-downs and disagreeable exercises in one-upmanship. Last year the two came to blows at a party. Their children had to separate them. Both went away without apologizing to the other.

Stories About Family Life

As additional examples of family life, I am including several stories that people have told me regarding their family relationships.

Recently, I met a woman of indeterminate age on a cruise, and we began to discuss the various problems parents have with their grown children. She told the following story about her relationship with her son. "We were always close. There wasn't anything he wouldn't do for me or me for him. When he was 42, he fell in love and married a very mean woman, and now we have no relationship at all. When I come to visit my son at his home, she stays in her room and doesn't come out to see me. I helped them find a home and she accused me of doing a poor job even though they saved thousands of dollars. It feels as if he sides with her on every concern she has about me and that nothing I do is right. It's been very hurtful to go from being so close to now not having any relationship at all. When I was growing up and misbehaved, my mother used to say, 'When they're small, they step on your toes, but when they grow up, they step on your heart.' Maybe there's something I've done to my daughter-in-law to upset her, but all she says when I try and talk to her is that I had him for 42 years and now it's time to give him up and let him have a different woman in his life. She also implies that I'm controlling and that I've caused my son to have serious emotional problems in his life. He's a very successful and charming man, and I suppose it's possible that I did some things wrong, but everybody tells me it's her and not me, so I keep my distance. I try and give them space while leaving the door open to a better relationship. My son calls me from work and it's like it always was, but when he's at home, he has nothing at all to say, a complete stranger, and it hurts a lot. Maybe it's good for children to gain their own identity, but I hurt. I've been a strong person all my life and this is something I just can't seem to deal with at all. It's frustrating.

"I put a lot of my energy into work and I have wonderful friends, and it helps. Maybe he'll come around in time, but I can't count on it, and I just get on with my life hoping for the best while accepting things as they are. An old Yiddish saying keeps coming back to me: *Kleine kinder, kleine tzooris. Groise kinder, groise tzooris* (Small children, small problems. Grown children, large problems). What can I tell you? You hope for the best, but you have to get on with life. Maybe God has His own reasons and maybe I'll have the wisdom to understand them better in time. I went to see my rabbi about it and he said he hears this same story often. He suggested that I not get so angry and hurt that I close the door on my son, and said that I should keep my loving feelings alive. You have to live with yourself, and being angry doesn't help anyone, but mostly it doesn't help you. The good ways you act in life, he said, are what makes you a strong person. I guess I believe that and I try to be extra good these days and give a lot of myself to helping other people. It makes me hurt a lot less and there are times when I'm even very hopeful."

Another woman, overhearing our conversation, joined in and said that she'd visited her oldest son for Christmas only to be verbally abused by his wife. "She criticized me all the time I was there and said the most vicious and untruthful things about me. What really hurt was that my son never stood up for me, and after 3 weeks I went home a complete mess and ended up in the hospital with a panic attack. I mean, I felt foolish. I'm a very tough woman and I've been a single parent for a long time, since my husband passed away. We're a very tight-knit family and my sons are all strong and successful men, but here is this young woman just beating up on me while my 6 foot 4 inch son stands and listens. When I complained to him he said that I was just taking it the wrong way and that she was like that with everyone.

"I went through a long period of really being angry with my son, but in time and with some professional help, I could see that he was doing what I've always done. I'm not a fighter, I'm a peacemaker. I have a hard time being attacked by someone who doesn't want to fight fair, so I just backed away and became very hurt by it all. I now hope for the best and get on with my life. I talk to my son at work and he's wonderful, but he doesn't want to make things better with his wife and me, and a little bit of me resents it. Children grow up and you have to let them go their own way, but you don't expect them to be so hurtful about it. I guess we all hope our kids won't change when they grow up and that the little man at 9 will be the same little man at 30, but people have minds of their own and you can't stop change. I put a lot of my energy into the arts in my community. Helping to create beauty is my way of dealing with a little bit of the ugliness in my own life."

A friend of mine told me a very similar story to tell about her son and daughter-in-law. "My daughter-in-law completely controls his life," she said. "She needs every toy in the world and they're in deep financial trouble. She doesn't talk to me when I come over to visit. Just recently I went to see them and she didn't answer the door even though she was home. Other times when she does answer the door and my son's not at home, she doesn't invite me in. This has been going on for 10 years now, so I can't see it changing. I've stopped blaming her and I now see that my son has control he doesn't exert because he just doesn't want to make waves. My way of handling it? I try not to get hurt, but it's always hurtful. You (the author) invited me to come visit for Thanksgiving and I said no because I thought my son and daughter-in-law were going to invite me over. They didn't, and I sat home alone on Thanksgiving and ate a turkey sandwich. I give them Christmas presents and get nothing in return. I try not to get too upset because it doesn't help to get upset over something you can't change, but I do, and it hurts. The only way I've been able to handle it is to think that all people change. maybe someday my son will see what his behavior is doing to the people who love him and he'll make some changes.

"I try and live a very balanced and spiritual life. When I feel really hurt, I look for information in books or I talk to people in the field and get some advice. Most of the time I can get on with my life and put my hurt feelings aside, but sometimes it gets to me and I feel as if my son has died and imagine that his death was heroic and that he fought for his loved ones to make us safe. It's a fantasy, of course, but it keeps me going."

What These Stories Say About Family Life

Many of the people I talk to are angry at members of their family or have negative views of the way they were raised, and yet, they are very competent and successful people. Blood doesn't guarantee love. A family is like a small organization with conflicting loyalties. While we often use the term *dysfunctional* to describe troubled families, it might be more helpful to view these families as having very different ideas about how best to do the job of surviving.

A troubled family may use put-downs or corporal punishment to instill toughness. It may deny love to prepare people for life as parents see life. A troubled family may turn child against child or play favorites among the children to make children more competitive. I'm not suggesting that these tactics are good, but I think it's important to understand why parents develop styles of child rearing that may leave children unhappy and distant from each other but, at the same time, resilient and emotionally tough. The amazing thing about troubled families is how differently each member of the family may view the problem. In the following dialogue, a son and his mother discuss the past. As this dialogue shows, the son sees his mother as an ogre, while the elderly mother cannot understand his animosity toward her.

The Son: When I was growing up, my mother and father were so enmeshed with one another that we kids pretty much felt like the hired help. When my dad died, my mom had secret alliances with all of the kids, which bordered on the perverse. Everything was slightly sexualized. She'd let us see her naked. She'd always wear sexy clothing around the house. I hated being around her. I thought she was this childish, immature old hag who ignored us when my dad was around and now was trying to seduce us.

I saw our home as being immensely unhappy. I couldn't wait to leave it, I hated it so much. And I hated her the most. My brothers and sisters and I keep some sort of peace. We manage, in a hollow way, to get along. But no one gets along with my mother. She's past seventy and she's still trying to seduce us. And hating her the most, guess who's stuck with caring for her? Me.

The Mother: When my husband died, it was very difficult. I had four small children. I was tired from working all of the time. I didn't go out with men because I thought it would upset the kids and, anyway, I was too tired from working all day. The kids were difficult after George died. They wouldn't mind me at all. I wondered if they thought that I was to blame for George's death. Kids have a funny way of seeing things, I guess.

I went to a counselor to get help, I even took the kids in a few times, but they complained about it so much that I stopped. I did the best I could, but the kids never helped out the way I needed them to.

> Now I'm staying with my son Johnny. He's so nasty to me it's worse than being in a nursing home. I ask to leave and then he becomes apologetic, and I stay. I have no idea why they're all so hateful. George and I were good parents. After he died, I tried real hard to be a good parent. You can only do so much for kids, I guess.

It's always interesting when two people discuss the past. In this dialogue, you see the animosity of the son and the confusion of the mother, and yet they survived. Like all resilient families, they put their problems aside and got on with the function of living and trying, in the process, to make their way in life, even though conditions in their past are still troubled and unlikely to ever be resolved.

Characteristics of Family Resilience

McCubbin and McCubbin (1993, 1996) believe that family resilience consists of two important family processes: (1) adjustment, which includes the strength of protective factors in mobilizing the family's efforts to maintain its integrity and functioning and fulfill developmental tasks in the face of risk factors; and (2) adaptation, which includes recovery factors that permit the family to effectively respond to a crisis. Family resilience is the ability of the family to deal with a crisis, to understand the potential risk factors associated with a crisis, and to develop recovery strategies that permit family members to cope and adapt to crisis situations. Family crises might include financial problems, health problems, unemployment, marital problems, abusive behavior by a caregiver, social and emotional problems of children, loss of a home, and any number of other problems that affect the entire family.

In listing the attributes of healthy families that help develop resilient children, an article in *Pediatrics* notes that a well-functioning family consists of two parents who are married and who offer their children a secure, supportive, and nurturing environment ("The Changing American Family," 2003). Children have more life success when raised by caring and cooperative parents who have adequate social and financial resources. Defining parental attributes that lead to resilient children, Spock and Rothenberg (1985) write, "Good-hearted parents who aren't afraid to be firm when it is necessary can get good results with either moderate strictness or moderate permissiveness. . . . The real issue is what spirit the parent puts into managing the child and what attitude is engendered in the child as a result" (p. 8). Baumrind (1966) writes that parents who combine warmth and affection with firm limit setting are more likely to have "children who are happy, creative, and cooperative; have high self-esteem; are achievement oriented; and do well academically and socially" (p. 887). Unresponsive, rigid, controlling, disengaged, overly permissive, uninvolved parents jeopardize the emotional well-being of their children, and these parental attributes consistently result in less emotionally strong and resilient children (Spieker, Larson, Lewis, Keller, & Gilchrist, 1999). Parents who monitor and supervise their children inside and outside of the home, who encourage growth-enhancing activities, and who then move toward shared decision making and responsibility with children as they mature are likely to have the healthiest and most resilient children.

In additional studies of resilience in children, Baldwin, Baldwin, and Cole (1990) suggest the importance of parental supervision and vigilance. Conrad and Harnmen (1993) emphasize the importance of maternal social support for children. In a study of 144 middle-class families, in half of which the parents were divorced, Hetherington (1989) indicates the importance of structured parenting to the health of families. Richters and Martinez (1993) found that low-income children living in a violent neighborhood did best when living in a stable and safe home environment. In their studies of resilient children, Wyman, Cowen, Work, and Parker (1991) report that children did best when the parenting style consisted of consistent discipline and an optimistic view of the children's future. Wyman and colleagues (1992) found that children who were most successful in grades 4–6 had nurturing relationships with primary caregivers and stable, consistent family environments. Werner and Smith (1992) reinforce the importance of family environmental factors, including self-confident mothers who value their children, supportive alternate caregivers, and supportive fathers.

In describing the factors that assist family recovery from a crisis, Hamilton, McCubbin, McCubbin, Thompson, Han, and Allen (1997) believe that the critical factors are these:

1. *Family integration,* which includes parental efforts to keep the family together and to be optimistic about the future.

2. *Family support and esteem building,* which includes parental efforts to get community and extended family support to assist in developing the self-esteem and self-confidence of their children.

3. *Family recreation orientation, control, and organization,* in which there is a family emphasis on recreation and family entertainment.

4. *Discipline,* where family life includes organization, rules, and procedures.

5. *Family optimism and mastery,* in which the more families have a sense of order and optimism, the healthier the children.

An article in *Pediatrics* ("The Changing American Family," 2003) reports that religious or spiritual involvement offers important supports for many families and that a growing body of research shows a positive association between religious or spiritual involvement and health and well-being, resulting in lowered risk markers among children for substance abuse and violence. In Glicken (2005b), similar findings have been reported regarding the positive impact of religiosity and spirituality on the health and mental health of individuals, but there is a caution that many research issues make this relationship a promising, but, as yet, unproven one.

Seiffege-Krenke (1995a, 1995b) and Wyman and colleagues (1991) have found that the following factors lead children to develop positive abilities to cope with stress in family life: (1) positive relationships with one, some, or all family members; (2) achieving personal growth within family life by being given opportunities to achieve independence and being rewarded for autonomous thought; (3) a family structure that provides a sense of order and rationality.

Chatterji and Markowitz (2000) report the negative impact of parental substance abuse, noting that it affects the social, psychological, and emotional well-being of children and their families. The researchers indicate that 10% of American adults are addicted to substances, and that this frequently causes them depression and leads to family life that is often disrupted, chaotic, and filled with conflict and may ultimately result in poverty, family violence, and divorce. Children in homes where one or both parents abuse substances are themselves more at risk of abusing substances and of experiencing behavioral problems.

Yet resilient children often come from families that do, in fact, have many of the risk indicators for social and emotional problems, and still they do remarkably well. Why? One reason, which we tend to underestimate, is the strength of the family to survive in the midst of trauma and to develop deep levels of resilience in children. Patterson (2002) believes that rather than looking at risk markers only, we should also consider the strengths of the families and their survival skills, abilities, inner resources, and emotional intelligence. Families with many risk markers often have elegant but unidentified strengths that lead to high levels of resilience in children. In all children? Perhaps not, since it's true that some children growing up in malfunctioning families develop significant psychosocial problems, while others are resilient, healthy, and survive family traumas. In addition to protective factors, perhaps resilient children also have the good fortune of reaching important developmental stages when family life may have provided a more positive and nurturing environment. We also know that dysfunctional families develop a type of triage where the children who can help the family are singled out for adult responsibilities that sometimes lead to high levels of resilience. These children are often found in immigrant families, families with severe emotional problems in parents, and families with substance-abusing parents, and these children behave more like co-parents in their families than like children.

Parker, Cowen, Work, and Wyman (1990) and Smith and Prior (1995) have found that children who perceive stressful events in the family positively are more likely to effectively cope with them after the event. As an example, Jackson and Warren (2000) report that children who received little family social support but could understand why and didn't define the lack of support as rejection displayed less internalizing and externalizing behavior than children with higher levels of family support but with lower positive ratings. These results suggest that positive perceptions act as a protective factor for children.

In very dysfunctional families, often the strongest child is singled out for special treatment because the child represents a degree of protection and stability for the family and suggests a possible means of survival through his or her success. When you listen to stories of family violence, for example, you hear about children who survived because although they were being badly abused, they were also asked to take on significant family functions which led to higher self-esteem and promoted attributes of resilience. These children know that even though their abuse is damaging, the family's need for their skills makes them likely to survive the abuse and to do better in life. Does the abuse have other more sinister and negative effects? Yes, and the fact that resilient people are sometimes affected by emotional problems and act in negative ways are good examples.

In summarizing the research on family resilience, Walsh (2003) identifies the key behavioral aspects of family resilience as follows:

1. Making meaning of adversity by normalizing the stressful situation through understanding and managing it.

2. Having a positive outlook by being optimistic and having confidence that the crisis will be resolved.

3. Using transcendence and spirituality to provide inspiration for new ways to resolve a crisis and to provide a bonding and supportive group of people who assist in resolving the crisis.

4. Being flexible so that the family is open to change and can adapt to new challenges.

5. Being connected so that the family shows mutual support, collaboration, and commitment.

6. Having social and economic resources that provide the family with economic security and allow family members to balance work with family time.

7. Having clarity in the way a crisis is viewed and the ability to communicate within the family to resolve difficulties.

8. Having open emotional expression that allows family members to share feelings and jokes and interact in a safe and positive way.

9. Doing collaborative problem solving that encourages creative brainstorming, proactive stances, building on success, and learning from failures.

In summarizing the concept of family resilience, Walsh (2003) writes,

Building on theory and research, on family stress, coping, and adaptation (Patterson, 2002), the concept of family resilience entails more than managing stressful conditions, shouldering a burden, or surviving an ordeal. It involves the potential for personal and relational transformation and growth that can be forged out of adversity (Boss, 2001). Tapping into key processes for resilience, families can emerge stronger and more resourceful in meeting future challenges. A crisis can be a wake-up call, heightening attention to what matters. It can become an opportunity for reappraisal of priorities, stimulating greater investment in meaningful relationships and life pursuits. Members may discover or develop new insights and abilities. Many families report that through weathering a crisis together their relationships were enriched and more loving than they might otherwise have been. (p. 3)

A Story About a Resilient Immigrant Family

My father came to the United States in 1921 from a small rural town in the Ukraine called Beliazerkov. It means "white church" in English. After the Second World War, there wasn't a single Jew left in Beliazerkov, and the reality of the Holocaust and hopelessness of the situation became apparent to my family from the seemingly endless Red Cross letters we received informing us that my father's 10 brothers and sisters were all dead and my mother's 8 brothers and sisters had also perished. Our assorted cousins and other members of both extended families had all perished, perhaps 200 or more people. We didn't know how they died and worried that it was in some horrible massacre of Jews like *Babi Yar,* or in the Nazi death camps. The news caused my mother to move into a depression that lasted the rest of her life.

Because my father was coming of age when the Communists came to power in 1918, he would have been forced into the military and almost certain death, an indignity because Jewish people in Russia were denied Russian citizenship. In the middle of the night, my father, my aunt, and my grandmother left Russia. Perhaps he was 14. It took them 3 years of walking across Europe to earn enough money for their passage to America. When he saw the Statue of Liberty, he and a thousand poor Europeans came up from steerage class at the bottom of the ship, stood on the deck, and wept.

America. My father could hardly say the word without tears welling up in his eyes. America.

> Give me your tired, your poor,
> Your huddled masses yearning to breathe free . . .

He knew the words on the Statue of Liberty by heart, and he would say them to me until I knew the words as well as he did.

My father had a way of avoiding the downside of the country. I guess his immigrant love of America created a sort of selective perception. When we couldn't move from our slum house across from the railroad tracks because no one would sell us a house in a better part of town (because there was so much bias against Jews that being Jewish was like having leprosy), my father said, "So, who wants to live with the bastards anyway? Better we should live among our own people where nobody makes jokes about us."

In the following story, an immigrant family is beset by the loss of the mother to illness and by poverty. I am the storyteller, and I started out by writing this story about my family and, particularly, about my father in highly positive terms, only to begin remembering what family life was really like and the angry feelings I had at my mother for getting sick and leaving us. This is why the story didn't end the way I intended it to. It was to be an homage to my father, but the memories the story created were bittersweet, and I experienced the complicated emotions all the storytellers whose stories are in this book have told me they've experienced.

My father went to work for the Great Northern Railroad when he was 17 and continued working as a blue-collar worker until he retired at 66. His job consisted of working outside in the freezing North Dakota cold, loading and unloading boxcars. Later, as he developed seniority, he had his pick of jobs and finally ended up working in the office where most of his co-workers were drunk by noon. He became secretary-treasurer of the railroad clerks union, whose boundaries went from mid-Minnesota to mid-Montana. He was a deeply committed union man who believed firmly in the right of working men and women to have a secure and well-paid future. We went together on Sundays on the milk train to small towns in North Dakota and Minnesota to preach the gospel of unionism to a largely drunk and unbelieving audience of railroad workers we met at the card halls and the pool joints, and who called my father the "Commie" and the "Jew Commie," but who nevertheless had a love for him that I found exasperating.

It was these same men who would come to our house on Saturday nights after beating up their wives to ask my father for a few dollars of union money to get out of town for a while, or who caused drunken accidents that cost the railroad millions of dollars and then would hide behind my father (who never failed to protect them). This same bigoted, alcoholic, wife-beating group of men would meet me on the platforms of railroad stations across the northern part of America as I traveled from North Dakota to graduate school in Seattle and bring me sack lunches or pastries, or buy me breakfast because my father had sent out smoke signals that his son was to be taken care of during the 2,000-mile railroad odyssey through the prairies, Glacier National Park, the Cascades of eastern Washington to Seattle, and then back home. When they handed me little sacks of food, they would try to hide the tears in their eyes when they told me stories about my father and how he'd saved them from being fired. They never knew my name and just called me by his name, Sammy.

He never gave up on anyone in the union. He believed in counseling for alcoholism and pushed for health benefits before either notion was popular. The well-known liberal politicians of our time knew him and sometimes came to our home or stood with him on Labor Day celebration platforms. I sat with Hubert Humphrey in 1948 and listened to the beauty of his language and felt chills go down my spine. My father was president of the Anti-Defamation League in the Dakotas, even though his English was legendarily fractured. He'd come home after a union meeting or a meeting of frightened Jewish men who knew that anti-Semitism was always ready to rear its ugly head and bang out letters on an old Remington typewriter, never using a comma or making a new paragraph, each clause perfect in his mind. While I was in graduate school, he'd write to me in beautiful longhand about the way his boots sounded in the frozen snow, or how the smoke stood absolutely still in the 40-degree-below North Dakota winter. His letters would go on for 30 pages with no punctuation marks and no logical progression. Page 1 had page 12 on the back and, by the way, he'd add on page 19, "your mother is in the hospital again. I don't think she'll make it." And then the descriptions would begin again, and he'd tell me that he saw a robin one morning and it made him cry because spring must be ahead, and maybe my mother would be able to come home for a visit.

My mother's illness made her a recluse and she would lie in bed all day while my brother, sister, and I did the shopping, the cooking, the cleaning, and the washing—chores that to this day I hate to do. My father always seemed bigger than life to me in his World War Two U.S. Air Force bomber jacket. He was a handsome man, with thick black hair and blue eyes, who was full of the gift of gab and eager to talk to everyone he saw on the street. With us, he could be charming, and hateful, and tyrannical. Having a sick wife, three children, and not enough money to even pay for my mother's care during her illness did that to him, and we cut him some slack. But in the moments when he was happy and full of life, he would tell me stories about Russia.

Very early in the morning, well before the birds would start to sing, I remember eating breakfast with my father, listening to him describe the Cossacks and the retreat of the White Russian Army during the Russian Revolution. My father is dressed in his long underwear and has pieces of toilet paper covering cuts on his face from a very used double-edged Gillette razor.

"You should have seen the women," he tells me. "They were more beautiful than you can imagine." I am maybe 5 years old. It sounds nice to listen to my father talk about beautiful women. I imagine that they all look like Mrs. Cooper down the street, a woman everybody considers to be very beautiful, although I think she seems mean and unfriendly and I worry that maybe she'll take my mother's place.

My mother, who used to be beautiful, lies in a hospital ward with an illness no one can explain. She is still a young woman, but she looks old and wrinkled and I try not to think of her when my father talks about beautiful women. In a while, we will take a streetcar to see my mother in the hospital. I don't want to go.

"We could hear the Cossacks hours before we saw them," he says, as he flips over the eggs and the kosher salami we will eat together for breakfast. "The horses, and there must have been thousands of them, made a noise like an earthquake."

My father adds a little coffee to my hot milk. It makes me feel grown up. I am his confidant in these early morning chats before he goes off to work for the railroad. I am unsure of what he does on the railroad, but his leather jacket looks dashing and I imagine that it's something important. Maybe he drives train engines or blows the whistle on the morning train I watch alone from our house near the railroad tracks.

"We all walked out of our houses and watched the Cossacks pass through our town," he continues, putting the fried eggs and salami on my plate. He never ruins the eggs, and I can always dunk toast into the yolk and watch it run down the bread. "We were poor people and my mother told us not to watch them or one of the Cossacks would put a sword through our stomachs. But we couldn't help ourselves. We watched them for hours. They were covered with frost and they had a mean look in their eyes."

My father walks to the window and looks outside. Even though it is still dark outside, he is certain that the day will be mean. "I hate the rain," he says. "I hate this endless warm weather. I miss the snow and the cold." I'm not sure how I feel about snow, since my mother became sick when it snowed and it makes me sad when the weather turns the frozen land bleak and desolate, but from my father's description of the Cossacks in winter, snow sounds wonderful to me, maybe like soft melting ice cream or fluffy feathers.

In this moment, this perfect moment before the dawn, before anything else intrudes on his time, I listen to his Russian stories and I am in love with him. I love the way he shaves and the way he smells after his shower. I want to be just like him, driving trains through the city, blowing the engine whistle to let everybody know I'm coming.

I help my father put away the dishes from breakfast and then dress for my trip to see my mother. When the apartment looks decent enough, as decent as it can look with a working father taking care of young children, we walk down the block to catch the streetcar. The first light of dawn is just coming through and the small city we live in looks lovely to me. It is all that I have ever known and the smells mesmerize me, call out my name, talk to me.

I don't want to take this ride with my father. I'd rather sit at home and listen to his stories about Cossacks, but we board the streetcar anyway so that my father can see my mother before work begins. I never want to go with him and use every excuse I can muster. My father looks hurt when I tell him my excuses. Secretly, he doesn't want to visit her either. My little fibs just confirm his own feeling that my mother has given up and that the rides we take to the hospital on the streetcar are pointless. Often we ride together in brooding silence, watching the people on the street and smelling the strange smells of foreign cooking that float through the open windows of the streetcar.

Sometimes on our rides to the hospital, my father tells me stories about the way he and my grandmother and aunt walked across Russia to escape the Communists, but I look out the window and try not to listen. The fact is that my mother has abandoned us and I don't want to give up my 5-year-old's anger for one second.

Once in a while, on our rides to the hospital, a lady smiles at him. He doesn't know what to do and smiles back, making sure that he waves his wedding ring so the ladies will know that he's married. It's such a half-hearted effort that it only encourages them more. More than a few times on our way to the hospital, he moves away from me and sits next to one of the ladies on the streetcar. It seems to me that he has every right to be friendly with other women. His woman has given up on us. I secretly wonder what some of the ladies would be like as mothers. Better than mine, I'll bet.

The streetcar leaves us off a few blocks from the hospital. The neighborhood is full of people who aren't like us at all. They speak different languages and seem happy and carefree. In our neighborhood, people keep to themselves and seem secretive about everything. My grandmother, who lives on the next block, says that we shouldn't talk to strangers and that we should keep our troubles to ourselves, but these people seem like they'd be happy to listen to a five-year-old's troubles. Once in a while, we stop at a bakery and have a pastry before we go to the hospital. I know my father is delaying the moment when we have to visit my mother and I don't care. We can stay here forever as far as I'm concerned.

The people in the bakery all speak another language, but the pastries are delicious and the people are nice to us. Sometimes they give me a cream soda and talk to me in their language. I don't know what they're saying, but I like the way the words sound and the way their faces seem so animated and full of life when they talk. I want to wait for my father in the bakery, but he says my mother would be hurt if I didn't come. I don't care.

We walk in silence to the hospital. Inside, the hospital smells of disinfectant and I want to leave as soon as we walk into the lobby. But we climb up the dark old stairs to the third floor where my mother lies in a charity ward. I'm not sure what a charity ward is, but it seems to me that all the women in the ward have sad looks on their faces, looks of hopelessness and defeat.

My mother sits up in her bed waiting for us. She tries to smile, but the effort is so great that her body slumps. I know that she is 28 years old, but she looks as old as my grandmother. Her hair has turned white. I hardly know what to say to her. She kisses me and I pull away, afraid, I guess, that I'll catch whatever she has. I can't be sure whether she notices, although I have become an expert at reading the signs of hurt in people. It is a burden to be 5 years old and worry so much about other people's feelings.

My father gives her a perfunctory kiss and begins to tell her about work and the gossip from our street. I watch the ladies in the ward and focus on a little girl sitting next to her mother. She is probably my age and has a very innocent look on her face. She is holding her mother's hand for all she is worth. Her mother, like the rest of the ladies on the ward, looks ill beyond repair. Little tears trickle down her mother's face, which the little girl wipes off with a tissue. The little girl has the same look of bewilderment I must have on my face.

I don't know why, but I start to cry just looking at the little girl. My father looks distraught and puts his finger over his lips, but I can't stop. The tears pour down my face and I feel ashamed to be causing such a scene.

One of the nurses comes over and speaks to me. She says that I'll have to leave if I don't stop crying, but the tears gush out of me and I sit on the chair next to my mother's bed and sob. The nurse takes me downstairs and makes me sit in the lobby next to the information booth. I want to stop crying, but I can't. The nurse tells the lady at the information booth that I'm a naughty boy and that if I can't stop crying, they won't let me see my mother anymore. I just want to be back in the bakery having a cream soda and eating warm pastries. I want someone to fuss over me and treat me like I'm 5 instead of like an adult.

On the way home, my father puts his head in his hands. I want to hug him, to give him a kiss, to let him know that I'm sorry his wife is sick and that he has to take care of me all by himself. But he just sits there in the streetcar with his head in his hands and says nothing. Maybe he's hurting, too, and we ride together, silently, keeping whatever is in our hearts to ourselves.

LESSONS TO BE LEARNED FROM THIS STORY

I've written the following list as objectively as I can, balancing my personal feelings about the situation with my attempt to provide you with the lessons to be learned.

1. When a family crisis occurs, it's not unusual for it to center around one person or for that person, in this case the mother, to be scapegoated. Both the

son and father believe that the mother has done something to badly upset their lives. The crisis they are experiencing goes beyond the practical aspects of trying to live without the mother's help in the home. The central issue is the sense of abandonment and that what is happening is the mother's fault.

2. The child in the story has shifted his love and identity entirely to his father as a way of maintaining his equilibrium. And, in a sense, he wants to make himself invisible to his mother, whom he thinks is responsible for the family crisis.

3. The fact that he cries in the hospital while attempting to control the ambivalent feelings he has for his mother is an example of his confusion. He can't understand why this is happening to his family and sees that his mother is doing very badly. He wants to be more sympathetic and loving, but his anger at his mother and his ambivalence collide in a burst of emotion that actually threatens the family's ability to cope. His feelings of guilt are quite clear.

4. The boy sees his father as his hero and has developed a fantasy life to romanticize his father's life. The father helps this along by telling exciting stories of his early life in Russia that cement his relationship with his son and direct their thoughts to faraway places and other times. This takes away some of the pain caused by trying to cope with the mother's illness and her absence from the home.

5. The son is taking on emotional responsibility for his family's survival through his concern about the impact he has on other people. He tries to listen to others and to understand the proper response. In effect, he is learning to be a positive factor in stabilizing the family, but at this troubled time in his life, the skills he needs and his own emotional needs conflict, and he ends up worried that the lapse in his behavior when he cried at the hospital will drive him and his father apart and cause further friction in the family.

6. The father is trying to keep the family together, and we should recognize his attempts without being judgmental or critical. Keeping the family intact has a very positive impact on the boy, who must be worried that the stress of life with his mother in the hospital, without any realistic expectation that she'll return home, could cause the father to send him away. The son knows, from the father's behavior with women on the streetcar, that the father's feelings about the mother and his desire for a different life parallel his own feeling that maybe life would be better with someone else as his mother. We shouldn't be too critical of the son for feeling this way, since his sense of survival has overcome his loyalty to his mother. The same is true of the father.

A family crisis is raw, and people don't always behave kindly or well. In my family, my mother remained ill throughout her lifetime, but we stayed together. We were poor and without many resources, other than our will to survive and contribute. Still, our home was lively and stimulating, with my father acting as a cheerleader. At some point in time, the family accepted my mother's illness and made do. I fear my mother came out of this the most wounded because, in her absence, we created our own family dynamic that essentially left her out. But she had a profound influence on all of us, and when she was well enough to be part of the family, she could be wonderfully warm and positive. Her resilience in coping with her illness and the way my family was able to survive a time in our lives that would have ruined many families are the reasons I wrote this book.

A Story That Needs No Explanation

The toughest thing I've ever done was to tell my dad he had to stop driving. He was 82 at the time. His memory was fading. His reflexes were slowed. It was a conversation we should have had long before he became a hazard to himself and others on Cleveland's highways. But it was a conversation no one in the family wanted to have. So we put it off until we could no longer ignore the obvious. Dad, like some of the nearly 19 million drivers age 70 and older in the United States, was a hazard on the highways.

We confronted him on a Sunday afternoon in 1997. My mom was in the hospital with two broken arms. The hospital's social worker had approached my brother Jim and me.

"We're concerned about your dad's driving," she told us. "Several people here at the hospital are worried about how he pulls into and out of the hospital parking lot. He's going to kill someone, including himself. It's simply a matter of time. Today, tomorrow, but soon," she said.

So, we devised a foolproof plan. First we'd talk to Mom. And she agreed. "Your father should not be driving," she told us.

We decided to meet in Mom's hospital room to talk to Dad. According to our plan, the social worker would open the conversation in a nonthreatening way. We'd second her concerns. Mom would agree with us. And Dad would hand over the keys. Simple. Do-able. Right? We rehearsed the meeting several times. Mom was fabulous. Jim, a psychologist, was excellent, too.

Dad arrived at noon. While he chatted with Mom, Jim and I went over the plan with the social worker. And then we walked into Mom's room.

"Saul," the social worker began, "we're worried about your driving. We care about you. We don't want you to hurt yourself or anyone else."

Jim and I jumped in at that point, echoing her words.

Dad looked like a kid who'd been cornered by bullies on the playground. His back literally against the wall, he looked from me to Jim, at the social worker, and then at Mom, who'd said nothing so far.

"What are you talking about?" he whispered. "I'd be the first to know if I had a problem driving. I've been driving for more than 60 years. I'm a good driver." There were tears in his eyes. In mine, too.

The following story was written by a very special friend, Ron Aaron, who has worked in the social service field in San Antonio, Texas, in many capacities and who now has a syndicated radio program whose emphasis is on the helping process and the many problems experienced in life by all too many people. The story originally appeared in the July 27, 2003, issue of the San Antonio Express-News.

That's when Mom jumped in. "Your father's a wonderful driver," she said. "The best. I should know, I've driven with him for more than 50 years."

And that was it.

Dad drove for another year or so until dementia made it impossible for him. At some point, he couldn't even remember how to start the car. We were lucky he didn't hurt himself or anyone else. But it was just dumb luck.

The fact is, people over 70 have a disproportionate number of accidents per miles driven, according to the National Highway Traffic Safety Administration. Indeed, their statistics show that not only do older drivers have more accidents; they are more likely than any other age group to kill themselves or others in an accident.

We knew Dad should have stopped driving long before he did. My guess is most family members know. But there's a long way from knowing to doing something about it. We need tough new laws to require annual driving tests, eye exams, and other physical tests for older people. It's in their best interests and ours.

What did we learn from our experience? Dad died in February 2000. Mom was still driving then, at 84. But we talked to her about our concerns and she agreed to sell the car. She's not happy about it, but today, at 87, she's alive and doing quite well.

Strict new laws could keep other older people safe, too (Aaron, 2003, p. 3k).

Summary

This chapter on family resilience notes the importance of family life in developing resilience in children. Several stories were introduced that suggest problems in family life, and a number of factors were discussed that define healthy family life. A story was provided that suggests the difficulty of maintaining resilience in the midst of family crisis.

CHAPTER 13

How Resilient People Cope With Acts of Random Violence

O ne of the primary emotional responses to acts of violence by victims is the development of posttraumatic stress disorder (PTSD). PTSD is linked to highly traumatic experiences which produce intrusive thoughts that are difficult to dislodge once they've reached conscious awareness. Those with PTSD may reexperience the original traumatic event, which produces in them a highly agitated state of arousal. Symptoms of PTSD usually begin within 3 months of the original trauma. In half the cases, complete recovery occurs within 3 months of the onset of symptoms, but many cases last more than 12 months (American Psychiatric Association, 1994, p. 426).

The core criteria for a diagnosis of PTSD include individuals' exhibiting the distressing symptoms of (1) reexperiencing a trauma through nightmares and intrusive thoughts; (2) numbing, feeling aloof, or being unable to express loving feelings for others; and (3) persistent sleep problems, irritability and angry outbursts, difficulty concentrating, hypervigilance, and an exaggerated startle response lasting more than a month and causing problems at work, in social interactions, and in other important areas of life (American Psychiatric Association, 1994, pp. 427–429). The *DSM-IV* calls the condition acute if it has lasted less than 3 months, and chronic if it has lasted more than 3 months, but symptoms may be delayed for 6 months or more from the original trauma (American Psychiatric Association, 1994, p. 429). Stein (2002) reports that physical pain is a common symptom of PTSD and writes, "Ongoing chronic pain may serve as a constant reminder of the trauma that perpetuates its remembrance" (p. 922).

Violent assaults are one of the primary reasons people develop and sustain symptoms of PTSD. Often, however, resilience plays a significant role in whether the symptoms will be minimized and time limited. Some evidence exists that symptoms of PTSD are more robust when certain conditions exists. In studies of women who have been sexually assaulted, PTSD was more likely to occur when women were injured in the assault, were threatened with death or injury if they reported the assault, had a history of prior assaults, or experienced blame or criticism for the assault from family members, peers, or law enforcement officers (Regehr, Cadell, & Jansen, 1999). The *Harvard Mental Health Letter* ("What Causes Post-Traumatic Stress Disorder: Two Views," 2002) reports that "the people most likely to have symptoms of PTSD were those who suffered job loss, broken personal relationships, the death or illness of a family member or close friend, or financial loss as a result of the [trauma] itself" (p. 8).

According to Ozer, Best, Lipsey, and Weiss (2003), no single variable predicts PTSD. Rather, the authors believe that a person's level of resilience is the best predictor of whether or not PTSD will develop. Highly resilient people seem to have lower incidents of PTSD following a trauma. Ozer and colleagues (2003) summarize their findings by writing, "This cluster of variables may all be pointing to a single source of vulnerability for the development of PTSD or enduring symptoms of PTSD—a lack of psychological resilience" (p. 69).

Reinforcing the relationship between violent behavior and PTSD, the National Vietnam Veterans Readjustment Study (Weiss et al., 1992) found that 9% of the men and 26% of the women serving in Vietnam had met the diagnostic criteria for PTSD at some point since their Vietnam service. However, 20 years after exposure to one or more violent experiences, evidence of continued symptoms of PTSD in Vietnam veterans is 2% for men and 5% for women, suggesting that 830,000 Vietnam veterans still be experiencing PTSD 20 years later (Schlenger et al., 1992). Further evidence of the impact of violence is noted in reports of lifetime rates of PTSD of between 30% and 50% in women who have been sexually assaulted or raped (Foa, Hearst-Ikeda, & Perry, 1995; Meadows & Foa, 1998; Resnick, Acierno, Holmes, Kilpatrick, & Jager, 1999). In addition, the October 2002 issue of the *Harvard Mental Health Letter* reports that PTSD is most likely to occur in those people who have experienced some form of assault. Seventy percent of the patients in this *Harvard Mental Health Letter* report who had current or lifetime PTSD said that the assault was their very worst traumatic experience ("What Causes Post-Traumatic Stress Disorder: Two Views," 2002).

While we now accept PTSD as a normal response to trauma, Ozer and colleagues (2003) report that in the early and middle 1970s, Vietnam veterans with PTSD were receiving diagnoses of schizophrenia at veterans hospital psychiatric units, even though similar problems of PTSD had been seen in World War Two and Korean War veterans. Those symptoms included "intrusive thoughts and images, nightmares, social withdrawal, numbed feelings, hyper vigilance, paranoia, especially about the government, and vivid dissociative phenomena, such as flashbacks" (Ozer et al., 2003, p. 54).

Cohen (1998) discusses the problem of using PTSD as a diagnosis for children and adolescents. Some PTSD symptoms, such as dissociation, self-injurious behaviors, substance abuse, and/or conduct problems, may obscure the original trauma and clinicians may miss the existence of PTSD. Children going through abrupt changes in development may demonstrate some of the signs of PTSD. Cohen urges clinicians to do a careful job of history taking to avoid overlooking the presence of a PTSD. To meet the criteria for a diagnosis of PTSD, a child must first have been exposed to an extremely traumatic event which results in the child's re-experiencing the event, avoidance and numbing, and increased arousal when memories of the event are triggered. Cohen (1998) suggests that re-experiencing the trauma may show itself in repetitive play with traumatic themes, recurrent upsetting dreams about the trauma, and intense anxiety when conscious and unconscious cues remind the child of the trauma. Avoidance and numbing may be observed in children's withdrawing from their usual activities and also in their use of techniques to avoid thinking about the trauma—techniques that may, in time, become obsessive. Children who have a complete loss of memory about the event or seem detached and lack future thinking may be examples of this. Persistent symptoms of increased arousal, if they are to be considered part of the response to PTSD, must be newly observed symptoms that may include sleep problems, irritability or angry outbursts, difficulty concentrating, hypervigilance, and an exaggerated startle response. Symptoms must be present for at least 1 month and cause clinically significant distress or impairment in normal functioning for the child to be assigned a diagnosis of PTSD.

Cohen (1998) indicates that experts agree that children should be asked about the traumatic event. Clinicians often fail to ask children about the event and its impact because they fear that reminding the child of painful events may trigger anxiety, or they may not want to become involved in disturbing discussions that may change the child's memory of the event. In situations that involve litigation, a discussion of the precipitating event may confuse the child's memory and could result in liability concerns about the clinician's role in the child's confusion about the event. Cohen believes that we often miss important evidence of the presence of PTSD: "There is a strong clinical consensus that if children are not asked, they are less likely to tell about their PTSD symptoms" (Cohen, 1998, p. 998). Cohen (1998) notes that several semi-structured interviews are necessary in order to discover traumatic events in a child's life and suggests that clinicians pay close attention to the criteria for PTSD when they collect information from the interviews.

Debriefing

A form of treatment with potential for use in work with PTSD victims following a tragedy such as 9-11 is a single-session treatment, or what has also been called *debriefing*. In this approach, clients who have experienced a trauma are seen in a group lasting 1 to 3 hours that meets within a week to a month of the original traumatic event. Risk factors are evaluated and the group participants are provided with information and the opportunity to discuss their experiences during and after the trauma (Bisson, McFarlane, & Rose, 2000). Most debriefing groups use crisis intervention techniques in a very abbreviated form and may provide educational information to group members about typical reactions to traumas, what to look for if group members experience any of these symptoms, and who to see if additional help is needed. They may also attempt to identify group members at risk of developing PTSD (van Emmerik, Kamphuis, Hulsbosch, & Emmelkamp, 2002).

Despite the considerable appeal of this approach, there is almost no evidence that debriefing works to reduce the number of people who experience PTSD following debriefing sessions. In fact, there is some evidence that debriefing is less effective than no treatment at all following a trauma and may actually lead to an increase in PTSD (van Emmerik et al., 2002). Gist and Devilly (2002) support these findings and write that "immediate debriefing has yielded null or paradoxical outcomes" because the approaches used in debriefing are often those "kinds of practical help learned better from grandmothers than from graduate training" (p. 742). They report that in 4 months after the 9-11 bombing, the estimated number of cases of PTSD was still high but had dropped by almost two thirds since the day of the tragedy. Gist and Devilly (2002) conclude that "these findings underscore the counterproductive nature of offering a prophylaxis with no demonstrable effect, but [with] demonstrated potential to complicate natural resolution, in a population in which limited case-conversion can be anticipated, strong natural supports exist, and spontaneous resolution is prevalent" (p. 742).

There are several reasons for the lack of effectiveness of debriefing: (1) Debriefing interferes with natural healing processes and sometimes results in bypassing trauma victims' usual support systems, such as family, friends, and religious groups (Horowitz, 1976); (2) after hearing that PTSD symptoms are normal reactions to trauma, some victims of trauma actually develop the symptoms as a result of the suggestions provided in the debriefing session, particularly when victims have not had time to process the various feelings they may have about the trauma (Kramer & Rosenthal, 1998); (3) Trauma victims seen in debriefing include both those at risk and those not at risk. Clinicians might obtain better results by screening for those who are at risk through a review of victims' past exposure to traumas that are potentially serving as catalysts for their current development of PTSD (Brewin, Andrews, & Valentine, 2000).

Responses of Resilient People to Violence

Gist and Devilly (2002) worry that PTSD is being predicted on such a wide scale for every tragedy that occurs that we've watered down its usefulness as a diagnostic category. They write, "Progressive dilution of both stressor and duration criteria has so broadened application that it can now prove difficult to diagnostically differentiate those who have personally endured stark and prolonged threat from those who have merely heard upsetting reports of calamities striking others" (p. 741). The authors suggest that many early signs of PTSD are normal responses to stress that are often overcome with time and distance from the event. Victims often use natural healing processes to cope with traumatic events, and interference by professionals in natural healing could make the victims' problems more severe and prolonged. In determining whether PTSD will actually develop, people must be given time to cope with the trauma on their own before we diagnose and treat them for PTSD. To emphasize this point, Gist and Devilly (2002) note that the immediate predictions of cases of PTSD in victims of the World Trade Center bombings turned out to be almost 70% higher than the number of actual cases of PTSD 4 months after the event. Susser, Herman, and Aaron (2002) report that 2,001 New Yorkers were interviewed by telephone between January 15, 2002, and February 21, 2002. The interview indicated a significant decrease in the stress-related symptoms subjects experienced during and after the World Trade Center bombings only several months earlier. Susser and colleagues note that "many affected New Yorkers are clearly recovering naturally, a tribute to the resilience of the human psyche" (p. 76). Of course, symptoms of PTSD may develop much later than 4 months after a trauma. Still, the point is well taken. People often heal on their own, and a premature diagnosis of PTSD may be counterproductive.

Asmundson, Coons, Taylor, and Katz (2002) observed that 70% of a sample of clients with pain who coped dysfunctionally (i.e., overly medicated themselves and/or had high numbers of doctor's visits) also met the diagnostic criteria for PTSD, as compared with 35% of the sample who met the diagnostic criteria for PTSD but who coped with pain in a functionally adaptive way. There is evidence to suggest that high sensitivity to anxiety in the midst of a traumatic event increases levels of fear, which may result in panic attacks and the greater likelihood of developing pain and related medical problems (Taylor, 1999, 2000). In fact, there is some evidence that elevated levels of anxiety during the traumatic event may be the primary factor in the development of chronic pain (Taylor, 2000), leading Asmundson and colleagues (2002) to conclude that

> when people with high anxiety sensitivity levels encounter a traumatic stressor, painful physical injury, or both, they are believed to respond with a more intense emotional reaction than do those with lower levels. In the case of PTSD, the degree of alarm caused by the stressor itself combined with alarm related to the anxiety sensations arising from the stressor amplifies the emotional reaction and thereby increases the risk of developing PTSD. (p. 933)

In a meta-analysis of the many factors that may predict the development of PTSD after a traumatic event, Ozer and colleagues (2003) found the following factors to be related to the development of PTSD:

- A history of prior trauma
- Psychological problems before the traumatic event
- Psychopathology in the family of origin
- The degree to which the person thought the traumatic event would endanger his or her life
- The lack of a support system to help the person cope with the trauma
- The degree of emotional response during and after the trauma
- Evidence of a dissociative state during and after the trauma

The authors believe that each of these variables helped explain, to some extent, how well the person could cope with the trauma and whether PTSD would develop.

However, when Ozer and colleagues (2003) tried to use individual variables to predict PTSD, they found that no single variable predicted of the onset of PTSD. Instead of the variables noted above, the authors believe that the person's degree of resilience is the best predictor of whether PTSD will develop. Highly resilient people appear to have lower incidents of PTSD following a trauma. Thus the authors suggest that those who are not highly resilient and develop PTSD may be compared to those who contract the flu and write, "It is tempting to make an analogy [between PTSD and] the flu or infectious disease: Those whose immune systems are compromised are at greater risk of contracting a subsequent illness" (Ozer et al., 2003, p. 69).

In a study of resilience among children directly exposed to terrorism and violence, Stahl (2004) reports that a majority of Israeli children and adolescents exposed to terrorism show a remarkable ability to rebound. These children were present, lost someone meaningful to them, knew someone who was injured, planned to be at the sight of the attack, or were there just before or a terrorist attack. Only about 5% of the children developed "full blown" symptoms of PTSD, while another 10% suffered isolated symptoms such as anxiety or depression. These statistics are very similar to those in the United States, where 2% to 5% of all children develop PTSD at some time because of physical and emotional traumas.

A Story About Random Violence

I was 53 when I was mugged and robbed on my way to the parking lot of the bank I worked for. I don't remember much about it other than I've never been so scared in my life. I thought he was going to kill me. I remember thinking something about his voice, and how he sounded desperate and I'd better cooperate. They give us courses at the bank about how to deal with bank robbers, and something flashed in my mind that this guy sounded like he was on some drug and he'd kill me for sure if I didn't cooperate. I know he hit me with his gun several times, and I can remember thinking that if I just relaxed my body and was passive that he wouldn't hurt me so much. He took my purse and my wedding ring and stole my car. It was February in Minneapolis and maybe 5 degrees below zero. Someone found me in the parking lot and told me later that my body temperature had dropped and I was close to freezing to death.

I was in the hospital for almost a week. The bank robber broke my nose and damaged my eye, so I have blurred vision in one eye. I still haven't been able to learn how to see well out of my good eye, and I get headaches a lot. The cuts he put on my face are permanent scars, so I have to use very heavy makeup to hide them. For a while, my husband didn't look at me the same way he did before this happened. We've talked about it and maybe he feels he should have been there to protect me and feels guilty. I'm not sure. He's a wonderful man and I think he's adjusting to it all. In many ways, our marriage is better than before this happened. Maybe the assault brought back old feelings of love that sometimes get sidetracked when you've been married as long as we have.

For about a year after the attack, I was very frightened. They said I had PTSD, which is pretty understandable. I went for counseling for a year and had a wonderful therapist who works with people who have been assaulted. She said that

I'd get better in time and was very supportive. She had me read about PTSD, and I found out that people who've been assaulted have the highest amount of PTSD.

I think I've always handled things pretty well, and soon after I came home I asked to return to work. The people at the bank were reluctant at first, not knowing how I'd be, but they let me come back and it was a godsend because it took my mind off what happened to me. My therapist suggested that I join a support group. It's been wonderful. All the people have been assaulted and some of them are doing badly. I felt pretty blessed to see that I was doing well compared to some of them. Some of them don't work anymore, and they're still young people. It's wrecked their lives.

I tried going back to synagogue, but I've never been religious, and I have to admit that I was pretty mad at God for letting this happen to me. I spoke to my rabbi about how I felt, but I just couldn't get over how mad I was at God. So I started going to a small church near my home. I don't know anything about Christianity, but the services are warm and the people are very caring. I started helping the church with financial matters and joined their relief society. We give food and clothing to needy people and take in children who need a place to stay when their parents are drunk or in trouble. I'd never done that before, and when I began, it suddenly made me very happy to help others. I can't quite explain why, but maybe I was finally getting over being mad at God and I was starting to be thankful I was alive and hadn't gotten killed.

My children have never been a source of support and have always been critical of me and my husband. They blamed me for the attack, saying that I should have had an escort, or I should have been more careful. They wanted me to sue the bank for not having a safe parking lot. I feel a little sorry for myself that my kids aren't more loving. So does my husband, who I think has become more deeply attached to me than ever. You're married 30 years and you lose a lot of steam, but after this happened I just felt a lot of real, tender love. It makes me very emotional sometimes when we're in bed together to rediscover love.

They caught the guy who did this to me and wanted me to go identify him. I did, but I was very frightened. I felt he had a lot of power over me, that he could see through the one-way mirror, and that he'd hurt me again. But I identified him and he's in jail for a long time. He'd done this a lot, and many people came forward during the trial, and the judge gave him the maximum sentence he could. He was a pathetic little man with a drug problem. I saw him in court and he seemed to shrivel up and disappear as the trial went on. I felt a little sorry for him, but I'm glad he's in jail. At the sentencing hearing his mother came and pleaded for leniency while apologizing for what he'd done. I could see that she was a good woman and a caring mother. My heart went out to her and I felt how she must feel knowing the harm her son had done and, because of my kids, how children can sometimes turn out pretty badly even though you've tried your best.

It's been 2 years now since the assault. I still have scars on my face and in my heart, and there are days when the nightmares scare me. But every day is a little better, and every day I can see that I'm changing and becoming a more caring person. I don't feel the bitterness some people feel who've been assaulted, and I don't want to sit around feeling full of hate.

You asked me to tell you why I was able to handle it so well when other people don't. I guess part of it is that my mother had cancer when I was a child, and the sicker she got, the more loving and gentle she became. She was an inspiration to me. I've always been a very logical person. I'm an accountant, and I've been able to sort things out and develop solutions to personal problems. I think I did that after the assault. I don't hold grudges and I don't blame people for my problems. And while I was angry at God after this happened to me, I always felt that God had been good to me most of my life, and as I became more involved with the church, I saw that God had protected me from greater harm. Finding the church, getting involved in helping other people, getting right back to work, and rediscovering love in my marriage were all part of getting over the assault.

I think you have to find the good out of the bad things that happen in life. I went to the Bible and I read Job and I thought, there is a lot of wisdom here, and maybe what I went through was a test of my strength and I'll be able to deal with this because I'm a strong woman. I don't know if any of this makes sense to you, but I hope it helps other people who go through what I did. Somebody told me they'd read something in a book, which said, "My strength is in my vulnerability." I now know that I'm vulnerable but that I can deal with it.

LESSONS TO BE LEARNED FROM THIS STORY

According to Resnick and colleagues (1999), PTSD may develop as early as 2 weeks after a violent trauma but doesn't necessarily have to last for a prolonged period of time. Our storyteller seems to have dealt with the early symptoms of PTSD by doing the following:

1. She returned to work as quickly as possible. Most studies of serious trauma suggest that returning to one's usual routines is one of the best immediate ways to deal with trauma, because routines bring people back to their pre-trauma state of life.

2. She entered therapy with someone specializing in traumas caused by assaults. Not everyone believes that therapy should immediately follow a trauma, and some writers indicate that therapy provided too early actually reinforces the potential for PTSD (Gist & Devilly, 2002; van Emmerik et al., 2002). Speaking about one of the most common forms of early therapy, debriefing, Gist and Devilly (2002) caution against the use of therapy with victims of violence whose symptoms are not yet evident, as therapy might interfere with natural healing and the positive impact of support systems. Gist and Devilly also believe that therapy sometimes encourages symptoms of PTSD, when clinicians suggest that a lack of symptoms may be symptomatic of denial, and that many victims of assault have spontaneous resolution of the trauma without professional help.

3. On the advice of her therapist, she joined a support group. Humphreys and colleagues (Humphreys, 1998; Humphreys, Mavis, & Stoffelmayr, 1994; Humphreys & Moos, 1996; Humphreys & Ribisl, 1999) have shown the positive benefits of self-help and support groups with a number of serious emotional, medical, and substance abuse problems.

4. The storyteller dealt with her anger at God by finding an outlet for coping with her meaning-of-life issues through a small church near her home where she helped with finances and provided assistance to people in need. One of the ways resilient people have of dealing with their inner conflict is to help others. Perhaps resilient people have been trained to be helpers early in life, since many resilient people have been caregivers to substance-abusing, mentally ill, or abusive parents as children. For many resilient people, however, helping others seems to have a curative effect. In her study of survivors of the Holocaust, Nachama Teck (2003) writes, "The more accustomed prospective victims are to performing nurturing and cooperative roles, the more likely they are to adapt to changing circumstances" (p. 353).

5. She used her logical way of dealing with life to develop coping strategies. Some writers on resilience have noted that "emotional intelligence" seems to be a characteristic of resilient people. In a review of the factors associated with people's resilience during highly stressful life events, Tiet, Bird, and Davies (1998) found that higher IQ seemed to be a factor in coping with stressful events. However, when successful resolution of traumas was evaluated, problem-solving skills were found to be the single most significant component of resilience and may or may not be associated with a higher IQ.

6. She remembered how her mother coped with a terminal illness and used that example to suggest various ways of coping with her assault. This example reinforces the idea that children who have been trained as caregivers, particularly if the experience was a highly positive one, resort to helping others as a way of resurfacing old feelings of competence as they struggle to regain their coping abilities.

7. While she was frightened at identifying the assault perpetrator, she did it and began to see him not as someone with power over her, but as someone who she felt was troubled and "pathetic." Along with Sechrest (Glicken & Sechrest, 2003), I have written previously about victims of violent crime actually confronting perpetrators. Some courts and prison systems have reunited victims and perpetrators to permit victims to gain emotional understanding of perpetrators and to share with them the harm done by their violent acts. Empathy training or victim awareness, as it is sometimes called, helps victims gain emotional power over perpetrators and can sometimes help to reduce the impact of traumatic assaults.

8. She found comfort in the perpetrator's mother's attempts to help her son. The realization that good parents sometimes fail helped her deal with the insensitive behavior of her own children. She now understands that while we try to be good parents, sometimes good results aren't apparent and we shouldn't punish ourselves for it.

9. She rediscovered love with her husband and formed a stronger bond with him than ever. The reality is that many victims of assaults find their spouses and family members unsupportive, blaming, and critical. It says a great deal about both her and her husband that the assault actually brought them together and strengthened their love for one another.

10. She used the experience and her ability to cope with it to further define herself as a strong person. Finding strength to cope with the assault did what

positive psychology and the strengths perspective said it would do. It made clear to her that "every maladaptive response or pattern of behavior may also contain the seeds of a struggle for health" (Saleebey, 2000, p.129). The more she did to cope with the problem, the more power she had over it. Because she had defined herself as a strong woman before the assault, she was able to use examples of her strength to cope with the problems she experienced as a result of the assault.

A Story About a Resilient Woman Coping With an Act of Terrorism

I worked for a Jewish agency in the Mid west. Just before we were to close for the day, a man entered the agency and held me hostage for the next 2 days. He had guns and knives, which he frequently pressed against my body. He kept telling me that he would kill me because the Israeli Army killed his entire family. I'm a social worker and I tried to calm him down, but as time went by, he became really agitated and violent. I got increasingly frightened and I was certain he was going to kill me. He beat me up pretty badly and broke my jaw and cut my face. He made me look at pictures of his family while they were alive and then pictures after their death. He spoke in broken English and another language I couldn't identify, and he kept on crying and screaming at me. On the second day, he finally gave up and I was released, but when he came out of the building, the police thought he had a weapon with him and shot him to death. I saw the whole thing. In a way, we'd bonded together, and maybe the shooting traumatized me even more than being held captive.

At first, I seemed numb but OK. I went back to work the next day and told everyone that I was fine and happy to be back. The staff wasn't so sure, and my supervisor cautioned me about PTSD. At the office, I seemed fine for months. People were pretty amazed. But at home I was a mess. I was afraid all the time and I really thought one of his friends would break into my house and kill me. To handle my fear I started self-medicating by using Ativan I'd gotten from a friend. And I began drinking a bottle of wine every night, something I'd hardly ever done before. I was irritable, anxious, and frightened. At work, I began to have severe mood swings. I couldn't handle many routine assignments and I'd hide in my office if I saw anyone who looked like the man who held me hostage.

My supervisor made me seek help and take a leave of absence. I was seen for 6 months by a therapist specializing in random violence who used cognitive therapy and exposure therapy, where I was told to talk about the event so that its emotional grip on me would change. Within 2 months of treatment my symptoms were in remission enough for me to go back to work. I still get frightened feelings and sometimes I can't sleep. I'm also jittery about leaving the house and sometimes I still use wine and Ativan. I'd say I'm back to about 90% of where I was before the event happened.

This story was first presented as a case study in Glicken (2005b, pp. 151–153). The subject was asked to tell the story from her point of view for this book, and to provide an update a year and a half after the initial interview for the case.

THE STORYTELLER'S SELF-ANALYSIS

You asked me to comment on why I was able to go so long without help after the event, and why I responded so well to therapy and I was able to return to work so fast. People become social workers for many reasons. My reason was that I was sexually molested when I was a child. I kept it to myself and learned to do well in many ways even though I often felt awful inside. Both my parents had drug and alcohol problems, and I took care of them when I was growing up. You learn to put your own problems away when that happens, and I was good at hiding my feelings. Often, I didn't even know what my feelings were, but I knew I had to be tough and strong and survive or my family would fall apart. My personal life was a mess and I had no support group, no romantic involvements, very few friends, and even before this happened to me, I'd begun suffering from anxiety, insomnia, and drinking too much.

In many ways this awful event has helped me change for the better. For one thing, I joined a support group for survivors of violence. I've made some nice friends from the group, and I've begun seeing a guy who works with me. We have a very close relationship and it's been wonderful to have a companion and good friend. I'm still frightened and I fall apart every once in a while, but in many ways, I'm better than before this happened. And I feel great empathy for the man who held me hostage. We Jews need to understand that some people have grievances against us. Rather than calling it anti-Semitism, we need to be more open to listening and understanding with our hearts. I've joined a group of Jews and Palestinians who dialogue every week about our mutual problems. I think the openness of our conversation is very healing for both sides. The group has helped diffuse some problems between [its members in] the two communities [and] that is a hopeful and empowering sign. We're all Americans. We live in this wonderful land in harmony. Maybe our example will help resolve problems in Israel. That idea is very strong inside of me and helps on those days that aren't so good and some of the anxiety and stress come back.

I think I had an exceptional therapist. He enlisted my help in finding out what we should do together. He asked me to look at the research literature and to help in the treatment plan. We both agreed that cognitive therapy with desensitization that allowed me to reduce my level of anxiety was the best treatment option, coupled with work on my ongoing problems with intimacy. He listened, consulted me, and treated me like a competent adult. I think the way he deferred to me and respected my ideas helped more than anything else. He also had a knack for reminding me about my positive behaviors, something I was all too ready to forget. I was at a point where I didn't believe I knew anything, and I was falling apart. It was really pretty scary. His encouragement and willingness to involve me was such a wonderful gift at a time when my self-esteem was very low, that I could have just hugged him for treating me so well.

Am I cured? No. I have problems to resolve that predate those awful two days. Most of the time I'm fine, better than fine, really. I don't think I'm responsible for everyone anymore and I'm taking better care of myself. It's made me a better social worker and a much healthier person. I'm optimistic about the future, but a little part of me will never be as trusting or feel as safe. I think I'll always live in a state of hypervigilance, and from the clients I've work with who are survivors of violence I know that you fight the feeling of being afraid all the time. So I won't say I'm cured, but I'm much better and I'm optimistic. And that's a long way from where I was during, after, and even before this happened to me.

Summary

This chapter on resilient people who cope with random violence includes discussions of the symptoms and prevalence of posttraumatic stress disorder and why some people are more resilient than others in coping with violence. Assault is one of the primary reasons for the development of symptoms of PTSD. Two case studies of assaults are provided. In one case, I provide reasons for the ability of a storyteller to cope so well with a violent act, while in the second story, the storyteller provides a self-analysis.

CHAPTER 14

Resilient Communities

In our effort to understand resilience, we need to remember that people live in communities and neighborhoods that assist or hinder their ability to cope with traumas. As Saleebey (1996) writes in his discussion of the importance of healthy community life,

> Membership [in a community] means that people need to be citizens—responsible and valued members in a viable group or community. To be without membership is to be alienated, and to be at risk of marginalization and oppression, the enemies of civic and moral strength (Walzer, 1983). As people begin to realize and use their assets and abilities, collectively and individually, as they begin to discover the pride in having survived and overcome their difficulties, more and more of their capacities come into the work and play of daily life. (p. 297)

While it is clear that community affects physical and emotional health and leads to resilience, it is not clear whether we have a healthy community life in America. A number of authors think we don't. In an interview with Robert Putnam on the isolating aspects of American life, Stossel (2000) quotes Putnam as saying that

> Americans today have retreated into isolation. Evidence shows, Putnam says, that fewer and fewer contemporary Americans are unionizing, voting, rallying around shared causes, participating in religious services, inviting each other over, or doing much of anything collectively. In fact, when we do occasionally gather—for twelve-step support encounters and the like—it's most often only as an excuse to focus on ourselves in the presence of an audience. Supper eaten with friends or family has given way to supper gobbled in solitude, with only the glow of the television screen for companionship. (p. 1)

Stossel goes on to quote Putnam (2000), who in describing the impact of our social isolation, the weakening of our social bond, and our loss of connectedness, notes that the most startling fact about social connectedness is how pervasive are its effects. We are not talking here simply about nostalgia for the 1950s. School performance, public health, crime rates, clinical depression, tax compliance, philanthropy, race relations, community development, census returns, teen suicide, economic productivity, campaign finance, even simple human happiness— all are demonstrably affected by how (and whether) we connect with our family and friends and neighbors and co-workers. (Stossel, 2000, p. 4)

Putnam (2000) believes we are all at risk when communities develop dysfunctional qualities and argues that violence exists in even the most affluent of communities. "The shooting sprees that affected schools in suburban and rural communities as the twentieth century ended are a reminder that as the breakdown of communities continues in more privileged settings, affluence and education are insufficient to prevent collective tragedy" (Putnam, 2000, p. 318).

This disconnectedness from one another has led Americans to a search for happiness in isolation, which indicates a growing rift in our social and spiritual lives. According to Seligman (2002), we have

myriad shortcuts to feeling good; drugs, chocolate, loveless sex, shopping, masturbation, and television are all examples. The belief that we can rely on shortcuts to happiness, joy, rapture, comfort, and ecstasy, rather than be entitled to these feelings by the exercise of personal strengths and virtues, leads to legions of people who, in the middle of great wealth, are starving spiritually. (quoted in ABCNews.com, 2002)

Wolff (2003) believes that "recent trends in American society [show] an emphasis on individuals rather than communities, with discrepancies between the haves and have nots growing dramatically, and with racial and social justice sliding to the back burner" (p. 110). The author continues, "The decline in civic engagement continues to stymie the problem solvers, and the dysfunctional organization of government that focuses on categorical funding and government silos is failing to address the whole community" (p. 110).

Gates (2000) argues that the reason for the lack of health in our communities is that

the energy Americans once exercised to address shared community concerns is now being expended on issue-specific debates that hamper citizens' ability to view community challenges in the total community context. The root of this condition can be found in the difference between public debate and public deliberation. In debate, points of view are argued and defended until one argument proves stronger. Conversely, deliberation is a discussion that uncovers underlying values between both similar and differing points of view. It is a deeper level of communication, requiring commitment from all parties involved to standards of conduct or ground rules through which they comport themselves. (p. 164)

Ryff and Singer (1998) argue that modern psychology has failed to develop a view of clients that extends beyond the presence or absence of dysfunctional behavior. As long as we hold this limited view of clients, our work will fail to account for the impact of communities and neighborhoods on clients. Sandage and Hill (2001) suggest that modern psychology has no model of the civic virtues that promote healthy individual and community behavior. In fact, they believe that much of psychology and perhaps most of the helping professions have no model of the positive values that should be stressed with our clients or the necessary constructive social behaviors that will lead to an increased sense of social responsibility and healthier community life.

Martin Seligman worries that Americans have become so caught up in a personal sense of entitlement that even helping professionals have gone along with, in fact encouraged, "the belief that we can rely on shortcuts to happiness, joy, rapture, comfort, and ecstasy, rather than be entitled to these feelings by the exercise of personal strengths and virtues, which results in legions of people who, in the middle of great wealth, are starving spiritually" (quoted in ABCNews.com, 2002). Seligman goes on to say that "positive emotion alienated from the exercise of character leads to emptiness, to inauthenticity, to depression, and, as we age, to the gnawing realization that we are fidgeting until we die" (quoted in ABCNews.com, 2002).

Resilience and Healthy Community Life

The Surgeon General's report *Healthy People in Healthy Communities* (Satcher, 1998) defines a healthy community as "one that is safe with affordable housing and accessible transportation systems, work for all who want to work, a healthy and safe environment with a sustainable ecosystem, and offers access to health care services which focus on prevention and staying healthy" (p. 1). The report goes on to say,

> The healthy city strives to provide a thriving economy and opportunities for individuals and families while adequately addressing public health, medical care, and other essential needs of its population. In addition, a healthy community demonstrates an element of interconnectedness. When a healthy community initiative is undertaken, a communal spirit develops, linking public, private, and nonprofit sectors to address the underlying causes of poor health. Healthy community participants represent the wide spectrum of interests and roles that make a community work. (p. 1)

Kesler (2000) defines a healthy community as one that has social connectedness, civic virtue, and socially responsible members. In healthy communities, there is "a sophisticated, integrative, and interconnected vision of flourishing of the individual and the human collective in an environmental setting" (Kesler, 2000, p. 272) that involves all sectors of the community, including the disenfranchised. People in healthy communities connect intimately with one another and are aware of special issues that need to be addressed with sensitivity and creativity. In healthy communities, a dialogue exists among people to help formulate public policy agendas that function with consensus among all community groups and political persuasions. Healthy communities are caring, mature, and aware communities that seek alliances with other community-based movements and "encourage all concerned to rise to higher integrative levels of thinking, discourse, research, policies, programs, institutions, and processes, so that they might truly begin to transform their lives, their communities, and the greater society" (Kesler, 2000, p. 271).

Lachman (1997) uses the term *sustainable communities* to describe communities with strong local economies, clean air and water, energy efficiency, recycling programs, sufficient jobs, lack of sprawl, a safe and cooperative population, and a political process with the maximum involvement of its residents. To achieve the goal of long-term sustainability, she suggests a political process that is able to develop consensus among residents and that develops long-term plans and remains loyal to those plans. In a discussion of sustainable communities, Srinivasan, O'Fallon, and Dearry (2003) write,

> The spare research on sustainable *communities* suggests that diligent planning is needed to create an environment that is conducive to the mental and physical well-being of humans as well as the natural environment. These studies contend that health benefits exist when people come into contact with the natural environment. The studies recommend both the creation of green spaces and the use of environmentally conscious construction. (p. 1448)

Putnam (2000) suggests that most Americans recognize that we need to reconnect with one another and that "figuring out how to reconcile the competing obligations of work and family and community is the ultimate kitchen table issue" (quoted in Stossel, 2000, p. 4). The lack of ability to find commonality with our fellow citizens and to develop mutual helping relationships often ends in what Taylor (1993) calls "entrapping niches" where membership in the community is based upon social alienation and stigma. In its place, Taylor (1993) calls for "enabling niches" where people are known for what they do and for their willingness to reach out to one another in time of need. Writing about the purest form of community outreach, the natural helpers who define the most elegant aspects of social responsibility, Waller and Patterson (2002) suggest that "informal helping sustains and extends resiliency in individuals and communities . . . and [is] consistent with the growing body of research suggesting that informal social support buffers the effects of stress on adaptational outcomes" (p. 80).

As I noted in Chapter 9, Robert and Li (2001) believe that while most researchers think there is a relationship between income and health, research actually suggests a limited relationship between the two variables. Rather, there seems to be a relationship between community levels of health and individual health. Lawton (1977) reports that older adults often think of their communities as a primary source of support, recreation, and stimulation. Lawton and Nahemow (1973) believe that communities are especially important when older adults have emotional, physical, or cognitive problems and for older adults who have disabilities and limited mobility.

Robert and Li (2001) suggest three indicators of healthy communities that relate directly to individual health: (1) a positive physical environment that provides an absence of noise, traffic, inadequate lighting, and other features of a community that may lead to functional loss in older adults; (2) a positive social environment that includes an absence of crime, the ability to find safe environments to walk in, and easy access to shopping; and (3) a rich service environment that includes simple and safe access to rapid and inexpensive transportation, the availability of senior centers, and easy access to meal sites.

In studying the impact of natural disasters on a population of elderly adults demonstrating predisaster signs of depression, Tyler and Hoyt (2000) found that elderly adults with high levels of social support (friendships, concerned neighbors, church involvement, volunteer activity) had lower levels of depression before and after a natural disaster. Tyler and Hoyt (2000) also report that "older people with little or no social support, perhaps due to death of a spouse and/or loss of friends, may have a more difficult time dealing with life changes and, as a result, are particularly vulnerable to increases in depression" (p. 155).

A STORY OF A RESILIENT COMMUNITY
CONSTRUCTING A VIOLENCE TREATMENT PROGRAM

Lakewood is a moderately sized city in the Mid west that had been beset by extraordinarily high rates of childhood and adolescent violence. It is a middle-class community with few pockets of poverty, little unemployment, and citizens who are generally involved in community affairs. Unfortunately, Lakewood is experiencing an escalating drug and alcohol epidemic among children and adolescents, while also experiencing a breakdown in the school system because bomb threats and school violence make it difficult for most children to get a respectable education. Rather than quickly adopting programs used by other communities with similar problems, the Lakewood City Council brought in two tough-minded consultants. The Council asked the consultants to find and review programs that had long-term effectiveness and to return with recommendations. Council members had spoken to representatives from other communities who complained that programs they developed on the advice of local consultants had very short life spans. Children seemed to improve as a result of treatment, but improvement rates were short term and the overall crime rate was unaffected. The Lakewood City Council told the consultants that they wanted a report showing a connection between treatment and prevention strategies and lowered crime rates over the course of the life span . . . a very tall order.

The following case, which describes the construction of a community violence treatment and prevention program, first appeared in a book I wrote on youth violence (Glicken, 2004b, pp. 116–118). The case is followed by the opinions of the key members of a committee to reduce violence who, when interviewed for this book, were asked whether the original program resulted in lower rates of youth violence 3 years later.

Two months later the consultants came back with their report. It said that there were few available studies showing lowered rates of violence over the life span. Some programs actually increased rates of violence (some substance abuse programs discovered that some participants were selling dangerous drugs to other participants, raising the violence level dramatically). Not all programs were equal, they said, and beyond that, one had to factor in the reality that programs had differential results based upon the competency and length of employment of the staff. Most programs that worked were politically unpopular and often resulted in termination before long-term results were noted. A case in point was a program paying youth $150 for guns they turned into the police. The consensus was that the guns were illegally obtained and that the community should not pay for illegal merchandise.

The cost of intervention and prevention would be very high, the consultants said, but compared to the cost of crime and violence, it was well worth the effort, even if the programs only helped a small cohort of children. Finally, it took time for programs to work. Changing long-term behaviors was difficult, and changing an environment that was currently experiencing high crime rates would take time.

The consultants said that programs should be made available to everyone in the community, but the target population should be at-risk children since they had a greater probability of youth violence. At-risk children included children who had been abused or neglected or were at risk of abuse and neglect; children whose parents abused substances; children with other siblings who had problems with violence; children from homes with poor health and nutritional practices; children whose parents undervalued or failed to support education; and children who were demonstrating early signs of aggression. The consultants went on to suggest adopting the following programs, while making certain that the lack of definitive effectiveness data should be kept in mind: (1) early assistance to at-risk families by providing financial, health, mental health, educational, and parenting skills services (at-risk families included families with an unusually high number of negative characteristics, including drug and alcohol problems, evidence of family violence, work-related problems, and unemployment); (2) appropriate counseling service to individuals and families in the high-risk group (the consultants said that treatment is an important aspect of violence intervention and prevention); (3) a close working relationship between schools and community agencies with instances of bullying and acting-out behavior and evidence of child abuse or domestic violence to be immediately referred to the appropriate agencies, and a supervisory committee set up to monitor results; (4) recreational facilities close to high-risk neighborhoods, with professionally trained staff who could spot troubled behavior and provide immediate help through counseling or referrals to mental health professionals; (5) a no drug or alcohol tolerance policy for youth in schools and at community events; (6) close supervision of high-crime areas by the police and an immediate response at the first sign of violence; (7) a no-tolerance policy for weapons in the possession of youth, with mandatory sentencing; (8) a juvenile court that would enforce a no-violence community response to youth violence; and (9) a no-violence policy in the school system, with a school board prepared to enforce the policy.

The consultants also told the Council a truism of all research: Because a program worked well in one location, it might not work well in another. Conditions varied in geographic locations and each community had its own set of dynamics that made it unique. Even so, the consultants said, it was wise to give the programs time to work, perhaps several years. Ongoing effectiveness evaluations were essential and should be used to make modifications in the programs as needed. If there was an immediate drop in violent behavior, the consultants noted, it would probably be the result of other forces and not the treatment programs. Perhaps, they suggested, the treatment programs would create concerns about violence and those concerns would be enough to cause a sudden decrease in rates of violence. Sudden impressive changes would probably not last and it would be a mistake to eliminate violence treatment and prevention programs before they had a chance to be empirically evaluated.

The consultants suggested, as a first step, that the City Council try and find out why the violence rate in Lakewood had been increasing so dramatically. The reasons could be transient or they could be related to systemic problems in the community. Transient reasons for increases in violence might include contagion from nearby communities and could include mobile violence caused by non-residents, rivalries with other communities that increased youth violence, and copycat violence that was short-lived. Community-based violence was violence that had its origins in community difficulties and included high tolerance for child abuse and neglect, easy youth access to weapons, an overly tolerant police force, schools that didn't work cooperatively with the police or with child welfare agencies, easy youth access to drugs and alcohol, and increased gang and violent subculture activity.

THE RESULTS OF THE PROGRAM: AN INTERVIEW WITH MEMBERS OF THE CITY COUNCIL

Member 1: A lot of people thought the problem would go away on its own and opposed the program. Youth violence was going down all over the country since its peek years in the early 90s. The problem was that the violence in Lakewood was taking place in 2001 and was way out of kilter with the rest of the country.

Member 2: And the cost of the program was high. We think Lakewood is a very healthy place to live. We have low taxes and our public labor costs are below average because people just love Lakewood and will work here for less pay. Most people don't have large public sector needs so there was plenty of opposition to a program that would add about $200 a year to property taxes.

Member 3: Most of us on the City Council have children in public school and we could see that school violence was a very serious problem. My daughter almost got raped in the girl's bathroom in her middle school. So the Council really pushed for the program. We got right on it, hired people, and put the plan into practice the consultants mapped out for us.

Member 2: The program has been working for almost 3 years now. All the things the consultant told us would happen did happen. Violence went down right away and then came back even worse. We almost lost the program . . . and then when we were trying to get a new business to come to town, a business magazine came out with best places to do business in America and the "also rans." We were an "also ran." The magazine wrote: "Lakewood is a wonderful community. Housing is moderately priced, the climate is moderate, and the people are moderate. The only immoderate thing about Lakewood is that children have a tendency to assault and kill in Lakewood. If you don't mind a great deal of youth violence in a community that otherwise has many good things going for it, Lakewood is the place for you." Because of the publication, the company changed its mind about relocating its headquarters to Lakewood and the person we were negotiating with told us, "We want our kids to live in a safe community. Lakewood has been remiss in its efforts to deal with youth violence."

Member 1: That really got us off our butts and led to the community getting behind the program, wholeheartedly. Since then, crime and violence are below national levels, and we think we can do even better. We're also looking at public transportation and whether Lakewood is such a good place for older adults, poorer families, and diverse groups. We found a bit of prejudice against certain people because of their skin color and we have programs in place to deal with that. No one likes to think the community we live in is prejudiced, but we've come to believe that about Lakewood and we're working hard to change that problem.

Member 3: When you do one thing with a community, you end up doing a lot. We want Lakewood to be the best place it can be and we want to someday be one of those communities everyone says is one of the best places in the country to live in. We are part of the healthy communities movement and it's been a blessing. Every year we ask citizens to rate the community. In 2000 the highest satisfaction rating was about 50%. Now about 80% of the citizens give us the highest possible score. We have more to do, but that certainly is a good start, don't you think?

Member 2: Once people get invested in the community, they want to do even more to make Lakewood the best place it can be. We have a significant beautification project where people plant flowers and trees all over town. We have a program of free rides for low-income or older people to see doctors and to do their shopping. Our standardized test scores have gone way up since we did something about violence in the schools. We all live in a community, and when you think of it as the most important part of your daily life next to family, it becomes very important to most residents.

A STORY ABOUT A RESILIENT COMMUNITY COPING WITH A DEVASTATING FLOOD

Grand Forks, North Dakota, is a community of 60,000 people in a mainly agricultural area 90 miles south of the Canadian border. The town sits on the banks of the contentious Red River of the North, which has a propensity for flooding and caused a massive flood that destroyed the entire downtown area, over 9,000 homes, and much of the city, causing an evacuation of 51,000 residents in the spring of 1997. Throughout the 5-week period of the flood, the local newspaper kept publishing a daily paper on the Internet by moving from one location and higher ground to another location or community. Because of this extraordinary effort, the paper won a Pulitzer Prize in 1998. In the stories, the newspaper's staff described the deep wounds suffered by the community as fires raged throughout the downtown area, and thousands of homes and historic buildings were lost, much of it unwitnessed by the evacuated townspeople. Thousands of people, helping to build dikes to hold the rising waters back, found the strength to help others. It was only "stuff" they lost, the people reminded one another, and so many others had it even worse (Jacobs & Maidenberg, 1997).

Weeks later, as the floodwaters continued to rise almost 28 feet above flood level, President Clinton came to see the ravaged community, landing at an airbase 30 miles away that housed 3,000 refugees from the flood. He took a helicopter tour and found most of the city submerged and water 40 miles in every direction flooding the flat, fertile Red River Valley. When he returned to the airbase, he was greeted with signs welcoming him to "Water World." According to Fedor, Bonham, Bradbury, and Paulson (1997), hundreds of people in the crowd rushed to the shake hands with the president after his speech.

Grand Forks is my hometown. I had been in town a month before the flood to watch a hockey series between the University of North Dakota and the University of Minnesota and to meet old friends. It was 44 degrees below zero and everything was closed except the hockey arena, the restaurants, and the bars. My ears froze from a block-long walk from the parking lot to the hockey arena. My brother, a newspaper editor from Long Beach, California, phoned Mike Jacobs, the editor of the *Grand Forks Herald,* and asked him what people did when it got that cold. "They put tee-shirts in boiling water and then throw them up in and air and see if they freeze before they hit the ground," he said. Smoke from chimneys and power plants went straight up, and the snowfall looked massive. But the people, the tough, resilient people of Grand Forks, were astonishing. I saw young men walking into restaurants with tee-shirts on, and nobody wore a hat. As it was when I was growing up, so it was now. You made the best of a bad situation and you were proud to have survived it. You reveled in your toughness and optimism.

I think it was this resilience that made it possible for a destroyed community to come back so quickly. Rather than 20% of the town folk not moving back, as had been predicted, it turned out to be less than 3%. Most people thought it would take many years to rebuild the city, but within several years, most of the 9,000 homes and all the destroyed downtown structures were rebuilt. My grade school and synagogue were among the destroyed buildings, and they have been rebuilt. Before the flood, my grade school, Belmont Elementary, was among the 100 best elementary schools in the country. It's even better now. It takes resilient people to cope with such a trauma, but it takes a resilient community with forward-thinking community leaders to pull them together. That, I think, is why communities like Grand Forks not only survive, but they become model communities.

When President Clinton met the mayor of Grand Forks, Pat Owens, in the hanger of the airbase where she and others were living, she told him that his presence had brought hope and inspiration to the people, and that she'd had a hard time deciding what to wear. When he told the mayor that she looked great, Mayor Owens replied, "What I wear is the heart and soul of my community" (Fedor et al., 1997).

Summary

In this chapter, material from the work of Robert Putnam, Martin Seligman, and Dennis Saleebey is offered as evidence that our communities have a long way to go before they qualify as being safe and healthy places for most Americans, particularly our most needy citizens. Two stories of resilient communities are provided that show the productive nature of what Hanifan (1916) refers to as "Social Capital," or "the good will, fellowship, sympathy, and social intercourse among the individuals and families who make up a social unit" (p. 130). When social capital exists, it can lead to healthy communities where natural healing and resilience are allowed to flourish.

PART IV

Practice Implications

CHAPTER 15

The Primary Behaviors of Resilient People

Application of Findings to Practice

The following attributes of resilient people, developed from the stories and the research presented, may help to summarize what we know about resilient people. After analyzing the stories told by resilient people, I find that my understanding of resilience differs from that in some of the research presented. This research portrays resilient people as continually stress resistant and endlessly resilient, which doesn't seem to be the case. Resilient people have doubts, moments of despair, high anxiety, and a range of debilitating emotions. Sometimes those emotions overpower them and they have periods of malfunction. For the most part, however, these amazing people are able to cope well with life in the everyday ways we think of when we consider positive social functioning. They get up in the morning, shower and dress, go to work, take care of others, contribute to the community, and do wonderfully inspiring things, even in the midst of feeling deeply dispirited and emotionally labile. It's a mistake to think of resilient people as superhuman. They are very human and are as emotionally unsettled when stress reaches critical levels as the rest of us. What differentiates resilient people from others is their ability to get on with their lives in elegant, unique, and contributory ways that suggest the very best in human behavior.

Resilient people are not necessarily nice people. Resilience is not a value judgment but an attribute based solely upon the ability to sustain oneself over the life span in ways that permit a very high level of social functioning. Some not terribly nice people survive traumas and are, by definition, resilient. We need to know a great deal more about them and how they differ from and are similar to the people we normally think of as the morally sound and emotionally gifted people we consider to be resilient.

Listed below are the attributes of resilience that were taken from the stories told in past chapters. Following each attribute of resilience, there is a section entitled

"Application to Practice" that contains the lessons learned from this book about how best to use resilience research with our clients.

The Attributes of Resilient People and Practice Recommendations

1. Better Coping Skills: Resilient people are more likely to cope well with serious stressors and traumas than nonresilient people. This isn't always the case, however. The specific trauma and its relationship to pretrauma functioning may result in a nonresilient response by a resilient person.

Application to Practice: The evidence presented in the chapter suggests that a thorough psychosocial history should be taken, making certain that prior traumatic events are discussed. One should find out how well the client coped with past traumas, if this traumatic event is similar to or dissimilar from the other events, and whether the client is using coping mechanisms that worked well in the past. Allow the client time to heal on his or her own before initiating treatment. The research on debriefing for traumas suggests that intervention applied too soon after an event may increase the probability of symptoms of PTSD, and that symptoms that may have been dealt with through self-healing might require more extensive treatment. In an article discussing the use of debriefing within 72 hours of traumas, such as those resulting from the World Trade Center bombing, Groopman (2004) reports on a ship explosion in Nova Scotia in 1917 in which over 2,000 people were killed and 9,000 injured. He writes, "Many of them [the victims] were blinded and dismembered. The night after the explosion, a blizzard descended on Halifax hindering the relief effort and many people whose homes were destroyed froze to death" (Groopman, 2004, p. 34). Large numbers of the victims were in such extreme shock that relief workers thought they were suffering from psychosis. Hallucinations were noted in many of the survivors. But within a week of the tragedy, "these disturbing symptoms spontaneously subsided in the vast majority of cases" (Groopman, 2004, p. 34). What has been learned from this and other traumatic events is that people need to be given time to heal on their own, and that intervention should initially be limited to caring for physical needs and offering basic emotional support to trauma victims.

2. Positive Social Functioning: While resilient people are generally able to maintain high levels of social functioning, they may also experience emotional side effects related to traumas that include depression, moments of despair, sexual problems when abuse and rape are involved, anxiety when symptoms of PTSD are also apparent, and a host of other emotional problems. Consequently, the term *resilience* refers more to social functioning than to an absence of emotional side effects. Resilient people function well in the midst of symptoms of emotional difficulty and generally recover from those symptoms faster and more completely than do nonresilient people. Good coping skills suggest that resilient people are open to new ideas, new directions, and new pathways to resolve life crises. Superior coping skills might be thought of as the "habits" people have developed to deal with adversity.

Application to Practice: Using supportive interventions that focus on client strengths is the initial way to work with most clients reacting to a traumatic life event. This suggests that empathic listening and cooperative approaches to treatment will be most beneficial because these approaches allow clients to mobilize their own resilience in a way that doesn't interfere with natural healing. Our efforts to help clients achieve positive social functioning also require that we consult the research literature and make certain that our treatment is supported by the best evidence of effectiveness. Evidence-based practice seems the most likely approach to help us provide treatments that will lead to positive social functioning.

Sackett, Richardson, Rosenberg, and Haynes (1997) define evidence-based practice (EBP) as "the conscientious, explicit, and judicious use of current best evidence in making decisions about the care of individuals" (p. 2). Gambrill (2000, p. 1) defines EBP as a process involving self-directed learning that requires professionals to access information that permits us to (1) take our collected knowledge and provide questions we can answer; (2) find the best evidence with which to answer questions; (3) analyze the best evidence for its research validity as well as its applicability to the practice questions we have asked; (4) determine if the best evidence we've found can be used with a particular client; (5) consider the client's social and emotional background; (6) make the client a participant in decision making; and (7) evaluate the quality of practice with that specific client.

In describing the importance of evidence-based practice, the American Medical Association Evidence-Based Practice Working Group (1992) asserts that a new paradigm is emerging that "de-emphasizes intuition, unsystematic clinical experience, and pathophysiologic rationale as sufficient grounds for clinical decision making, and stresses the examination of evidence from clinical research" (American Medical Association Evidence-Based Practice Working Group, 1992, p. 2420). Timmermans and Angell (2001) indicate that evidence-based clinical judgment has five important features: (1) It is composed of both research evidence and clinical experience; (2) There is skill involved in reading the literature that requires an ability to synthesize the information and make judgments about the quality of the evidence available; (3) The way in which information is used is a function of the practitioner's level of authority in an organization and his or her level of confidence in the effectiveness of the applied information; (4) Part of the use of evidence-based practice is the ability to independently evaluate the information used and to test its validity in the context of one's own practice; (5) Evidence-based clinical judgments are grounded in the Western notions of professional conduct and professional roles, and are ultimately guided by a common value system.

Gambrill (1999) points out that one of the most important aspects of EBP is the sharing of information with clients and the cooperative relationship that ensues. She believes that in EBP, clinicians search for relevant research to help in practice decisions and share that information with clients. If no evidence is found to justify a specific treatment regimen, the client is informed and a discussion takes place about how best to approach treatment. Gambrill (1999) thinks that the use of evidence-based practice can help us "avoid fooling ourselves that we have knowledge when we do not" (p. 342).

Hines (2000) suggests that some fundamental steps are required for the practitioner of EBP to obtain usable information in a literature search. They are (1) developing a well-formulated clinical question; (2) finding the best possible answers to your questions; (3) determining the validity and reliability of the data found; and (4) testing the information with your client. Hines (2000) also says that a well-formulated clinical question must accurately describe the problem you wish to look for, limit the interventions you think are feasible and acceptable to the client, include a search for alternative approaches, and indicate the outcomes you wish to achieve with the client. The advantage of EBP, according to Hines, is that it allows the practitioner to develop quality practice guidelines that can be applied to the client, identify appropriate literature that can be shared with the client, communicate with other professionals from a knowledge-guided frame of reference, and continue a process of self-learning that results in the best possible treatment for clients.

3. A Present and Future Orientation: Resilient people are present and future oriented. They are usually able to put the past in context, not dwell on it, and move on with their lives. Their notions of the future may be very short term and may be indistinguishable from living in the present. Another way of looking at this is that resilient people live their lives a day at a time.

Application to Practice: Approaches that examine the past to explain the present are probably not terribly effective with most resilient people and will very likely meet with resistance if they are used. Cognitive-behavioral approaches seem more likely to help because they focus on the here and now instead of the then and there, and they provide the client with many options for problem solving. Evidence-based practice, which stresses a cooperative relationship and asks the client to do a great deal of the research to find the best evidence of treatment choices, would also provide clients with a here and now orientation.

4. Invisibility: Resilient people have often been able to lessen the emotional impact of a trauma by making themselves "invisible." For resilient people in traumatic situations, being invisible has two meanings: being absent from the source of the trauma to the extent possible, and when in the midst of the traumatic experience, thinking of themselves as neither being in the situation nor feeling troubled by it. This may also include avoiding potentially negative people or situations that cause discomfort.

Application to Practice: Anderson (1997) indicates that the professional literature often reports an association between child maltreatment and emotional problems. She gives as an example the observation that many maltreated children use wishful thinking or daydreaming to emotionally distance themselves from the abuse. Anderson suggests that, rather than seeing these coping mechanisms as dysfunctional, we should recognize all of the child's survival strategies as elegant ways to cope with an ongoing trauma. The child's coping strategies should be seen as strengths and not as impediments or dysfunctions. Another way to deal with invisibility is to use approaches that place the client in the present or that focus on life meaning (existential) issues. Posing a question that has often been associated with existential therapy, Frankl (1978) asks highly suicidal clients why they don't follow through on suicidal thoughts. The question often brings out deep-seated feelings of guilt, shame, and fear that, when voiced by clients, bring them back to the present and help them begin to cope with the problem.

5. Optimism: Resilient people are generally optimistic about the future, have a strong belief in themselves, and have unusually ambitious dreams and aspirations that motivate them to succeed in life. Positive self-identity helps people who are unable to immediately change their situation to stabilize themselves in times of stress with activities that keep them from feeling emotionally trapped.

Application to Practice: As Tech (2003) notes in her work on surviving inmates of the concentration camps, even though conditions in the camps were horrendous, "many inmates created for themselves make-believe worlds—a blend of dreams, fantasies, friendships and resistance—as an antidote" (p. 351). Prisoners found these fantasies very gratifying. "Such escapes into fantasy may have improved the prisoners hold on life. . . . Prisoners created bonding groups which, however illusory, forged links with the past and the future" (Tech, 2003, p. 351). Using approaches suggesting that dreams are unrealistic and unachievable will probably be ineffective effective with resilient people. Dreams and aspirations should be supported, however unobtainable. Resilient people need dreams to stay resilient. Without hope, they may lose their ability to cope.

Positive views of life can have a significant impact on physical and emotional health. In a longitudinal study of a Catholic order of women in the Mid west that included many life variables, Danner, Snowdon, and Friesen (2001) found that the positive and optimistic nature of personal statements written by very young women to gain entrance into the religious order correlated positively with the life span of women in the study. The more positive and affirming the personal statements written when applicants were in their late teens and early twenties, the longer the life span, sometimes as long as 10 years beyond the mean length of life for the religious order, as a whole, and up to 20 years or more longer than the general population. Many of the women in the sample lived well into their 90s and beyond. In a sample of 650, 6 women were over 100 years of age. While some of the women in the sample suffered serious physical problems, including dementia and Alzheimer's, the numbers of those with such problems were much smaller than in the general population and the age of onset was usually much later in life. The reasons for increased life span in this population included good health practices and an environment that focused on spiritual issues, optimism, and helping others. The order also has a strong emphasis on maintaining close, supportive relationships among its members, so that when illness *did* arise in these women, a network of positive and supportive help was available.

This need to focus on positive behavior in clients to increase optimism suggests the use of the strengths perspective with many clients. I define the *strengths perspective* as a way of viewing the positive behaviors of all clients by helping them see that problem areas are secondary to areas of strength and that out of what they do well can come helping solutions based upon the successful strategies they use daily in their lives to cope with a variety of important issues, problems, and concerns (Glicken, 2004a).

The central elements of the strengths perspective provide common themes (Glicken, 2004a; Goldstein, 1990; Saleebey, 1985, 1992, 1994; Weick, Rapp, Sullivan, & Kisthardt, 1989), which are detailed in the following list.

1. The strengths perspective focuses on the coping mechanisms, problem-solving skills, and decision-making processes that work well for the client and that result in an abundance of generally positive and successful behaviors. There is usually more about the client that is positive and functional than is negative or dysfunctional. Helpers must reassess the way they diagnose client behavior to recognize these largely positive behaviors (Turner, 2002).

2. The focus on positive behaviors can be critical in that it helps motivate and energize clients to effectively resolve problems in areas of difficulty in their lives and not to "give up" hope that they will get better.

3. The worker using the strengths perspective must do an "asset review" of the many positive behaviors that result in life success to include all areas of life as defined and recognized by the client.

4. The worker must have a basic understanding of the client's belief system, including recognition of the client's spirituality, religious involvement, and social and political philosophies, as well as the cultural beliefs that shape a client's worldview. Understanding the client's deeply felt beliefs is crucial to the helping process, since they are the core beliefs that help motivate the client to change.

5. The worker can help by understanding the client's aspirations, dreams, hopes, and desires. These unspoken dreams are the hidden motivators that help clients cope with serious social and emotional problems and to continue on in life even when the path seems hopeless.

6. Effective professional helping enlists the client in the process of change. All change comes from the client's willingness to provide direction and information to the worker.

7. The use of labeling in mental health often suggests client problems that may be difficult, if not impossible, to resolve. The strengths perspective does not use labels that imply pathology, since they are often misleading, pejorative, unhelpful in treatment, and often provide an excuse for not providing services.

8. The strengths perspective always views the client in a hopeful and optimistic way, regardless of the complexity of the problem, the length of time the client has experienced the problem, or the difficulty the client has experienced in resolving the problem. As Saleebey (2000) writes, "Healing, transformation, regeneration, and resilience almost always occur within the confines of a personal, friendly, and dialogical relationship. . . . The more the power of a caring relationship is actualized with those served, the better the individual's future" (p. 128).

9. The worker using the strengths perspective should be fully engaged, optimistic, and positive, and should respond to the client in an honest and open way.

10. The strengths perspective is oriented toward what clients do well and not toward what they do badly. This doesn't negate a problem or eliminate the fact that clients may be involved in behavior that is destructive to themselves or others. Negative and judgmental worker responses about a client's behavior will almost always result in resentment and opposition to treatment.

11. The strengths perspective is very much aligned with knowledge-guided and evidence-based practice approaches to treatment. It also requires the worker to encourage clients to seek as much independent information about their treatment as possible.

12. The struggle to overcome life problems usually contains elements that are healthy and positive. In listening to clients discuss their attempts to change, practitioners using the strengths perspective may find many examples of positive, purposeful, and adaptive behavior. As Saleebey (2000) reminds us, "Every maladaptive response or pattern of behavior may also contain the seeds of a struggle for health" (p. 129).

13. The recognition that the social and cultural environment of the client is rich in opportunities for support, encouragement, and assistance from others is important in this approach. Within the client's social environment are the family, friends, co-workers, religious leaders, neighbors, and acquaintances who form the client's external world. The worker's task is to help clients identify those people in their social and cultural environment who possess positive and reinforcing skills that can be used to help the client in times of need and to maintain gains made in treatment.

14. The strengths perspective believes that the work we do with individuals has a synergistic impact on the community and, ultimately, on society. This notion of help that touches many lives is a core ingredient of the strengths perspective.

6. Higher Aspirations: Resilient children and adolescents often have higher educational aspirations than nonresilient children and adolescents and, in many ways, show superior school performance and extracurricular skills that strongly suggest successful functioning in the future.

Application to Practice: Don't confuse positive social functioning with an absence of emotional difficulty. Resilient people seek help when their emotions become difficult to control, not because their social functioning is impaired. When clients' aspirations are limited, you might do well to help them identify their dreams, however limited, and to discuss the impediments, if any, to achieving their dreams. Tiet, Bird, and Davies (1998) indicate that high educational aspirations serve as goals and motivators for resilient youth and provide them with meaning and purpose in life. The authors write, "The relationship between educational aspiration and youth adjustment is robust and cannot be explained completely by academic achievement" (p. 1194). They go on to note, however, that the presence of high achievement does not necessarily suggest the absence of emotional turmoil. Tiet and colleagues point out that even in the midst of emotional difficulty, resilient youth do well in school because of their high aspirations. Consequently, helping clients define their goals, dreams, and aspirations could result in better social and educational achievement.

7. The Ability to Take Full Responsibility: Resilient people don't blame others for their own difficulties in life. They often have an internal locus of control and believe that they have control over their lives, no matter how traumatic their lives have been in the past. This belief in the ability to control their lives suggests a practice approach in which clients are highly involved in finding solutions and the best evidence in the research literature regarding the effectiveness of treatment choices.

Application to Practice: Having an internal locus of control has positive implications for treatment, specifically because clients want to be part of the solution. For this reason, clients should have a cooperative role in treatment. As Henry (1999) suggests, "Resilient children often acquire faith that their lives have meaning and that they have control over their own fates" (p. 522). Gambrill (1999) points out that one of the most important aspects of EBP is the sharing of information with clients and the cooperative relationships that ensue. She notes that in EBP, clinicians search for relevant research to help in practice decisions and share that information with clients. If no evidence is found to justify a specific treatment regimen, the client is informed and a discussion takes place about how best to approach treatment. This discussion includes the risks and benefits of any treatment approach used. Clients are involved in all treatment decisions and are encouraged to independently search the literature. As Sackett and colleagues (1997) suggest, new information is constantly being added to our knowledge base, and informed clinicians and clients may often find elegant treatment approaches that help provide direction where none may have existed before.

8. The Desire to Help Others: Resilient people often get strength and satisfaction from helping others. The desire to help is not felt to be an obligation but resides in the belief that helping others is a positive outlet for the wisdom they've gained as survivors of traumas.

Application to Practice: Tech (2003) observed in her interviews with survivors of the Holocaust that while war preoccupies people with self-preservation, it often leads to cooperation: "There is strength in cooperation and mutual help. . . . In extremely threatening environments, only the minority are able to effectively engage in mutual help and cooperation. This, in turn, mirrors reality; in threatened circumstances only a few have a chance to survive" (p. 344). As people who believe they've gained wisdom during their lives that might be of value to others, resilient people often reach out and offer support and mutual encouragement. This finding can be used in treatment by allowing resilient people to take part in self-help groups and to be in a position to act as natural helpers. It also means that less resilient clients should be encouraged to develop values and beliefs that add to the civic health of communities and, when they are ready, to become involved in some type of help to others.

9.   Problem-Solving Skills: Resilient people are excellent problem solvers. In a sense, they have high emotional intelligence, which means they have a great deal of common sense and practical wisdom. Some researchers also say that the ability to solve problems is tied to higher intellectual functioning.

Application to Practice: The ability to problem solve in a rational and objective way is a core goal of many systems of therapy, and for good reason. Resilient people demonstrate the positive results of logical thinking when problems are encountered. Writing about his experiences in the South during racial desegregation, Robert Coles (1964) tells us how he was continually amazed by the ability of people to deal with the racial, social, and educational crises throughout Southern life. He writes, "Again and again I was struck by the distinctly different kinds of psychological adaptations a political crisis can bring into being" (Coles, 1964, p. 380). In describing the way African American children in the South coped with conflict (a distinct problem-solving skill) during the critical and often violent initial phases of desegregation, Coles (1964) writes,

> It must be said that under grave stress they have done more than persist, more than endure. They have prevailed in the way Faulkner knew they would by summoning every bit of their humanity in the face of every effort made to deny any of it to them. In so doing, they have become more than they were, more than they themselves thought they were, and perhaps more than anyone watching them could quite put into words: bearers and makers of tradition; children who in a moment—call it existential, call it historical, call it psychological—took what they had from the past, in their minds, out of their homes, and made of all those possessions something else: a change in the world, and in themselves, too. (p. 365)

10.   Help With Self-Righting: When coping with an original trauma, resilient people often find adult mentors and support systems to help them achieve "self-righting" abilities. In times of a crisis, resilient people may call upon their support systems for assistance. These support systems are often composed of old friends, some of them from a very young age in the client's life (showing an early ability to make and maintain long-term relationships). Resilient people take friendships seriously and are able to distinguish the difference between friends and acquaintances. Most resilient people don't try to cope with their problems alone. Even when they don't have a strong family support system, they are able to ask for help or recruit others to help them. Resilient adults are often more likely to talk to friends and co-workers about events in their lives than are nonresilient people.

Application to Practice: Perhaps the best-known study of resilience in children as they grow into adulthood is the longitudinal research begun in 1955 by Werner and Smith (1992). Werner and Smith (1982) found that one out of every three children evaluated by several measures of early life functioning to be at significant risk for adolescent problems had actually developed into well-functioning young adults by age 18. In their follow-up study, Werner and Smith (1992) report that two out of three of the remaining two thirds of the children at risk had turned into caring and healthy adults by age 32. One of Werner and Smith's (1982, 1992) primary theories to explain these findings is that people have "self-righting" capabilities. From their studies, the authors concluded that some of the factors that lead to self-correction in life can be identified. They also concluded that a significant factor leading to better emotional health for many children is a consistent and caring relationship with at least one adult. This adult (in a few cases, it was a peer) does not have to be a family member or physically present all of the time. This relationship provides the child with a sense of protection and serves to initiate and develop the child's self-righting capacities. Helping professionals sometimes assume mentoring relationships with troubled children, particularly when they work in school systems where mentoring is seen as an established role for teachers and human services professionals. The success of this role seems clear from the research provided by Werner and Smith (1982, 1992).

11. Ongoing Self-Righting: Even children who initially experience social and emotional problems as a result of a trauma and are not seen as resilient may develop self-righting abilities as they move through the life cycle. This suggests that resilience may be a learned characteristic taught to children by other resilient people rather than an attribute they are born with that is innate to people in unpredictable ways. There is no timeline or set period for becoming resilient. It can happen at any time and under a variety of circumstances.

Application to Practice: Lifton (1993) believes that out of the chaos of modern life, a highly resilient and flexible "protean self" is developing. Rather than succumbing to the chaos and confusion of modern life, Lifton believes that people use a number of coping mechanisms or, "bits and pieces here and there that somehow help us to keep going" (p. 1). Lifton thinks that modern men and women are evolving and, though our path may seem chaotic and confused, the evolutionary process is helping us to define not only ourselves, but also modern life. Lifton writes,

> The protean self emerges from confusion, from the widespread feeling that we are losing our psychological moorings. Leaders appear suddenly, recede equally rapidly, and are difficult for us to believe in when they are around. We change ideas and partners frequently, and do the same with jobs and places of residence. Enduring moral convictions, clear principles of action and behavior: we believe these must exist, but where? Whether dealing with world problems or child rearing, our behavior tends to be ad hoc, more or less decided upon as we go along. We are beset by contradictions: schooled in the virtues of consistency or constancy or stability—whether as individuals, groups, or nations—our world and our lives seem inconstant and utterly unpredictable. We readily come to view ourselves as unsteady, neurotic, or worse. (p. 1)

Lifton goes on to suggest that modern life now requires shifts in friendships, lifestyles, jobs, family ties, and other important factors that cause life to be fleeting, uncertain, and continually in flux throughout the life span. The formal rites of passage are no longer present, and in their place is a flexibility that permits the pro-tean self to define new ways of viewing the meaning of life, morality, relationships, and intimacy. Flexibility and the lack of ties to the past give modern men and women a resilience which is quite different from our traditional notions of resilience. It is Lifton's belief that resilience develops from need rather than from sustaining internal and external support systems.

12. Negative Responses to Some Traumas: Resilient people are not impervious to all traumas. Traumas involving force and assault seem to lower the level of resilience in many people, but highly resilient people are, nonetheless, able to cope with very serious traumas involving assault and force.

Application to Practice: In describing the recovery process of women who were sex-ually assaulted, Hensley (2002) indicates that while treatment research suggests good results, the recovery process can be long and difficult. "Survivors are vulnera-ble to victim-blame, self-blame, unwillingness to disclose the rape to others, and an overall lack of support in addition to PTSD symptoms and other significant nega-tive psychological and physiological outcomes" (Hensley, 2002, p. 342). Hensley reports that women who survive sexual assaults need validation of their experiences and positive reinforcement for their attempts to deal with the traumas they've expe-rienced. Instead, they must often deal with limited support and even skepticism from family, friends, professionals, and the legal system. This concern for the limited support of rape victims as they try and recover from the trauma they've experienced can be generalized to many other victims of traumas.

In writing about treatment and recovery myths of PTSD, Rothbaum and Schwartz (2002) express their belief that many people think that clients suffering from PTSD will recover in time without help, but the prolonged suffering of those with PTSD suggests that this may not be the case and that interventions should be introduced when client symptoms are intrusive and the client voluntarily seeks help. The authors also note that a trauma doesn't need to be current for the client to require help with recovery. Many clients who have experienced child abuse and other early life traumas benefit from therapies such as exposure therapy, which focuses on their worst memory of a trauma. Clients find that reducing the stress involved with traumatic memories has carryover benefits in that it increases their ability to cope with other traumas. Rothbaum and Schwartz (2002) report that exposure therapies are often useful in treating clients' non-PTSD symptoms that predate the traumatic event causing PTSD and help to provide a more complete recovery. Exposure therapies help reduce "feelings of depression, rage, sadness, and guilt [in addition] to reducing related problems, such as depression and self-blame" (Rothbaum & Schwartz, 2002, p. 71).

13. Spiritual Beliefs and Religious Convictions: Spiritual and religious beliefs may help people become and stay more resilient since they often help answer meaning-of-life questions. When people experience traumatic events, meaning-of-life questions are particularly relevant, and resilient people search for answers

through available sources. Faith in the future, the continuity of life, and a higher power are essential ingredients of resilience because they help resilient people perceive bad times as temporary.

Application to Practice: One aspect of people's search for meaning is their development of spirituality in the midst of trying to understand life-changing or life-ending disabilities or illnesses. Finn (1999) writes that spirituality leads to "an unfolding consciousness about the meaning of human existence. Life crises influence this unfolding by stimulating questions about the meaning of existence" (p. 487). Balk (1999) suggests that three issues must be present for a life crisis to result in spiritual changes: "The situation must create a psychological imbalance or disequilibrium that resists readily being stabilized; there must be time for reflection; and the person's life must forever afterwards be colored by the crisis" (p. 485).

Boorstein (2000) indicates the difference between traditional psychotherapy and spiritually based psychotherapy:

> I believe that traditional psychotherapy is basically pessimistic (though called "realistic") in its outlook. There is the oft-quoted line attributed to Freud that psychoanalysis attempts to convert "neurotic misery to ordinary misery." Transpersonal psychotherapy attempts to open awareness to this and to other psychic realms where joy, love, serenity, and even ecstasy are present. As I have stated, without a basic belief in and/or experience of these transpersonal or spiritual realms, I do not think one can be a transpersonal or spiritual psychotherapist. (Boorstein, 2000, p. 413)

14. Unanticipated Resilience: Resilient people cope in ways we cannot predict. Our lack of knowledge about these intriguing types of coping skills is the result of research that has focused on pathology rather than on strengths. What we know about traumatized people comes from clients seeking help for traumas rather than from those who have been able to resolve the effects of traumas, largely by themselves. This means that the impact of certain traumas may be less intense for many people over the life span than had been previously thought, and that resilience is more prevalent in the population than we may think.

Application to Practice: Writing about the aftermath of the 9-11 tragedy in New York City, Groopman (2004) reports that most of the debriefing and early counseling done with people closest to the bomb site was done by nonprofessional relief workers who focused on the absence of pathology and used a strengths perspective. Groopman quotes psychiatrist April Naturale, who evaluated the amount of PTSD following the bombing, as saying, "Non-mental health professionals do not pathologize. They don't know the terminology, they don't know how to diagnose. The most helpful approach in the aftermath of a tragic event in which people are potentially in crisis is to employ public health models, using people in the community who aren't diagnosing you" (p. 34). By this, Groopman means that in a crisis, nonprofessionals are often able to see the need for help more clearly than professionals can, because they seek to help with observable problems in straightforward ways rather than using more complex and sometimes incorrect notions of what needs to be changed and why. A public health approach emphasizes "primary prevention—that is, prevention taking place before the onset of disease or injury. Primary prevention identifies behavioral or environmental risk factors associated with traumas and harmful social and emotional health problems and takes steps to educate the community about, or protect it from, these risks" (Hamburg, 1998, p. 43).

15. Focusing on Strengths Rather Than Pathology: Resilient people have attributes that should be recognized and studied. Studying resilient people and the way they cope with life might offer more effective solutions to the problems associated with traumas than the solutions generated by studies of people who function poorly following traumas.

Application to Practice: While a pathology model is generally certain that most people will suffer social and emotional problems as a result of trauma, a more positive orientation that focuses on people's strengths suggests that most people recover from traumas with only moderate levels of dysfunction, and that some people suffer even less than moderate levels of dysfunction. As Saleebey (1996, p. 297) writes,

> Practicing from a strengths perspective does not require social workers to ignore the real troubles that dog individuals and groups. Schizophrenia is real. Child sexual abuse is real. Pancreatic cancer is real. Violence is real. But in the lexicon of strengths, it is as wrong to deny the possible as it is to deny the problem. The strengths perspective does not deny the grip and thrall of addictions and how they can morally and physically sink the spirit and possibility of any individual. But it does deny the overweening reign of psychopathology as civic, moral, and medical categorical imperative. It does deny that most people are victims of abuse or of their own rampant appetites. It denies that all people who face trauma and pain in their lives inevitably are wounded or incapacitated or become less than they might. It decries the fact that the so-called recovery movement, now so far beyond its original intended boundaries, has pumped out a host of illnesses and addictions that were by earlier standards, mere habits, some good, some bad. Everywhere in public we find people talking freely, if not excitedly, even proudly, about their compulsion—whether it be gambling, sex, shopping, exercise, or the horrible desire to please other people. We are awash in a sea of codependency, wounded inner children, and intimacy crises (Wolin & Wolin, 1993, p. 7).

16. Humor: Resilient people sometimes use self-deprecating humor to reduce stress and to cope with unimaginable grief, agony, and despair. Anderson (1997) says that humor "channels pain and discomfort in imaginative ways" (p. 597). Self-deprecating humor has also been referred to as gallows humor. An old Jewish joke might serve as an example. In those of us who grew up in immigrant homes after the Holocaust, there was a fear that what happened in Germany might also happen in the United States. To cope with that possibility, Jewish children were often taught to keep their public opinions to themselves and to not create attention,

while at the same time achieving at a high level. The joke that epitomizes this dilemma is about two Jewish prisoners who are about to be executed and are asked by the captain of the firing squad if they have any last requests. One of the prisoners says, "Yes, I'd like a cigarette," to which the other prisoner whispers, "Shhhhh. Don't make waves." The underlying premise of the joke is that if the two prisoners had been more vociferous in their defense, they may not have been shot. Jokes like this one permeated many postwar Jewish households and had a strong positive impact because they helped children see the absurdity of keeping quiet if their lives were in danger or if there was nothing to lose by voicing an opinion.

Application to Practice: Humor often has metaphorical meaning for people and can have a very positive impact if used correctly. An example of a joke with metaphorical meaning was used with a client who was losing his temper at the noise made by his next-door neighbors. Unable to just go over and talk to his neighbors, the client obsessed about the situation to the point of being in a continual rage. To help him better deal with the situation, the worker told him the following joke.

> A writer is sitting at his computer trying to write, when his parrot starts calling him names. "You're so stupid, you're lazy, you don't feed me enough, I hate you," the parrot screeches. The writer tries to calm the parrot down, but to no avail. Starting to do a slow burn, the writer threatens the parrot.
>
> "If you don't stop making that noise, and I mean stop it now," the writer yells, "I'm putting you in the freezer, and I mean it."
>
> The parrot doesn't take the warning seriously and keeps up a steady flow of criticism. "You're a pet-hater, you have a thing against birds, my beak is bigger than yours," and so on until, in a rage, the writer throws the parrot in the freezer.
>
> Twenty minutes later, the writer takes the parrot out. Shivering and full of frost, the parrot apologizes. "I'll never do that again," he says. "I've learned my lesson. I know what I did wrong and I'll never interrupt you again while you're writing. But tell me," the parrot asks, "I'm really curious. Just what did the turkey do?"

This joke about going too far with anger and about the one being punished getting the last laugh, helped the client see how troubled his behavior had become. After listening to the joke and discussing its meaning with the worker, he was willing to go to his neighbors and talk to them in a calm and reasonable way. And if the noise level didn't decline, or if the neighbors were unwilling to comply, the client understood that there were legal options. However, the alternatives turned out to be unnecessary. When asked to lower the noise level, the neighbor readily agreed, apologizing in the process. The joke had held special metaphorical meaning for the client since it was the way his parents often spoke to him, preferring to tell stories or jokes about important issues rather than using direct statements with clear meaning.

To explain the Jewish immigrant's way of making bad luck and misery somehow funny, Rosen (2003) describes his immigrant father's use of black humor:

The humor and the odd link to more conventional elements of Jewish tradition (the Messiah, for example, has been about to not come for a long time now) somehow saved these utterances from seeming like embodiments of despair. They were, in a complicated way, an answer to despair. Or at least they captured an aspect of Jewish tradition that has always fascinated me—a wise pessimism that emphasizes the perpetuation of tradition rather than individual salvation. As Kafka memorably said, "There's plenty of hope in the world—just not for us." (p. 87)

The use of humor should be linked to the client's presenting problem. It should also help the client have an awareness of how the problem might be better resolved. Never assume, however, that what is funny to you might be funny to your client. Before using humor with metaphorical meaning, test out small bits of humor without any particular meaning to gauge the client's sense of humor. And never tell ethnic, religious, or gender jokes or you run the risk of offending the client. Use humor, but use it with caution and discretion.

17. Possible Changes in Resilience During the Life Cycle: Resilience may be affected by changes in the life cycle. Adults who were able to cope well with a trauma in childhood may find their resilience decreasing with age as they progress into more complex expectations of relationships and employment. Resilient adults may find it difficult to maintain resilience as they age, and we should not assume that resilience will follow a person throughout the life cycle.

Application to Practice: The notion of resilience has become so all encompassing that we sometimes forget that those who were resilient in childhood have very different pressures in their lives when they reach adulthood. Workers should be prepared to work with resilient people when their ability to cope begins to deteriorate and to find out the reasons for the loss in resilience. Often biological issues such as illness may affect a person's resilience, or as Kramer (2005) suggests, people may move from resilience to depression many years after they seem to have coped with a trauma successfully. "Beset by great evil," he writes, describing why some people cope so well when victims of genocide and war, "a person can be wise, observant and disillusioned and yet not be depressed. Resilience confers its own measure of insight" (Kramer, 2005, p. 53).

18. Superior Biological Functioning: Resilience may, in part, be a function of a superior biological ability to withstand stressful and traumatic experiences and may be due to very good physical health. However, Masten (2001) believes that resilience is part of the genetic makeup of humans and that it is the norm rather than the exception. "Resilience does not come from rare and special qualities, but from the everyday magic of ordinary, normative human resources in the minds, brains, and bodies of children, in their families and relationships, and in their communities" (Masten, 2001, p. 9).

Application to Practice: Making certain that our clients receive proper diets and live in decent and nurturing environments would go a long way toward increasing their resilience. Given our awareness of the biological impact on social and emotional functioning, we should assume that before a problem is treated, a medical evaluation is necessary to eliminate the possibility of a physical reason for the client's behavior.

19. Decreased Resilience With Multiple Traumas: The more serious and frequent the traumas experienced by a person, the less resilient he or she may become. One of the primary findings regarding resilience is that frequent severe traumas during times of reduced ability to cope tend to decrease resilience in otherwise resilient people, and that physical assaults are primary destroyers of resilience.

Application to Practice: We should expect domestic violence, rape, assaults, terrorism, and random violence to be extraordinarily harmful to all clients, even those who are highly resilient. PTSD is always a concern, and prolonged symptoms of PTSD are always possible when clients are victims of assaults. One of the confusing symptoms of PTSD, which I believe may be associated with resilience in people, is that symptoms of PTSD may be delayed. Delayed symptoms may occur in resilient people when the weight of the trauma and an inability to cope with it collide after many months of utilizing what are normally successful coping skills. Resilient people may delay seeking help well beyond the point when it makes sense to do so because they are so accustomed to successfully coping with traumas and stress. Resilient people may also seek medical help for physical symptoms related to a trauma before they seek help for their emotional concerns. If you work in a medical setting, the symptoms of fatigue, insomnia, panic attacks, chest pains, headaches and backaches, depression, and anxiety in otherwise very healthy people should always include an evaluation of prior traumas. The question "Why now?" is always a good one to ask the client. Why is this happening to someone who appears to be healthy and hasn't been seen for prior emotional problems?

Rothbaum and Schwartz (2002) describe a type of treatment, based on an emotion-processing theory they call exposure therapy. Practitioners of exposure therapy assume that PTSD develops as a result of memories eliciting fear that trigger escape and avoidance behaviors. Since the development of a "fear network" functions as a type of obsessive condition, the client continues to increase the number of stimuli, which serves to increase his or her fear. To reduce the number of stimuli that elicit fear, the client must have his or her "fear network" activated so that new information can be provided that rationally contradicts the obsessive network of emotions reinforcing the PTSD symptoms. Rothbaum and Schwartz (2002) believe that the following progression of treatment activities, which they call exposure therapy, serves to reduce the client's fear network: (1) Repeated reliving of the original trauma helps to reduce anxiety and correct a belief that anxiety will necessarily continue unless avoidance and escape mechanisms are activated; (2) Discussing the traumatic event reduces negative reinforcement of the event and helps the client see it in a logical way that corrects misperceptions of the event; (3) Speaking about the trauma helps the client realize that it's not dangerous to remember the trauma; (4) The ability of the client to speak about the trauma provides the client with a sense of mastery over his or her PTSD symptoms.

Hensley (2002) provides an explanation of exposure therapy as it might be given to a client who has been raped:

- Memories, people, places, and activities now associated with the rape make you highly anxious, so you avoid them.
- Each time you avoid them you do not finish the process of digesting the painful experience, and so it returns in the form of nightmares, flashbacks, and intrusive thoughts.
- You can begin to digest the experience by gradually exposing yourself to the rape in your imagination and by holding the memory without pushing it away.
- You will also practice facing those activities, places, and situations that currently evoke fear.
- Eventually, you will be able to think about the rape and resume your normal activities without experiencing intense fear. (p. 338)

20. The Ability to Learn From Others: Resilient people learn from others and often believe that there is great wisdom to be gained in their day-to-day interactions with people. They are consequently curious, inquisitive, and questioning. Resilient children often develop friendships with other children who make up, in social and emotional skills, what they may lack. Friends become a source of support, knowledge, and modeling and are often extremely important in the lives of resilient people.

Application to Practice: Don't be surprised if resilient people see you more as a friend than as a professional. Resilient people tend to personalize their relationships and to discount differences in status and knowledge. "He puts his pants on the same way I do" is indicative of the attitude of many resilient people. Resilient people have been through tough times, they've done well, and they feel entitled to respect. Don't be offended if resilient clients want to call you by your first name, and don't assume they have transference issues if they want personal information about you. This is the natural inquisitiveness and friendliness that work so well for them. Don't be surprised if these lovely people are terrible clients. Remember that they've done well on their own, and now they're not doing well. It's natural for them to resist change when things have worked so well for them in the past. Treatment with these clients may need to be paced slowly, focusing primarily on support and empathic listening at first.

This same resistance to treatment may also appear in clients who seem less resilient. While their problem-solving skills may not be well developed, many clients distrust change, even when their current decision making is leading to painful results. Cooperative relationships with clients in which their wisdom and past experience are utilized to assist in the helping process can go a long way in reducing client resistance and improving self-healing.

Entwistle, Sheldon, Sowden, and Watt (1998) suggest that people can be actively involved in decisions regarding their treatment in the following ways: (1) through the care [they] will or will not receive; (2) through the research information indicating the effectiveness of certain interventions, including their risks and benefits; (3) through the use of recommended approaches showing good research validity, or doing nothing; and (4) through involvement in all decisions regarding treatment. The American Medical Association Evidence-Based Practice Working Group (1992) writes that all practitioners must be sensitive to the emotional needs of clients and that "understanding patients' suffering and how that suffering can be ameliorated by the caring and compassionate practitioner are fundamental requirements for practice" (p. 2422). The Working Group also calls for much more research to better understand how the interaction between clients and practitioners affects the outcome of treatment.

21. Creativity That Enhances Resilience: Resilient people often use creativity as a way of expressing inner feelings and intense emotions. The term *creativity* is defined broadly here as outlets that allow inner feelings to be expressed. These outlets may take conventional or unconventional forms, but to resilient people, the activities are creative.

Application to Practice: One way to tap creativity in clients is through *bibliotherapy,* the use of literature to facilitate the therapeutic process. Myers (1998) defines bibliotherapy as "a dynamic process of interaction between the individual and literature, which emphasizes the reader's emotional response to what has been read" (p. 243). Pardeck (1995) gives six goals of bibliotherapy: (1) to provide information; (2) to gain insight; (3) to find solutions; (4) to stimulate discussion of problems; (5) to suggest new values and attitudes; and (6) to show clients how others have coped with problems similar to their own. "Bibliotherapy provides metaphors for life experiences that help clients verbalize their thoughts and feelings and learn new ways to cope with problems" (Myers, 1998, p. 246).

It is important to recognize that most of us have creative outlets that help us cope with stress and trauma. Writing and painting may be clear signs of creativity, but so are woodworking, building engines, growing gardens, decorating, and any number of outlets that are more than just hobbies because they immerse clients in positive emotions and strengthen the client's self-image. Finding out about clients' hobbies and other creative endeavors might help us better understand the ways in which many nonresilient clients cope with emotional and social concerns. Obviously, not all hobbies are necessarily healthy, and those that involve drinking or highly risky behavior should be understood while not necessarily being encouraged.

22. Work: Resilient people are often able to work very hard. They may even be thought to be workaholics. Often this is not the case. Work may be a creative outlet for the desire to achieve and may be thought of as a continuation of the academic achievement seen in abused children and adolescents. However, when a person works excessively or compulsively, it may suggest a decrease in resilience because it fills time rather than provides joy.

Application to Practice: Many resilient people get immense pleasure from work or use it to achieve and increase their level of security. Letting resilient clients talk about their work can give great meaning to their lives and is important to all clients. Work, however, can be a very troubled environment for many clients, and talking about the work environment in an open and positive way can be very helpful to clients who experience work-related difficulties. Stillman (1994) explores the difficulties that arise in the workplace and the mistake we sometimes make in encouraging women to puruse "gender politics." Stillman (1994) writes that

> women have made a grave mistake in not examining broader issues, such as that of office harassment in general. What men have had to put up with over the years to rise through the corporate and bureaucratic marketplace, frankly, is as odious to me as sexual harassment. But men have never lobbied against such wage-slave requirements as mandatory lying to cover up company crimes, mandatory company retreats, mandatory obsequiousness toward higher-ups, mandatory cocktails with the boss's brother-in-law, and so on. Maybe they should. However, in their fight against sexual harassment, women have failed to take into account that power always resists challenge, and change is always met with resistance. If women could stop taking the general unfairness of the workplace so personally, they would find allies rather than enemies among their fellow worker-bees. (p. 32)

Additional Attributes of Resilient People

The following are characteristics of resilient people that are also applicable to practice, but such application seems self-evident and thus is not discussed in detail here.

1. A Sense of Adventure: Resilient people have a sense of adventure and enjoy taking personal risks to see if goals can be accomplished. Some people might find this behavior courageous.

2. Moral Development and Conviction: Resilient people often have a high level of moral development and conviction. They often place the needs of others before their own and are socially responsible, with a high degree of personal integrity and honesty. Anderson (1997) defines morality as the "expression of an informed conscience" and writes that it "is demonstrated through empathy, compassion, and caring toward others " (p. 596).

3. An Introspective Nature: Resilient people are often introspective and insightful about themselves and others. They are also very rational and try to see connections between events and their responses to them. They think seriously about their interactions with others. When in conflict, they evaluate their behavior and try to understand its impact on the problem and their role in resolving that problem. The insightful person is able to understand that a situation of importance in a person's psychosocial development may actually differ from that person's memory of it and may "not [be] what it's supposed to be" (Wolin & Wolin, 1993, p. 73).

4. Cultural Strengths: A person's culture assists him or her in being resilient if it has a positive, helpful view of people. Sometimes cultures take negative stands about independence and autonomy while encouraging behavior that may be harmful, including the use of substances and spousal abuse. We would therefore see culture as a positive if it strongly opposes the abuse of alcoholism and drugs and the abuse of spouses and children. Culture would also play a positive role if it urges people to seek help for health-related and social and emotional problems and if it values its traditions and its history.

5. A Strong Degree of Social Responsibility: Resilient people usually have a strong need to make the world a better place. This might include supporting social change, responsible involvement in social justice, and an active role in their community. It might also include voting and being informed about social and political issues, tolerance for other political beliefs, and a desire to leave a positive legacy for future generations.

6. Curiosity: Curiosity in this context is the desire to learn more about self, community, and others. Resilient people often want to experiment with new ideas, behaviors, and life directions. One would expect resilient people to have a sense of intellectual adventure, to permit new life experiences to take place, and to share a sense of curiosity and adventure with significant others, particularly children. That curiosity continues on as resilient people age.

7. Persistence: Resilient people are able to stay with work assignments, educational challenges, difficult but rewarding relationships, career expectations that require the ability to continue on without giving up, difficult family situations, and complex financial arrangements that require careful planning and time to complete.

8. Determination: Determined clients have strong positive notions that they will be able to master most life situations. Determination is the desire to master and complete assignments, resolve life problems, and meet career requirements that may include retraining or gaining new skills. Determination is the mind-set that leads to persistence.

9. Recognizing the Realities of Traumatic Life Events: While resilient people are often amazing in their ability to cope with terrible life events, the persistence of poverty, crime, abuse, and violence take a toll on everyone, including resilient people. The concept of resilience sometimes offers an overly simplisitic view of why some children succeed despite terrible hardships. Forgetting those hardships makes us believe, erroneously, that children thrive in the midst of harmful environments when, in fact, many children falter and develop severe problems. Recognizing resilience should also lead to a more dynamic approach to lessening the liklihood of traumas in early childhood that, regardless of a child's abilty to cope, often have negative ramifications throughout the life cycle.

A Story About a Young Worker Finding Resilience in His Clients

Early in my career as a social worker, and before I had a usable theoretical framework to help people, I worked for The Sister Kenny Foundation in Minneapolis, a rehabilitation center. Quite without knowing why, I would buy ice cream after work and go from room to room visiting my clients in the evening when the facility suddenly became empty and quiet and my clients were left with their own thoughts. Many of my clients had serious disabilities brought on by strokes, polio, or accidents. There was rawness to these evening visits, and my clients would often despair about their lives as we sat together in their rooms. I was too young to know what a disability was like, physically, but I saw my patients struggle through their daily regimens of physical therapy, and sometimes they would collapse in exhaustion and despair. The physical therapists had a way about them I admired as I watched them coax my clients on. It was tragic, and it was wonderful.

In my evening visits, my clients would tell me about their fears, their sorrows, their deepest anguish, and something in me reached out to them, and we held hands in the night and comforted one another. I was wise enough to listen and to remain silent, for the most part. But the urge to be a cheerleader was very strong, and sometimes I would say something so palpably optimistic and positive that my clients would smile, nod their heads, and say, in that way clients have of telling you how off base you've been, "Bravo for trying, but maybe you don't quite know what you're talking about." The impulse to say something positive is strong in most of us, and it may help, but I've come to realize that listening and sitting with a client in the moment can do wonders. These brave people endure such pain that I want to embrace them all and give them little love messages. Wisely, I've learned to listen, to be empathic, and to respond only when I'm invited to. In a sense, this is a very optimistic and positive approach, since no one listens to people in pain, or to the people who are afraid of death, or to the people who will never do the things again that we all take for granted. The knowledge of what life is like for our disabled and terminally ill clients always touches me deeply. Like most of us, I cannot imagine a life of immobility and pain, or a terminal illness that takes a life before it's possible to be ready for death. And like most of us, I don't think I could cope with such situations, and it makes me very humble when I work with people who are not only coping well but are, in a real sense, evolving. The process of evolving in the midst of pain, disability, and possible death seems quite beautiful to me and I am in awe of it.

Clients I have worked with ask me my notion of death. I haven't a very firm one, and I can never give them a very good answer. Instead, I wonder about their idea of death. Often, like me, death bewilders them. They haven't thought about it and admit that it's a subject they've always avoided. But often, they want to finish unfinished business with family, some of it painful and disturbing. Frequently, they want to remember the good moments in their lives and to have someone confirm that they're good people. Often, they want to talk to a religious figure and share their worries about the afterlife. And quite frequently, they are angry. Why shouldn't they be? And I listen to their anger, some of it directed at me because I represent someone healthy when they are not, and I think it's a small price to pay if I can help them with what they're enduring.

In the end, death isn't clean, or pleasant, or uplifting. It is often filled with pain, misery, and fear. The one thing you realize when you work with dying patients is that they want to make their time with you meaningful. What they talk about, the empathic way you respond, the gentle listening you do can help them move gracefully from this place to the next. As one of my clients faced the end of a long and painful illness, he wrote me,

I will go to the river and I will lie in peace.
And when the sun sets, I will sleep the peaceful sleep
of a child.
And when it is dark and night comes,
I will go from this place to the next.
And I will be with God, and I will know
His tender mercies.

Final Words

I have approached this book in a very subjective and impressionistic way because I believe the concept of resilience, important as it is, is still a nebulous one. And I approached this book with a belief that sharing the life stories of resilient people is a positive way of conveying the reality of resilience and acts as additional information to augment the resilience research. Some of these stories touch me very deeply. I hope you've had the same response. I grew up with resilient people. From these resilient immigrant people, many of them terribly poor, I learned that inner toughness isn't limited to a few people but belongs to many of us. I also learned that even resilient people suffer, and some never make it through the moments in their lives when sorrow and despair become too great a burden to bear. I wanted to write a book about people's personal experience of resilience. I hope that as a result of this approach you have come to appreciate, as I have, the heroic ways that ordinary people deal with despair and trauma too great to comprehend. And I hope you are touched by the wonder of the human condition and why we should be optimistic about people, even in the midst of bad times when the human condition seems full of excess.

Warm Regards and Best Wishes,
Morley Glicken

References

Aaron, R. (2003, July 27). Taking the car keys from elderly is tough—I know first hand. *San Antonio Express-News*, p. 3k.

ABCNews.com. (2002). *Authentic happiness: Using our strengths to cultivate happiness.* Retrieved October 14, 2002, from http://abcnews.go.com/sections/GMA/Good Morning America/GMA020904Happiness_feature.html

Abrams, M. (2001). Resilience in ambiguous loss. *American Journal of Psychotherapy, 55*(2), 283–291.

Altarriba, J., & Bauer, L. M. (1998). Counseling the Hispanic client: Cuban Americans, Mexican Americans, and Puerto Ricans. *Journal of Counseling and Development, 76,* 389–396.

Amato-von Hemert, K. (1994). Point/counterpoint. Should social work education address religious issues? Yes! *Journal of Social Work Education, 30,* 7–11.

American Medical Association Evidence-Based Practice Working Group. (1992). Evidence-based practice: A new way of teaching the practice of medicine. *Journal of the American Medical Association, 268,* 2420–2425.

American Psychiatric Association (APA). (1994). *Diagnostic and statistical manual of mental disorders* (4th ed.). Washington, DC: Author.

American Psychological Association. (2005). *The help line.* Retrieved May 14, 2005, from http://helping.apa.org/articles/article.php?id=31

Anderson, K. M. (1997). Uncovering survival abilities in children who have been sexually abused. *Families in Society, 78*(6), 592–599.

Angier, C. (2002). *The double bond of Primo Levi.* New York: Farrar, Straus & Giroux.

Anthony, W. A. (1993). Recovery from mental illness: The guiding vision of the mental health service system in the 1990's. *Psychosocial Rehabilitation Journal, 16,* 12–23.

Antonovsky, A. (1980). *Health, stress, and coping.* San Francisco: Jossey-Bass.

Arend, R., Gove, F., & Sroufe, L. (1979). Continuity of individual adaptation from infancy to kindergarten: A predictive study of ego-resiliency and curiosity in preschoolers. *Child Development, 50,* 950–959.

Asmundson, G. J. G, Coons, M. J., Taylor, S., & Katz, J. (2002). PTSD and the experience of pain: Research and clinical implications of shared vulnerability and mutual maintenance models. *Canadian Journal of Psychiatry, 47*(10), 930–938.

Asser, S. M., & Swan, K. (1998). Child fatalities from religion-motivated medical neglect. *Pediatrics, 101,* 625–629.

Baca Zinn, M. (1980). Gender and ethnic identity among Chicanos. *Frontiers, 2,* 18–24.

Backer, K. L., & Walton-Moss, B. (2001, October). Detecting and addressing alcohol abuse in women. *Nurse Practitioner, 26*(10), 13–22.

Baetz, M., Larson, D. B, Marcoux, G., Bowen, R., & Griffin, R. (2002). Canadian psychiatric inpatient religious commitment: An association with mental health. *Canadian Journal of Psychiatry, 47*(2), 159–167.

Baldwin, A. L., Baldwin, C., & Cole, R. E. (1990). Stress-resistant families and stress-resistant children. In J. Rolf, A. Masten, D. Cicchetti, K. Neuchterlein, & S. Weintraub (Eds.), *Risk and protective factors in the development of psychopathology* (pp. 257–280). Cambridge, UK: Cambridge University Press.

Baldwin, A., Baldwin, C., Kasser, T., Zax, M., Sameroff, A., & Seifer, R. (1993). Contextual risk and resiliency during adolescence. *Development and Psychopathology, 5,* 741–761.

Balk, D. E. (1999). Bereavement and spiritual change. *Death Studies, 23*(6), 485–493.

Barnard, C. (1994). Resiliency: A shift in our perception? *American Journal of Family Therapy, 22,* 135–144.

Barnas, M., & Valaik, P. L. (1991). Life-span attachment: Relations between attachment and socioemotional functioning in adult women. *Genetic, Social & General Psychology Monographs, 117*(2), 177–200.

Baron, L., Eisman, H., Scuello, M., Veyzer, A., & Lieberman, M. (1996). Stress resilience, locus of control, and religion in children of Holocaust victims. *Journal of Psychology, 130*(5), 513–525.

Batson, C. D., & Ventis, W. L. (1982). *The religious experience: A social-psychological perspective.* New York: Oxford University Press.

Baumrind, D. (1966). Effects of authoritative control on child behavior. *Child Development, 37,* 887–907.

Beardslee, W. R., & Podorefsky, D. (1988). Resilient adolescents whose parents have serious affective and other psychiatric disorders: Importance of self-understanding and relationships. *American Journal of Psychiatry, 145,* 63–69.

Beekman, A.T., Bremmer, M. A., Deeg, D. J. H., van Balkom, A. J., Smit, J. H., & de Beurs, E. (1998). Anxiety disorders in later life: A report from the Longitudinal Aging Study Amsterdam. *International Journal of Geriatric Psychiatry, 12*(10), 717–726.

Beeler, J., & Diprova, V. (1999). Family adjustment following disclosure of homosexuality by a family member. *Journal of Marital and Family Therapy, 25,* 443–459.

Bidstrup, S. (2000). *Homphobia: The fear behind the hatred.* Retrieved June 17, 2005, from http://www.bidstrup.com/phobia.htm

Biernacki, P. (1986). *Pathways from heroin addiction: Recover without treatment.* Philadelphia: Temple University Press.

Billings, A. G., & Moos, R. H. (1981). The role of coping responses and social resources in attenuating the stress of life events. *Journal of Behavioral Medicine, 4,* 139–157.

Billings, A. G., & Moos, R. H. (1984). Coping, stress and social resources among adults with unipolar depression. *Journal of Personality and Social Psychology, 46,* 877–891.

Bisson, J. I., McFarlane, A. C., & Rose, S. (2000). Psychological debriefing. In E. B. Foa, T. M., Keane, & M. J. Friedman (Eds.), *Effective treatments for PTSD* (pp. 39–59). New York: Guilford Press.

Blatt, S. J., Zuroff, D. C., Bondi, C. M., & Sanisolow, C. A., III. (2000). Short- and long-term effects of medication and psychotherapy in the brief treatment of depression: Further analyses of data from the NIMH TDCRP. *Psychotherapy Research, 10,* 215–234.

Blazer, D. G. (1993). *Depression in late life* (2nd ed.). St. Louis, MO: Mosby.

Blazer, D. G., Hughes, D. C., & George, L. K. (1987). The epidemiology of depression in an elderly community population. *Journal of the American Geriatric Society, 27,* 281–287.

Blundo, R. (2001). Learning strengths-based practice: Challenging our personal and professional frames. *Families in Society, 82*(3), 296–304.

Bly, R. (1986, April-May). Men of wisdom. *Utne Reader,* pp 37–41.

Boorstein, S. (2000). Transpersonal psychotherapy. *American Journal of Psychotherapy, 54*(3), 408–423.

Boss, P. (2001). *Family stress management: A contextual approach.* Thousand Oaks, CA: Sage.

Bostwick, J. M., & Pankratz, V. S. (2000). Affective disorders and suicide risk: A re-examination. *American Journal of Psychiatry, 157,* 1925–1932.

Braithwaite, D. O. (1996). Exploring different perspectives on the communication of persons with disabilities. In E. B. Ray (Ed.), *Communication and disenfranchisement: Social health issues and implications* (pp. 449–464). Hillsdale, NJ: Lawrence Erlbaum.

Brent, D. A., Holder, D., Kolko, D., Birmaher, B., Baugher, M., & Roth, C. (1999). A clinical psychotherapy trial for adolescent depression comparing cognitive, family, and supportive therapy. *Canadian Psychologist, 40,* 289–327.

Brewin, C. R., Andrews, B., & Valentine, J. D. (2000). Meta-analysis of risk factors for posttraumatic stress disorder in trauma-exposed adults. *Journal of Consulting Clinical Psychology, 68,* 748–766.

Brooks, R. (1994). Children at risk: Fostering resilience and hope. *American Journal of Orthopsychiatry, 64,* 545–553.

Brown, D. R., & Gary, L. E. (1991). Religious socialization and educational attainment among African Americans: An empirical assessment. *Journal of Negro Education, 3,* 411–426.

Brown, W. K., & Rhodes, W. A. (1991). Factors that promote invulnerability and resilience in at-risk children. In W. K. Brown & W. A. Rhodes (Eds.), *Why some children succeed despite the odds* (pp. 171–177). New York: Praeger.

Burgess, C., Morris, T., & Pettingale, K. W. (1988). Psychological response to cancer diagnosis—II. Evidence for coping styles. *Journal of Psychosomatic Research, 32,* 263–272.

Burt, J. M., & Halpin, G. (1998). *African American identity development: A review of the literature.* Paper presented at the annual meeting of the Mid-South Educational Research Association on November 4–6 in New Orleans.

Bustillo, J. R., Lauriello, J. H., Keith, W. P., & Samuel, J. (2001). The psychosocial treatment of schizophrenia: An update. *American Journal of Psychiatry, 158*(2), 163–175.

Butler, C. K. (2005, April 11). The pressure mounts. *U.S. News & World Report, 138*(13), 47.

Butler, R., Lewis, M., & Sunderland, T. (1991). *Aging and mental health: Positive psychosocial and biomedical approaches* (4th ed.). New York: Macmillan.

Byrd, R. (1994). Assessing resilience in victims of childhood maltreatment (Doctoral dissertation, Pepperdine University, 1994). *Dissertation Abstracts International, 55*(03), 74.

Caffrey, T. A. (2000). The whisper of death: Psychotherapy with a dying Vietnam veteran. *American Journal of Psychotherapy, 54*(4), 519–530.

Caldwell, J. (2004). Gay men, straight lives. *Advocate, 924,* 55–58.

Carpenter, J. (2002). Mental health recovery paradigm: Implications for social work. *Health & Social Work, 27*(2), 86–94.

Carver, C. S., Pozo, C., Harris, S. D., Noriega, V., Scheier, M. F., & Robinson, D. S. (1993). How coping mediates the effect of optimism on distress: A study of women with early stage breast cancer. *Journal of Personality and Social Psychology, 65,* 375–390.

Carver, C. S., Scheier, M. F., & Weintraub, J. K. (1989). Assessing coping strategies: A theoretically based approach. *Journal of Personality and Social Psychology, 56,* 267–283.

Caserta, M. S, & Lund, D. A. (1993). Intrapersonal resources and the effectiveness of self-help groups for bereaved older adults. *Gerontologist, 33*(5), 619–629.

Casey, D. A. (1994). Depression in the elderly. *Southern Medical Journal, 87*(5), 559–564.

Chafetz, J. S. (1974). *Masculine/feminine or human.* Itasca, IL: Peacock.

Chambless, D. L., & Ollendick, T. H. (2001). Empirically supported psychological interventions: Controversies and evidence. *Annual Review of Psychology, 52,* 685–716.

Chang, S. C. (1982). The self: A nodal issue in culture and psyche: An Eastern perspective. *American Journal of Psychotherapy, 36*(1), 67–81.

The changing American family: A report of the task force of the American Academy of Pediatrics. (2003, June). *Pediatrics: The Journal of the American Academy of Pediatrics, 3*(6), 1541–1572.

Chatterji, P., & Markowitz, S. (2000). *The impact of maternal alcohol and illicit drug use on children's behavior problems: Evidence from the children of the National Longitudinal Survey of Youth* (Working Paper No. 7692). Cambridge, MA: National Bureau of Economic Research.

Chen, C. C., David, A., Thompson, K., Smith, C., Lea, S., & Fahy, T. (1996). Coping strategies and psychiatric morbidity in women attending breast assessment clinics. *Journal of Psychosomatic Research, 40,* 265–270.

Chinman, M. J., Weingarten, R., Stayner, D., & Davidson, L. (2001). Chronicity reconsidered: Improving person-environment fit through a consumer-run service. *Community Mental Health Journal, 37*(3), 215–229.

Chung, R. C., & Bemak, F. (2002). Revisiting the California Southeast Asian mental health needs assessment data: An examination of refugee ethnic and gender differences. *Journal of Counseling & Development, 80*(1), 111–120.

Classen, C., Koopman, C., Angell, K., & Spiegel, D. (1996). Coping styles associated with psychological adjustment to advanced breast cancer. *Health Psychology, 15,* 434–437.

Cohen, J. A. (1998). Summary of the practice parameters for the assessment and treatment of children and adolescents with posttraumatic stress disorder. *Journal of the American Academy of Child and Adolescent Psychiatry, 37*(9), 997–1001.

Cohler, B. (1987). Adversity, resilience, and the study of lives. In E. J. Anthony & B. J. Cohler (Eds.), *The invulnerable child* (pp. 363–424). New York: Guilford Press.

Coleman, L. M. (1997). Stigma: An enigma demystified. In L. J. David (Ed.), *The disability studies reader* (pp. 216–231). New York: Routledge.

Coles, R. (1964). *Children of crisis: A study of courage and fear.* New York: Atlantic-Little, Brown.

Comstock, G. W., & Partridge, K. B. (1972). Church attendance and health. *Journal of Chronic Diseases, 25,* 665–672.

Congress, E. (1990). Crisis intervention with Hispanic clients in an urban mental health clinic. In A. Roberts (Ed.), *Crisis intervention handbook* (pp. 221–236). Belmont, CA: Wadsworth.

Conrad, M., & Harnmen, C. (1993). Protective and risk factors in high and low risk children: A comparison of children with unipolar, bipolar, medically ill, and normal mothers. *Development and Psychopathology, 5,* 593–607.

Courbasson, C., Endler, M. A., Kocovski, N. S., & Kocovski, N. L. (2002). Coping and psychological distress for men with substance use disorders. *Current Psychology, 21*(1), 35–50.

D'Augelli, A. R., Hershberger, S. L., & Pilkington, N. W. (1998). Lesbian, gay, and bisexual youth and their families: Disclosure of sexual orientation and its consequences. *American Journal of Orthopsychiatry, 68,* 361–371.

Danner, D. D., Snowdon, D. A., & Friesen, W. V. (2001). Positive emotions in early life and longevity: Findings from the Nun Study. *Journal of Personality and Social Psychology, 80*(5), 804–813.

Davidson, L., Chinman, M., Moos, B., Weingarten, R., Stayner, D. A., & Tebes, J. K. (1999). Peer support among individuals with severe mental illness: A review of the evidence. *Clinical Psychology: Science and Practice, 6,* 165–187.

Delson, N., & Kokish, R. (2002). *Treating sexually abused children: Disturbing information about effectiveness.* Retrieved November 25, 2002, from http://www.delko.net/CSA%20kid%20treatment.htm

Dixon, L., Krauss, N., & Lehman, A. L. (1994). Consumers as service providers: The promise and challenge. *Community Mental Health Journal, 30,* 615–625.

Druss, B. G., Marcus, S. C., Rosenheck, R. A., Olfson, M., Tanielan, T., & Pincus, H. A. (2000). Understanding disability in mental and general medical conditions. *American Journal of Psychiatry, 157*(9), 1485–1491.

Dudley, J. R., & Helfgott, C. (1990). Exploring a place for spirituality in the social work curriculum. *Journal of Social Work Education, 26*(3), 287–294.

Duffy, A. (2000). Toward effective early intervention and prevention strategies for major affective disorders: A review of risk factors. *Canadian Journal of Psychiatry, 45*(4), 340–349.

Edlund, M. J., Wang, P. S., Berglund, P. A., Katz, S., Lin, E., & Kessler, R. C. (2002). Dropping out of mental health treatment patterns and predictors among epidemiological survey respondents in the United States and Ontario. *American Journal of Psychiatry, 159*(5), 845–851.

Egeland, E., Carlson, E., & Sroufe, L. (1993). Resilience as process. *Development and Psychopathology, 5,* 517–528.

Elizur, Y., & Ziv, M. A. (2001, Summer). Family support and acceptance, gay male identity formation, and psychological adjustment: A path model. *Family Process, 40,* 125–144.

Elkin, I., Shea, T., Watkins, J. T., Imber, S. D., Sotsky, S. M., & Collins, J. F. (1989). National Institute of Mental Health Treatment of Depression Collaborative Research Program: General effectiveness of treatments. *Archives of General Psychiatry, 46,* 971–982.

Ell, K. O., Mantell, J. E., Hamovitch, M. B., & Nishimoto, R. H. (1989). Social support, sense of control, and coping among patients with breast, lung, or colorectal cancer. *Journal of Psychosocial Oncology, 7,* 63–89.

Ellison, C. G. (1993). Religious involvement and self-perception among black Americans. *Social Forces, 71,* 1027–1055.

Ellison, C. G., Boardman, J. D., Williams, D. R., & Jackson, J. S. (2001). Religious involvement, stress and mental health: Findings from the 1995 Detroit area study. *Social Forces, 80*(1), 215–235.

Ellison, C. G., & George, L. K. (1992). Religious involvement, social ties, and social support in a southeastern community. *Journal for the Scientific Study of Religion, 33,* 46–61.

Ellison, C. G., & Levin, J. S. (1998). The religion-health connection: Evidence theory and future directions. *Health Education and Behavior, 25,* 700–720.

Emrick, C. D. (1987). Alcoholics Anonymous: Affiliative processes and effectiveness as treatment. *Alcoholism: Clinical and Experimental Research, 12,* 416–423.

Endler, N. S., & Parker, J. D. A (1999). *Coping Inventory for Stressful Situations (CISS): Manual* (Rev. ed.). Toronto: Multi-Health Systems.

Enns, R. A., Reddon, J. R., & McDonald, L. (1999). Indications of resilience among family members of people admitted to a psychiatric facility. *Psychiatric Rehabilitation Journal, 23*(2), 127–136.

Enstrom, J. E. (1978). Cancer and total mortality among active Mormons. *Cancer, 42,* 13–19.

Enstrom, J. E. (1989). Health practices and cancer mortality among active California Mormons. *Journal of the National Cancer Institute, 81,* 1807–1814.

Entwistle, V. A., Sheldon, T. A., Sowden, A., & Watt, I. S. (1998). Evidence-informed patient choice: Practical issues of involving patients in decisions about health care technologies. *International Journal of Technology Assessment in Health Care, 14,* 212–225.

Farber, E., & Egeland, B. (1987). Invulnerability among abused and neglected children. In E. J. Anthony & B. J. Cohler (Eds.), *The invulnerable child* (pp. 289–314). New York: Guilford.

Fedor, L., Bonham, K., Bradbury, R., & Paulson, M. (1997). M. Owens: "You bring us hope." *Grand Forks Herald.* Retrieved March 27, 2005, from http://grand-forks-herald.ask .dyndns.dk/

Felton, C. J., Stastny, P., Shern, D., Blanch, A., Donahue, S. A., Knight, E., & Brown, C. (1995). Consumers as peer specialists on intensive case management teams: Impact on client outcomes. *Psychiatric Services, 46,* 1037–1044.

Fergusson, D. M., Horwood, L. J., & Beautrais, A. L. (1999). Is sexual orientation related to mental health problems and suicidality in young people? *Archives of General Psychiatry, 56,* 876–880.

Fetto, J. (2000). Lean on me. *American Demographics, 22*(12), 16.

Filipp, S. H., Klauer, T., Freudenberg, E., & Ferring, D. (1990). The regulation of subjective well-being in cancer patients: An analysis of coping effectiveness. *Psychology and Health, 4,* 305–317.

Finn, J. (1999). An exploration of helping processes in an online self-help group focusing on issues of disability. *Health & Social Work, 24*(3), 220–231.

Fleming, M., & Manwell, L. B. (1998). Brief intervention in primary care settings: A primary treatment method for at-risk, problem, and dependent drinkers. *Alcohol Research and Health, 23*(2), 128–137.

Foa, E. B., Hearst-Ikeda, D., & Perry, K. J. (1995). Evaluation of a brief cognitive-behavioral program for the prevention of chronic PTSD in recent assault victims. *Journal of Consulting & Clinical Psychology, 63,* 948–955.

Frankl, V. E. (1978). *Psychotherapy and existentialism: Selected papers on logotherapy.* New York: Simon & Schuster.

Franklin, A. J. (1992). Therapy with African American men. *Families in Society: The Journal of Contemporary Human Services, 26*(6), 350–355.

Friedrich, W. (1993). Sexual victimization and sexual behavior in children: A review of recent literature. *Child Abuse and Neglect, 17,* 59–66.

Furr, S. R., Westfield, J. S., McConnell, G. N., & Jenkins, J. M. (2001). Suicide and depression among college students: A decade later. *Professional Psychology: Research and Practice, 32,* 97–100.

Furstenberg, F. F. (1998). Paternal involvement with adolescence in intact families: The influence of fathers over the life course. *Demography, 35*(2), 201–216.

Furuto, S. M., Biswas, R., Chung, D., Murase, K., & Ross-Sheriff, F. (Eds.). (1992). *Social work practice with Asian Americans.* Newbury Park, CA: Sage.

Galanter, M. (1988). Zealous self-help groups as adjuncts to psychiatric treatment: A study of Recovery, Inc. *American Journal of Psychiatry, 145*(10), 1248–1253.

Gambrill, E. (1999). Evidence-based practice: An alternative to authority-based practice. *Journal of Contemporary Human Services, 80*(4), 341–350.

Gambrill, E. (2000, October 14). *Evidence-based practice.* Handout to deans and directors of schools of social work, Huntington Beach, CA.

Gardner, J. W., & Lyon, J. L. (1982). Cancer in Utah Mormon men by lay priesthood level. *American Journal of Epidemiology, 116,* 243–257.

Garmezy, N. (1983). Stressors of childhood. In N. Garmezy & M. Rutter (Eds.), *Stress, coping and development in children* (pp. 43–84). New York: McGraw-Hill.

Garmezy, N., Masten, A., & Tellegen, A. (1964). The study of stress and competence in children: A building block for developmental psychopathology. *Child Development, 55,* 97–111.

Gartner, J., Larson, D. B., & Allen, G. D. (1991). Religious commitment and mental health: A review of the empirical literature. *Journal of Psychology and Theology, 19,* 625.

Gates, C. T. (2000). Toward a healthy democracy. *National Civic Review, 89*(2), 161–168.

Gaw, A. C. (1993). Psychiatric care of Chinese Americans. In A. Gaw (Ed.), *Culture, ethnicity, and mental illness* (pp. 245–280). Washington, DC: American Psychiatric Press.

Gentilello, L. M., Donovan, D. M., Dunn, C. W., & Rivara, F. P. (1995). Alcohol interventions in trauma centers: Current practice and future directions. *JAMA, 274*(13), 1043–1048.

George, L. K. (1992). Social factors and the onset and outcome of depression. In K. W. Schaie, J. S. House, & D. G. Blazer (Eds.), *Aging, health behaviors, and health outcomes* (pp. 137–159). Hillsdale, NJ: Lawrence Erlbaum.

George, L. K., Larson, D. B., Koenig, H. G., & McCullough, M. E. (2000). Spirituality and health: What we know, what we need to know. *Journal of Social and Clinical Psychology, 19*(1), 102–116.

Gilden, J. L., Hendryx, A. S., Clar, S., Casia, F. P. & Singh, S. P. (1992). Diabetes support groups improve health care of older diabetic patients. *Journal of the American Geriatrics Society, 40,* 147–150.

Gist, R., & Devilly, G. J. (2002). Post-trauma debriefing: The road too frequently traveled. *Lancet, 360*(9335), 741–743.

Gladwell, M. (2002, August 12). Political heat. *New Yorker,* pp. 76–80.

Glasner, S. V. (2004). Motivation and addiction: The role of incentive processes in understanding and treating addictive disorders. In W. M. Cox & E. Klinger (Eds.), *Handbook of motivational counseling: Concepts, approaches, and assessment* (pp. 29–47). Hoboken, NJ: John Wiley & Sons.

Glick, H. A. (1994). Resilience research: How can it help city schools? Retrieved August 1, 2004, from http://www.ncrel.org/sdrs/cityschl/city1_1b.htm NCRAL

Glicken, A. J. (2002). Building on our strengths. *Park Record, 122*(59), A15.

Glicken, M. D. (1991, July 7). Who to trust at work. *National Business Employment Weekly,* p. 27.

Glicken, M. D. (2004a). *Using the strengths perspective in social work practice: A positive approach for the helping professions.* Boston, MA: Allyn & Bacon/Longman.

Glicken, M. D. (2004b). *Violent young children.* Boston, MA: Allyn & Bacon/Longman.

Glicken, M. D. (2005a). *Ending the sex wars: A woman's guide to understanding men.* Lincoln, NE: iuniverse.

Glicken, M. D. (2005b). *Improving the effectiveness of the helping professions: An evidence-based approach to practice.* Thousand Oaks, CA: Sage.

Glicken, M.D. (2005c). *Working with troubled men: A contemporary practitioner's guide.* Mahwah, NJ: Lawrence Erlbaum.

Glicken, M. D., & Garza, M. A. (1996, October, 26). *Crisis intervention with newly immigrated Latino clients.* Paper presented in Sacramento at the California Conference for Latino Social Workers.

Glicken, M. D., & Garza, M. A. (2004). Clinical work with traditional and newly immigrated Latino men. In M. D. Glicken (2005), *Working with troubled men: A contemporary practitioner's guide* (pp. 245–259). Mahwah, NJ: Lawrence Erlbaum.

Glicken, M. D., & Sechrest, D. K. (2003). *The role of the helping professions in treating the victims and perpetrators of violence.* Boston, MA: Allyn & Bacon/Longman.

Golan, N. (1978). *Treatment in crisis situations*. New York: Free Press.

Goldstein, H. (1990). Strength or pathology: Ethical and rhetorical contrasts in approaches to practice. *Families in Society, 71*, 267-275.

Gong-Guy, E. (1987). *California Southeast Asian mental health needs assessment*. Oakland, CA: Asian Community Mental Health Association.

Gordon, E. W. (2000). The myths and realities of African-American fatherhood. In R. D. Taylor & M. C. Wang (Eds.), *Resilience across contexts: Work, family, culture, and community* (pp. 217–232). Mahwah, NJ: Lawrence Eribaum.

Gordon, K. A. (1996, June 20–23). *Infant and toddler resilience: Knowledge, predictions, policy, and practice*. Paper presented at the Head Start National Research Conference in Washington, DC.

Granfield, R., & Cloud, W. (1996). The elephant that no one sees: Natural recovery among middle-class addicts. *Journal of Drug Issues, 26*, 45–61.

Grant, B. F., & Dawson, D. A. (1997) Age at onset of alcohol use and its association with DSM-IV alcohol abuse and dependence: Results from the national longitudinal alcohol epidemiologic survey. *Journal of Substance Abuse, 9*, 103–110.

Greenstein, M., & Breitbart, W. (2000). Cancer and the experience of meaning: A group psychotherapy program for people with cancer. *American Journal of Psychotherapy, 54*(4), 486–500.

Greer, S. (1991). Psychological response to cancer and survival. *Psychological Medicine, 21*, 43–49.

Groopman, J. (2004, January 26). The grief industry. *New Yorker*, pp. 30–38.

Haight, W. L. (1998). "Gathering the spirit" at First Baptist Church: Spirituality as a protective factor in the lives of African American children. *Social Work, 43*(3), 213–223.

Hamburg, M. A. (1998). Youth violence is a public health concern. In D. S. Elliott, B. Hamburg, & K. R. Williams (Eds.), *Violence in American schools: A new perspective* (pp. 31-54). New York: Cambridge University Press.

Hamilton, I., McCubbin, H. I., McCubbin, M. A., Thompson, A. I., Han, S. Y., & Allen, C. T. (1997, June 22). *Families under stress: What makes them resilient?* American Association of Family and Consumer Sciences Commemorative Lecture, Washington, DC. Retrieved August 4, 2004, from http://www.cyfernet.org/research/resilient.html

Hanifan, L. J. (1916). The rural school community center. *Annals of the American Academy of Social Science, 67*, 130–138.

Hanson, M., & Gutheil, I. A. (2004). Motivational strategies with alcohol-involved older adults: Implications for social work practice. *Social Work, 49*(3), 364–373.

Harding, C. M., Brooks, G. W., Ashikaga, T., Strauss, J. S., & Breier, A. (1986a). The Vermont longitudinal study of persons with severe mental illness: I. Methodology, study sample, and overall status 32 years later. *American Journal of Psychiatry, 144*, 718–725.

Harding, C. M., Brooks, G. W., Ashikaga, T., Strauss, J. S., & Breier, A. (1986b). The Vermont longitudinal study of persons with severe mental illness: II. Long-term outcome of subjects who retrospectively met DSM-II criteria for schizophrenia. *American Journal of Psychiatry, 144*, 727–735.

Hardwig, J. (2000). Spiritual issues at the end of life: A call for discussion. *The Hastings Center Report, 30*(2), 28–30.

Harrington, R., & Clark, A. (1998). Prevention and early intervention for depression in adolescence and early adult life. *European Archives of Psychiatry in Clinical Neuroscience, 248*, 32–45.

Hawker, D. S. J., & Boulton, M. J. (2000). Twenty years' research on peer victimization and psychosocial maladjustment: A meta-analysis review of cross-sectional studies. *Journal of Child Psychology and Psychiatry, 41*(4), 441–55.

Health Canada. (1998). *Suicide in Canada: Update of the Task Force on Suicide in Canada.* Ottawa: Mental Health Division, Health Services Directorate, Health Programs and Services Branch, Health Canada.

Heim, E., Valach, L., & Schaffner, L. (1997). Coping and psychosocial adaptation: Longitudinal effects over time and stages in breast cancer. *Psychosomatic Medicine, 59,* 408–418.

Henry, D. L. (1999). Resilience in maltreated children: Implications for special needs adoptions. *Child Welfare, 78*(5), 519–540.

Hensley, L. G. (2002). Treatment for survivors of rape: Issues and interventions. *Journal of Mental Health Counseling, 24*(4), 331–348.

Herbert, E. A. (1950). *A Confucian notebook.* London: Butler & Tanner.

Hernandez, R. (1990, September 9). Please stand up if you are a real Hispanic. *Los Angeles Times,* pp. 5–7.

Hetherington, E. M. (1989). Coping with family transitions: Winners, losers and survivors. *Child Development, 60,* 1–14.

Hines, S. E. (2000, February 29). Enhance your practice with evidence-based medicine. *Patient Care, 60*(2), 36-45.

Hingson, R., Scotch, N., Day, N., & Culbert, A. (1980). Recognizing and seeking help for drinking problems. *Journal of Studies on Alcohol, 41,* 1102–1117.

Ho, M. K. (1987). *Family therapy with ethnic minorities.* Newbury Park, CA: Sage.

Horowitz, M. J. (1976). *Stress response syndromes.* New York: Jason Aronson.

Horton, C. B., & Cruise, T. K. (2001). *Child abuse and neglect: The school's response.* New York: Guilford Press.

Hsu, F. L. K. (1983). *Rugged individualism reconsidered: Essays in psychological anthropology.* Knoxville: University of Tennessee Press.

Huber, G., Gross, G., & Schuttler, R. (1975). A long-term follow up study of schizophrenia: Psychiatric course of illness and prognosis. *Acta Psychiatrica Scandinavica, 52,* 49–57.

Human Rights Watch. (2001). *Hatred in the hallways: Violence and discrimination against lesbian, gay, bisexual and transgender students in U.S. schools.* New York: Human Rights Watch. Retrieved April 13, 2005, from http://www.hrw.org/reports/2001/uslgbt/

Humphreys, K. (1998). Can addiction-related self-help/mutual aid groups lower demand for professional substance abuse treatment? *Social Policy, 29*(2), 13–17.

Humphreys, K., Mavis, B. E., & Stoffelmayr, B. E. (1994). Are twelve step programs appropriate for disenfranchised groups? Evidence from a study of post-treatment mutual help involvement. *Prevention in Human Services, 11*(1), 165–179.

Humphreys, K., & Moos, R. H. (1996). Reduced substance-abuse-related health care costs among voluntary participants in Alcoholics Anonymous. *Psychiatric Services, 47,* 709–713.

Humphreys, K., & Ribisl, K. M. (1999). The case for partnership with self-help groups. *Public Health Reports, 114*(4), 322–329.

Idler, E. L. (1987). Religious involvement and the health of the elderly: Some hypotheses sand an initial test. *Social Forces, 66,* 226–238.

Idler, E. L., & Kasl, S. V. (1992). Religion, disability, depression, and the timing of death. *American Journal of Sociology, 97,* 1052–1079.

Idler, E. L., & Kasl, S. V. (1997). Religion among disabled elderly persons II: Attendance at religious services as a predictor of the course of disability. *Journal of Gerontology: Social Sciences, 97,* 1052–1079.

Ino, S. (1985a). *Close relationships: Their subjective construction and contribution to the sense of self.* Ann Arbor, MI: University Microfilms International.

Ino, S. (1985b, August 22). *The concept of an Asian American collective self.* Paper presented at the Pacific/Asian American Research Methods Workshop (P/AAMHRC), Ann Arbor, MI.

Ino, S. (1987, August 27). *The sense of collective self in Asian American psychology.* Paper presented at the national convention of the Asian American Psychological Association, New York.

Ino, S. (1991). *The sense of collective self in Asian American psychology.* Paper presented at the American Psychological Association (APA): 99th Annual Convention on August 16-20 in San Francisco.

Ino, S. M., & Glicken, M. D. (1999). Treating Asian American clients in crisis: A collectivist approach. *Smith College Studies in Social Work, 69*(3), 525–540.

Ino, S. M., & Glicken, M. D. (2002). Understanding and treating the ethnically Asian client: A collectivist approach. *Journal of Health and Social Policy, 14*(4), 37–48.

Jackson, Y., & Warren, J. (2000). Appraisal, social support, and life events: Predicting outcome behavior in school-age children. *Child Development, 71,* 1441–1453.

Jacobs, M., & Maidenberg, M. (1997, March 25). The day that changed everything. *The Grand Forks Herald.* Retrieved March 27, 2005, from http://www.draves.com/gf/gfhhw.htm

Jacobs, S., & Prigerson, H. (2000). Psychotherapy of traumatic grief: A review of evidence for psychotherapeutic treatments. *Death Studies, 24*(6), 479–496.

Jamison, K. R. (1995). *An unquiet mind.* New York: Knopf.

Jimenez, M. A. (1988). Chronicity in mental disorders: Evolution of a concept. *Social Casework, 69,* 627–633.

Joiner, T. E., Jr., Catanzaro, S., Rudd, M. D., & Rajab, M. H. (1999). The case for a hierarchical, oblique, and bidimensional structure of loneliness. *Journal of Social and Clinical Psychology, 18,* 47–75.

Kaczorowski, J. M. (1989). Spiritual well-being and anxiety in adults diagnosed with cancer. *Hospice Journal, 5,* 105–126.

Kann, L. (2001). Commentary. *Journal of Drug Issues, 31*(3), 725–727.

Kaplan, S. J., Pelcovitz, D., & Labruna, V. (1999). Child and adolescent abuse and neglect research: A review of the past 10 years. Part I: Physical and emotional abuse and neglect. *Journal of the American Academy of Child and Adolescent Psychiatry, 38*(10), 1214–1222.

Kaufman, C. (1995). The self-help employment center: Some outcomes from the first year. *Psychosocial Rehabilitation Journal, 18,* 145–162.

Kauffman, C., Grunebaum, H., Cohler, B., & Gamer, E. (1979). Superkids: Competent children of psychotic mothers. *American Journal of Psychiatry, 136,* 1398–1402.

Kazdin, A. E., Holland, L., Crowley, M., & Breton, S. (1997). Barriers to treatment participation scale: Evaluation and validation in the context of child outpatient treatment. *Journal of Child Psychology and Psychiatry, 38*(8), 1051–1062.

Kesler, J. T. (2000). The healthy communities' movement: Seven counterintuitive next steps. *National Civic Review, 89*(3), 271–284.

Kessler, R. C., Frank, R. G., Edlund, M., Katz, S. J., Lin, E., & Leaf, P. (1997). Differences in the use of psychiatric outpatient services between the United States and Ontario. *New England Journal of Medicine, 336,* 551–557.

Kessler, R. C., Mickelson, K. D., & Zhao, S. (1997). Patterns and correlates of self-help group membership in the United States. *Social Policy, 27,* 27–46.

Kissman, K., & Maurer, L. (2002). East meets west: Therapeutic aspects of spirituality in health, mental health and addiction recovery. *International Social Work, 45*(1), 35–44.

Kline, R. B. (1998). *Principles and practice of structural equation modeling.* New York: Guilford Press.

Kramer, P. D. (2005, April 17). There's nothing deep about depression. *New York Times Magazine*, pp. 50–53.

Kramer, S. H., & Rosenthal, R. (1998). Meta-analytic research synthesis. In N. R. Schooler (Ed.), *Comprehensive clinical psychology: Vol 3. Research and methods* (pp. 351–368). Oxford, UK: Pergamon Press.

Kruger, A. (2000). Schizophrenia: Recovery and hope. *Psychiatric Rehabilitation Journal, 24*, 29–37.

Kubler-Ross, E. (1997). *On death and dying.* New York: Simon & Schuster. (Original work published 1969)

Kurtz, R. C. (1988). Mutual aid for affective disorders: The manic derpressive and depressive association. *American Journal of Orthopsychiatry, 58*(1), 152–155.

Kyrouz, E., & Humphreys, K. (1996). Do psychiatrically disabled people benefit from participation in self-help/mutual aid organizations? A research review. *Community Psychologist, 29*, 21–25.

Lachman. B. E. (1997). *Linking sustainable community activities to pollution prevention: A sourcebook.* Santa Monica, CA: Rand Corporation.

Lajoie, D. H., & Shapiro, S. Y. (1992). Definitions of transpersonal psychology: The first twenty-three years. *Journal of Transpersonal Psychology, 24*(1), 79–98.

Lambie, G. W. (2005). Child abuse and neglect: A practical guide for professional school counselors. *Professional School Counseling, 8*(3), 249–259.

Lang, A. J., & Stein, M. B. (2001). Anxiety disorders. *Geriatrics, 56*(5), 24–30.

Larson, D. B., Koenig, H. G., Kaplan, B. H., & Levin, J. S. (1989). The impact of religion on men's blood pressure. *Journal of Religion and Health, 28*, 265–278.

Last, U. (1989). The transgenerational impact of Holocaust trauma. Current state of the evidence. *International Journal of Mental Health, 17*(4), 72–89.

Laszloffy, T. A., & Hardy, C. B. (2000). Uncommon strategies for a common problem: Addressing racism in family therapy. *Family Process, 39,* 35–50.

Lawson, E. J., & Sharpe, T. L. (2000, July 7). Black men and divorce: Implications for culturally competent practice. *Minority Health Today.* Retrieved July, 8, 2003, from http://www.findarticles.com/cf_0/m0HKU/5_1/66918338/print.jhtml

Lawton, M. P. (1977). The impact of the environment on aging and behavior. In J. E. Birren & K. W. Schaie (Eds.), *Handbook of the psychology of aging* (pp. 276–301). New York: Van Nostrand Reinhold.

Lawton, M. P., & Nahemow, L. (1973). Ecology and the aging process. In C. Eisdorfer & M. P. Lawton (Eds.), *The psychology of adult development and aging* (pp. 619–674). Washington, DC: American Psychological Association.

Lazarus, R. S. (1966). *Psychological stress and the coping process.* New York: McGraw-Hill.

Lee, E. (1996). Asian American families: An overview. In M. McGoldrick, J. Giordana, & J. Pearce (Eds.), *Ethnicity and family therapy* (2nd ed.). New York: Guilford Press.

Levi, P. (1995a). *If not now, when?* New York: Viking Penguin. (Original work published 1982)

Levi, P. (1995b). *The periodic table.* New York: Random House. (Original work published 1975)

Levin, J. S., & Vanderpool, H. Y. (1989). Is religion therapeutically significant for hypertension? *Social Science and Medicine, 29*, 69-78.

Lewis, E. A., & Suarez, Z. E. (1995). Natural helping networks. *Encyclopedia of Social Work* (19th ed., pp. 1765–1772). Silver Spring, MD: National Association of Social Workers.

Lifton, R. J. (1993). *The protean self: Human resilience in an age of fragmentation.* New York: Basic Books.

Livneh, H. (2000, April 1). Psychosocial adaptation to cancer: The role of coping strategies. *Journal of Rehabilitation.* Retrieved April 14, 2005, from http://www.findarticles.com/p/articles/mi_m0825/is_2_66/ai_62980227/print

Livneh, H., Livneh, C. L., Maron, S., & Kaplan, J. (1996). A multidimensional approach to the study of the structure of coping with stress. *Journal of Psychology, 130*(5), 501–513.

Lock, J., & Steiner, H. (1999). Gay, lesbian, and bisexual youth risks for emotional, physical, and social problems: Results from a community-based survey. *Journal of the American Academy of Child and Adolescent Psychiatry, 38,* 297–304.

Loewenberg, J. (1988). *Caring and responsibility: Crossroads between holistic practices and traditional medicine.* Philadelphia: University of Pennsylvania Press.

Lukefahr, J. L. (2001). Treatment of child abuse [Book review]. *Journal of the American Academy of Child and Adolescent Psychiatry, 40*(3), 383.

Luthar, S. (1991). Vulnerability and resilience: A study of high risk adolescents. *Child Development, 62,* 599–616.

Luthar, S. (1993). Annotation: Methodology and conceptual issues in research on childhood resilience. *Journal of Child Psychology and Psychiatry, 34,* 441–453.

Luthar, S., & Zigler, E. (1991). Vulnerability and competence: A review of research on resilience in childhood. *American Journal of Orthopsychiatry, 6,* 6–22.

Lyon, L., Klauber, M. R., & Gardner, J. Y. (1976). Cancer incidence in Mormons and non-Mormons in Laah, 1966–1970. *New England Journal of Medicine, 294,* 129–133.

Majors R., & Billson, J. M. (1992). *Cool pose: The dilemmas of black manhood in America.* Lexington, MA: Lexington Books.

Maltz, W., & Holman, B. (1987). *Incest and sexuality: A guide to understanding and healing.* Lexington, MA: Lexington Books.

Mandleco, B. L., & Peery, J. C. (2000). An organizational framework for conceptualizing resilience in children. *Journal of Child & Adolescent Psychiatric Nursing, 13*(3), 99–112.

Manfred-Gilham, J. J., Sales, E., & Koeske, G. (2002). Therapist and case manager perceptions of client barriers to treatment participation and use of engagement strategies. *Community Mental Health Journal, 38*(3), 213–221.

Manheimer, R. J. (Ed.). (1994). *Older Americans almanac.* Detroit, MI: Gale Research.

Mannion, E. (1996). Resilience and burden in spouses of people with mental illness. *Psychitric Rehabilitation Journal, 20*(2), 13–24.

Markowitz, F. E. (1998). The effects of stigma on the psychological well-being and life satisfaction of persons with mental illness. *Journal of Health & Social Behavior, 39*(4), 335–347.

Marmar, C. R., Horowitz, M. J., Weiss, D. S., Wilner, N. R., & Kaltreider, N. B. (1988). A controlled trial of brief psychotherapy and mutual help group treatment of conjugal bereavement. *American Journal of Psychiatry, 145,* 203–209.

Masten, A. S. (1989). Resilience in development: Implications of the study of successful adaptation for developmental psychopathology. In D. Cicchetti (Ed.), *The emergence of a discipline: Rochester symposium on developmental psychopathology* (pp. 261–294). Hillsdale, NJ: Lawrence Erlbaum.

Masten, A. S. (2001). Ordinary magic: Resilience processes in development. *American Psychologist, 56,* 227–238.

Masten, A. S., & Coatsworth, J. (1998). Resilience and development: Contributions from the study of children who overcame adversity. *Developmental Psychology, 2,* 425–450.

McCallion, P., & Toseland, R. W. (1995). Supportive group interventions with caregivers of frail older adults. *Social Work with Groups, 18*(1), 11–25.

McClain, C. S, Rosenfeld, B., & Breitbart, W. (2003). Effect of spiritual well-being on end-of-life despair in terminally-ill cancer patients. *Lancet, 361*(9369), 1603–1608.

McCrae, R. R. (1984). Situational determinants of coping responses: Loss, threat, and challenge. *Journal of Personality and Social Psychology, 46,* 919–928.

McCubbin, M. A., & McCubbin, H. I. (1993). Family coping with health crises: The resiliency model of family stress, adjustment, and adaptation. In C. Danielson, B. Hamel-Bissell, & P. Winstead-Fry (Eds.), *Families, health, and illness.* St. Louis, MO: Mosby.

McCubbin, M. A., & McCubbin, H. I. (1996). Resiliency in families: A conceptual model of family adjustment and adaptation in response to stress and crises. In H. I. McCubbin, A. I. Thompson, & M. A. McCubbin (Eds), *Family assessment: Resiliency, coping and adaptation—Inventories for research and practice* (pp. 1–64). Madison: University of Wisconsin.

McFadden, S. (2000). Religion in the lives of older adults. Retrieved April 9, 2000, from http://www.lutersem.edu/cars/newsletters/ARTUS.HTM

Meadows, E. A., & Foa, E. B. (1998). Intrusion, arousal, and avoidance: Sexual trauma survivors. In V. Follette, I. Ruzek, & F. Abueg (Eds.), *Cognitive-behavioral therapies for trauma* (pp. 100–123). New York: Guilford Press.

Medalie, J. H., Kahn, H. A., Neufeld, H. N., Riss, E., & Goldbourt, U. (1973). Five-year myocardial infarction incidence II: Association of single variables to age and birthplace. *Journal of Chronic Disease, 26,* 329–349.

Miller, L. (1999). Juvenile crime statistics 1998. *Victim Advocate,* U.S. Department of Juvenile Justice. Washington, DC: U.S. Government. Printing Office.

Miller, L. H., & Smith, A. D. (2005). The different kinds of stress. *American Psychological Association Help Line.* Retrieved May 13, 2005, from http://www.apahelpcenter.org/articles/article.php?id=21

Miller, W. R., & Rollnick, S. (2002). Motivational interviewing (2nd ed.). New York: Guilford Press.

Mills, T. L., & Henretta, J. C. (2001). Racial, ethnic, and socio-demographic differences in the level of psychosocial distress among older Americans. *Research on Aging, 23*(2), 131–152.

Mirande, A. (1979). A reinterpretation of male dominance in the Chicano family. *Family Coordinator, 28,* 473–497.

Mishel, M. H., & Sorenson, D. S. (1993). Revision of the ways of coping checklist for a clinical population. *Western Journal of Nursing Research, 15,* 59–76.

Montgomery, H. A., Miller, W. R., & Tonigan, J. S. (1995). Does Alcoholics Anonymous involvement predict treatment outcome? *Journal of Substance Abuse Treatment, 22,* 241–246.

Monti, P. M., Colby, S. M., Barnett, N. P, Spirito, A., Roshenow, D. L., & Meyers, M. (1999). Brief intervention for harm reduction with alcohol-positive older adolescents in a hospital emergency department. *Journal of Consulting and Clinical Psychology, 67*(6), 989–994.

Morris, T. (1986). Coping with cancer: The positive approach. In M. Watson & S. Greer (Eds.), *Psychosocial issues in malignant disease* (pp. 79–85). New York: Pergamon Press.

Moxley, D. P., & Olivia, G. (2001). Strengths-based recovery practice in chemical dependency: A transperson perspective. *Families in Society, 82*(3), 251–262.

Mueller T. I., Leon, A. C., Keller, M. B., et al. (1999). Recurrence after recovery from major depressive disorder during 15 years of observational follow-up. *American Journal of Psychiatry, 156,* 1000–1006.

Murray, C. J., & Lopez, A. D. (1997). Alternative projections of mortality and disability by cause 1990–2020: Global burden of disease study. *Lancet, 349,* 1498–1504.

Myers, J. E. (1998). Bibliotherpay and the DCT: Deconstructing the therapeutic metaphor. *Journal of Counseling and Development, 76,* 243–251.

Nasar, S. (1998). *A brilliant mind: The life of mathematical genius and Nobel laureate John Nash.* New York: Simon & Schuster.

National Institute of Alcohol Abuse and Alcoholism. (2000). *NIAA Alcohol Alert* (NIAA Publication No. 49). Bethesda, MD: Author.

National Institute of Mental Health (NIMH). (1999). *Schizophrenia* (NIMH Publication No. 99–3517). Retrieved October 13, 2002, from http://www.nimh.nih.gov/publicat/schizoph.cfm

National Institute of Mental Health (NIMH). (2001). *Bi-polar disorder* (NIMH Publication No. 01–3679). Retrieved October 13, 2002, from http://www.nimh.nih.gov/publicat/bipolar.cfm#intro

National Institute on Aging/Fitzer Institute Working Group. (1997). *Measurement scale on religion, spirituality, health, and aging.* Bethesda, MD: National Institute an Aging.

Neighbors, B., Forehand, R., & McVicar, D. (1993). Resilient adolescents and interparental conflict. *American Journal of Orthopsychiatry, 63,* 462–471.

Newman, L. (1979). Emotional disturbances in children of Holocaust survivors. *Social Casework: The Journal of Contemporary Social Work, 60*(1), 43–50.

Oates, R. K., & Bross, D. C. (1995). What have we learned about treating child physical abuse? A literature review of the last decade. *Journal of Child Abuse & Neglect, 19,* 463–473.

O'Connor, R. (2001). Active treatment of depression. *American Journal of Psychotherapy, 55*(4), 507–530.

O'Connor, T. P., Cayton, T., Taylor, S., McKenna, R., & Monroe, N. (2004). Home for good in Oregon: A community, faith and state re-entry partnership to increase restorative justice. *Corrections Today, 66*(6), 72–77.

Okun, A., Parker, J., & Levendosky, A. (1994). Distinct and interactive contributions of physical abuse, socioeconomic disadvantage, and negative live events to children's social, cognitive, affective adjustment. *Development and Psychopathology, 6,* 77–98.

Olweus, D. (1993). Victimization by peers: Antecedents and long-term outcomes. In K. H. Rubin & J. B. Asendorpf (Eds.), *Social withdrawal, inhibition and shyness in childhood* (pp. 315–341). Hillsdale, NJ: Lawrence Erlbaum.

Ozer, E. J., Best, S. R., Lipsey, T. L., & Weiss, D. S. (2003). Predictors of posttraumatic stress disorder and symptoms in adults: A meta-analysis. *Psychological Bulletin, 129*(1), 52–73.

Pardeck, J. T. (1995). Bibliotherapy: An innovative approach to helping children. *Early Childhood Development and Care, 110,* 83–88.

Pargament, K. I. (1990). God help me: Toward a theoretical framework of coping for the psychology of religion. *Research in the Social Scientific Study of Religion, 2,* 195–224.

Parikh, S. V., Wasylenki, D., Goerung, P., & Wong, J. (1996). Mood disorders: Rural/urban differences in prevalence, health care utilization, and disability in Ontario. *Journal of Affective Disorders, 38,* 57–65.

Parker, G. R., Cowen, E. L., Work, W. C., & Wyman, P. A. (1990). Test correlates of stress resilience among urban school children. *Journal of Primary Prevention, 11,* 19–35.

Parkes, K. R. (1984) Locus of control, cognitive appraisal, and coping in stressful episodes. *Journal of Personality and Social Psychology, 46*(3), 655–668.

Parkes, K. R. (1986). Coping in stressful episodes: The role of individual differences, environmental factors, and situational characteristics. *Journal of Personality and Social Psychology, 51,* 1277–1292.

Patten, S. B. (2000). Incidence of major depression in Canada. *Canadian Medical Association Journal, 163,* 714–715.

Patterson, J. (2002). Integrating family resilience and family stress theory. *Journal of Marriage and the Family, 64,* 349–360.

Patterson, S. L., & Marsiglia, F. F. (2000). Mi casa es su casa: Beginning exploration of Mexican Americans' natural helping. *Families in Society, 81*(1), 22–31.

Pearlin, L. I., & Schooler, C. (1978). The structure of coping. *Journal of Health and Social Behavior, 19,* 2–21.

Pearlin L. I., & Skaff, M. (1996). Stress and the life course: A paradigmatic alliance. *Gerontologist, 36*(2), 239–248.

Peele, S. (1989). *The diseasing of America: Addiction treatment out of control.* Lexington, MA: Lexington Books.

Pena, J. M., Bland, I. J., Shervington D., Rice, J. C., & Foulks, E. F. (2000). Racial identity and its assessment in a sample of African-American men in treatment for cocaine dependence. *American Journal of Drug and Alcohol Abuse, 26,* 97–112.

Peplau, L. A., & Perlman, D. (1984). Loneliness research: A survey of empirical findings. In L. A. Peplau, & S. E. Goldston (Eds.), *Preventing the harmful consequences of severe and persistent loneliness* (pp. 13–47). Bethesda, MD: National Institute of Mental Health.

Peterson, A. L., & Halstead, T. S. (1998). Group cognitive behavior therapy for depression in a community setting: A clinical replication series. *Behavioral Therapy, 29,* 3–18.

Phillips, R. L., Kuzma, J, & Beeson, W. L. (1980). Influence of selection versus lifestyle on risk of fatal cancer and cardiovascular disease among Seventh Day Adventists. *American Journal of Epidemiology, 712,* 296–314.

Piper, W. E., Ogrodniczuk, J. S., Joyce, A. S., & McCallum, M. R. (2002). Relationships among affect, work, and outcome in group therapy for patients with complicated grief. *American Journal of Psychotherapy, 56*(3), 347–362.

Polk, L. V. (1997). Toward a middle-range theory or resilience. *Advances in Nursing Science, 1*(3), 1–13.

Pollak S. D. (2002). Early experience is associated with the development of categorical representations for facial expressions of emotion. *Proceedings of the National Academy of Sciences, 99*(13), 9072–9076.

Poussaint, A. F. (1993). Enough already. *Ebony, 48*(4), 86–89.

Powell, T. J., Yeaton, W., Hill, E. M., & Silk, K. R. (2001). Predictors of psychosocial outcomes for patients with mood disorders. *Psychiatric Rehabilitation Journal, 25*(1), 3–12.

Pratt, L. A., Ford, D. E., Crum, R. M., Armenian, H. K., Gallo, J. J., & Eaton, W. W. (1996). Depression, psychotropic medication, and risk of myocardial infarction. Prospective data from the Baltimore ECA follow-up. *Circulation, 94,* 3123–3129.

Prevent Child Abuse America. (2003). *What everyone can do to prevent child abuse: 2003 child abuse prevention community resource packet.* Chicago: Author.

Project Match Research Group. (1997). Matching alcoholism treatments to client heterogeneity: Project MATCH posttreatment drinking outcomes. *Journal of Studies on Alcohol, 58,* 7–29.

Putnam, R. D. (2000). *Bowling alone.* New York: Simon & Schuster.

Radke-Yarrow, M., & Brown, E. (1993). Resilience and vulnerability in children of multiple-risk families. *Development and Psychopathology, 5,* 581–592.

Radloff, L. S. (1977). The CES-D scale: A self-report depression scale for research in the general population. *Applied Psychological Measurements, 1,* 385–407.

Ramos, S. (1962). *Profile of a man and culture in Mexico.* Austin: University of Texas Press.

Randolph, W. M., Stroup, C., Benham, C., & Black, S. A. (1998). Alcohol use among Cuban-Americans, Mexican-Americans, and Puerto Ricans. *Alcohol Health and Research World, 22*(4), 265–269.

Raphael, B. (1977). Preventive intervention with the recently bereaved. *Archives of General Psychiatry, 34,* 1450–1454.

Rauch, J. (2003). Let it be. *Atlantic Monthly, 291*(4), 34.

Reece, R. M. (2000). *Treatment of child abuse: Common ground for mental health, medical and legal professionals.* Baltimore, MD: The Johns Hopkins University Press.

Regehr, C., Cadell, S., & Jansen, K. (1999). Perceptions of control and long-term recovery from rape. *American Journal of Orthopsychiatrty, 69,* 110–114.

Reidy, A. (1992). Shattering illusions of difference. *Resources, 4,* 3–6.

Reis, S. M., Hebert, T. P. D., Eva, I., Maxfield, L. R., & Ratley, M. E. (1995). *Case studies of talented students who achieve and underachieve in an urban high school* (Research Monograph No. 95120). Washington, DC: U.S. Department of Education.

Remick, R. A. (2002). Diagnosis and management of depression in primary care: a clinical update and review. *Canadian Medical Association Journal, 167*(11), 1253–1261.

Resnick, H., Acierno, R., Holmes, M., Kilpatrick, D., & Jager, N. (1999). Prevention of post-rape psychopathology: Preliminary findings of a controlled acute rape treatment study. *Journal of Anxiety Disorders, 13,* 359–370.

Richman, J. (2000). Introduction: Psychotherapy with terminally ill patients. *American Journal of Psychotherapy, 54*(4), 482–486.

Richters, J. E., & Martinez, P. E. (1993). Violent communities, family choices, and children's chances: An algorithm for improving the odds. *Development and Psychopathology, 5,* 609–627.

Riessman, F. (1965). The helper-therapy principle. *Social Work, 10,* 27–32.

Riessman, F. (1997). Ten self-help principles. *Social Policy, 27,* 6–11.

Riessman, F. (2000). Self-help comes of age. *Social Policy, 30*(4), 47–49.

Rind, B., & Tromovitch, P. (1997). A meta-analytic review of findings from national samples on psychological correlates of child sexual abuse. *Journal of Sex Research, 34*(3), 237–255.

Robert, S. A., & Li, L. W. (2001). Age variation in the relationship between community socioeconomic status and adult health. *Research on Aging, 23*(2), 233–258.

Roberts, A. R. (1990). *Crisis intervention handbook: Assessment, treatment, and research.* Belmont, CA: Wadsworth.

Rogler, L., & Malgady, R. (1987). What do culturally sensitive mental services mean? The case of Hispanics. *American Psychologist, 42*(6), 565–570.

Roizen, R., Cahalan, D., Lambert, E., Wiebel, W., & Shanks, P. (1978). Spontaneous remission among untreated problem drinkers. In D. Kandel (Ed.), *Longitudinal research on drug use.* Washington, DC: Hemisphere.

Root, M. (1993). Guidelines for facilitating therapy with Asian American clients. In D. Atkinson, G. Morten, & D. W. Sue (Eds.), *Counseling American minorities: A cross-cultural perspective* (pp. 349–356). Madison, WI: Brown & Benchmark.

Rosen, J. (2003). My Kafka problem. *American Scholar, 72,* 85–91.

Rotenberg, K. J., MacDonald, K. J., & King, E. V. (2004). The relationship between loneliness and interpersonal trust during middle childhood. *Journal of Genetic Psychology, 165*(3), 233–250.

Rothbaum, B., & Schwartz, A. C. (2002). Exposure therapy. *American Journal of Psychotherapy, 56*(1), 59–75.

Rouse K. A. G., Longo, M., & Trickett, M. (1999). The definition of resilience. In Fostering resilience in children. *Bulletin 875–99.* Retrieved January 16, 2006, from http://ohioline.osu.edu/b875/b875_1.html

Rowe, J. W., & Kahn, R. L. (1998). *Successful aging: The MacArthur Foundation study.* New York: Random House. Retrieved January 14, 2005, from http://www.egyptianaaa.org/Q&A-SuccessfulAging.htm

Rubin, K. H., & Mills, R. S. L. (1991). Conceptualizing developmental pathways to internalizing disorders in childhood. *Canadian Journal of Behavioral Science, 23*(3), 300–317.

Rush, A. J., & Giles, D. E. (1982). *Cognitive therapy: Theory and research in short term psychotherapies for depression* (pp. 143–181). New York: Guilford Press.

Russell, D. E. (1999). *The secret trauma: Incest in the lives of girls and women* (Rev. ed.). New York: Basic Books.

Rutter, M. (1979). Protective factors in children's responses to stress and disadvantage. In M. W. Kent & J. Rolf (Eds.), *Primary prevention of psychopathology, Vol III. Social competence in children* (pp. 49–74). Hanover, NH: University Press of New England.

Rutter, M. (1990). Psychosocial resilience and protective mechanisms. In J. Roll, A. S. Masten, D. Cicchetti, K. Nuechterlein, & S. Weintraub (Eds.), *Risk and protective factors in the development of psychopathology* (pp. 181–215). New York: Cambridge University Press.

Rutter, M. (2003). Genetic influences on risk and protection: Implications for understanding resilience. In S. S. Luthar (Ed.), *Resilience and vulnerability* (pp. 489–509). Cambridge, UK: Cambridge University Press.

Ryff, C. D., & Singer, B. (1998). The contours of positive human health. *Psychological Inquiry, 9,* 1–28.

Sackett, D. L., Richardson, W. S., Rosenberg, W., & Haynes, R. B. (1997). *Evidence-based medicine: How to practice and teach EMB.* New York: Churchill Livingstone.

Safren, S. A., & Heimberg, R. G. (1999). Depression, hopelessness, suicidality, and related factors in sexual minority and heterosexual adolescents. *Journal of Consulting and Clinical Psychology, 67,* 859–866.

Saleebey, D. (1985). In clinical social work practice, is the body politic? *Social Service Review, 59,* 578–592.

Saleebey, D. (1992). *The strengths perspective in social work practice.* White Plains, NY: Longman.

Saleebey, D. (1994). Culture, theory, and narrative: The intersection of meanings in practice. *Social Work, 39,* 352–359.

Saleebey, D. (1996) The strengths perspective in social work practice: Extensions and cautions. *Social Work, 41*(3), 296–305.

Saleebey, D. (2000). Power in the people: Strength and hope. *Advances in Social Work, 1*(2), 127–136.

SAMSHA. (2001). *The CMHS approach to preventing violence.* Washington, DC: United States Department of Health and Human Services. Retrieved May 14, 2005, from http://alt.samhsa.gov/grants/content/2002/YouthViolence/need.htm

Sandage, S. J., & Hill, P. C. (2001). The virtue of positive psychology: The rapproachment and challenge of an affirmative postmodern perspective. *Journal for the Theory of Social Behavior, 31*(3), 241–260.

Satcher, D. (1998, June). *Healthy people in healthy communities: A guide for community leaders.* Washington, DC: U.S. Department of Health and Human Services, Office of the Surgeon General. Retrieved August 15, 2004, from http://odphp.osophs.dhhs.gov/pubs/healthycommunities/hcomm2.html

Satcher, D. (1999). *Mental health: A report of the surgeon general.* Retrieved August 12, 2004, from http://www.mentalhealth.org/features/surgeongeneralreport/chapter8/sec1.asp #ensure

Satcher, D. (2001a). *Mental health: A report of the Surgeon General.* Retrieved August 3, 2003, from http://www.surgeongeneral.gov/library/mentalhealth/chapter8/sec1.html#tailor

Satcher, D. (2001b). *Mental health: Culture, race, and ethnicity. A supplement to Mental health: A report of the Surgeon General.* Retrieved August 2, 2003, from http://www.surgeon-general.gov/library/mentalhealth/cre/release.asp

Savin-Williams, R. C. (1998). The disclosure to families of same-sex attractions by lesbian, gay, and bisexual youths. *Journal of Research on Adolescence, 8,* 49–68.

Savin-Williams, R. C. (2001). Suicide attitudes among sexual minority youth: Population and measurement issues. *Journal of Consulting and Clinical Psychology, 69*(6), 983–989.

Schlenger, W. E., Kulka, R. A., Fairbank, J. A., Hough, R. L., Jordan, B. K., Marmar, C. R., & Weiss, D. S. (1992). The prevalence of post-traumatic stress disorder in the Vietnam generation: A multimethod, multisource assessment of psychiatric disorder. *Journal of Traumatic Stress, 5,* 333–363.

Schnoll, R. A., Mackinnon, J. R., Stolbach, L., & Lorman, C. (1995). The relationship between emotional adjustment and two factor structures of the Mental Adjustment to Cancer Scale. *Psycho-Oncology, 4,* 265–272.

Schwarz, K., & Mazer, C. (2003, December 3). Transcript of an adolescent panel on Resilience at the Alisos Institute, Santa Barbara, CA.

Seaborn-Thompson, M., & Ensminger, M. E. (1989). Psychological well-being among mothers with school age children: Evolving family structures. *Social Forces, 67,* 715–730.

Seattle Youth Risk Survey Results. (1995). *Youth Risk Behavior Survey* (Table 4, p. 10; Table 6, p. 15). In B. Reis & E. Saewyc (1999), *Eighty-three thousand youth.* Retrieved May 14, 2005, from http://www.safeschoolscoalition.org/safe.html

Sechrist, W. (2000). Health educators and child maltreatment: A curious silence. *Journal of School Health, 70*(6), 241–243.

Seiffege-Krenke, I. (1995a). Changes in stress perception and coping style as a function of perceived family climate. In I. Seiffege-Krenke (Ed.), *Stress, coping and relationships in adolescence.* Mahwah, NJ: Lawrence Erlbaum.

Seiffege-Krenke, I. (1995b). Stress, coping and relationships as risk and protective factors in explaining adolescent depression. In I. Seiffege-Krenke (Ed.), *Stress, coping and relationships in adolescence.* Mahwah, NJ: Lawrence Erlbaum.

Seligman, M. E. P. (1992). *Learned optimism: How to change your mind and your life.* New York: Pocket Books.

Seligman, M. E. P. (1994). *What you can change and what you can't.* New York: Knopf.

Seligman, M. E. P. (2002). *Authentic happiness: New positive psychology to realize your potential for lasting fulfillment.* New York: Free Press.

Sheridan, M. J. (2000). *The use of spiritually-derived interventions in social work practice.* Proceedings of the 46th Annual Program Meeting of the Council on Social Work Education (pp. 1–22). Washington, DC: Council on Social Work Education.

Sheridan, M. J., Bullis R. K., Adcock C. R., Berlin S. D., & Miller, P. C. (1992). Practitioners' personal and professional attitudes and behaviors toward religion and spirituality: Issues for social work education and practice. *Journal of Social Work Education, 28,* 190–203.

Sheridan, M. J., Wilmer, C. M., & Atcheson, L. (1994). Inclusion of content on religion and spirituality in the social work curriculum. *Journal of Social Work Education, 30*(3), 363–377.

Shworles, T. R. (1983). The person with disability and the benefits of the microcomputer revolution: To have or to have not. *Rehabilitation Literature, 44*(11/12), 322–330.

Simpson, W. F. (1989). Comparative longevity in a college cohort of Christian Scientists. *Journal of the American Medical Association, 262,* 1657–1658.

Sireling, L., Cohen, D., & Marks, I. (1988). Guided mourning for morbid grief: A replication. *Behavior Therapy, 19,* 121–132.

Skaff, M. M., & Pearlin, L. I. (1992). Caregiving: Role engulfment and loss of self. *Gerontologist, 32,* 656–664.

Sloan, R. P., & Bagiella, E. (2001). Spirituality and medical practice: A look at the evidence. *American Family Physician, 63*(1), 33–34.

Smith, J., & Prior, M. (1995). Temperament and stress resilience in school-age children: A within families study. *Journal of the American Academy of Child and Adolescent Psychiatry, 34,* 168–179.

Smith, R. B., & Brown, R. A. (1997). The impact of social support on gay male couples. *Journal of Homosexuality, 33,* 39–61.

Snow, M. (1973). Maturing out of narcotic addiction in New York City. *International Journal of the Addictions, 8*(6), 932–938.

Sobell, L., Sobell, M., Toneatto, T., & Leo, G. (1993). What triggers the resolution of alcohol problems without treatment? *Alcoholism: Clinical and Experimental Research, 17*(2), 217–224.

Solomon, D. A., Keller, M. B., Leon, A. C., et al. (2000). Multiple recurrences of major depressive disorder. *American Journal of Psychiatry, 157,* 229–233.

Solomon, P., & Draine, J. (1995d). The efficacy of a consumer case management team: Two year outcomes of a randomized trail. *Journal of Mental Health Administration, 22,* 135–146.

Solomon, R. (1996). Coping with stress: A physician's guide to mental health in aging. *Geriatrics, 51*(7), 46–51.

Spieker, S. J., Larson, N. C., Lewis, S. M., Keller, T. E., & Gilchrist, L. (1999). Developmental trajectories of disruptive behavior problems in preschool children of adolescent mothers. *Child Development, 70,* 443–458.

Spilka, B., Shaver, P., & Kirkpatrick, L. (1985). A general attribution theory for the psychology of religion. *Journal for the Scientific Study of Religion, 24,* 1–20.

Spock, B. & Rothenberg, M. B. (1985). *Baby and child care.* New York: Dutton.

Srinivasan, S., O'Fallon, L. R., & Dearry, A. (2003). Creating healthy communities, healthy homes, healthy people: Initiating a research agenda on the built environment and public health. *American Journal of Public Health, 93*(9),1446–1251.

Stahl, J. (2004, May 28). Israeli children show "amazing resilience, " experts say. *CNSNews .com.* Retrieved May 7, 2005, from http://www.cnsnews.com/ViewForeignBureaus.asp ? age=\ForeignBureaus\archive\200405\FOR20040528e.html

Stall, R., & Biernacki, P. (1989). Spontaneous remission from the problematic use of substances. *International Journal of the Addictions, 21,* 1–23.

Stanton, A. L., & Snider, P. R. (1993). Coping with a breast cancer diagnosis: A prospective study. *Health Psychology, 12,* 16–23.

Stark, K., Rouse, L., & Livingston, R. (1991). Treatment of depression during childhood and adolescence: Cognitive-behavioral procedures for the individual and family. In P. C. Kendall (Ed.), *Child and adolescent therapy* (pp. 165–206). New York: Guilford Press.

Stein, M. B. (2002). Taking aim at posttraumatic stress disorder: Understanding its nature and shooting down myths. *Canadian Journal of Psychiatry, 47*(10), 921–923.

Stillman, D. (1994, February 24). Has feminism missed the point? *Los Angeles Times,* p. 32

Stober, J. (2003). Self–pity: Exploring the links to personality, control beliefs, and anger. *Journal of Personality, 71*(2), 183–221.

Stossel, S. (2000, September 21). Lonely in America. [Interview with Robert Putnam]. *Atlantic Unbound.* Retrieved June 12, 2002, from www.theatlantic.com/unbound/interviews/ ba2000-09-21.htm

Strengthening American families: Reweaving the social tapestry. Final report of the ninety-seventh American Assembly (2000, September 21–23). Retrieved August 9, 2001, from http://www.americanassembly.org/programs/ uas_families_TOC.htm

Stressed out and traumatized [Editorial]. (2005, March 5). *Economist, 374,* 84–86.

Stroebe, M. S. (2001). Bereavement research and theory: Retrospective and prospective. *American Behavioral Scientist, 44*(5), 854–865.

Sue, S., & Morishima, J. K. (1982). *The mental health of Asian Americans: Contemporary issues in identifying and treating mental problems.* San Francisco: Jossey-Bass.

Susser, E. S., Herman, D. B., & Aaron, B. (2002). Combating the terror of terrorism. *Scientific American, 287*(2), 70–78.

Taylor, J. (1993). *Poverty and niches: A systems view.* Unpublished manuscript, University of Kansas, Lawrence.

Taylor, S. (1999). *Anxiety sensitivity: Theory, research, and treatment of the fear of anxiety.* Mahwah, NJ: Lawrence Erlbaum.

Taylor, S. (2000). *Understanding and treating panic disorder: Cognitive-behavioural approaches.* Chichester, UK: John Wiley & Sons.

Tech, N. (2003). *Resilience and courage: Women, men, and the Holocaust.* New Haven, CT: Yale University Press.

Theuninck, A. (2000). *The traumatic impact of minority stressors on males self-identified as homosexual or bisexual.* Master's dissertation, University of the Witwatersrand, Johannesburg.

Tiet, Q. Q., Bird, H., & Davies, M. R. (1998). Adverse life events and resilience. *Journal of the American Academy of Child and Adolescent Psychiatry, 37*(11), 1191–1200.

Timmermans, S., & Angell, A. (2001). Evidence-based medicine, clinical uncertainty, and learning to doctor. *Journal of Health & Social Behavior, 42*(4), 342.

Tobias, M., Morrison, J., & Gray, B. (Eds.). (1995). *A parliament of souls.* San Francisco: KQED Books.

Trice, H., & Roman, P. (1970). Delabeling, relabeling, and Alcoholics Anonymous. *Social Problems, 17*, 538–546.

Tsuang, M. T., Woolson, R. F., & Fleming, M. S. (1979). Long-term outcome of major psychoses. *Archives of General Psychiatry, 36*, 1295–1301.

Turner, F. (2002). *Diagnosis in social work.* Toronto: Allyn & Bacon.

Tyler, K. A., & Hoyt, D. R. (2000). The effects of an acute stressor on depressive symptoms among older adults. *Research on Aging, 22*(2), 143–164.

U.S. Department of Health and Human Services. (2000a). *Healthy people 2010* (2nd ed.). *With understanding and improving health and objectives for improving health.* (2 vols.). Washington, DC: U.S. Government Printing Office.

U.S. Department of Health and Human Services. (2000b). *National household survey on drug abuse.* Retrieved October 13, 2002, from http://www.samhsa.gov/oas/dependence/chapter 2.htm

U.S. Department of Health and Human Services. (2005). *Results from the 2004 national survey on drug use and health* (DHHS Publication No. SMA-4062). Retrieved Sept. 22, 2005, from http://www.samsha.gov/hsduh/2k4results/2k4results.htm

Uba, L. (1994). *Asian Americans: Personality patterns, identity, and mental health.* New York: Guilford Press.

Uruk, A. C., & Demir, A. (2003). Loneliness. *Journal of Psychology, 137*(2), 179–194.

Vaillant, G. E. (1993). *The wisdom of the ego.* Cambridge, MA: Harvard University Press

Vaillant, G. E., & Mukamal, K. (2001). Successful aging. *American Journal of Psychiatry, 158*(6), 839–847.

van Emmerik, A. P., Kamphuis, J. H., Hulsbosch, A. M, & Emmelkamp, P. M. (2002). Single session debriefing after psychological trauma: a meta-analysis. *Lancet, 360*(9335), 766–772.

Velasquez, R. J., Arellano, L. M., & McNeill, B.W. (2004). *The handbook of chicana/o psychology and mental health.* Mahwah, NJ: Lawrence Erlbaum.

Waern, M., Runeson, B. S., Allebeck, P., Beskow, J. (2002). Mental disorder in elderly suicides: A case-control study. *American Journal of Psychiatry, 159*(3), 450–455.

Wagner, M. K., Armstrong, D., & Laughlin, J. E. (1995). Cognitive determinants of quality of life after onset of cancer. *Psychological Reports, 77,* 147–154.

Waldorf, D., Reinarman, C., & Murphy, S. (1991). *Cocaine changes: The experience of using and quitting.* Philadelphia: Temple University Press.

Waller, M. A., & Patterson, S. (2002). Natural helping and resilience in a Dine (Navajo) community. *Society, 81*(1), 73–84.

Wallis, M. A. (2000). Looking at depression through bifocal lenses. *Nursing, 30*(9), 58–62.

Walsh, F. (1998). *Strengthening family resilience.* New York: Guilford.

Walsh, F. (2003). Family resilience: A framework for clinical practice—theory and practice. *Family Processes, 42,* 1–18.

Walzer, M. (1983). *Spheres of justice.* New York: Basic Books.

Weick, A., Rapp, C., Sullivan, W. P., & Kisthardt, W. (1989). A strengths perspective for social work practice. *Social Work, 34,* 350–354.

Weiss, D. S., Marmar, C. R., Schlenger, W. E., Fairbank, J. A., Jordan, B. K., Hough, R. L., & Kulka, R. A. (1992). The prevalence of lifetime and partial post-traumatic stress disorder in Vietnam theater veterans. *Journal of Traumatic Stress, 5,* 365–376.

Weiss, R. S. (1973). *Loneliness: The experience of emotional and social isolation.* Cambridge, MA: MIT Press.

Werner, E. (1989). High-risk children in young adulthood: A longitudinal study from birth to 32 years. *American Orthopsychiatric Association, 59,* 72–81.

Werner, E. (1993). Risk, resilience, and recovery. Perspectives from the Kauai longitudinal study. *Development and Psychopathology, 5,* 503–515.

Werner, E. (1996). Vulnerable but invincible: High risk children from birth to adulthood. *European Journal of Child and Adolescent Psychiatry, 5*(Supplement 1), 47–51.

Werner, E., & Smith, R. S. (1982). *Vulnerable but invincible.* New York: Adams, Bannister & Cox.

Werner, E., & Smith, R. S. (1992). *Overcoming the odds: High risk children from birth to adulthood.* Ithaca, NY: Cornell University Press.

Werner, E., & Smith, R. S. (2001). *Journey from childhood to midlife: Risk, resilience and recovery.* Ithaca, NY: Cornell University Press.

Whaley, A. L. (2001). Cultural mistrust: An important psychological construct for diagnosis and treatment of African Americans. *Psychology: Research and Practice, 32*(6), 555–562.

What causes post-traumatic stress disorder: Two views. (2002, October). *Harvard Mental Health Letter, 19*(4), 8.

Wilkes, G. (2002a). Abused child to nonabused parent: Resilience and conceptual change. *Journal of Clinical Psychology, 58*(3), 261–276.

Wilkes, G. (2002b). Introduction: A second generation of resilience research. *Journal of Clinical Psychology, 58*(3), 229–232.

Williams, O. J. (1992). Ethnically sensitive practice to enhance treatment participation of African American men who batter. *Families in Society, 26*(12), 588–595.

Winfield, L. F. (1991). Residence, schooling and development in African American Youth. *Education and Urban Society, 24*(1), 5–14.

Winick, C. (1962). Maturing out of narcotic addiction. *Bulletin on Narcotics, 6,* 1.

Wituk, S., Shepherd, M. D., Slavich, S., Warren, M. L., & Meissen, G. (2000). A topography of self-help groups: An empirical analysis. *Social Work, 45*(2), 157–165.

Wolff, T. (2003). The healthy communities movement: A time for transformation. *National Civic Review, 92*(2), 95–112.

Wolin, S. J., & Wolin, S. (1993). *The resilient self: How survivors of troubled families rise above adversity.* New York: Villard.

Wuthnow, R. (1994). *Sharing the journey: Support groups and Americas' new quest for community.* New York: Free Press.

Wyatt, S. T. (2004). *Identifying factors that affect the development of adolescent African American males.* Retrieved August 1, 2004, from http://www.imgip.siu.edu/journal/afamdev.html

Wyman, P. A., Cowen, E. L. & Work, W. C. (1999). Caregiving and developmental factors in at-risk urban children showing resilience versus stress-affected outcomes: A replication. *Child Development, 70*(3), 645–659.

Wyman, P A., Cowen, E. L., Work, W. C., & Parker, G. R. (1991). Developmental and family milieu correlates of resilience in urban children who have experienced major life stress. *American Journal of Community Psychology, 19*(3), 405–426.

Wyman, R A., Cowen, E. L., Work, W. C., Raoof, A., Gribble, P. A., Parker, G. R., & Wannon, M. (1992). Interviews with children who experienced major life stress: Family and child attributes that predict resilient outcomes. *Journal of the American Academy of Child and Adolescent Psychiatry, 31*(5), 904–910.

Yntema, S. (Ed.). (1999). *Americans 55 and older* (2nd ed.). New York: New Strategist.

Zimmerman, M. A., & Maton, K. I. (1992). Life-style and substance use among male African American urban adolescents: A cluster analytic approach. *American Journal of Community Psychology, 20,* 121–138.

Zuckerman, D. M., Kasl, S. V., & Ostfeld, A. M. (1984). Psychosocial predictors of mortality among the elderly poor: The: role of religion, well-being, and social contacts. *American Journal of Epidemiology, 179,* 410–423.

Zuniga, M. E. (1992, January). Using metaphors in therapy: Dichos and Latino clients. *Social Work, 37*(1), 55–60.

Index

About the Author

 **Dr. Morley D. Glicken** is the former dean of the Worden School of Social Service in San Antonio, Texas; the founding director of the Master of Social Work Department at California State University, San Bernardino; the past Director of the Master of Social Work Program at the University of Alabama; and the former executive director of Jewish Family Service of Greater Tucson in Arizona. He has also held faculty positions in social work at the University of Kansas and Arizona State University. Dr. Glicken received his BA degree in social work with a minor in psychology from the University of North Dakota, his MSW degree from the University of Washington, and MPA and DSW degrees from the University of Utah. He is a member of Phi Kappa Phi honorary fraternity.

Dr. Glicken's recent books include *The Role of the Helping Professions in the Treatment of Victims and Perpetrators of Crime* (with Dale Sechrest) and *A Simple Guide to Social Research,* both published in 2003 by Allyn and Bacon/Longman; *Violent Young Children* and *Understanding and Using the Strengths Perspective,* both published in 2004 by Allyn and Bacon/Longman; *Improving the Effectiveness of the Helping Professions: An Evidence-Based Approach to Practice,* published by Sage in 2005, and *Working With Troubled Men: A Contemporary Practitioner's Guide,* published by Lawrence Erlbaum Associates, also in 2005. He has two books forthcoming from Sage in the near future: *Social Work in the 21st Century: An Introduction to Social Welfare, Social Issues, and the Profession* will be published in 2006 and *Competency-Based Supervision* will be published in 2007.

Dr. Glicken has published over 50 articles in professional journals and has written extensively on personnel issues for Dow Jones, publisher of the *Wall Street Journal.* He has held clinical social work licenses in Alabama and Kansas and is a member of the Academy of Certified Social Workers. He is currently Professor Emeritus in Social Work at California State University, San Bernardino, and Director of the Institute for Personal Growth: A Research, Treatment, and Training Cooperative in Los Angeles, California. The Institute's Web site may be found at: http://www.morleyglicken.com, and Dr. Glicken can be reached online at mglicken@msn.com.